Amazing Amanda

My Journey Through Mito

by

Amanda Perrotta

With Dave Hart

Amanda Perrotta

This is a work of non-fiction detailing the struggles and milestones of one suffering from Mitochondrial Depletion Syndrome. All of the characters mentioned herein are real people.

Amazing Amanda
My Journey Through Mito

Please support local and national efforts to eliminate Mitochondrial Disease. For more information, visit the website of the United Mitochondrial Disease Foundation or other professional organizations fighting to end Mito.

www.umdf.org
www.amandasjourney.org

Read these other books by Dave Hart

The novel:

DARK DAY OF THE SOUL
A quiet man hides his friendship with a fugitive until their discovery forces them to flee into the seclusion of the Adirondack Mountains.

The travel memoir:

SOLOMON BOY:
AND ISLAND JOURNAL:
ADVENTURES AMONG THE PEOPLE OF THE
SOLOMON ISLANDS
Recounts Dave's life in a rural village in the Solomon Islands while helping to establish one of the country's first nationally-staffed eye clinics. Join him in this often humorous account of the joys and pitfalls of working cross-culturally. There's so much adventure, even the bat meat sounds delicious.

Amanda Perrotta

The Perrottas thank:

• God and our Lord and Savior Jesus Christ for giving us our miracle of Amanda's life for 16 years and blessing us to continue through life without her;
• Dave Hart, our editor;
• Dr. Darius Adams, Cheryl Clowe, Kayt Marra, Albany Medical Center Pediatrics PCAs and staff on C-7 and D-7 North, Dr. Sanchez, Dr. Pretty P, Dr. Qualia, AMC nursing staff—Debbie , Misty Seams, Allie Keith, Maude Kaye, Kristen Daniels, Stephanie Vanderbilt, Peggy Morelli, Elma, Klem, Kathy Hagadorn, Ashley, Chrystal, and especially Bethany Murray, aka Pippy. Also we thank Scott Whipple for all his help with medical equipment, and Margaret and Anthem Medical Supply for their care and training. Also, we cannot forget our beloved Uncle Tony and Maryanne for all of their wonderful and sacraficial in-home care.;
•Catholic Charities' Denice LaBier, Nicole, and Yolanda, and also Alicia VanKleek.;
• Denise Boniface our Respite worker;
• Father Rodino, Pastor James DuJack, his wife Karen, and Sam Messina of Pastoral Care at AMC;
•Certainly we thank the committee of Amandasjourney.org for all their hard work, dedication, and support, and all of the beautiful family and friends who have stood by us through every day of this journey.
•Abby's trainer, Maria Rauche, her husband, Matt Smith, and their Therapy Dog, Maggie;
• A special thank you to Wildwood School teachers and staff in units 6 and 8 for all of their dedication, love, and support through Amanda's years there. Also to Oakwood Christian School and St. Jude's Parish;
• All the friends Amanda made on CaringBridge and at Double H Ranch;
• The support of the United Mitochondrial Disease Foundation and the doctors and staff of the VIR department at AMC and the Childlife Specialists Amy and Brenna and all the volunteers.
• Aunt Kim, for continuing Amanda's entries on the CaringBridge site.

• There are so many of you who have been so helpful and dedicated through the years, and we regret if we have forgotten any of you. Please forgive us.

Amanda Perrotta

Dave Hart thanks:

• Fernando Gomes, for vouching for me to the Perrotta family for this project;

• Jacki and Lou Perrotta and daughter Carolyn, for trusting me in the editing and creating of this book. I value the friendship we have made and am truly changed and blessed through the privilege of making this story happen;

• The Lord Jesus, for His gifts of talent and words.

This book is dedicated to:

All families who have lost a child through Mitochondrial disease or who continue to fight this terrible, merciless illness every day;

Amanda's special friends Malisa, Jaden, Erik, Emilie, Gina, Kylie, and Josh;

Amanda's best friend Mike Silvia, and;

Her service dog, Abby;

With a special dedication to Amanda's cousin Emma Marie Hamilton.

Always B+ and F.R.O.G.

Amanda Perrotta

Hi!

My name is Amanda Perrotta, I'm 16 years old, and I have a rare, life-threatening disease called Mitochondrial Depletion Disease. Please take a few minutes to look through my pictures and read through my story. B+!!!

"The cure Mito is living life!"

—Amanda Perrotta

So began the journaling of Amanda Perrotta, a sweet, sensitive girl growing up in the outskirts of Troy, NY. Once diagnosed with Mito, she would never be the same, of course. Who of us would? But part of what changed was her focus, turning almost immediately from her own ails to those of others. Her life became such a witness of strength and courage, and as such, a beacon of hope and encouragement, that this book came to be through her own desire to help others in their needs and to offer her own insights and understandings to those struggling through the sadness and desperation that come with the diagnosis of a terminal illness.

Here, after a short introduction to her on-line friends, are Amanda's journals. She entered them at a web site called CaringBridge. There, people can "support and connect loved ones during critical illness, treatment and recovery." The site allows individuals to develop and maintain their own pages, correspond with others in recovery, and inform others of their prognosis and progress. Please visit CaringBridge at: www.Caringbridge.org.

Please note: All of the journals remain the way Amanda wrote them, which is the way she wanted them to be presented. It is understood that present-day use of lower case letters, especially at the start of a sentence, can run against the grain of many readers who know that this is unacceptable, but it must be remembered that these were on-line journals of a casual nature, where Amanda was writing to friends and others dealing with medical issues.

This is the way Amanda wrote, so, for her sake, and to preserve the integrity of her writing, they have been left untouched as she entered them.

The only corrections have been in proper spacing, correct use of most commas and sentence punctuation, certain consistent spelling errors, capitalization, and a few instances of awkward wording. Any spelling errors remain only where she made note of them.

A few editorial additions were necessary to clarify Amanda's meaning, which have been added within the text in brackets. Some headings to mark particularly important entries were added later.

~~~~~

My Journey began the second I was born, almost two months early. I was in the neonatal ICU for a while. After I came home from the NICU, I seemed fine until I turned two years old, that's when I had my first seizure. The doctors diagnosed me with epilepsy and autism.

After that, I didn't have a seizure until I was 11. My Family and I had just gotten back from vacation, and I was looking forward to school starting the next day. My throat felt funny, so I told my mom, and when I went to go tell her, I fell to the ground and had a seizure. That seizure took a lot away from me. A lot of it I got back, but I'm still learning the things it didn't give back.

I then began at a Special Ed. School. One Day when I went to get a regular school checkup, a special Dr. was there and asked the nurse if I ever got tested for Mitochondrial Disease. At that point I had hearing loss in both ears, and I had to wear a brace on my right foot because it kept giving out. My mom and dad decided I should get tested. I had a muscle biopsy, which confirmed I have Mito.

Almost a year later, I went in for a skin biopsy, and that confirmed that I have Mitochondrial Depletion Syndrome. Since a year ago, I can no longer walk long distances, only a few steps. I'm in my electric wheelchair. I cannot eat because my stomach shut down, and my bowels also shut down. I have a G-J [gastro-jejunum—inserted directly into the second portion of the small intestine] tube. I'm currently not on feeds. My tubes just drain into bags. I wear oxygen 24/7. When I'm sleeping, I'm on a Bi-Pap [oxygen] because I can't take deep enough breaths from being low on energy.

Having Mitochondrial Disease changed my life. Partly in a good way and partly in a bad way. I wake up every morning and thank God I'm alive because usually kids with Mito die before they reach their teen years. I thank God I'm not one of those kids. I try to appreciate life to the best, and my goal in this lifetime is to teach people about life and how to live it. Maybe some day there will be a cure. I hope so, but for now, all we can do is Hope, Pray, and Live.

THURSDAY, FEBRUARY 05, 2004
hi again! lately I've been feeling tired. more then usual anyways. i don't know why exactly... i think my body might just need some extra sleep, but i don't know. OK, well I'm going to go get some sleep. I'll try to write later this week. amanda   xoxo

WEDNESDAY, MARCH 24, 2004
OK, this is gonna be short because I'm typing on my PSP because my body won't let me get to the computer. I have been on the couch all day (except when i took a shower, which didn't help). I haven't really eaten anything all day, so I've been on my feeds for most of the day. My energy level is at like a one right now. I'm just trying to conserve it for a special birthday (wink, wink). OK, well, i just thought i should update. amanda

SUNDAY, OCTOBER 08, 2006
Hey Everyone! ... OK, so this is my first time doing this, so bear with me (actually my third, but never mind...lol). So, tomorrow I'm going in to have surgery. An indocopy (which i know I didn't spell right!) It's not really a big deal because I had one when i was one year old, so I'm not scared. The only thing I'm scared about is if they can't find a vein. :-/ But other then that, I'm good!

My legs have been getting worse. The stairs have been getting harder to go up. I used to be able to run up them, but now I have to take them one by one. Some days two-by-two (if it's a good day). On the 19th I'm going to see the AFO Dr. [An AFO, or ankle foot orthosis, stretches the Achilles tendon to keep the foot from pronating or pointing in. As children age, they need to get refitted]. I have to get a new AFO for my right leg. And i might have to get one for my left cause it's been getting weaker.

OT [occupational therapy] has been going pretty good! I LOVE the scooter rides and going on the swings! The only thing i don't like is the stretches. Last year I was able to do ten without stopping, but this year I'm only able to do 5 and then stop for a break. I guess my legs are just getting worse, but it's part of my disease. I can't control it. The one thing that stinks about my disease is that i can't have kids. I'm fine with it now, but when i found out i wasn't (i had a hissy fit!) But, I'm OK with it now 'cause my goal is to become an LPN for a children's hospital. And that's all I really need. :-)

~Amanda~

MONDAY, OCTOBER 09, 2006
Hey Guys!
So my surgery went pretty well. There was only one tiny problem. I had to take this yucky stuff to make me relax, and it was supposed to put me to sleep (key word supposed). Anyway, the nurse was like, "wait 5 minutes and we'll see." So five minutes passed, and i wasn't asleep. So they did an IV, but it kinda blew out. So the nurse was like, "well, let's take her into the OR, and we'll do the mask." So they took me in, and the NICE nurse said, "OK I'm going to put some medicine into your IV, and it will make you sleep along with the mask." So I didn't mind that until the mask was put on me. It felt like they were smothering me! I was about to say take it off until i fell asleep...lol. But anyway, other than that, the surgery went well. they did a little biopsy in my throat where they took out five pieces or something like that. So I'm good right now. I'm just relaxing until tomorrow for school (which i can go to!). Hallelujah! So I'll update you guys at the end of the week.

~Amanda~

MONDAY, OCTOBER 16, 2006

Hey guys!

So, as i promised i would, I'm updating. I went to the Dr. today for my legs. It wasn't the visit i was looking forward to (let me tell you). So we got there. He made me walk as usual, and then he came back in and was like, "OK, well, your foot can hardly move up and down. if it gets any worse or if it stays like this, we're going to have to operate on it," and i'm like, oh OK. so that was fine. The next part he said to me, well i was a little scared at first (i thought he was kidding). he says, "OK it's getting harder for you to walk around, especially when it's far, like the mall. So i'm going to order you a part-time wheelchair." i'm like, woahhhh!!! But i'm fine with it now 'cause it's only part time for now. I'm also getting new AFO's. So other than that, everything went fine. My mom's going to see if she can get me in to get fitted for my new AFO's tomorrow afternoon because the Dr. wanted them for me ASAP. OK, so i just wanted to update you on that. i'll update you soon.

Amanda :-)

THURSDAY, OCTOBER 19, 2006

hey!

So i know a lot is not supposed to happen in three days, but a lot can. I found out that within this year i will be having surgery done to put a GI [gastro-intestinal] tube in me to get extra nutrients. I'm kinda nervous about that... But i'll handle it. :-)

Next i found out i'm going to be using those crutches that hook

16

onto your elbows and they have handles... does anyone know what i'm talking about? And i'll be using those a lot probably.

In PT today, i got my legs measured for how far they can go up and how far i can point and flex them. The results weren't that good, though. But for good news...lol [laughing out loud], on Saturday i MIGHT be going horseback riding!!!!! So, i'm excited about that. It's therapeutic, so it will be so much fun. And I know the person who is going to teach me (even though i already know how to ride a horse...lol). And i'm going to get my crutches. So other than that, i'm good. Just wanted to make sure i updated you. I'll update when there's more to come, and i'm sure there will be. :-)

MONDAY, OCTOBER 23, 2006
Hey Everyone!
i'm not sure if i told you or not, but i got my crutches and my wheelchair. I got them Saturday. I was hoping for some color in my wheelchair, but they just gave me plain old black (ewww). But i'm going to make it stylish with stickers...he-he. i'm using my crutches almost every day. Tomorrow is going to be the first time i bring them into school. I can already tell it's going to be hard walking into my classroom and watching everyone's expressions on their faces...and asking, what happened to you? That's what always happens. I'm kind of nervous, but hopefully, when i get it over, i will be relieved. I'm not, like, embarrassed. i'm just nervous about the questions...you know? Well, hopefully it will be fine tomorrow. I just won't be as fast as the others...lol. I'll update you soon.

Amanda :-)

Amanda Perrotta

THURSDAY, OCTOBER 26, 2006
Hello!
So my first day of school with the crutches actually went GREAT!
I thought it would be the worst day of my life, but it was like a
normal day. I'm using my crutches every day for about 4-5 hours
(that's what i would say at least on a good day). On bad days, i
use them the whole day (with a partial break). Today i go to the
AFO Dr. to get fitted for new AFO's. I also have to go see a
nutritionists (spelling?). And i'll explain that right now. This Dr.
put me on this medicine for my swallowing yesterday, so i took
the day off in case there were any side effects (which there were).
So they took me off it, and now they're putting me on these
nutritional drinks that i have to drink i think three or four times a
day. And if that doesn't go well, then it's G-tube time. Which i
really don't want! My mom sent over a prescription to the nurse
saying I can't run in gym anymore, which really means i can't play
gym, right, because that's really all we do in gym is run, run, run.

Amanda :-)

TUESDAY, OCTOBER 31, 2006
Hello!
Happy Halloween is the very first thing i can say..lol.

So not much has been happening but i just wanted to insure you
that i'm still here...lol. Yesterday my parents and my teachers had
a meeting after school to make sure they all knew what i had. I
think some of them were surprised when they saw this video

about Mito because now every day a different T/A [teacher's assistant] is with me walking right besides me. I get my new AFO'S next week. I put butterflies on them. Hopefully they will look OK..maybe even GREAT!   Well, that's really all. I'll give you an update probably either the end of this week or next week when i get my AFOS. BYE!

Amanda :-)

THURSDAY, NOVEMBER 02, 2006
Hello!
So i know i just updated like two days ago, but i've been, not frustrated, but i don't know what word. i can't think of it...overwhelmed? Anyways, I've been using my crutches in school lately (as almost everybody knows..lol). and i thought it would be easy using crutches, and i know they help me and everything, but it's still kinda hard getting around with them when you have stuff in your hands, or in gym. Like today when i was walking to get to my bus to go home, i dropped my book bag by accident, and a teacher had to keep helping me pick it up. i wanted to say so bad, I CAN DO IT!   But the fact is, i need more help than i used to. I can't run in gym anymore, which saddens me. :-(I LOVE running, but if i keep running, i'm going to wear down, and i won't have any strength left in my body. So now i can only do an hour of gym and have to limit my gym activity. But the good thing is i've been getting more strength in my arms because of the crutches, so i now can do 15 push-ups in a row!   I know it's not a lot, but i used to only be able to do three...lol. I guess, when bad things come, good things come, too.   OK, i've got to go.   i'll update soon.

Amanda Perrotta

Amanda :-)

Drooling

SUNDAY, NOVEMBER 05, 2006
Hello...everybody!
So where to start...where to start. Let's start with my drooling..lol. I've been drooling a lot these past two days (over the weekend). I have no idea what's going on?!?! Ever since i have been diagnosed, I have been drooling, but it seems like it has been getting worse. Like I cannot control my muscles in my mouth or something. I hate it because, in school, when i'm in lunch, it's just terrible! I haven't told my mom yet that it's gotten worse, but after I write this, I am because she checks these...lol.

I tried eating a roll today, and I nearly choked on it! It seems also that it's getting harder to swallow things, such as rolls and bread. The muscles in my mouth are getting weaker, so I can't swallow some things that i LOVE to eat.

I found out on Friday night I have to watch the carbohydrates that i eat because they stick. they don't burn like they're supposed to. I'm not really worried about burning them, though, because I've lost 3 lbs. in one week! I was, like, woahhh when i stepped on the scale. They're trying to get the nutrient drinks into me ASAP, but, hmm, i just don't know.

I also forgot to tell you...i'm getting some extra OT/PT [occupational therapy/physical therapy] time. Well, more PT actually. They're doing an extra 15 minutes on Tues. for me. Not that it will help really, but that's OK. i enjoy getting away from the class for a little while...he-he. OK, well that's pretty much it! I'll update when my new AFO's come, and they're supposed to come this week! CAN'T WAIT!!!!

Amanda :-)

SUNDAY, NOVEMBER 12, 2006
Hi Everyone!
So I went to Maine this weekend, and i've never had so much fun in my LIFE!...OK, well except for California. My cousins came up with us, and we had a BLAST together. My mom actually let me ride a scooter, which i thought would never happen, since I will never be able to drive (unless i don't have a seizure for five years). My mom let me drive a scooter on a main road going 35 MPH!!!! I was so thrilled with that. Another thing was, i know i will not be able to get up in a top bunk bed in another year, so my sister slept in the top bunk, and my cousin slept in the other top bunk, and i actually climbed up!   The hard part was getting down...lol. We did sparklers and played sardines, although i had to use my crutches more then ever (because we did a lot of walking!). I was so happy just to be in Maine.

The thing I didn't like about Maine was telling my cousin about my disease and how it is going to affect me. After i told her half of what i'm going through, she interrupted and asked, "Are you going to be OK?" I said, yea, i might just be in the hospital a lot. I could tell she was kinda worried and sad after i told her about the wheelchair, but she was fine after a little while. She knew I was having the time of my life.

Anyway, i had a 20 minute video tape taken of me through the whole adventure, and when it gets developed, i'm going to TRY to put some of it up here. Oh, i got my new AFO's. i'm still trying to break them in. They're very nice, though. OK, well that's pretty much it.

Amanda :-)

SATURDAY, NOVEMBER 18, 2006
Hey!
So let's start with the AFO's. I'm going to visit the AFO Dr. on Mon. because my AFO's are really hurting me! I know i have to break them in, but i've been breaking them in for two weeks now, and they still hurt like nuts. Every day when i come home and take them off, I have like weird blister things on my feet (its disgusting!). So My mom said the choices he is PROBABLY going to offer me are: get my AFO fixed or have the foot surgery (but i don't know those details). I think if I get the choice, I will pick the surgery only because then I can flex and point my toes instead of not moving them, and right now the Dr. said i'm a perfect candidate.

On other hands, some time before Christmas, I'm going to go and test those [protein] drinks out (which i'm not looking forward to!). In my opinion, I would rather have the G-tube. I don't want to drink those nasty drinks every who knows how many times a day. But i have to go and test them out (i hope i do not throw up!). I just really want to get it over with, but the fact is, this adventure will never end. It's always going to be something new.

I'm getting a new bedroom—an easy access one with ramps (for some day when a need a wheelchair and a bath with, like, a Jacuzzi thing in it), so i don't have to go out and get my aquatherapy somewhere else. It's an edition to the house, so it's going to take a while, but it will come out nice. And the nice thing about it is that I get to choose the colors of my walls...lol. And all new furniture for the room, so i'm excited!

Amanda :-)

MONDAY, NOVEMBER 20, 2006
Hello everybody!
So as most of you know, i went to the AFO Dr. today. He said I might need new AFO's. But I have to go see the other AFO Dr. before i'll know. It's really confusing in a way (really!). He was talking about the surgery, and he said he's looking into it right now because with general anasthesia(sp?) your Mito can get worse or something like that. So he has to talk to other Drs., like my pediatrician and neurologist. He said if it's a good chance, then we will take it. The thing is with the surgery, well, my foot is getting worse week by week, and it's barely moving anymore, but, when it stops moving, i WILL need some type of surgery, or otherwise I will end up in a wheelchair pretty early. So if I get the chance to do the surgery now while my foot still moves a little, then i only have to be in a cast for three weeks, but, if my foot stops moving, i have to be in a cast for three months!!!!!

But on another note, my hands have been getting numb for no apparent reason. My feet, too. It's kinda strange. They stay numb for about half an hour, then i can feel them again. My mom is going to talk to my neurologist on Dec. 3rd when i go. So I'll eventually know what's happening sometime later. So that's pretty much it. Update soon

Amanda :-)

FRIDAY, NOVEMBER 24, 2006
Hey!

So first things first. I'm having trouble swallowing my pills and some other certain foods, like bread, turkey and etc. The thing is, when i have trouble swallowing my pills, i try to get them back up by throwing up. So my mom was talking to me about getting a G-tube. She really doesn't want me to get it right now, but if i'm throwing up just trying to get my pills down, then that's a problem. I really don't want a G-Tube, but if it stops me from throwing up, then i'm all for it!

OK, hope everyone had a GREAT Thanksgiving!!!!

Amanda :-)

TUESDAY, NOVEMBER 28, 2006
Hey,
Ughh. so right now, i'm not feeling so well (sick wise). Last night i started getting Infant Tigo [Impetigo—a contagious skin condition, usually of children, characterized by pustules and yellow, crusty scabs]. My mom thought it was a cold sore, but i knew it wasn't. I hate when i get it because i always get it bad! I

have a really bad swelled up lip. i can hardly speak, and my lips that aren't puffed up are really dry! I'm going to the Dr. today, and i already know he's going to give me medicine because he's dealt with me with this particular situation a million times or so.

On pill terms, last night was horrible! My mom tried to put the whole pill in apple sauce, and on 7 out of 15, i choked on those. But after i took most of them except for three, i was like, ughh, i don't fell good, so i ran to the bathroom, and i threw two up. It's just not going well. If I keep doing this, i'm soon going to be throwing all of them up within the next month or two. I'm going to my neurologist and three other Dr. appts., so we'll see. Until then, I'll leave you with that.

Hope you all had a GREAT Thanksgiving!!!

Amanda :-)

MONDAY, DECEMBER 04, 2006
Hi,
So as some of you may know, I went to NYC for the weekend. I went to visit my aunt who has CF [Cystic Fibrosis]. She's really sick right now, so if you could pray for her, that would be great! Anyways, i also had a great time while i was there, too.

While I was there, my mom went out to get my aunt and me pizza, so my aunt and I had a talk. We were talking about G-Tubes and ports and how they're kinda the same. I told her that it's getting harder and harder for me to swallow every day. But i don't want to get a G-Tube. My aunt said, "You'll know when it's time. I didn't want to get one either, but i knew when i HAD to get one." The only thing is, she didn't tell me how i'm supposed to know how to know? Am i supposed to get this feeling like i can't do it anymore? Because i'm way past that, but i'm stubborn, so i keep pushing myself. I guess she's right, though. i will know. Anyways, i'm going to the swallowing Dr. on Wed., and he's going to tell me about the G-Tube and stuff, so i'll update then. until then, bye.

Amanda :-)

THURSDAY, DECEMBER 07, 2006
Hey,

As promised, i am updating from yesterday's Dr. appts. It went pretty well compared to other ones. Let's start with the swallowing. The Dr. for the swallowing was going to put me on some medicine, but then my mom forgot that I got an allergic reaction to it. So what they're going to do is a procedure where i am awake (i don't know what it's called, and you probably do)— it's where they stick a little string tube down your nose and into your throat, and they see what's going on down there, and they make you swallow and see how much your muscles can swallow and how much they're weakening. So that's really all that's going on with the swallowing.

I've been having a hard time breathing lately, too, and they finally figured out why (i have a funny story to tell you after, but for right now...). they drew blood (took them four tries), and they tested it for low lactaid [lactic acid] or potassium. So we got the results today, and we found out that, when i have a hard time breathing, i need more potassium. If my potassium doesn't go up within the next week, i'm going to need injections through an IV (which i don't want).

Abby (my [cairn terrier] dog) graduated from puppy class last night. It was so funny because they actually had real graduation hats for the puppies. It was hysterical. And i'm VERY surprised she passed the test because she was so excited when she was going through it.

Anyways funny story: While i was getting my blood tested yesterday (after four tries), they finally got it and were so happy, and they put the tube on it, and it popped off and spilled all over me and the floor and them! I was, like, Oh no, not another four sticks! So what they did was take what was left in the tube and give one drop in each of the other tubes. And they actually had enough. But you should have seen the room! It was a mess! Anyways, i'll update soon. Have a great weekend!

Amanda :-)

MONDAY, DECEMBER 11, 2006
Hi,
I'm kinda nervous and scared right now as i'm typing, so don't mind me. The nutrition drinks have not been working because they have a side effect on me. So my mom called the Nutritionist today and told her, and then one thing led to another, and now i'm getting a G-Tube, then a Mickey Button to replace it (Over Christmas Break!!!!) [A mickey button is an entry point for feedings which is inserted through the belly into the upper intestine. It eliminates the tube and looks somewhat like the

blow-up valve on a beach ball] I'm not too fond of the Christmas break idea, but whatever works, i guess. I guess what scares me is that it's my first real BIG surgery.... i mean, before it was just a muscle biopsy or tonsils or sticking a tube down my throat, but now they're actually putting something in my stomach permanently! And i guess that's what i'm scared about. So i just wanted to get that out.

I guess i just realized that everyone always needs prayers, but only some people need special prayers. Anyway, i hope everyone has a terrific week! I'm going to play some arcade games tomorrow with my friends, so i will. and i'm going shopping with my friends on Thursday!

Amanda :-)

MONDAY, DECEMBER 18, 2006
Hello again,
So i finally found out what day i am officially going to have my G-Tube placed in me. It's believe it or not the day after Christmas!...lol. I laugh about it now because it's just my luck... but i can deal with it. And then, two weeks after the surgery, i have to have another one to have the tube replaced with the Mickey Button i don't know all the details yet, but when i do, i'll definitely let you know.

So my music teacher did the nicest thing for me today. She told me so at least. I have a private music class learning the piano every Tuesday, and i play pretty good. So my music teacher came up to me today and said, "I know your going through a ruff patch right now, and your emotions are all over, so i thought you might want to put all of your emotions in a song and then play it on the piano." So i am really looking forward to that.

Dahea is coming January 7th! If you don't know who Dahea is, she is a foreign exchange student who is coming to live with us from Seoul, South Korea. She's 15, and we have been exchanging emails, and she's getting very excited to learn all the American traditions. She thought Easter was before Christmas...lol.
Hope everyone has a VERY MERRY CHRISTMAS!!!!

Amanda :-)

FRIDAY, DECEMBER 22, 2006
Hi,
This morning i woke up to pink eye (nice before Christmas). But hopefully it will be gone by Christmas day. I'm very excited about Christmas and Christmas Eve! I love it because everyone, well most people, are very joyful, and it's kinda the best time of the year for me because i really don't think about all of my seizures, muscle problems and etc. at that time.

I'm starting to come around with the G-Tube and not be so scared (even though i have a right to be). I know that it's probably the biggest operation that i've had yet in my life, so i think that's what i was afraid of, and other silly stuff. But i came to terms that, if i could handle other surgeries, i can handle this. I know i am going to have to have another operation two months after i get this one, so why am i afraid of this?

I'm getting more excited about Dahea coming than anything else.

There's this other little girl that came from Korea (a foreign exchange student), and she came in September. Her name is Jisue (Je-Sue). And she follows my sister like a puppy. I went to my sister's Christmas concert last night, and all i saw was Jisue following my sister, but my sister doesn't care. So she gave Jisue a card, and one of the words said 'inspiration', and she asked what it meant, and my sister had to explain to her for 15 minutes what it meant, so that made me laugh, and she had no clue why. i didn't mean to laugh at her, but i couldn't help it.

So this will be my last post until after my surgery and when i'm better enough to type. But if like a week goes by, them i'll get my sister or mom to write in here. So i hope everyone has a Happy Holiday and Happy New Year!

Amanda :-)

TUESDAY, DECEMBER 26, 2006

OK quick update. My surgeon who was supposed to perform my surgery TODAY...is taking a little more of a Christmas break than we thought. My mom called the surgeon's secratary (sp?) today, and we're having a meeting Thursday because they're trying to fit me in Friday. So, on Thursday, there going to go through all of the anesthesia, what i can and can't eat, etc. So, i just thought i would let you all know that because i know most of you thought i was going in for surgery today (so was i), so i just wanted to let you know. Hope you all had a splendid holiday!

Amanda :-)

FRIDAY, DECEMBER 29, 2006

OK, i was getting pretty mad yesterday, and i'm sure at least two or three of you know why...lol. I have a new surgeon who is going to operate on me...next Friday!!!! Yea. i was kinda mad when i heard NEXT FRIDAY because the exchange student, Dahea, is coming the day after, and i have to spend the night [in the hospital] after i get the tube, and if anything goes wrong and i have to spend the night, i won't be able to pick her up. But someone pointed out to me that she's going to be living with me for a whole year so.... well, i'm probably at one point going to get sick of her...lol. They decided instead to do a smaller surgery. it's called a peg [Another form of G-tube inserted directly into the stomach]. I really can't explain it because it was really hard to concentrate on the date and all that, so....sorry. :-(I Know i will have the G-Tube in for eight weeks, and then i have to go back and get the mickey button replaced with [instead of] the G-Tube. So that's what i know. I'll update when or if i know more. Sorry to confuse you guys. Have a Happy New year!

Amanda :-)

THURSDAY, JANUARY 04, 2007

Hey!

Hope everyone had a Happy New Year!

Well, tomorrow is definitely the day. they just called and made sure we had all of those weird instructions and everything of what to eat and when to stop eating. Last night, i was getting nervous about getting sick, and i was really freaking out that i actually thought i was getting infatigo [impetigo]. Hopefully i won't freak out tonight and i will just go to bed..lol. I can't wait for this surgery to be over with, and then i don't have to drink chocolate milk every morning and every night (cause, to tell you the truth, i'm getting VERY sick of chocolate milk!). I just want to be able to get my pills down me in a tube (how weird does that sound...lol).

Anyway, we were having this chat on BraveKids about how people name their tubes, and i want to name mine. i just don't know what to name it...lol. I've been thinking all day, yesterday and today. But, if you have any ideas, just let me know so that i can put it on its birth certificate... ;-)

Hope everyone has a GREAT weekend!

Amanda :-)

All About getting the G—Tube

MONDAY, JANUARY 08, 2007
Hi!!!!

This is Amanda!   And i am finally updating about my surgery! I'm so excited to be home!!!! I just got home, actually, and, as soon as i walked in, i told my mom i HAVE to update!   So anyways, i have a lot to tell you guys.   let's start with this: my surgery went GREAT!   The surgeon said i was the best patient she has EVER had!   I walked right into the OR, and then they put on the mask (yes the mask where you breathe in that yucky paint smell). So i stayed in the ICU, and it was OK. i got my own private room, and it wasn't colorful or anything because they called it a suicide room (it's a room where they put crazy people)... lol. So i had the BEST nurse anyone could possibly have. her name was Alishia... she was like an old mother hen...lol. She sat with me when my mom wasn't there, and she gave me pain meds every five minutes... The pain was HORRIBLE! I thought i was going to die the first night. I said to myself, why did i have to have this?! But the second night was a little better. i got some sleep, but i had the worst night nurse in the history of night nurses.

I just started my feedings that day, and i only started with 150 mls. [milliliters, about 5 ounces], so that night she put two bags of that into me, and i started to get a stomach ache, and i asked her if i could hold it for a while, and she said, yes, for five minutes, and i said OK! So, five minutes went by, and my stomach was still in so much pain, and she came in, and was like, times up! and i'm like what?! My stomach hurts like i am dying here, and your telling me to keep putting more stuff into my stomach!? I was flipping on the inside, but it got better.

I am now currently at home doing feeds from 6:00PM-6:00AM and some in the afternoon. It depends, though, what i eat that day. I never knew how much pain that could be. i thought it would be like an ouch or two, but WOW! I never experienced that much pain in my life! Now i know how other people with Mito and have G-Tubes feel.

One more thing. Dahea came, and let me be the first to tell you, she's the cutest thing! She doesn't understand English that well, but she's very nice and doesn't care that she had to come to the hospital to meet me for the first time, and stay there.

So that's pretty much it. my birthday is Wed., so hopefully i can go to school because i have a little plan for my teacher (he-he). Have a GREAT week!

Amanda :-)

THURSDAY, JANUARY 11, 2007

Hi!

I know i just updated but i thought i would give you just a brief little update on things. I've been doing OK with the G-tube. It mostly hurts at night because i think i really over do it during the day. And, trust me, i get the full payback! The other night, i was up for two hours laying in my mom's bed, and i couldn't move... i tried to move but didn't succeed. Last night was a little better. i didn't have any pain during the night, but, right when i woke up, i had A LOT! I know it's going to take at least one more week to heal and for me to not have all of this pain.

I had a wonderful birthday last night! Even though it wasn't at school with all of my friends, i think it may have been better! Dahea (our foreign exchange student) bought me gold earrings from Korea and a pencil case and a book mark, and it's all from Korea. I'm getting to know her better, and she's actually starting to laugh at my jokes. But the only thing i don't think she liked was when the nurses had to come. she walked into the other room. I felt bad... but maybe she didn't feel comfortable.

I'll update in a few days

Amanda :-)

TUESDAY, JANUARY 16, 2007
Hellooooo!!!!

So, as i last updated, i was in pain with my G-Tube (i think?). anyways, i am in no pain any more (officially!). I start school today, and i am feeling soooo much better with the nutrition, and i feel like i'm five years old again...lol. I know i sound stupid, but i really do. it feels so weird, but good!   There's just been some leakage that's been bothering me, but that's not really a problem compared to what was before.   I have this pain in my back, though, for some reason, and my mom thought it was knomonia (sp?), but it isn't, so i have no idea what that is, of course, so....

Dahea is getting along perfectly well in this family. She has so many jokes no one can count them. Last night she pulled a good one on me. I was getting a blanket, and all of a sudden i heard the door shut, and i was, like, Carolyn (my other sister), come on open the door! and she wouldn't open it for three minutes. finally, she let go, and i fell, and i was like, Dahea, you're mean!   It was so funny, though, because it's good to see her laugh.

I have a couple people in prayer requests tonight... Malisa, that she keeps getting stronger. my Aunt Dawn who has CF, that she keeps fighting for her life. and Mumbles, that she gets well soon!

Hope everyone has a GREAT week!

Amanda :-)

Amanda Perrotta

MONDAY, JANUARY 22, 2007
Hey!
So, i have a prayer request today. It's actually for my sister. She found out last night that she has pneumonia. The Dr. said it was pretty bad, too. She's had it for two weeks, but we thought it was broncidous (sp?) and so did the Dr., but it turned out it was pneumonia. So she's not feeling to well right now. so if you could just keep her in your prayers.

My terms: My legs were killing me the other night, and you probably want to know why, right? Well, my mom skipped my feeds, and i felt tired all day! Then, at the end of the day, my legs were throbbing, and i had no idea why, and i didn't even notice that my mom didn't give me my feeds, so then my mom's like, i guess she needs it... So then i was hooked up to an IV all night (ughh!)

OK, i have to tell you this story because i wanted to ask you a question after it. So the other night i was watching the first anniversary of High School Musical. And i was thinking, what was i like last year at this time? I thought, well i only had one AFO, i didn't need crutches, i didn't have a tube in my stomach, and i wasn't underweight. Then i thought, what will it be like next year for the High School Musical 2 reunion? Will i have another tube in my stomach?, will i be in a wheelchair? I just thought about that... if anyone ever thought about that, would you let me know 'cause i never thought about that, and i wanted to know if it was normal...lol.

Amanda :-)

FRIDAY, JANUARY 26, 2007
Hey!
So, i guess i found out there's truly a reason for everything. Last night, my sister Carolyn, who has pneumonia, was talking to a friend on her cell phone, and she was saying how she couldn't go anywhere, and she was sick of all the Dr. appts. and no one else knows what it's like. Well, i guess she got a dose of my life for a couple weeks. I don't know if she wanted to know, but i know she didn't know how i felt everyday, and now i know she will appreciate how my pace goes and all of my Dr. appts. I mean, i know how it feels to be in the hospital... why wouldn't i?!?!? I've only been there about 1,000 times! Anyways, i just wanted to tell you that because my journal wasn't talking back...lol.

Amanda :-)

TUESDAY, JANUARY 30, 2007
Hey!
I have a lot going on right now, so let's get right on it. A couple days ago, i thought my [G-tube] site was infected because it was all red around the opening, and it hurt like crazy! But it turned out it was just ...well it just hurt. So i have no worries about that right now. My legs have been hurting more often. I know all of the nutrition stuff is supposed to help me, but for some reason it doesn't help my legs or it's just a bad week for them. I'm also very tired it seems this week also. I need some extra sleep, let's say two hours? I feel like i'm going to fall asleep in class (and no not like a regular person). My body just seems to be falling apart this week. But i just don't know why.

Amanda Perrotta

I'm not sure if i told you guys this, but my mom dropped off my Double H Ranch Camp papers to my Dr. last week, and she is returning them tomorrow for my mom to fill out the rest. I'm so excited about the Summer...well, just because of Double H![1]   I finally finished my song from music that was a secret project, and still is until right now, and you guys can't show anyone until i put all of the stuff together because i'm making a video, too. OK, so here're the lyrics. the music is from "Hanging On" by Cheyenne.

"Hanging on"

My legs Hurt
I'm so tired; i've got no energy.
I sleep all day.
I got no appetite.

I don't cry, but i still feel sad
And i don't want no sympathy!
There could be worse things.
I'm gonna write about it.

And I'll be fine. I just need some time.
(Chorus)

I'm hanging on today, and nothing's gonna stop me anyway.
I'm holding on, i'm strong.
I'm the only one who can make a change.

---

[1] Double H Ranch is a special summer camp in Lake Luzern, NY for kids with disabilities and special needs. It is associated with the Paul Newman camps.

I don't wanna fight. I gotta live my life.
I'm gonna make it right.
I'm hanging on... and nothing's gonna stop me anyways.

My mom didn't know
That i knew kids could die from Mito
But I'm not
Gonna let it get me down.

I know in the future I'll need more help.
I'll probably be in a wheelchair.
But God made me that way.
And i like who i am.

And i'll be fine
I'm gonna be alright
(Chorus)

People don't know about Mito
There's no cure for it yet.
Keeping my head up.
Keeping my head up.
Keeping my head up.

(Chorus)

I've had a bad day.

So that's it. sorry if it took up time. how was it?

Amanda Perrotta

MONDAY, FEBRUARY 05, 2007
Hey!

So I just wanted to update you on what's going on. I had to take a day off from school today because of my dumb tiredness. I was so tired today! I couldn't believe how much i slept. I think i was only awake for, like, maybe four hours? It was really amazing how tired my body was.

The other thing that's going on right now is that, at night, once again, i'm freezing cold! It's like i'm bare in the arctic...lol. My mom called the Dr. to see if that was normal and what to do about that. She said it's normal because, with Mito, my energy level is down right now, so if i want to get my temperature up, i have to walk around for about ten minutes, and i will feel a little more heated.

EXITING NEWS!
I was talking to my mom last night, and about a month ago, i asked her if i could do Make-a-Wish. She always said no, its for children that are dying. So I asked her again last night, and when i told her what i wanted to wish for, she said yes. I'll tell you what i wished for, and then i'll tell you why she said yes. I wished that i could go to the Bahamas and swim with the Dolphins with my aunt who has CF. My mom said yes because my aunt, i don't think she ever did Make-a-Wish. I want my aunt to come because she kind of has a disease like me. She's a fighter, though, because she lived past her life expectancy. So i want to take her to the Bahamas to celebrate what she is doing and what she is going through. My aunt is submitting me, so that's my exiting news! OK, well, i'll try to update you later.

Amanda :-)

MONDAY, FEBRUARY 12, 2007

Hey,

Sorry i'm lacking here. So my breathing problems are not getting any better. But i'm going to see the Pulmonologist (sp?) soon. So hopefully he will have some answers. I'm home today because my energy source was also lacking...lol. I think i know why i was tired, though—I want to hang out with Dahea and Carolyn at night, so i try to go up the stairs, and i think that takes some energy away from me. But last night i went up the stairs A LOT! That's really all for medical conditions.

I may have told you this or may have not. Last month, i got my papers to fill out for my Double H Ranch Camp. My Dr. had to fill some of it out so my mom dropped it off [to him]. And i think this week we're mailing it out! I think this summer might be the BEST summer ever because this camp looks like it will change my life. One of my teachers told me that in my class. He worked there one summer, and he said it was AWESOME!

Prayer requests I have a couple prayer requests. For Malisa, that she keeps getting stronger. for my Aunt Dawny, that she is not sad about her Grandma dying. and for all of the families who are going through a ruff patch right now, that they will get some relaxation.

I'll try to update in a few days.

Amanda Perrotta

Amanda :-)

FRIDAY, FEBRUARY 16, 2007
Hey Everyone!

So i'm not sure if i told you last time (i have such a short term memory loss...lol), my nutrition supplements at night were giving me the low energy because they had too much carbs in them. And as i know at least, i'm not supposed to have many carbs in one day. So i'm on a different feed, and its working out pretty well. I tried it last night, and i can definitely manage more.

My mom and dad finally put a limit to the stairs, and i get frustrated sometimes at them because i want to go hang out upstairs with Dahea and Carolyn, but i just can't climb that much anymore because #1, my legs are exhausted, and #2, i use up most of my energy when i'm in school, and coming home and climbing stairs doesn't make it much better. But i'm getting used to it now, and i think Carolyn and Dahea are, too.

I think Abby [the service dog] MIGHT actually have the potential to become a therapy dog after all. Last week in training class, we worked on something for therapy dogs, and on the second day she got it to an A+! I'm so excited for this summer when we can see if she is really ready to be a therapy dog! Next year (when or if she becomes a therapy dog), i want to bring her to hospitals (Children's Hospitals, to be exact) and just let her sit with the children for a while because, if you knew Abby, you would want that while to spend with her.

Amanda :-)

TUESDAY, FEBRUARY 20, 2007

Hey

So i got an update on my Mickey Button and when i am going to get it today. I was supposed to get it next month in March, but my mom called my surgeon who performed the operation for my G-Tube and asked her when i am getting my mickey, and she said in April! I can't believe that i am keeping this G-Tube for another month and a half! And another thing is, when they put the mickey in, they have to do it in the OR because of my Mito, and the breathing thing that's been happening, and they MIGHT have to keep me overnight! I am so bummed about that, but i guess i better start getting use to it. The only thing that really bums me is that i can't do gym for another month and a half. And i LOVE gym! It's sooooo fun!

i got my hair cut. I think i told you i was doing Locks of Love because #1, i couldn't really handle my hair any more, and #2, i have to have some EEG's[2] and stuff, and with long hair it makes it so much worse! But i LOVE my new haircut, and it is so much easier. My mom says i look like you, Malisa...lol. I always tell her i tried not to make my haircut look like you, but it kind of does, and she also said I look like your daughter Malisa...lol. I was cracking up on that one.

Amanda :-)

---

[2] Electroencephalogram, to measure brain function.

Amanda Perrotta

SATURDAY, FEBRUARY 24, 2007
Hey,
So, this weekend has been a BLAST!   Except my not being able to walk around like most kids in a mall. I finally realized this week that i need more help with my muscles than i ever needed. I found out this week that going up the stairs, down the stairs, walking in stores is taking away sooooo much energy it's UNBELIEVABLE!   I mean, i already take up much needed energy in school. So when i get home and get out of the shower, i just want to relax and get my energy ready for the next day. I know it's going to get worse through the years, and that's what i fear. I don't want to go around in a wheelchair by the time i'm 17 or 18. I'm already in a wheelchair when i need to go to stores, but i thought, what about next year? What if i'm going to need a wheelchair 24/7? I'm not ready for that, so i'm trying not to think about it. I hate that more people don't know about Mito. I wish there was some way we could get it out there so people could raise money to help us find a cure.

Anyway on the up side...i found not a colored wheelchair but a colored SCOOTER!   And it's not just a regular scooter, it's a medical scooter, and it purple, has a horn! and has a mirror!   I'm really excited about getting it because i can finally be independent! So i'm looking forward to that!   The other things that have been GREAT this week have been that I went to go see "Bridge to Terabithia" and, let me tell you, if you haven't seen it, GO SEE IT! It's the best movie! I LOVED it! I fell in love with it, and i think i may actually marry it...lol.
I went to the mall and built a bear. its name is Champ, and half of the money i paid for it goes to kids with Cancer, AIDS and other

stuff. I bought it a wheelchair and Hello Kitty clothes. So now every time when i go to the hospital, Champ can, too.

Nothing else has been happening except that school starts Monday. i'm so excited for that...i'm excited to see my friends again, and for them to see my haircut! ...I'll try to update later on next week.

Amanda :-)

THURSDAY, MARCH 01, 2007
Hey!
What a hard and exhausting week it has been for me and my family. I never thought that going back to school after a one week break was going to be so hard for my muscles...but i guess i was wrong. At recess time, we walk three laps around the school...well, the hallways in the school for now. And i realized on my first lap that my legs were hurting a little (and that normally doesn't happen), so i just knew i had to build myself up again for Wed, so i think that's why i took Tuesday off, because of my legs.

PT is getting a little harder for me to do. at the beginning of the year, i was able to do everything and not take breaks and go out the door not hurting or have a muscle cramp. But right now during PT, that's what's happening.... sometimes it hurts so bad i can't control my legs, and they collapse. I think one leg did it two weeks ago before break. Maybe one day i'll get back up to that point again, like at the beginning of the year (i can dream).

My Make-a-Wish is coming along good... i actually found out that my Dr. recommended me for Make-a-Wish, and he put my name in, and the next day the Make-a-Wish people called my mom and asked her a 1,000 questions...lol. The lady said once she gets the Drs'. signatures she's going to come to my house and ask me a couple questions. So i'm kinda looking forward to that!

My scooter should be coming tomorrow or Saturday, so watch out everyone. Amanda is on the roads...lol.

OK, so my last thing is prayer requests: For Malisa, that she keeps getting stronger. For my dad, that his BP [blood pressure] will go down. and for Erik, that he will get better soon.

Amanda :-)

SATURDAY, MARCH 03, 2007
Hey,
So i went to see the Pulmonologist (sp?) yesterday, and i told him what i've been going through, and he said, "CPAP"! [Continuous Positive Air Pressure: a mask and gentle, continuous forced oxygen over the face to prevent sleep apnea.] So the plan for this is that first i have to go to St. Peter's, and they have to see how much oxygen i have to be put on at night. I hate doing these kinds of things because they watch you with that tiny camera in the corner, and the Dr. said they're going to monitor my dreams and my breathing. I have no clue why they are going to monitor my dreams, but they must have a reason. So once that is said and done, they will find out how much oxygen i will need at night, and then they will supply it. I just wish it could be done at Albany Med because i have never been to St.Peter's (i don't think, at

least), and i trust Albany so much more!   My mom asked the Dr. if the breathing COULD get any worse, and he said NO!   I hope he is right...i'm pretty sure he is.

Prayer Requests: Right now Erik really needs all the prayers he can get, so please pray for Erik, that he will rebuild his strength.   also that Malisa keeps building her strength. Thanks

Amanda :-)

SUNDAY, MARCH 04, 2007
OK,
So this is going to be quick because i'm not supposed to be up, and i'm going to explain why. Here we go. it's been a VERY long night and morning.   My G-Tube had been killing me the past night and morning, so my mom called the Dr. today, and he told my mom that tomorrow i'm going in for surgery because either it's infected or the bubble thingy blew because i lost more weight. So i just wanted to tell you guys that so you have a heads up in case you don't hear from me. I'm really not excited about this because i was supposed to meet my Pen pal this week, and i've been looking forward to that since last week!   I'm so NOT happy, but whatever makes this killing pain go away, it's fine with me.   The other thing is Anesthisia(sp?).   I hope i come out of it OK. Sometimes my eyes go nuts when i come out of it, and once in a while i shake a little.   So this is what's going to happen. either i'm going to get my Mickey Button early, or i'm going to have to get ANOTHER G-Tube. I'll try to get my sister to update tomorrow night and tell you what's going on.   Please keep praying for Erik who is in the same hospital i'm going to be in, that he gets better! And that i get through this OK without another G-Tube!

Amanda Perrotta

Thanks,
Amanda

MONDAY, MARCH 05, 2007
Hey,
Well, i'm back from the ER from last night. Last night i woke up
in sooo much pain around 12:00, and my mom and dad decided
they had to call the ambulance. So i was off to the ER and was
throbbing in pain. I got there, and they hooked me up to an IV,
gave me morphine (that works, and i LOVE it!), and did a CT
scan. I waited for a while with loads of morphine, and i found out
my tube was in place, but they just caught an infection starting to
spread. It's called cellulitis. They gave me some antibiotics and
pain meds to go home with at 5:30 am. My thought was they
shouldn't have sent me home because i'm still in a lot of pain, and
i'm white as a ghost. I meet with the surgeon on Wed., and they
might end up doing the Mickey Button on Thursday. My mom
said most likely they will do the Mickey Button on Thursday,
which means no Pen Pal time on Friday. I'm OK with that as long
as i get out of this throbbing pain. My strength is unbelievable
right now. I can't stand in the tub like i usually do. I can hardly
walk-in, just lay in bed all day. and last night i was, like, shaking
when i stated to get up. I'll try to update on Wed. to tell whether
i'm getting the Mickey or not.

Amanda :-)

Please keep praying for Erik and Malisa

TUESDAY, MARCH 06, 2007

Hi everyone. This is Amanda's mom. Manda is not doing very well right now. She is so weak!! This is the first time I have had to update you all for her, and that makes me sad. Malissa, if you read this, Manda is pulling from the strength you have shown her, and all the love and support. Darcy, also, the same. Louis (dad) and I want to thank you two so very much. To everyone out there, I thank you all so much for the support and love that you have given and will continue to give. We only ask for your prayers right now, and love and support. Love,

The Perrotta Family

WEDNESDAY, MARCH 07, 2007

Hey!

It's Amanda. I'm finally up at the computer doing much better! The last three days have been not so much fun. I had to go to the ER on Monday morning because of the awful pain i was having from the G-Tube. So then i came back home, and i started on my antibiotics and pain meds and, of course, they made me start throwing up Monday night and Tuesday. I felt so weak the last two days. I couldn't get to the bathroom, the computer, my room. I really couldn't get anywhere. I just laid and stared in one spot all night and day. I haven't eaten anything really. I've been going on feeds. Last night i kind of came around. So i thought i would give you an update myself!

Amanda :-)

Amanda Perrotta

THURSDAY, MARCH 08, 2007
Hellooooo!!

So today's Dr. appt went GREAT! I talked to the surgeon who did my G-Tube about getting my Mickey Button (or, as i call it, Minnie), and she said we could either do it today or wait two more weeks. So I decided to do it today! It hurt a little since she didn't give me anything. But it's so much easier and comfortable! And there's not much leakage either. I still have to turn it, which is a down, but the rest is all good!

I got my scooter yesterday! It is the neatest thing i ever rode on. It said you can only go five on it, but i think you can go at least 15 mph. It goes so fast! And it's like driving a car (that's what my sister said anyways). I already hit two things so....

I got to meet Erik yesterday, which was so thrilling for me because i never met anyone (in person) with Mito before. He needs more prayers, so if you could pray for him. I'm going to try to go to school tomorrow to meet my pen pal Haley.

Amanda :-)

MONDAY, MARCH 12, 2007
Hi,
I'm home today...i'm really not so thrilled about that, but it's kind of my fault in a way. This weekend i cheated on my carb diet. I ate chocolate, ice cream, and spaghetti. i usually don't eat all of that, but it was such a craving! What kid at age 15 doesn't crave chocolate? But then look what happens to me. I have no energy

for school on Monday. But overall, i did pretty well this weekend. I took my scooter out for a ride in the neighborhood, and it was so funny because i took Abby (becoming a therapy dog), and as soon as she saw a car, she hopped on the scooter and rode with me until the car was out of sight. I took it as a, 'Don't hurt my Mommy' thing, but i don't know if she was just tired or was protecting me because it was my first time out on my scooter in the neighborhood.

Malisa is home!!!! I am so proud of you, Malisa, and hope you are nice and comfy in your house again. Keep up the excellent work!!!

OK, well, i'll update later on this weekend.

Amanda :-)

WEDNESDAY, MARCH 14, 2007
Hi...this might be a little long.
So, today was a FANTASTIC day!!! I wish i could have these days everyday sometimes. FINALLY got to go back to Gym! And let me tell you, it was the best feeling i have had in a long time. It felt like i was back on my tracks again. We played volleyball, and i spiked that ball so hard it almost got caught in this net thing in the ceiling...lol. But i had to spike it that hard because it felt so good! And i was the only girl in the class... ;-) And we went outside for a walk it was just so nice. We had music today, and for some reason i just think the Spring air caught me today. Music was so fun! We listened to Hey Oh (Snow) by The Red Hot Chili Peppers. Then, once we were done doing that, we just played the drums to the music. I just thought i would share that...lol.

My parents had a meeting with the teachers yesterday after school to talk about my goals and everything, and what i will be doing next year (yes, i am staying in classroom 8 next year!). I was so excited to hear that! And i had even better news with it. I will be helping out in my school during the summer with little kids (while i get my OT, PT, and Speech). I personally think that's a GREAT deal because i LOVE little kids and helping them out.

There are two down things for next year. They are upping my OT and PT, and i think my Best Friend in the school might be leaving to go to another school, so i'll have to deal with that, but i'll get through it.

Everyone have a Happy St. Patrick's Day!
Amanda :-)

MONDAY, MARCH 19, 2007
Hi,
Sorry i haven't updated...i wasn't feeling so well for the past 3-4 days. It really started on St. Patrick's Day. I had no energy whatsoever. I slept most of the day. i tried to get up, but my body was a little shaky. I then took a shower once i started to feel a little burst of energy, but for my advice, DON'T EVER DO THAT! because it took away the rest of my energy, and my hands were shaking, and i tried to update you all, but my hands were literally shaking on the keyboard. Yesterday i hardly ate anything except for when my mom hooked me up to my feeds, and a shook. I never felt such a lack of energy in my whole entire life!!! But i'm just glad that i'm feeling a little better now, and i can

finally type and get up and walk. I'm trying to conserve my energy for a very special birthday tomorrow (hint hint...wink wink). So, right now, i'm hooked up to my IV and getting my feeds so that i can have loads and loads of energy for tomorrow!

Amanda :-)

TUESDAY, MARCH 20, 2007
OK, quick update,

MAKE-A-WISH UPDATE!!!

Make-a-Wish called yesterday afternoon, and they are sending two Wishers out here next week!!!! I have to think of my wish fast. I already know i want to go to Discovery Cove and swim with the dolphins, but they said i could go to Disney World, too, and stay in Cinderella's Castle. So i might actually think about that. If you guys have any opinion, please don't hesitate to tell me.

I'm doing something else that's really special for Family Night [at school], but i can't tell because i know my mom checks in on my site, so if you want to really know, you can email me.

Amanda :-)

FRIDAY, MARCH 23, 2007
Hey!

So, overall my week was pretty good (i can't complain). I didn't go to school on Thursday because i didn't sleep very well on Wed night. I'm not sure if it was because of my breathing issues or i just couldn't get to sleep. I personally think the breathing issues are getting worse. But for the past few nights, they have been the same. Today was a pheww day! I went to a Garden Show because it benefited my school. And we walked and walked. But my teacher was great about going upstairs and letting me take the Elevator (I'm glad i have her next year!).After that we went to Pizza Hut, and i ate a little bit because we're having pizza tonight....hehe.

This morning was a little bit of a surprise. I went out to get on my bus, and i went down the stairs and fell on ice...lol. It seems funny now, but it wasn't then. I was thinking, "Great, what about my minnie, and what if it fell out?" and then i thought, "oh great, i might have to go to the ER." But everything turned out OK.

My Minnie Button started bleeding last night, and i know the reason. I pick the yucky crusty stuff off of it to try to make it clean, but the fact is, it makes it dirty because it will make an infection on it. So i'm trying not to get my hands anywhere near my Minnie right now. I'm doing VERY well so far.

Amanda :-)

SATURDAY, MARCH 24, 2007
Oh were do i start,

Let's start with yesterday. I got a nice, HUGE cold sore on my lip, and now i look like i have new lips. This morning i felt a lack of energy, and my throat hurt. I was coughing, and my chest hurt....so my mom went to the Dr. with me, and i have a sinus bug and a high temp of 101.2°. I haven't had my regular appetite all day. I ate some eggs, drank half of a shake, and then had some rice and broccoli. Trust me, that's not my normal appetite. I feel so lazy, but i think it's just my energy level taking a spin. Thank goodness i caught the sinus bug in time, otherwise i would have had Bronchitis!   Abby hasn't left me all day, and if someone was to pick her up when she was lying next to me, she would growl (that's how protective she is of me).

On a good note I had such an AWESOME time last night! Two Koreans came over along with two of Carolyn's friends. I have to tell you they were the cutest things. I wish i got a picture with just them, but i got a picture with the group.

That's really all. I just wanted to update (in case i'm not on for a couple days) but hopefully the antibiotics will help! ?

Amanda :-/

WEDNESDAY, MARCH 28, 2007
OK, this is gonna be quick,
I've been really sick for the past couple days, and weak. I'm still very weak right now, so that's why i'm being quick about this. But i think i'm almost over the sickness (hopefully!) I was running a fever of 102-102.7°!   And, trust me, that's not my usual temp. I haven't moved (except today is really my first day of moving). I haven't eaten one single thing in the past 2-3 days. all i have been going on is feeds. I have lost five pounds. I'm now down too 121. I think i'm almost done coughing up green mucus stuff. But my nose is still going, and i can't control it!   Anyways, i just wanted

to update you on that.

One more thing....Abby (who's going to be a Therapy Dog) passed her test last night coming in 3rd! Her trainer said she doesn't even need to go to the next level. she can go get tested right after she graduates (which is next week). But we're still going to the next level.

OK, well i'm gonna go lay down.

Amanda :-/

FRIDAY, MARCH 30, 2007
Hey Guys!
Well, it's been a ruff week, but, all-in-all, the end turned out pretty well (except for my dad getting what i had). So I feel SO much better now!   I think i started to feel all the way better the other day. But i was still coughing up stuff and weak and etc. I'm still coughing, but just a cough, not hacking anything up (thank goodness!) Thank you guys for all of the messages and prayers while i was sick. I checked them everyday on my PSP[3] (since i really couldn't get up).

So yesterday i had a Dr. appt. with the surgeon who did my G-Tube and my Minnie Button (my mickey). she just showed my mom what to do in case it ever fell out, and it looks so simple that a monkey could do it, but i probably wouldn't have the guts....lol. Then they weighed me, and i think i lost another pound or two

---

[3]Play Station Personal, a compact game system that also has wireless Internet.

because i had my AFOs on and a sweater, and it was the same weight, and they didn't take any off...but who knows? all i know is i want to gain at least 5 pounds! They also ordered me another mickey button in case the other one fell out, but they ordered the other one a little bit bigger in case i gain weight.

I found out another amazing thing yesterday....my AFOs fit into my Crocs (thanks to Emily!). I was so amazed that i could walk in them and they fit, and i don't have to JUST wear sneakers anymore. I was just like, YEA!

Amanda :-)

MONDAY, APRIL 02, 2007
Hey!
Such an AWESOME first day back at school (let me tell you!). It's probably because it's been a while since i've been at school and i love being back in a schedule and just seeing my friends and knowing what's going on again. But the best thing that happened today was the Hip Hop class! I didn't think i could last through the whole thing, but i DID! It was amazing, and i wanted to keep going and going like the Energizer Bunny (ha-ha). It was so fun because it was my best friends, and we danced to a song from "Step Up," and i just can't explain the feeling it was.

Make-a-Wish UPDATE
So i know you will all want to know about this one. The Wish Makers called, and they will be coming April 20th. I am super excited!!!!!! So i just thought you would want to know that. ;-)

One of my friends, Allison (who has my disease, Mitochondrial

Disease), died last week, and she was only a kid, yet i guess her work was done. If you could please pray for her family, i know they must be going through a ruff time.

Amanda :-)

WEDNESDAY, APRIL 04, 2007
Hey Everyone!

Last night was an exiting night for Abby and me because Abby graduated Intermediate Dog Class (which means one more step closer to becoming a Therapy Dog!) I was excited because the trainer's dog (who is a therapy dog) was there. and she was so nice and calm, and i just wanted to take her home. Abby is starting the next and last level to training on Saturday, and it will be for only six weeks this time instead of eight!!!!!

I forgot to tell you all that papers came for my sleep thing for my breathing problems at night. My mom finished filling them out today, and i think i might be going either next month or May?

Well, that's pretty much it. Thanks goodness (in a good way!)
Amanda :-)

SUNDAY, APRIL 08, 2007
Hi Everyone!

First of all HAPPY EASTER! I hope all of you had a great Easter. Not much has been happening (in a good way). I'm on Spring

Vacation from school, which is a good thing because i can sleep in and just relax and conserve my energy. A couple days ago, i found out I went down another pant size (weight loss), which i'm not too happy about, so i've been stuffing my face with foods i can eat and putting as much formula into me as i can handle. I just want to get back to 127 lbs. at least. It makes me sick when my sister says she can see my spine bone through my shirt when i get hot. I'm working on it though :-).

Today my dad showed me this cool trick. It's where you put a needle on a piece of thread and you swing it above your wrist eight times and then if it goes side to side it means you will have a baby boy when you get older, if it keeps circling a baby girl, if it stops no kids. It worked for my mom when she was younger, and it was exactly correct—two girls. So, my dad swung it above my wrist eight times and it went side to side. I felt kind of happy because i do still want a baby in a way when i get older, but in another way i don't because i know i won't have the strength. So my dad swung it again to see if i was going to have more kids and it stopped. I was glad! I just thought i would share this with you in case you wanted to try because it worked for my mom, and it was 100% correct.

NEWS ON ABBY
Abby started Advanced [Training] Sat. Morning and was doing pretty well. She is now up to a four-minute stay and did one thing better then a Therapy Dog (which impressed me). I think she will make a GREAT Therapy Dog!

My Double H Ranch Camp papers came back from the Dr's. yesterday (FINALLY!), and they have to get to there [Ranch headquarters] by the 14th. I'm worried because they still have to go

Amanda Perrotta

through another Dr. Next month we're going there to visit.

Amanda :-)

THURSDAY, APRIL 12, 2007
Hi,
The week has been passing by so quickly, and i hate it but like it (if you get what i mean). So my Double H papers are going out today, and i so hope they make the date they are supposed to be there by.I think it's April 15th?? I was worrying about it last night so badly. I just want to have a little fun in my summer this year!

Last night I went up the stairs (i can do it once a day if i get hooked up to my feeds) to play with my sisters, and toward the end of the game, my legs started to cramp...you know that cramp where it feels like a growing pain? I told my sister because my mom and dad were asleep at 12:00 am, lol. And she said, "Is it a growing pain?" Then, after a minute, she was like, "oh yea, sorry i forgot." I started to laugh because i thought if i had that many growing pains i would be at least 6'4"...lol. But then last night when i came downstairs, i finally knew what triggered it (at least i think so). I went up the basement stairs earlier from riding my scooter in the neighborhood. So i think going up and down the stairs too many times did it.

*Make-a-Wish NEWS! *
So i've been forgetting to put this into all of my entries, but we had to reschedule our meeting with our Wish Makers because my sister has a Sports banquet that she has to attend on the 20th, and my mom and dad have to go because my dad was a part of the

team (sorta). But they're trying for that weekend, so i'm not too worried.

I have two Dr. apts. coming up. Next week i get my new PURPLE hearing aids!!!!!!! I've been waiting for them for forever because they had to order the colored backs and everything so.....

Amanda :-)

SUNDAY, APRIL 15, 2007
Hey!

I started out with a nice cold sore on my top lip the other day (which is nice because i always think i'm going to get sick when i get those things). Last time when i got a cold sore, i came down with a bad cold thing. I'm happy that didn't happen this time *knock on wood*. It might just be the weather change or that i get one of these things every month! My lip looks like i got punched...lol.

School starts back up tomorrow (if the snow stops!). It's April, and it's snowing. when was the last time this happened? The only thing i'm worried about is getting up. i've been used to sleeping in until like 9:00. But i'm sure if i get all my feeds into me right now i'll be fine. I'm excited to see my friends and teachers!

Make-a-Wish NEWS!!!!
So you know how i told you that my Wish Makers couldn't come on the 20th? Well, my mom called, and they are coming (drum roll please! ....) NEXT SUNDAY !!!!!!!!!! Can you see my excitement?!??! I hope you can because, when they called and

my mom said, "yes, next Sunday is great," i was jumping and screaming and yelling! I was just so happy!!!! And I can't wait to write about it next weekend!

I have NO idea if i am going to be going to Double H now because my mom still hasn't finished my papers. It's really my Dr's. fault. He took three months to fill out two sheets of paper (CAN YOU BELIEVE THAT?!?!???!). If i don't get in, i'm going to be so sad and angry. But the only thing i can do is wait and hope that i get in and have a GREAT summer!

Amanda :-)

WEDNESDAY, APRIL 18, 2007
Hi,
FOUR MORE DAYS UNTIL MY WISH MAKERS COME!!!!

Well, this week isn't going so well for me. I knew it was coming. Monday i went to school, and i felt GREAT! But Monday night, i started not to feel so, well.... tired, stomach aches, etc. I haven't been to school since Monday because i haven't been able to move really. When i get my feeds in me, i get a boost of energy, but then, when night falls, i'm back down again. This will be over probably by Sat. or Sun. because i know what is causing the fatigue and everything else. Hopefully i'll be up and feeling GREAT by Sunday.

Well, you probably know my Wish Makers are coming on Sunday, and i finally know what i'm wishing for. But i'll tell you on Sunday ;-). I'm so excited!!!!! I wish i had the words to express how excited i am.... this and Double H is putting me on overload, so i'm trying not to think about both at the same time. Just one at a time. Because, if i think about both at the same time, i might end up in a seizure mode. And i DON'T want that to happen.

I have A LOT going on next week. Family night at school, my cousin's birthday party in Utica, and just a lot of practicing for Family Night. Family Night is going to be AWESOME!

Amanda :-)

SUNDAY, APRIL 22, 2007
Oh my!

I'm so overwhelmed right now that i don't even now where to start?!   OK, well, my Wish Makers came today, which you probably know. They came in with a $15.00 gift certificate for me and my sisters. I never really expected that, but it was nice of them. One of them said she was sorry she forgot my T-shirt, but it didn't really matter to me at that point. The next step was that she asked me what was my wish, and i told her I wished i could go to Discovery Cove and spend two nights in Cinderella's Castle. They said that was a great wish, and then they asked me, "if we can't make that happen, what would you want?" I said just to stay in Disney. They asked me all of these questions (which i have no idea what they are going to do with). they asked me what's my favorite color, favorite band, favorite movie etc. Then they told me about the place in Disney. I will be getting $20.00 a day to spend for suvaniers (sp?), and everything else is paid for, too—food , snacks EVERYTHING!!!!!   I was so shocked!   They next asked about the date. I told them i wanted to go in the fall around

November or even in December. They are going to check around November 10th or something like that. This was such an exiting day for me, and i can't WAIT for the next six months!

Amanda :-D

TUESDAY, APRIL 24, 2007
Hey...Quick Update.

So I had my Neuro appt. on Monday, and they weighed me, and again i lost two or three pounds!   For some reason, i cannot seem to keep my weight on me no matter how much i eat or how many feedings i get. But i'm trying, i really am. Right now i weigh 119 pounds (which isn't good for a teen my age and my height!).   So i'm trying to at least get up to 125 pounds. My Neuro nurse said i am doing good with my seizures (knock on wood). I got my hearing Aids....they're purple with sparkles.   The only problem with that is they don't seem to fit correctly, so i'm wearing my old ones again...lol. I have an AFO Dr. appt. next Tuesday because, since i'm losing more weight, my AFO's are getting bigger on me, so i need new Velcro® and to tighten them a up a little bit.

*Make-a-Wish NEWS! *
OK, so my Wish Makers called my mom, and they called my Dr. also. I found out i cannot go swimming with the dolphins....BUT, they are setting me up with something to do with dolphins (i do not know what because they won't tell me, and my mom won't either!) But i'm still very excited!   So instead of going to Discovery Cove, i'm going to be staying at Give Kids the World. Have any of you ever heard of that?   It's such a beautiful place,

and i think they said it's right next to Disney!   If you want to check it out, i think there's an address in Google.

Well, tonight i'm going to a Birthday Celebration at PetsMart [since standardized to PetSmart] with Abby, and tomorrow is Family Night, so i'm excited, and i'm ready!

Amanda :-)

THURSDAY, APRIL 26, 2007 09:30 PM,
Hey,

So Family Night went GREAT!!!!!! I think I did pretty well. But everyone did GREAT last night.   I think most of the families enjoyed the Hip Hop Dance. I did...lol. The other thing I did was sing to a song called "My Wish" by Rascal Flatts. Everyone said they were crying...lol. It was a GREAT night for me, but it took it's toll. today I couldn't get up because I had school yesterday and family night right after it!   I guess that's just the price you pay, though.

I have a lot going on this weekend, so i'm not sure about Monday for School, but maybe, if i get a lot of feeds in me.... First, tomorrow i'm going on a field trip for playing volleyball!   On Saturday, i have training class with Abby (YES, FREEDOM TIME!) Then, right after that, were leaving to go to Utica for my cousin's birthday party. On Sunday, were walking for The March of Dimes because we're on a Team, Emma's ACES. It stands for Amanda, Carolyn, Emma and Sarah. Then, whew, i'm done!!!

On Tuesday, I have an appt. for my AFO's to get them shrunk a little bit. I'm excited because they have been sliding up and down my legs, which kinda doesn't support my legs. Other than that, i don't think anything else is really going on. I'm really excited about this summer and what's going to be going on!

Amanda :-)

MONDAY, APRIL 30, 2007
Hey!
So, this weekend was busy, and busier than i thought it would be. Saturday was up and go, go, go! As soon as i woke up, i got myself ready, then Abby for her training classes. And in between all of that, i tried to pack some fun stuff to do in the car on the way to Utica. After Abby's training class, my dad and I had to quickly stop in the dollar store and then try to get a pizza for the family. As soon as we got home, i had to let Abby out and get myself together, and then we left for Utica! On the way there, i started my feeds because i wanted some energy to play with my cousins, and i didn't eat anything all day. I have to admit, Utica was the highlight (along with Abby's class) of my weekend. I got to see my cousins, Liam and Belle. I hardly ever get to see them, which is sad because they are the cutest things. We didn't stop after we went home! we sat for like 15 minutes and then went out to Friendly'. I ate a nice salad along with a Monster Mashsundae...lol. It was good, but it took its toll again.

On Sunday, we woke up, showered, and went to a park and walked (i didn't walk. i rode my scooter). It was for The March of Dimes. But what really surprised me is, even though i was on my scooter, once i got home, i slept for three hours! It wore me out so much!   I couldn't believe that just THAT could wear me out. And i know it's going to get harder in the future, so i'm trying to conserve energy right now. I didn't go to school today (i knew i wasn't going to be able to get up at 6:30 AM and go, go, go at school. It will just wear me out more, and that's what i hate because school is the best thing for me. I LOVE school!   And the sad thing is, i miss at least one or two days out of five days in the week. Tomorrow i have my AFO appt. to shrink them, and then i'm going to school. Wed. i have no school, then Thursday and Friday school! On Wed., i'm going to paint the bakery and try to call a friend. ;-).

This Sunday, i'm going to the Double H for Open House. I'll let you guys in on a little secret: Ty [Pennington] from Extreme Home Makeover redid some of Double H. My Wish Makers told me, and I'm going to see it before it's on TV. It will be on TV on the Last episode. it's going to be a 2-hour special. Have a GREAT week!

Amanda :-)

THURSDAY, MAY 03, 2007
Ughh. such a hard but kinda rewarding day.

So, yesterday I found out I have to use a wheelchair in school (only sometimes). I wasn't fond of it at first, but then, when i thought about it, it kinda added up, i guess. It's just hard, though, because my friends know me as the funny girl who walks around and jokes. So it was REALLY hard telling them today. Their expressions were kinda odd, but then they came around. My teacher, Diane, asked me if I wanted to tell them or just come in tomorrow and surprise them. I figured that it would be worse if i came in and was in a wheelchair because then they would be asking questions, and i really wouldn't want to answer. So i decided to tell them today. I told them that i will be using a wheelchair. I will use a wheelchair for laps when we do recess and field trips. And when i'm in the wheelchair, i DO NOT want to be treated differently! Then they asked questions. well mostly Cody (big surprise!)...lol. But he said how he needed a relaxation thing, so that made me feel a little bit better, and then i realized that Zack needed something that talked for him So basically i just need something i can use to lift up my legs for big walks or whatever.

The other cool thing Diane thought about was decorating my wheelchair in class for Art...lol. And all my friends can help, too, (if they want to). I'm going to spray paint it red or purple, put some sparkles on it, and stitch some things on the back. I think then it will look much cooler!

Amanda :-)

SUNDAY, MAY 06, 2007
Hey!

So today was such an AMAZING day! I went to Double H Ranch Camp (where i WILL be going this summer!). When we got there, i just couldn't believe i actually was there because i watched that thing that was on TV about 30 times, and said i'll never get to go there, but i was there! After my big open mouth part, we went inside where you hang out and stuff. there was pool, Pac Man, and other cool games!   I played Pac Man for a while waiting for our tour.   After like 15 minutes, we met our tour guide. ours was named, Weirdo (yea, don't ask, but he was so funny and cool). First we went into the Dining Hall, which i was thrilled to see!   Then we saw the cabins, and i saw which cabin i will be staying in this summer. Then to the High Ropes course. That was the 2nd best part. I'm not sure if i'm going to be able to do it (not physically, but courage!) It looked so big!   Then we went inside a cabin and saw what the beds looked like, and they look like a little home. After that, we went to see the basketball courts and The Happy Barn For Happy Campers where i got to meet my favorite buddy—this horse i loved!!!! I kept petting it and petting it. I think i was there for, like, 20 minutes...lol. That was my favorite part. Then we went to the BODY SHOP. We saw the rooms [where we'll go] if we're not feeling well or something. Then we went to the Stage area and costume area for The Talent Show night. The stage is so much bigger in life than on TV!   Then we saw the outdoor pool, and we went back into the dining hall for something to eat, where i got to meet Carrie and Tara. They said i have a definite chance of getting in because we live so close, and there're not many who live so close, so that made me feel better.   That was really fun, and i'm looking so so forward to August!

Amanda :-)

WEDNESDAY, MAY 09, 2007
Hey!

So, I have so far made school Monday, Tuesday, and WEDNESDAY!!!!!! That's such a HUMONGOUS change for me!   Usually i go Monday then skip Tuesday because i'm too exhausted, but since i've been in my wheelchair for laps i'm going to school every day, and i'm planning on being there everyday from now on. My wheelchair turned out GREAT!   It's purple, and it doesn't look anything like how it used to. I'm still getting a new one that's manual and electric so that i can be independent when we go to stores and such. I'm so proud of the progress i've made this week just Mon, Tues, and Wed. It's amazing what a wheelchair can do to save.   i'm going to the neuro so that they can see how much of the feeds i've been getting into me and to start shots. Yes, the shots that go into your body. I think my mom said their D12 [vitamin B12, to support energy production]. i'm just gonna need to get used to the idea of getting shots three to five times a week?!   But it's a quick adjustment for me since i LOVE shots...lol. I know, weird. They're also adding some oil to my formula to put some extra pounds on me. That's really all in the medical world...lol.

On Friday, i'm going to visit Erik who had his G-Tube placed in today. I'm praying for him and, everyone who reads this, if you can, please do the same. i went through that whole ordeal, and i know how he feels. it's a little bit of pain. But maybe i can cheer him up once i walk in the room Friday morning. :-). OK, well, i'll update this weekend

Amanda :-)

SATURDAY, MAY 12, 2007
Hey Everyone!

I MADE IT THROUGH THE WHOLE SCHOOL WEEK!!!!!!!! OK, i'm just so excited about this because i haven't done that since December maybe. I was just so happy when Friday ended, and then i could write in here and put this in. I'm proud of the progress i made this week, and i'm going to try to make a record for two weeks in a row. Just wanted to let everyone know quick...lol.

Everyone at school seems to enjoy my wheelchair at some point. For some weird reason they enjoy it more then me. And that's weird, but i guess it would be normal if i wasn't in a wheelchair and someone in my class was. They LOVE pushing me and making things up like, "oh, let's put a motor on it, and you can go full speed," or they try to put me into the ditch sometimes (which isn't mean, it's a joke between us). I just thought it would be different, like they would treat me differently, but NOPE, and i'm glad they don't.

Abby is graduating in three weeks from her last class, Advanced. She has come so far, and, when i think back of when i first brought her into PetSmart, and she was so excited and barked, and she didn't even know 'sit' or anything, now it's like she's a totally different dog. There was a man last weekend who came up to me when our class was doing a trick in an aisle, and he came RIGHT up to me and said in the middle of everything, "excuse me, but is she a Cairn Terrier?" And i said, "yes'" So he said, and this is mean!..."You will never be able to train that dog! that dog will never be off of that weird Gentle Leader® [collar], stop barking, or obey commands. i had Cairn Terriers for three years, and i had to get rid of them because of all of that." Well, i got so mad because she knows everything a Therapy Dog is going to need to know, and she just came off her Gentle Leader® today (thank you very much!). Then my instructor came up and said a few words, so.... Just showing people out there that, even if they're a breed that wets or whoever says they CAN'T be trained, don't listen because my dog is going to become the youngest [Cairn Terrier] Therapy Dog in NY.

Mothers' Day is coming tomorrow, so make sure you wish your moms a Happy Mothers' Day! I have a special gift for my mom.

Amanda :-)

PS: Please pray for Erik...i didn't get to see him, but keep praying for him with the G-Tube, that the pain will stop

TUESDAY, MAY 15, 2007

Wow!!! Busy weekend and week! I didn't make it to school Monday because i was so wiped out from Mothers' Day (but in a good way). On Saturday, i had classes with Abby and then went shopping! Sunday was the eventful day. We woke up, showered, and went to my mom's parents' house. My cousins were there, so i played with them, and i also taught Dahea how to play baseball and krocay (sp?). So that took A LOT out of me. Then after that, we went to my dad's parents' house, and we just sat and talked and everyone could tell i was wiped out because i was just sitting there hardly talking. So, i'm getting the hang of when i know i can go to school and when i think its a bad idea.

OK, well, i'll update later on next week.

Amanda :-)

FRIDAY, MAY 18, 2007
Hey,

All i can say is WOOOWWWW!!!   OK, let's start with Wed. I had a GREAT day. i did a half hour of gym and just had an awesome day!   Thursday, i had my Dr. appt., and here it comes. My mom helped me word this so remember—this isn't all correct wording in my words. I found out from my mom that my Dr. said i have to go back to NYC because my muscles have gotten weaker.   I'm going to see my original Dr. (Dr Harono) at Columbia Hospital. He's the only one in the area that deals with Mito and what's happening to my muscles. It's really just so that he can keep track of me and to see how good or bad my muscles have gotten because they have gotten a little worse. We leave on June 25th with my mom and my grandparents. The Dr. might help me with my wheelchair (get me an electric one) or start me on D20 [B12] or decide to put a port in me, but i won't know for a while. As soon as i know more i will update. So, yea, that's pretty much been the exiting news for the week.

Abby's last class before she graduates is tomorrow!!!   I'm so proud of her, and i can't wait to see her graduate in two weeks!

Next week is going to be busy. we have Sibling Day on Tuesday. Wed. i'm going bowling with my pen pal (don't ask me how i'm going to do that with my AFO's, but, where there's a will, there's a way). And on Thursday and Friday were selling poppy thingsies for the Vets that served in the war, so busy week=need lots of rest.

Amanda Perrotta

Amanda :-)

WEDNESDAY, MAY 23, 2007
Ahhhh!

My busy week is almost over!   I went bowling today, and it was sooooo much fun!   I was thinking to myself when was the last time i went bowling, and i remembered. the last time i went bowling was when i only had one AFO, and i could bowl without it. But i had to wear my AFO's this time, but it didn't really matter to me because, as long as i was bowling and having fun.... I decided for my birthday i want to go bowling with friends because today i found out that even people in wheelchairs can bowl. I thought that you only can bowl if you wear those shoes, so i was wrong!

*Make-a-Wish UPDATE! *

My Wish Makers called and said our date to go is in October, and we will be gone for Halloween!   I'm so excited because that's the date i really wanted!   Also they're coming not this weekend but next weekend, along with Abby's graduation party with her friends. So that's something to look forward too.

This week wasn't bad at all for me in school. It went by quick (as usual). it seems the whole year went by very quickly!   I hate how the year is ending so fast!!!! OK, well, i'll update next week.

Amanda :-)

SUNDAY, MAY 27, 2007

Amazing Amanda: My Journey Through Mito

Hey!

I first wanted to wish everyone a Happy Memorial Day (early)! I hope everyone is enjoying their time off and time with their family. Note: This is a long entry

So the evaluation with the PT went pretty good. It hurt a little, but all-in-all went better than i thought. The first half hour was the worst because i just sat there while my mom and her went through what i had and my meds and etc. Then she stretched my legs to see the strength and how weak my muscles were in my legs. I can already tell you some days they're really bad. Then she went around and looked at the house, and i had to show her how i got into bed and how i got into and out of the shower. She decided we needed adjustments on our house (which we already know, and we are planning to get, i think). The last thing was, she finally determined i need an electric wheelchair sometimes, so she called a man who designs them, and he will be coming this Friday to measure me for one and see how i do in one. I'm kind of nervous because i never would have thought i would be in an electric wheelchair this soon, but whatever helps, i guess.

This week for school i'm kind of disappointed because i'm only going two days out of five. I have Monday off, then i go [to school] on Tuesday, Wed. a Dr. appt, Thursday i go, Fri. i can't because the man is coming. The only thing i hate about how i can't go on Friday is that two of my teachers are leaving the school, and we're having a surprise party for them right when we get off the bus. I won't be there. :-(i feel so bad because they did so much for us. But i'll see them again.

We have a new addition to our family...i'll give you a little hint....he has a beak and has feathers....yes, a parrot. He's an African Grey Parrot (if i got that correct). His name is Henry, and he's a rescue bird. He's so cute and friendly...i'm going to try to take some pictures to put up. He's going to start talking soon so....wish us good luck...lol.

OK, now this you don't have to read, but it's a freaky story about how Abby knows something's wrong. OK, yesterday, well, first off i have been having sugar problems where my sugar drops and i need sugar, but then i crash. but anyways, yesterday i was sitting in the family room watching TV when Abby came up to me and started staring at me. i thought she had to go out, so i was, like, "OK, let's go Abby," and usually she follows me, but she just stood there and stared at me, so i tried again, and she wouldn't budge. All of a sudden, i felt my sugar drop, and i knew i had to get something in me, so Abby kind of led me into the Kitchen where there was candy. It was really funny how she knew i was going to have a sugar moment.

OK, have a GREAT week!

Amanda :-)

SATURDAY, JUNE 02, 2007
Phewww, this is going to be a long one....

So my Dr. appt. on Wed., i got weighed, and i wasn't really happy, but i'll get into that later on. Without my AFO's i weighed 112, with them i weighed 115. I lost seven pounds!   I keep losing weight. My stomach seems like it can't hold anything, but my mom and I finally found out a reason (maybe). After i eat something, i usually always get either a stomach ache or gas or it just comes out of me. I'm not sure what it's called, but my mom does, so i'll check up on that next time.

My Wheelchair fitting on Friday went GREATTTT!!!!! We looked through electric wheelchairs to see which one would suit me best for my needs, and the one i was looking at and liked was the best one suitable for me! It reclines, has a head rest, a gel cushion for my bottom, and a support for my back, too. I'm also very excited because i got to pick out a really cool color....lime green. It's actually a little darker than lime green, but i say lime green. I'm kind of nervous [about] when i get it because i have to get used to it...like, i know i need it, but sometimes i think i don't. i want to think i'm a normal "can skip and jump" kid. And i HATE how everybody looks at you when you are in a wheelchair or scooter or even just have AFO's on. it bothers me because they don't even understand, and its rude, staring. But i'll get used to it.

Abby graduated today!!!!!! She got two certificates—one for click a trick and one final certificate because it's her last class ever!!!! All we have to do know is just practice and practice, so maybe by fall or winter she will be ready to be tested. I'm not worried about her, though, because she will be a GREAT therapy dog! Maria (her trainer) got her a present, and it was The Wizard of Oz...lol. You know how Toto is a Cairn Terrier? Well, Abby is a Cairn Terrier and looks JUST like her, so i LOVE it, and i watch anything that has Abby in it, and plus i love that movie!

Next week i have a neuro appt. on Thursday, and that's all, so four days of school!!!!

Amanda Perrotta

Amanda :-)

TUESDAY, JUNE 05, 2007
Hey,

So Sunday went GREAT!!!! I think it was the best Sunday i ever had in my life...lol. My Wish Makers came around 1:00 with pizza, soda, and a shake for me. They really just talked about what's going on and paperwork and stuff, so it wasn't really anything for me...except i got a surprise. When i go to Disney, we're going to Sea World, and they're setting my family and I up so we can have dinner with Shamu!!!! I was so excited to hear that!!! i didn't even know that we were going to Sea World...lol.

The Party on Sunday was even better. now, everyone has to know by now i LOVE dogs more then anything in this world, so having three dogs over plus our three dogs was heaven to me. I played with the dogs out in the pouring rain, and they love to play fetch, so i kept tossing the ball for like an hour. They kept bringing it back to me, so i was like, let's keep going! There was a special dog there, though, whom i LOVE so much (not as much as Abby, but second), and her name is Maggie, and she is Abby's trainer's dog, and she is also a Therapy Dog. She is so gentle and kind, and she obeys anyone in one second.

I didn't make it to school on Monday because i was too tired from Sunday (who wouldn't be?). Abby slept until 2:30PM, and i slept until about 1:00PM.

Later that day i started getting headaches. i think, and my mom thinks, they were more auras, but they didn't really feel like them to me. They just were headaches, and my head felt a little weird. So that lasted until i fell asleep last night. I stayed home today because i was afraid i was going to get those headaches again in school, so i was being extra safe. Tomorrow i'm definitely going to school though!!! I'm excited it's June because that's when all the fun school stuff begins, like a lot of field trips and ending math, reading, and everything else.

Amanda :-)

FRIDAY, JUNE 08, 2007
Hey,

So i was wrong with the neuro. it was actually the Endochronologist (sp?) [a doctor specializing in electrolyte and hormone balance, and other bodily functions]. It was pretty much a long day because we left the house at 9:30 and came back at 2 or 3:00. They weighed me, and i'm going to unmark that too. i actually weigh 110 pounds, which is kinda yucky!

Anyways, first. Cheryl (my nurse) came in and talked about everything that has happened (which, if you have been reading, you basically know), so that was that, and then she started talking about how maybe we should start thinking about a port [inserted under the clavicle or collar bone for direct entry of medications or withdrawal of blood]. I was like, "woahhh" at first, but then, when she explained what it could do, i was like, yea...sure! My dad didn't look so happy about it because, well, admit it, it's another operation (but not as big as my G-Tube). Then Dr. Adams came in and talked more about the port and how it may help me gain weight and how it might not. I'm willing to take the chance because they can always take it out if it doesn't work.

The nutritionist also came in and decided my stomach aches are coming from my formula because it has too much fiber in it, so, instead of Fibersource, i'm just going to be having RCF (with three cans and water) [A formula specifically designed for those who have difficulty digesting or managing the high carbohydrate content of regular dietary formulas]. So hopefully that will help my stomach aches.

They took my blood, which was painful because they had to stick me twice, and both of my veins blew, so they really hurt right now and are fragile...lol.

Hope everyone has a GREAT weekend!

Amanda :-)

WEDNESDAY, JUNE 13, 2007
Oh my gosh, this is such an exiting day for me, but i'll tell you in a while.

OK, so this week so far has been going well. Yesterday i had school, and math was so much fun because i am finishing up my fractions unit, and the fun part about finishing up is that i got to make smoothies figuring out how many cups or whatever of ice cream or etc. i have to put in. And then, of course, i got to eat it...lol. But then, after i ate it at lunch time, i wasn't hungry because i ate the smoothie, so i only took two bites of my salad. But Diane, Chris, and I figured out that if i make the smoothies, eat lunch, then have my smoothie later at 2:20 (before i go home), i won't be full (maybe?) We'll try!

Karaoke was so much fun yesterday. i sang "Stand In The Rain" by Superchic. I think it was a good choice. I liked everyone else's performances also. But it was GREAT getting up and holding a mic and just having fun!

Today, i'm taking it easy and resting for all my end-of-the-year feild trips coming up. Next week i have FunPlex, Jumpin' Jack's, the park and who knows what else?! I'm sure i will be worn out by next weekend, though.

OK, so for the too much exiting news! OK, so you know the song/music video i have been doing? Well, my music teacher (Beth) e-mailed the artist who originally sang it—her name is Cheyenne, and i LOVE her songs and her voice. Anyway, she didn't just get in touch with Cheyenne, she got a PHONE CALL from her mother and Cheyenne!!!! Cheyenne wants to talk with me on the phone and wants to learn more about Mito. She said we can put the music video public!!! Oh my gosh, this is way too much for me to handle!!! On top of that, she wants to donate dresses for the poker run for Erik...but i don't know why dresses. i'm sure i will find out, though! I'm way too over excited right now!!! This means way too much for me, and this is one of my biggest dreams come true!!!

Amanda :-) (such big smiles!)

Amanda Perrotta

SATURDAY, JUNE 16, 2007
Hey!

So almost everyone at my school is flipping out about the whole Cheyenne thing...i'm trying not to make a big thing out of it so that i won't get all hyper and go into a seizure or something...lol. So i'm trying to keep that off my mind for a while until someone brings it up again.

So the same day i found out about all of that, i also found out that they have a spot for me in Double H!!!! I'm leaving July 5th and coming home the 10th or 11th. I'm so excited!!!! because i've been waiting eagerly for them to call and say that i have a spot. And my mom called from Californian from the UMDF [United Mitochondrial Disease Fund] conference and said that she met a lady there that has a daughter 14 years old who has Mito and will be going to Double H the same week i am going!!!!!! So that just made it better!! The day i get back from Double H, i have to move fast because, two days after i get back, we leave to go to West Palm Beach Florida. so i have a busy schedule this summer!

My mom is having a GREAT time in California! She got to meet Jack Black. She found out he has a nephew who has Mito, and that's why he is involved with the fundraisers. My mom got me a Jack Black T-Shirt and a UMDF blanket (because i LOVE blankets, don't ask...lol). i loved Jack Black when he played in Nacho Libre, so i asked my mom if she could get him to sign a T-Shirt saying a line from the movie (my favorite line): "I sing and I dance at the party," lol. But i don't know if she did. All i really know is that she's finding a lot of information and meeting a lot of people.

Ughh. this week is going to be exhausting!! Monday is a regular school day, Tuesday we go to FunPlex, Wednesday we have graduation, Thursday we're going out to eat at Jumpin' Jack's and Friday were going to the park!...whew! So that's my last week of school and a busy schedule! So that's really all that's been going on. I'll update Tuesday because i'm sure Beth (music teacher) will have more to tell me about Cheyenne.

Amanda :-)

PS: To all the Fathers, Have a Great Fathers Day!!!

Probably Not Going to Double H Ranch

WEDNESDAY, JUNE 20, 2007
Ughhh!!!

I HATE Drsssssssssssss!!!!!!
Ughhh!!!...I'm so mad and sad right now at the same time i can't even explain what i'm feeling, but some of you might know. i know some of you know what i'm going through. I went to the Dr. today, and i lost three more pounds. I was waiting to update because i wanted to see what was going to happen and, of course, something BAD happened. Anyway, i lost three more pounds, which now makes it 107 pounds. So the Dr. was worried about that, so he moved my port date up, and i wasn't really concerned about that until he said i have to have it in before June 5th (and i was supposed to be going to Double H that week), and he wouldn't allow me to go at that weight anyway. So, i'm not going

83

to Double H. He promised me i would get another spot, which i doubt, and i'm going in for two operations tomorrow...a pick[4] line [an exposed intravenous line for the administration of medications, often near the collar bone] and a port the next day.

I started crying in the room when i found out i couldn't go to camp before i got the port. I cried the whole way home. It bugs me a lot because i've been looking forward to this for one year now, and i finally got a spot, and it feels like it got taken away from me from my disease. So i will be spending my last two days of school in the hospital without seeing my best friend for the last time for a year. :-(I'm so sad i won't be able to see him again. i didn't even say goodbye to him today. So that's my annoying and sad and mad news today.

I had my moving up day today, which was the only highlight of my day...seeing my friends. that's sad if that was the only highlight of my day. Ughh, i'm so frustrated right now, i can hardly type, so i'm sorry for that. I'll update more if i can in the hospital.

Amanda :-/

FRIDAY, JUNE 22, 2007
Hi!
I'm actually updating from Albany Med., so if the words get all mixed up, sorry, because the computer is kind of weird...lol. So today i get my port between 3 and 5PM. I'm really not that nervous. it's weird because usually i am, but i'm not this time....i'm excited to gain weight and be as healthy as Carolyn. I started my

---

[4]PICC line, for a Peripherally Inserted Central Catheter

lipids last night...they didn't fill me up!!!!!!!! I was shocked, but then i found out they go through an IV so...well, that's why. The dumb Drs. want me to talk to someone about my disease. i hate how people think when teens come in with a disease and they're underweight that they have an ED [emotional disturbance] or something like that....well, guess what, I DON'T!!!!

I wish i could eat everything in this entire world, but i can't....they don't even understand that. Right now i'm thirsty, starving for ice cream, and can't wait for this to be over and for friends to visit me. I met a nice friend who is my roommate while i'm here. her name is Rochelle (if i spelled that right)...i always misspell it...lol. She's very nice...she's 13, and we have a lot in common. She has some problems with her legs and muscles and has tremors. She's a very talkative girl...lol. The [new] Dr. came in yesterday and told me i will definitely have a spot in Double H this year!!!!! He said I may even make it for July, but he doesn't know. it depends on my weight. OK, well, i'll fill you guys in later when i come out of it and feel better.
Amanda :-)

SATURDAY, JUNE 23, 2007
Hey!
Updating still from Albany Med today. Umm, my surgery went well. I went in the OR at about 1:15. I didn't come back up until about 7:00 PM because i slept a lot after the anesthesia. I did good with it, but, after about an hour, i hurt, and i just wanted to sleep! I'm doing pretty good now. I didn't eat anything yet except cereal last night, about half a bowl, but nothing this morning. i drank like a hog last night and this morning. The surgeon came by this morning and made sure i wasn't in to much pain. Dr. Betzhold

(my GI [Gastro-Intestinal] Dr.) came by this morning and said i'll probably be here for a while because i'm not tolerating my feeds at all. I only took about 100 ml [about 3.3 Oz] last night, maybe not even that much so....

A new Dr. came by this morning (a Resident). I don't really like residents because they hardly ever know what they're talking about. But anyways, she said they're going to try to bolus me every 4-6 hours [give a dose of medication or, in this case, nutrients] (OK, that doesn't seem right to me because you know that i get full very easily, and i also want to eat food! but the weird resident wants me just to be bolused and have TPN [Total Parenteral, or intravenous, Nutrition] and lipids...so i'm pretty frustrated with her right now. My mom always said, if i don't keep swallowing, the muscles in my throat might get weaker, and i love food and don't want to get rid of eating...so i don't know.
I'm doing two or three tests today for my stomach. I'm not sure what they're called, but i'll find out. I had them done before. Thy put dye through my mickey and see what happens or something like that.

I get to start using my port today!!! At 5:00 PM they're going to start me on TPN and see how i do. Run it until tomorrow. This is my last night with lipids until i'm not sure because i've had it for two nights already, so this will be my third. Let me tell you, the lipids are like heaven! They make me stay up until 12:00 and wake up at like 6:00 AM...lol. And i still have energy all day. I think my mom and the Drs. can see it too. They still have me on IV fluids until i start my TPN.

Today i'm going to see a magic show and do games in the Ronald McDonald House to try to win some prizes. Yesterday i won Dominos from Bingo.

Amanda :-)

SUNDAY, JUNE 24, 2007
Hi!
So I talked to my Dr. today, and guess what?!?!?! I'm going to Double H!!!!!! But the only down side is that i have to stay here for this whole week and maybe next weekend to boost me up for the camp. I'm so excited!!!!   I have no words to express how excited i am!!!!   I'm trying to update you guys every day so that you know what's going on.:-)

The tests are happening on Tuesday and Wed. And just relaxing for the rest of the week...trying to boost myself up!   They weighed me today because they started me on TPN last night, and i've been on lipids since Thursday. i still weigh 107...but, you know what, i decided i'm not that worried about how much i weigh anymore, even if i lose another pound because, as long as i stay over 100 and my energy is like it is right now, i'm OK and i'm feeling GREAT!!!!   And i know i will be feeling AWESOME for Double H!   I know when i first heard that i was going to get a port before Double H, i freaked out because i thought it was going to be harder, but i finally figured out it's going to be so much easier for me, and i'm going to be climbing that high rope course like i'm a champion.

I've had lots of visitors, and i thank all that came and visited me so far and even those who left me messages on here or comments on my MySpace. They really bring my spirits up, and i thank you! I'll update when i hear more and when i have more good news! Amanda!!!! :-)

TUESDAY, JUNE 26, 2007
Hey!
Here at Albany Med still....chilling out i guess you could call it....or waiting for my booster to come up! My feeds are going pretty good. Let's say they're going better than they use to go. I'm getting about 500 mls. in a day (i think). i used to only get in about 300, so i think i'm making progress! The lipids are running every night, and they are giving me A LOT of energy!! TPN i'm on 24/7. That's giving me all my nutrients, and i think some energy as well. I'm maintaining my weight!!!! (FINALLY!!!!). I'm not losing any more. i'm finally keeping the weight i have, and that's what i have to do to get out of here. Every morning they weigh me, and this morning was funny because i usually take off my AFO's because that's shoes and braces. But this morning i was about to go for a walk when they weighed me, so i didn't [have time to take off my AFOs] so thy weighed me, and i was 108, so my mom was like, "yayyy, you gained a pound," and i was like, "mom, look down at my feet." She looked down and was like, "well, at least you're not losing any." So the Drs. think i gained a pound, but the nurses know and are going to keep it quiet...lol.

I moved to another bedroom last night because a roommate moved into my bedroom, and she was a little noisy. My new roommate is Emma, and she is 6. She is such a pretty young girl.

The testing went well yesterday. everything looked fine. My stomach doesn't have any leachage (sp?) problems, so tomorrow they're going to see if it's something else with another test. I'm getting very sick of hospital food! Even though i don't really eat it. ;-)

Today is a very special missed day for me. It's Abby's 1st birthday, and i haven't seen her since i left, and today i was going to have her tested to be a Therapy Dog, but my plans got changed. So i'm missing her birthday, but, most of all, i'm missing her. hAPPY bIRTHDAY aBBY!

Amanda :-)

THURSDAY, JUNE 28, 2007
Hey!
So, i have a lot of new news to share with you guys. I had my test yesterday, the emptying study where they inject dye into my stomach and water and see how fast or slow it comes out. My results came back, and they were normal. my stomach emptied normally (which is good). Then later on that day, we saw the [old] Dr., and he talked to my mom and told her something about me being anerexic (sp?) because all of the tests came back normal, he wants to blame it on anerexeia. He doesn't have anything else to blame it on. So he's pushing me, really pushing me, to get 250 [ml] feeds in me every four hours, and if i can't, i have to get what i can until i throw up! I think that's berserk!!!! They're trying to push the feeds until i throw up! So my mom is mad because of the Dr., and i'm mad because of the feeds, so last night was really horrible!

Maria (Abby's Teacher) stopped by yesterday with her husband, Matt, which was so nice, and i loved it! She was telling me how Abby might not have to go for the therapy test. she just might want to go straight to the Service Dog test. I was whammed with that one because i never expected that. So i'm happy for her and for me...lol

Amanda :-)

THURSDAY, JUNE 28, 2007

Hey!
I'm doing this for you Darcie! So guess what!??! I have an 80% chance of going home tomorrow!!!!! I'm so excited!!! The Dr. said i've been doing so good with my lipids and TPN and getting better with my feeds that i'm about ready to go home. You have no idea how exciting this is for me because i haven't been in the hospital for over a week since i was little. So, it's been tuff. I was crying this morning because i'm so homesick...i miss Abby, my dad and my sisters. I mean, who doesn't get homesick while they're in the hospital? So that's exciting news for me. I can go shopping now for the rest of my stuff for double H next week now! I can't believe it's going to be six days tomorrow until i leave...it's amazing how time flies...when you're busy, i'll say this time... ;-)

So i guess that's pretty much all i can say...I'm going home to a place where i belong, where your love has always been enough for me!

Amanda :-)

SATURDAY, JUNE 30, 2007 11:29 AM,
Hey!

So I'm home, as most of you should know by now. It was so hectic yesterday because i was so happy i was going home, yet i was sad because i got so close to some of my nurses and care partners. So it was kinda hard for me to say bye, but i know i'll see them soon (but hopefully not in any kind of situation like that...lol). But i'm really happy i'm home in my own bed and stuff.

When i got home yesterday, there were nurses here and like 20 boxes of medical equipment. I was so overwhelmed. I didn't know that having a port could kind of change you (not your life, but what you can do). I'm on IV fluids because i guess i'm not drinking enough throughout the day, lipids three days a week (Friday, Saturday, and Sunday, and i'm off TPN for now until i need it again). But the good part is the IV fluid and the lipids run during the night until i wake up, and then i'm free until the night so.....it's pretty good.

Yesterday at AMC [Albany Medical Center], my mom had to access the needle for the first time because it was a week and she was so nervous, but she did well. I was a bit nervous, too, because, well, she isn't a nurse first off, and, well, it's my mom sticking a needle into me! But everything turned out well.

My pump for the fluids and lipids didn't come with a backpack, so we're trying to change the pump right now, so i have no idea what we're going to do if we don't have a new pump before two weeks because that's when we leave for Florida.

So i'm leaving for Double H for SURE this Thursday, and i've been hearing so many excellent things about it at AMC, and i think i just might want to stay there after my session is over...lol. Lindsey (the person who ran the play room at AMC) said she might be up there when my session is going on, so i'll be happy if she's up there, and i met a girl at AMC that is going the same week i am, but she's a little bit younger. I met so many nice people at AMC, there's just not enough room to tell you about them all. OK, well, i'll try to update sometime this week if i have time between finding a bathing suit and packing, etc.

Amanda :-)

TUESDAY, JULY 03, 2007
Hey guys!

I wanted to update everyone before i leave for Double H!!!

Yesterday was a scare because the Dr. that originally told me if i could build myself up again i could go, and i did (i spent a week and a half in the hospital doing that), well, he decided to take me off the Double H list. So my other Dr...Dr. Adams (the one who's been rescuing me through this entire thing) called everyone at Double H and got me a spot. I was so mad at that other Dr. yesterday because he made a promise, if i built myself up enough. that i could go...and i did that. But he just pushed me into the dust after I had an operation and spent all that time in the hospital proving to him i could build myself up. Not mentioning almost puking from pushing the feeds. But Dr. Adams came to my rescue (AGAIN!). SO.....the next time i see him, i'm going to bow to him, i think...lol

Last night was my first night without my lipids, and it was so easy! I only had one line hooked up to me, and that was just for IV fluids. But i'll be on them this Fri-Sun when i'm at camp. :-/ I can tell they make a little bit of a difference...my mom says they make a lot, so does my dad, but i probably just can't see it because it's my body.

I'm maintaining (sp?) my weight. 107.6. Everyday i weigh myself when i get up. It varies through the day because of my feeds. But i'm glad i'm not losing any more, i'll tell you that.

This week and next week are going to be bang-bang moments because, right after i get home from Double H, i leave for Florida (not my Make-a-Wish). So i might not update as much. I'm pretty much packed, excited, ready to go. my dad isn't ready for me to leave, but i am! That's pretty much it. I'll try to update when i get home.

Amanda :-)))

TUESDAY, JULY 10, 2007
HEYYYYY!!!!!!
Oh my gosh. i'm so overwhelmed right now!!! I just got back from Double H and, woahhh, what and experience!!!! I don't know where to start. OK, let's start with the counselors. Oh...they were like my older sisters/mothers while I was there. I felt like I was at home. They kissed me good night every night. they made

sure when i was crying that I was OK. And they just made me have an AWESOME time!!!!! I got to get so close to them, and today, when i left and last night after the wish boat ceremony, i cried like nuts. And let's face it, i never cry. But i think i'll always remember those amazing counselors and what a great time they gave me for my first year....and maybe some of them will be back for my second?

Next is my friends that i made. I made two AMAZING friends. One was Cassie....this was her last year, and i know it was emotional for her, but she always made me laugh, and we always had plans for the other girls...lol. The other one was Joslyn. She was so funny!!!!! I can not even explain how funny she was, and she was always curios about why i had an IV pole or had a port or stuff like that...that's what i liked about her.

We went to the Great Escape this week (which didn't turn out so well because it rained after i went only on like five rides, but that's OK because i enjoyed just that many rides and just going there). Tess (One of my counselors) won me a [stuffed] puppy because we played games while waiting for the bus to come, so that was nice of her. :-)

We also went water rafting. that was fun also...i only got a little wet, but wet enough where my clothes stink right now because i put them in a bag [until now] and am washing them.

Ohhh, the high ropes course... I was scared to death about that, but I did it!!!... I made it through the whole thing like a bird. Everyone said i breezed through it, but i thought i went as slow as a turtle....i also got a courage bracelet from that.

I had so much fun at the dances....i dressed up kind of Gothic and then put on mascara and lipstick and went in my wheelchair, and we sang all of these songs, all of the counselors and us....its was to much fun!!!

The talent show was amazing, too.... Our cabin did a fashion show... i started...lol. I think i just was letting go there, not being my normal self as i would at home because i knew there were kids/teens like me, and they knew what it felt like.

The Wish Boat ceremony was AWFUL!!!!! I cried so hard..... I didn't want to leave. I did want to go home, but that place was like heaven for me. There were kids like me there. they understood exactly what i was going through. They didn't stare at me when i was in a wheelchair or ask questions. we were all just one body, one voice, one team.

All I have to say is, I loved it too much, and i'm going back next year!!!!

Amanda :-)

SATURDAY, JULY 21, 2007
Hey!

I just got back from Florida...and WOW, was it hot down there. But it was nice because I didn't have to worry turning blue. I LOVE the warm weather! I had a BLAST! I just relaxed most days, but every day i tried to go down to the beach for a swim. I only got to go down there three or four times, though, because a couple times i was accessed, and once or twice i was too tired. The beach was so nice...it was perfect temperature. I just floated in a tube with the waves...lol.

On the days I didn't go to the beach, i hung out at the computer room or at the game room which was fun. I got to e-mail my friends and counselors at Double H. Oh...i got my pictures back from Double H...they're AMAZING!!! I look at them every day...lol. I decided for my birthday in January i'm going up there to ski and maybe i'll try to get some of my counselors to meet up with me.??

I can't really get into other details right now because my nurse is coming in a minute, but i wanted to update you guys to let you know i'm home!

Amanda :-)

PS: Harry Potter is out!!!!!

MONDAY, JULY 23, 2007
Hey!

OK...so i'm finally ready to update since i'm unpacked and caught up on almost everything. My weight is down (yet again) to 102 now. it goes up and down because we have a weird scale. But this morning it was 102. My mom and i discovered I take more feeds when i'm on my lipids, and its true...i caught myself today taking more. So Dr. Adams i guess is putting me on lipids five days a week to start me off, and, if that doesn't work, then i'm on for seven. So well see what works and what doesn't. The only down side of when i'm on my lipids is that i have so much energy, and my mom says i have to conserve it, but how can I when I feel like I want to run a marathon or something?! I guess i'm going to have to figure that out as well. My goal is to build my energy level back up for September for school! I'm so excited for school! I miss all of my teachers (because i usually see them during the summer, but, since I just don't have enough energy this summer, i can't go). So that's my main goal!

I finally got one picture up [on CaringBridge] of my sisters and me on the train ride down to Florida...ohh was that an experience i'll never forget. :-/ It was horrible, let me be the first to tell you! Our whole day revolved around going to dinner, lunch, and breakfast....lol. My dad always kept saying 30 minutes to dinner or however many minutes to whatever meal we were going to. It was ridiculous but funny.

My sisters and I are planning to see Harry Potter on Sunday!!!!! I'm so looking forward to that! That's all i've been looking forward to since before I went to Florida. I already know it's going to be better then expected.

My new room is going to be under construction soon. I'm really excited! I'm painting it light blue, and then i'm going to get sponges and white paint and sponge paint white clouds on the side and the ceiling. The bathroom is going to be under construction as well. They're making it handicapped accessible. So it's going to be a LOT easier for me to get in and out of (thank goodness!).

I'm waiting very patiently for my new electric wheelchair to come...it's getting harder everyday to wait, though, because i hate being pushed around...i want freedom like every other teenager does. So i'm waiting on that, too.

Amanda :-)

SATURDAY, JULY 28, 2007 09:11 AM,
Hey!

Sorry I haven't been updating as much. I haven't gotten my lipds in about four days, and i've been feeling soooo ickkk. Yesterday i was going to update, but I could hardly hold my head up because i was so low on energy. I'm feeling GREAT today! So full of energy and ready to go see Harry Potter tomorrow!!!! OK, let's see what's going on.

My mom has been calling a lot of people since we got back home, so my electric wheelchair should be here in about a week! I'm so excited...its puke green...yea make fun of the name of the color, but, when you see the picture of it, you're going to LOVE it!..The whole wheelchair itself reminds me of Malisa's wheelchair.

My mom also talked to my nurse who comes every week, and he's going to get me some OT, PT and speech because i usually get it when i'm in summer camp (through school), so we'll see what goes on with that.

I'm trying to get my weight up, but it's not going anywhere. I'm doing all of my feeds lately (except for yesterday because i wasn't feeling well), and I eat a bowl of my mushy cereal like once in a while, so i don't know. Last night was kind of interesting. I ordered a salad (don't ask me how I can still swallow that...because i have no idea!) and, when I ate it, it didn't taste good to me. Salad doesn't taste good to me anymore. The only thing that tastes good to me these days are cereal and ice cream (once in a while). That's my diet...it's scary when you can't eat regular foods...fries, salads, fruits just don't taste the same to me anymore.

Tomorrow, i'm going to help my grandma cook (i've really been into cooking lately!) while my sisters help my grampa weed. i can't really weed right now because of my situation, and i want to be healthy enough to go to school in the fall (that's so important to me...school!) Last year was a bummer because I missed soooo much school because of my energy, but this year is going to be a LOT better i think because i have lipids, D-5 [5% dextrose solution intravenously], and MY wheelchair. I just have a feeling it's going to be better. Maybe not the winter, but the Fall and Spring definitely!

Also, when i'm up to it, I'm going to start taking Abby back to classes just for some extra stuff to put in her medium-sized brain. so, this week i'm going to try to make Wed. maybe my mom can give me lipids Tues? Oh talking about that....

My mom accessed me last night and WOW!...did that ever hurt...she poked at me three times (better than last time). But it hurt a little more than normal. She always cries when she accesses me because she feels no one should have to do that to their child, and it's true, but I don't really care because i seriously love needles (yes, i'm weird), and it doesn't bother me. We're still trying to get a nurse (i think full time) so that my mom actually gets some sleep at night.

Amanda Perrotta

OK, well, as you can see with my lipids, i could go on all day, but i'll save some for another. I'll tell you how Harry Potter was....i know who dies in the last book....so sad. :-(

Amanda :-)

TUESDAY, JULY 31, 2007
Hi!

Ahh today i'm a little drowsy. I think i'm due for my lipids. It's been four days! I'm just like in a blah mood. I need them tonight because, otherwise, I will NOT have the strength to bring Abby to her extra class tomorrow and other stuff that's going on this week.

So I made a mistake if i told you on my last update about my hearing appt. It's not until next month...lol. I'm glad because I woke up and at 9:30. My mom was like, "don't you have a Dr's. appt. today?" and I was like, "yea, my hearing." And so she went rushing to get her planning book, and she was like, "phew, it's not until next month." So that was a relief. I don't think i have any Dr. appts. this week. maybe next week, but not this week (besides nursing coming to my house every week!)

As I already said, Abby is supposed to be going to extra class tomorrow, so we'll see if I can get my mom to give me my lipids tonight. She [Abby] still needs a lot of practice if she wants to be my Service Dog...trust me when i say that. But for some reason she's gotten better...she is getting better every day! So props to her.

That's pretty much what's going on.

Amanda :-)

FRIDAY, AUGUST 03, 2007
Hey!

Well, my new portable pump came!!!!! It's so small...i never thought a pump for my lipids could be so small. I asked my nurse how am i supposed to put this on my IV pole, and he said just put it in the backpack and hang the backpack on the IV pole. So i'm going out backpack shopping sometime this week because the backpack they gave me is dark blue...kinda depressing if you think about it...and its HUGE!!!! It would drag down to my legs probably. But i'm excited to use it....some days i need my lipids during the day, so that's when it comes in use (the backpack anyways).

My Service Coordinator came over yesterday and talked to my mom and dad about bringing a hospital bed into my new room because yesterday i was kinda pooped out of energy for a little while, and she said the Drs. and she thought it would be a good idea for me to have one so that, if i want to sit up and i don't have enough strength, the bed would help (just like in the hospital). So i really don't like the idea because, well, let's really think about it....what kind of teen would want a hospital bed in their room!?!?!? My house already looks like an OR itself, for goodness sakes, and now a hospital bed. what next?... an elevator?!... i'm thinking about it, but i still don't like the idea. We also talked about, in the future, me living in a residential house...so....

Maggie, Matt, and Maria (the three M&M's) came over yesterday. My mom and dad took Matt and Maria out to dinner for a thank you for taking Abby while we were gone, and we stayed home and got to baby-sit Maggie!!! I LOVE her so much...she's so easy to take care of. And it was good practice for me because i want at least two or three dogs when i get older, and i want one big one, so, last night, i was in charge of three dogs, and it wasn't that hard actually. Except for making sure one dog wasn't around while the other one was eating...lol.

My weight is going all over lately. It was steady at 102, but this morning I weighed myself, and it wasn't good, let's put it at that. But maybe it's because i haven't been eating? I just haven't been up to eating the last two days. Maybe today i'll try some cereal?...I don't know. I've been doing the same with me feeds. So I don't know what's going on. All I know is, i need to get up to 105 before school starts so i CAN go to school. I need to do it!!!!!!!!!!

Today i'm going over to our [family] bakery to make covadeils [bread] with my grandma and then maybe later going up to the hospital to visit a friend. Then (whew, i'm going to be pooped out, so thank goodness, for lipids tonight!) I'm going to an extra class with Abby. it's not advanced, it's intermediate, but it's still good practice for her.

Next week i'm going to Maine...I'm not really that excited, but i'll probably be when i get there. Then the day when we get back it's my dad's birthday. What i'm giving him for his birthday is, i'm making him a birthday cake. It's going to be a yellow cake with pudding in the middle and chocolate frosting on the top and peanut butter morsels. yummm!!!!

Amanda :-)

SUNDAY, AUGUST 05, 2007
Hi,

Ughh what a disgusting three days it has been.

A couple days ago, I felt like i was half dead. I slept most of the day, didn't eat one thing, barely drank anything, and could hardly hold my head up. All because I didn't have my lipids and because i was getting a stomach bug on top of that. My mom called Dr. Adams to see if I had to be admitted to the Hospital (Thank goodness he said 'No' because, if he did, i knew i would just feel worse. But at that time maybe it would make me feel better?) It felt like i was gazing [off into space]. My mom, after she hooked me up to the D-5, i wanted to lay down and she said OK lets get you over to the couch. I really didn't or couldn't walk but i had to get to that couch because at that time i felt like i was going to throw up. Every second i was walking i felt like i was going to fall. I think it was the worse i've ever felt.

The next day i felt better with energy because i had my lipids(of which, Dr. Adams put me on a new schedule with lipids), but my stomach felt like i was going to throw up. All day again I didn't eat, I drank a little, and couldn't bear to smell or look at food. My temp was normal, but i just slept all day and didn't feel good. This is still going on. i've lost two pounds because i haven't eaten in three to four days. I can't afford to lose anymore weight, otherwise, no school in September. :-(That's all i've been looking forward to.

I'm not going to Maine next week because I can't in this condition (Dr. Adams won't let me). I really don't blame him, but i feel bad for my cousins because they've been looking forward to us coming up. We only get to see them maybe once or twice a year. And one of them was their birthdays two days ago so i feel kinds bad.

So right now my goal is to feel better by Wed so I can get my last extra class in with Abby and get my weight back where it was so I can get myself back to school by September. School starts in less then a month already! I'm excited but nervous because, if i get that saying from my mom, that I can't go to school, i'll be so disappointed in myself and my body that this happened to me this summer, and all i want to do is go to school and see my teachers and my friends.

Amanda :-)

TUESDAY, AUGUST 07, 2007
Hey!

Well my stomach bug is mostly gone!!!! YEAAAAA!!! The only thing that's really left of it is the eating issue. I tried some cereal last night, and it didn't taste at all good to me and ten minutes after I ate it, my stomach hurt a little. So maybe today i'll try something more bland, like rice or oatmeal. I'm just hoping i don't catch all this stuff that happens during the winter....ughh, i can already see it. Bugs and colds and, ughhh, i'm not looking forward to the winter. But i have some good things happening in the winter so that will keep me NOT thinking about it. I'm taking most of my normal feeds again, which is helping, but my stomach still hurts a little after that. I'm sure this whole thing will pass. I'm not worried.

So on to the good news. My mom is looking into going to Philadelphia to see Malisa!!!! and do the UMDF walk!!!!! I was super excited when I heard that that. i just wanted to jump out of my chair. If we can do it, i'm ready to pack my bags NOW!!!...lol.

I guess they're starting my new room at the end of August, and they will finish in a week. They will give me a paint chart, and i get to pick out the color i want, and they paint it....good deal, huh? I hope they have the color i want, though. I'm really excited because, i have to tell you, last night was the first night i slept in my own bed in about a year!!!! So i was so proud of myself for doing that. I figured yesterday i had to get myself ready for my new bed, and i'm 15 going on 16. i can't sleep with my mom, in the same room with her anymore. So i've actually accomplished one of my goals. So i'm super proud of myself!!!!

Amanda :-)

THURSDAY, AUGUST 09, 2007
Hey!

So much to tell in two days...lol.

Well. I didn't end up going to my Neuro yesterday because my OT came and did the evaluation. She seems really nice, and i hope she's my regular one. The next time she comes, she's bringing putty!!! Oh, how much i LOVE that stuff. So she'll be coming back tomorrow with all that and work (ugh). I need it though. :-)

I've lost more weight (what else is new?) It goes up, then down, then up, then down. Some days i just want to stomp on the scale and make it stay in one place! But the goal is to get up to at least 105 so that i can go to school. I'm doing more feeds and trying to eat a little.

My mom and some other people have been talking about a G-J Tube. I guess it's a tube that goes through my small intestine so that I don't get full that easily, and I can put on a little more weight? My goal right now is to get me up to 105, but, in the future, i just don't want to be a little kid's weight. i want to be a normal adult's weight. So we'll see what my path is.

Last night was the most thrilling night i could have ever asked for. My mom is making me put on an Oxygen mask for everywhere i go (except for outside stuff), so i had Abby's class last night, and it was one of my first times wearing a mask in a store. I was complaining the whole way in there and put on a face (which she really couldn't see, but i did!). So before i entered the classroom, Maria (Abby's trainer) asked me to take a short walk, so i thought it had something to do with the other dogs' graduation practice, coming in and out. Then, when Maria called Abby and me back in, everyone had masks on and even Maggie, too! They had ones on with faces. It made me feel a lot better. Matt (Maria's husband) kept his on the whole time. i give him props for that! So now i know next week i will totally feel very comfortable.

Today i'm going to try to visit my school and see some of my teachers! But i have to see if one of them is going to be there first, though. This weekend, i'm going to the fair (where i don't have to wear a mask) and ride some rides. And baking on Sunday for my dad's birthday. So that's my weekend plans.

Amanda :-)

SUNDAY, AUGUST 12, 2007
Hey!

OK, let's start with Friday.

Friday was absolutely normal chaos because the first thing i noticed when i woke up was Abby wasn't acting right. Now, Abby usually follows me around everywhere when i get up in the morning, but, for some reason, she just laid there. So i just let her lay there. Then, around 9 AM, she was still laying there but awake. I tried to feed her, but she wouldn't come to her bowl, so i brought it to her. That's when we noticed she couldn't put any weight on her left back leg. We tried to see if she could walk and she could, but she was limping. So we called the vet, brought her over. She had some X-Rays done and a Lyme disease test done. I guess it showed that one of her bones or nerves slip out when she runs, but it goes back into place after a while. So right now, she's on pain medicine. She acts fine one minute, but then her leg hurts the next. If it doesn't get better within a couple months, then they have to perform surgery. So that was my Friday morning chaos.

The Dr. called Friday also and told my mom i'm not eligible for the J-Tube because i don't take overnight feeds. So, i guess i'm going to have to gain this weight by myself. I'm up to taking 470 ml. [about 16 oz.] now. My goal is 500 by next week maybe? I gained some weight, on the bright side! (This is yesterday's weight because my mom and i decided we're not going to worry about weighing myself every day): 100.2 lbs. I know it doesn't seem like a big deal, but it's better then when i was 99 lbs. I'm up a pound, and that's all i care about. Now just five more pounds to go....wheewww!

Yesterday i went to my grandma's and made glumpkies (sp?) with her. I'm so into baking right now, its like out of control, but I guess its a good thing because i'll make a good wife...lol. Last night I also went to the Cheesecake Factory for dinner, which was good. I ate a little bit but not as much as usual. Then we went back-to-school shopping. I got some clothes and sweatpants for pajamas in the winter because i turn to blue/purple in the winter, so hopefully they will keep me warm. All i need to get now is my backpack. Then, after that, we went to the Korean Market, and i bought my favorite cookies that i can actually eat (hopefully they will help me gain some weight...lol). they're really good! Then we went home. got hooked up to lipids and D-5 for today because we have a party to go to today, and tomorrow, i have a Neuro Dr. appt., and i'm going to visit my school!

I also got some bad news this week. I'm not going to have the same teacher that i've had for the past two years. :-(I was so devastated! I wanted to cry, and i probably will at some point. I'll see her tomorrow, but i still can't get over the fact that she's leaving. I don't want to believe it. But i will at some point. OK, well...i'll update some time this week or sooner.

Amanda :-)

PS: Can you tell I've had my lipids?...lol

WEDNESDAY, AUGUST 15, 2007
Hey!

So last weekend and this week have been going GREAT!   On
Monday, I went to my school, and i was in total shock! It felt like
i was in a totally different school!   I had to wear a hard helmet
and get in a wheelchair because it's so big now to take a tour.
They're still working on it, but they're pretty sure it will be done
by the time school starts. I got to see two of my teachers, Joan
and Beth...that made my day! Beth gave me a tour of the school,
and i have to say the best part of the school is that it is now all
handicapped accessible. They built a stage, and there's this huge
thing you have to climb to get on it, so they built a wheelchair lift
for kids that can't jump or step that high. I think that was a
GREAT idea!   They also made all of the classrooms handicapped
accessible. I didn't get to see my classroom because they're still
working on it, but i'm sure it will look FANTASTIC!   I didn't get
to see Diane or Dianna, but Dianna and I are going to try to meet
up with each other before school starts.

Monday was also my dad's birthday and my mom and dad's
anniversary, so i made a cake for them. it was a coconut cake with
vanilla frosting. And then we heated up my glumkies (sp?) and
Dahea made a Korean meal for my dad. My cake tasted delicious, i
guess, but, when i [had] flipped it over, it all was kinda in
crumbles because it was so fresh and warm...but my mom and i
fixed it up with the frosting to put it back together. My grandpa
and grandma didn't even notice...lol.

OT and PT are going GREAT! I love both of the therapists that are helping me. I have to tell you, it's really helping me out during the week. Speech is supposed to start this week, i think, but i'm not sure.

OK, so these are the things i'm getting excited about.... Erik's fundraiser next weekend!, High School Musical II coming out Friday!, the UMDF walk, meeting Malisa and Darcie in Sept., school starting up in September, and, last but not least, my Make-A-Wish trip in October! I can't believe it's only two months and two weeks away! Yea, i have a countdown for it...lol.

Amanda :-)

SUNDAY, AUGUST 19, 2007
HEYYYYY!!!!

Do I have such good news to tell you! But first, i have to think of what's coming up and all of the medical stuff...lol

* So, Tony (my home care nurse) finally came and showed us how to use my portable pump for my lipids. My mom said it was easy, but we didn't use it yet, so i'm not sure. I think we might be using it tonight, so i'll tell you how it works out.

* I have a Dr. appt. at AMC on Tuesday with Dr Betzhold (how i'm not looking forward to that). I think it's just for a follow-up with the swallowing and the port. He was the Dr. who lied to me about camp...so i can't wait to see him!

* My mom decided, since i'm doing so well with my lipids and energy, that I might be able to go to the first day of school!!!! But the only down side is that i'm going to have to be in my wheelchair most of the time, but, hey, i say it's worth it for school.

* Yesterday, I filmed an ad for my grandfather's friend. he's going for the county judge, so we were in the ad...it was so fun because it felt like we were on the set of a movie. it was like, "Cut!," lol.

* Yesterday, my family also went up to Schroon (sp?) Lake to just spend a night. I had fun... this is where the HUGE surprise comes in. I brought Abby, and my dad brought one of our other dogs and our bird (yea, we're living in a farm..lol), so Dahea and I decided after dinner to take a walk. I brought Abby, and we went into the town. My dad met us there and said he had to stop at Grand Union [Supermarket] to buy aluminum foil. So Abby had her backpack on, and i was like, let's try to see how Abby acts in a store because nobody will ask about her because she has her backpack on. So I brought her in (some people looked), and it was AMAZING!!! She heeled the whole time, sat when i told her to, and didn't bark at all! I was literally in shock! I wanted to, like, scream when i got out of the store because it was the best feeling FINALLY having her come into a store with me and behave. So, since she did that good, the next day i decided to take her into a gift shop while i shopped for a sweatshirt....she was AMAZING!!! She just watched me as i looked through the sweatshirts, and I just can't describe how WONDERFUL it was for her to be with me and behave every second. So the next step FINALLY is for her trainer to sign the papers, my Dr. to sign the papers, and her vet to sign the papers. She might be my OFFICIAL Service Dog by the end of September, meaning she

might go on my Make-A-Wish trip with me!   So that was the highlight of my trip last night into today.

Amanda :-)))))))!!!!!

WEDNESDAY, AUGUST 22, 2007
Hi!

OK, this might be long because last night I got my lipids...lol.

So, yesterday was very interesting. The night before I had terrible pain near my port...yea.   I thought it was because I have been laying on it a couple nights, but I didn't lay on it that night, so I thought I would wait until the morning. So the morning came, and the pain was still there. When i touched it, it hurt really bad, and when i moved, it hurt also. So I told my mom, and what else would she do but panic because the first thing you think of is infection! So My mom called the Visiting Nurses, and they came out around 3:00PM right before Charlie came. The nurse undid the dressing and looked for redness just in case. It looked fine, so she just re-dressed it and said that if I kept having pain, and if it got worse, just go to the ER (luckily that didn't have to happen!). Then, Charlie came, and I think I know why it hurt so much. One of my exercises in OT is wall push-ups, and, when i do them, i bend forward with my chest, and i guess somehow the port stretches, so that probably irritated it. So that was kind of a nice way to start off the day.

OT was kinda tiring yesterday. The crab walk is getting harder and harder because Charlie is making me go from the Family Room out to the kitchen and then back to the computer room. And it was harder yesterday because i didn't have my D-5 or lipids in me, so i was kind of tired after. We also did things with a weight lift, which tires your arms out so bad! My arms literally felt like they were going to fall off...lol. But if it will help me get back to school the first day, i'm all for it!

This weekend is Erik's fundraiser!!!! I'm really looking forward to that also! I've been looking forward to that ever since i've heard about it. I hope he's ready to pose for the camera...lol. Just kidding Erik. ;-)

I'll get into all the Dr. appts. later on this weekend because i just hate going to them...lol. But i think i might get my mickey changed tomorrow by my visiting nurse! So YAYYYY!!!

Amanda :-)

SUNDAY, AUGUST 26, 2007
Hey!

So, we'll get to the medical stuff first before I talk about what an AWESOME time I had at the fundraiser today!

Friday was my weighing day, and when i got on the scale, I probably would have weighed less if I didn't have all the heavy clothing on, but, with all the heavy sweaters and socks on, i weighed in on 101.4 (plus i just ate and drank), so my mom took two pounds off and weighed me later, and i weighed 99.4. So let's just say were not doing too good still with the weight. My mom called my Primary Nurse, and he's going to have a Nutritionist come out and see what he/she can do. I just have to get a balanced weight where i can say to one person, "i weigh this much," without going on the scale or switching it everyday. So that's that.

Thursday, I got my New Electric Wheelchair FINALLY!!! It's AWESOME, too! It's the perfect color, and its so comfortable that when i sit in it (unlike my manual), my bottom doesn't hurt. I could probably sit in it for hours. It reclines and all of that. The guy that did it for me was so nice he made sure like 20 times that everything was in place and fitted correctly, and he's donating a portable ramp for the car so we can travel with it.

Yesterday, i got the rest of my back-to-school shopping done. And i got a haircut. When I was shopping for my jeans, I was thinking of last fall when i was shopping for jeans for back to school. I was a size 11. Then, in the Winter, i started going into a size 9 but didn't totally fit into them yet (that's when i really started to lose weight). then in the spring I went into a size 7. In the summer, size 5.

Now, i was scared yesterday to see what size I was because it seems every season i just get into a lower size. I take a size 1 now. Yea, the lowest size you can get before shopping at a whole different store. The people, when i wanted to try them on, just looked at me weird because they had to see how many pairs I had, and i guess either they didn't like me...lol, or they thought i was a stick?....I HATE how some people don't think before they show emotion or act or speak. Anyways.....

Today, I had SUCH a GREAT time!! I went up to Bingumton

(sp?) to Erik's fundraiser. When I first saw Erik, I was like, what should I say.....what should I say?!??!! I was getting so nervous, but it was weird because usually i'm so shy, and i warned him too...lol. But it seemed like we knew each other forever once i said hi, and then off we went chatting. It was GREAT! And I thought he would have to do the talking for me. Abby came, and she did good as well... Erik seemed to have a sweet spot for her (i'm glad he did). Just with selling car magnets, shirts, pins, and bracelets they raised over $150!!! I was so happy to hear that! Then with all the raffle and the bidding on the bench that Erik's dad made, they raised over $1,000!!! They reached such an accomplishment tonight, and if Tammy's speech didn't make you want to know more about Mito or make you cry, then you need to go see a Dr.....OK?!

When Tammy mentioned the Prom that Erik asked me to over an email about three to four months ago, I totally forgot about it for a second, and I was like, wait....what?...I'm seriously going to a prom that my sisters might never have a chance to go to with such a GREAT friend, and i would never go with anyone else. I can't wait, and i'll start picking out the color of my dress, Tammy.;-)

Amanda :-)

THURSDAY, AUGUST 30, 2007 o
Hi!

Monday, Charlie (my OT) came and discussed that maybe we should just do stretches because I guess (so my mom says) i've been taking naps and getting tired after OT. So were just going to continue doing stretched and the putty in OT. He called Dr.

Adams, and i guess he agreed with that.

Tuesday, Dahea and I took a stroll in my new electric wheelchair down to get ice cream. It's so comfortable! I had to go to the bathroom half way down (and it takes about 20 minutes to get to the ice cream place where we were going), and i told Dahea i had to go to the bathroom, but i'll hold it because i didn't want to get out of my chair because it was so comfortable! Also on the way there, these stupid immature boys decided to pull a nice joke on me. Dahea and I were just talking and strolling...lol. When these stupid boys yelled out of a car window, "Why don't you just walk?" Dahea of course didn't understand because they said it so fast! But I explained to her what they said and that it didn't bother me because they don't understand my circumstances, and if it were them, maybe they would. But when we got home, and I told my mom and dad, my dad went full blown. he was like, "If I was there, I would have...." so yea.

Yesterday, my sisters had to go get their uniforms, so we decided to go out for dinner. Then my sister also had to get sneakers, and I wanted to get a pair, but i couldn't find any, so my mom and I decided to go look just for fun in PayLess, and they had a perfect pair that would fit my AFO's and were my kind of style! So i'm excited to wear them. Then we went to Wal-Mart because i still need to get a cheap lunchbox, but of course couldn't find one there because the lunchboxes that were left were all kiddie ones. so my dad was looking at heat blankets since I get so cold in the Fall/Winter. But i didn't like the texture, so we decided we're going to go to Target one of these days and get a lunchbox and see if they have a good heat blanket.

Today my old Speech teacher, Dianna, is coming over for pizza! I'm so excited to see her because i haven't seen her since June. I'm baking this brownie cake for dessert (it's not exactly that, but i forgot the name of it). I have no idea when i'm going to have time to bake, though, because today i have OT, PT, and maybe Speech. But i'll get it done even if i have to rush!

This weekend, i'm not doing much (at least i don't think i am). I'm probably just going to enjoy my last few days of sleeping in and watch the [Muscular Dystrophy] telethon.

I watched the show Malisa put on her website, Crazy, Sexy, Cancer, with my family. My dad and I really enjoyed it, but my mom was like, "we don't need to be watching this. we see enough medical stuff." But i'm going to keep on watching it because it's interesting.

Amanda :-)

MONDAY, SEPTEMBER 03, 2007

Ughh. this morning was ruff, but i'll get to that after because you won't understand it right now if i tell you.

So, this weekend i was supposed to go to the Fair but didn't end up going because the day before i think i got a 24-hour bug. I woke up not feeling too great, and i tried to eat some cereal, and right after i ate it, it went right through me....three times. So I decided not to eat anything for the rest of the day because nothing seemed appetizing to me, and i didn't want to go through the bathroom thing again. My mom said maybe if I felt better the next day we could go.

So the next morning, i felt better, but my mom and I didn't want to take a chance of going there with the germs, and if i had to go to the bathroom, they only had port-a-potties. So we decided to go to the movies. We saw Halloween, and, for those of you who want to see it or are going to see it, DON'T!   It was the most gory, sick movie i ever saw. They had a lot of sexual content in there.   My sister and I just covered our eyes and talked to each other through most of it, but on one part it was scary, so we decided to watch it, and it ended up being gory, so we both turned our heads at the same time, the same way, and bumped and started laughing...i think that was the highlight of the movie...lol.

Last night was the night I dread...Sunday=weighing night...which also=trying to put it off. I weighed myself, and it ended up being 98. 2. And i also had a sweatshirt and my slipper socks on, so i wasn't so pleased. Then this morning, my mom wanted to see what i weighed after my lipids, so i got on the scale, and i was 97.8. I wanted to literally kick myself. This morning wasn't a happy morning. I was really down about stuff. My mom ended up calling Cheryl because [of] my weight with going back to school.

I guess my mom wants me to start with half days, and that's where i got mad at myself and just with my disease. I shut right down and was quiet for the morning, didn't talk to anyone, just was thinking until my brain fried. My mom told me I could go to school the first day, which made me feel better, but I still wasn't happy. I felt this morning like it's my fault that i'm losing weight and [that the] school that i've been working and trying so hard to get back to was failing, and i have to work for it again. Like my disease is playing tricks on me, and i can't catch it. I eventually just decided to go lay down in my bed because my brain was so fried of thinking. I first cried a little and had a pity party (i know it doesn't sound the best, but i needed to get it out!) And then i fell asleep for a good hour and a half. I feel much better now. i think i just need to get through this ruff patch and i'll be fine. It was just one of those days where i needed to hate my disease.

Anyways, tomorrow I have an orthopedic Dr. appt. to either shrink my braces or get fitted for new ones. I'm hoping they can do something with them!

Wed- My mom and I are going to see if we can stop by AMC and see Erik, my friend who got admitted. He's going through a ruff patch right now also, so, if you could pray for him and his family, that would mean a lot to him.

Thur- SCHOOL!!!!!   I just need to rest up and get some energy for school. It might be exhausting my first day, but i'm sure i'll be able to handle it...i know i will in fact.

Amanda :-)

THURSDAY, SEPTEMBER 06, 2007
Heyyyy!!!!!!

So you can guess where I just got back from...right? SCHOOL!!!!!! Oh my gosh it was the best feeling in the world getting on that bus this morning, let me tell you!   Last night it was so hard to get to sleep because I was so excited about today. I woke up at 6:00AM when I didn't even need to get up until 6:45...lol. But I couldn't get back to sleep, so I just woke up and got dressed and watched TV until my beautiful bus came!!!! When I got on the bus, I realized I should have worn a mask on the bus because they're all little kids this year, and the whole mini bus is full, and some of the little kids were coughing and sneezing, so I was like, ughhh. But that's OK because I knew it wouldn't ruin the day.

When I got to school, I got butterflies in my stomach because I worked so hard for this, and it felt like a dream. I got off the bus, and Mark (one of my TA's [teaching assistants]) greeted me. I was so happy to see him because I wasn't sure if i was going to have him again this year, so that just made my day better. When I got in the building, it felt like I was in a different school...it was HUGE!!!!! Now I know why i'm going to need my wheelchair so much...lol. I got to my classroom, and all of my same TA's and speech teacher hugged [me] and were cheering because some of them didn't know I was coming back to school the first day or this month. So they were extremely happy to see me! I met my new teacher who was very nice....she helped me out a lot during the day! I saw four of my same friends from last year, so that made me feel a little bit more comfortable, but there were new students....a lot of new students! So I kinda had to get used to that. But it was good because my TA's had everything ready for me...my cushion seat, my headphones, and my [therapeutic] weighted blanket. They even planned out the scooter rides for Ted and me...lol. We first went on a tour of the WHOLE school...which, yes, i was in my wheelchair for, then we had snack, made birthday signs, ate lunch, had recess, made place mats, came up with a student and teacher contract, and then ended the day by picking something for free time. I picked my usual scooter ride with my weighted blanket. It was a GREAT first day, i have to say, and the whole day I was smiling (my TA's even noticed i think?). I'm so happy that I made it the first day, and i think i'll be smiling everyday just to know that I made it that day.

I'm packing for Pennsylvania in a minute...yes if I didn't tell you yet, i'm going to Pennsylvania!!!! And you will never guess why?! I'm going there for a walk for the UMDF and to visit Darcie and Malisa!!!!!! I'm so excited to meet her in person and can't wait!!!!! Tonight I have to start my lipids extra early because I have to get up at 5:30AM and de-access [detach from all tubes], take a shower then access again...lol. Yea, its going to be a go, go, go morning (thank goodness for the lipids!)

Please continue to pray for my good friend Erik who is still in the hospital. He's not doing so well, and, if I have this correctly, he has to have another surgery. I hope I had that correct.

Amanda :-)

MONDAY, SEPTEMBER 10, 2007
Hey!

This is going to be such a quick update because i'm leaving for school in like 15 minutes.

OK, so we left for Philly (My grandma, mom, and I) on Friday, and boy was it a little bit of an exhausting trip, but it was kinda worth it. When we got there, my bottom hurt so much because, these days (sounds like i'm getting old...lol), i can hardly sit for an hour without my bottom hurting or getting sores on it. So I had to walk...and plus I had my lipids the night before, so i was energized. Once we got settled into our hotel, we decided to walk a little and just see what was around us, then we came back and decided what we wanted to see and do.

On Saturday, we had to get up really early (which i hated!) because, first of all, i didn't get my lipids and D-5, and [second,] on the weekends i'm not a morning person...lol. So we headed for the walk, and we met up with Malisa's mom (who was very sweet!) and her husband, Dave, and her neice (sorry i forgot her name). But anyways, I was exhausted after the walk, and, when Malisa's mom told me that the hospital was an hour away, I just knew I didn't have the strength to do that ride. I was so disappointed in my body and me, but I knew, if I did that, my body would pay BIG time! So i thought maybe next year we could meet up, so that will be my goal next year.

But one thing good came out of it I got to meet Darcie!!!!! I didn't get to say much to her because, at that point, i was so tired and i just wanted to relax and lie down for a while, so I'm sorry, Darcie, we didn't get to talk for very long or at all...lol. But at least i got a picture with her to remember when I met her.

After I rested up that night, we took the ride to see the sites. It was nice because I didn't have to walk, and I could still see the different sites. I enjoyed it! Then finally after that, what i've been wanting to see, the real Liberty Bell!!!!! I saw it!!!! And I got my sweatshirt and key chain...lol. So, then I was pooped out for the night. I could hardly hold my head up. I knew I overdid it. But luckily, that night I got my lipids...lol. And the trip home was just a bumpy one and more bottom hurting...lol.

OK, well this week it's back to school (YAY!!!) and more Dr. appts...boooo! So I think I may only get to go to school twice this week because we have Thursday off, and I have an appt. Wed. and maybe Fri.

Quick Note: I've been having more breathing problems during the night and day so...i guess my mom is going to call the Dr.

Also please pray for my friend, Erik, who is going in for surgery today. OK, well i better get going. I'll update sometime later on this week.

Amanda :-)

THURSDAY, SEPTEMBER 13, 2007

Hi all. I am updating Manda's journal for her this AM. Amanda is not feeling well. She is very tired and weak. I think last weekend and traveling didn't help, but she needed to see her friends. Sometimes you have to sacrifice to live LIFE! She knows what is important at 15 years of age, that is one thing we have learned from her!!! How simple, and she never complains.

They are trying to keep Manda out of the hospital as of now, but that could change at any point. We are going to have nurses come in five days a week and on weekends for four to five hours a day. No school since Tuesday, and we will see if she can go back. Manda is running a low grade fever, 99.4, and having trouble catching her breath during the day and night. We see the doctors tomorrow. Hopefully Manda can update you next. It takes me forever to type. Thank you all who take the time to sign [the

guestbook on the CaringBridge site] and think of Amanda. We can't thank you enough, it means the WORLD to her. That is the first thing she does in the morning and the last before bed. God Bless you all!
Jacki (Manda's mom).

P.S From Amanda, Hi to Erik and Malisa. you're in our prayers. hope you're home SOON!!!! Hi to Darcy, Emilie, Carrie, Natalie.

FRIDAY, SEPTEMBER 14, 2007
Hi!

wheww, what a ruff couple of days it has been. I'm sorry I didn't update yesterday. I didn't really have the strength to get up and type a whole page. My mom pretty much explained what was going on, but more happened yesterday after she updated, so i'm going to fi'll you in on that.

So, as most of you know, I've been having A LOT of breathing issues during the night and day now. It's gotten to the point where I can't really stand them anymore, and someone needs to take care of them. So today i'm going to the Pulmonologist (sp?), and we'll see what he says. I'm also going to see Erik! That's something i'm looking forward to, and seeing my nurses, too.

Yesterday, when Tony came (my Primary Nurse), I finally got my Mickey changed, and, let me tell you, i feel so much better with the new one! It doesn't feel like its going to fall out and it doesn't itch! When Tony took it out, he said it really was time to change it. It had a big blob inside like tissue, so he had to sting it (that's what he called it anyway...lol). that stung a little, but it will shrink it down and get rid of it. He has to do it once a week until it's gone, if I got that correct. I also got de-accessed yesterday, which felt so good because I got to take a shower!!!!   Ahhh, it felt so good! And i get to take one more today before my mom accesses me again. On the down side, Tony also had to weigh me...yea the dreadful part, so i got on the scale, and the day before i was 97 something, but yesterday I was 95.8...yea.   I dropped two pounds in one day. I thought the darn scale was playing a joke on me or something, but it wasn't. I hate being like this!!!   If I get sick this Fall/Winter, I know how much trouble I'm going to be in....trust me, I know, because, last winter, my sister came down with Knemonia (sp?), and she lost 20 lbs! If i lose 20 lbs, i'm in for a LONGGGG road. A seriously long road!

I'm trying to up my feeds more. It's really hard because, since i've been upping my feeds, i haven't been eating as much. The most i've been eating is a shake. It stinks when you have your feeds and then you feel full for the rest of the day and you see your family and people around you in class eat and you want to eat but feel so full that, if you eat, you're going to explode!!!! I try to eat, but, after that, i feel so nauseous! So that's why i've been trying to get at least a shake down every night from McDonald's. Because, to be honest, those are really the only shakes i drink and like. But I know I can't have those every night. I'm trying to get my feeds up to 520 ml. for now, so we'll see what happens. My mom and Dr. think that i'm loosing weight because i'm using all of my energy trying to catch my breath. I guess well find out more today when i see the Dr.

My mom JUST gave me the news that I might still have a chance of going in the hospital because of my breathing things, but we won't know until my Dr. appt. is over, and one today. I'm definitely going to keep you updated about that. And, if they decide to admit me, don't expect a good update (just a warning). I was really planning this year out good—School !!!! That's the only thing I want! If I could rewind time, and the Wish Makers asked me what I wanted to wish for, I would say not to be admitted to the hospital and go to school every day. But I know that's not reality. And i'm still happy with my wish, and i'm really looking forward to that! I think that's what's keeping my mood really up!

OK, well i'll keep you updated.

Amanda :-/

PS: Please continue to pray for my friend, Erik, who is still in the hospital, that he recovers well.

MONDAY, SEPTEMBER 17, 2007
Hey!

Most of this Journal entry is going to be about how my Pulmonolgy (sp?) or, as i call it, the Breathing Dr. went.

So I went to the Breathing Dr. appt. Friday, and he talked to me and asked me about what my breathing episodes feel like. I told him, and he then knew exactly what was going on (even with my disease). He explained it kind of like this: He said that when I go into a deep sleep and dream, all my muscles relax, and especially my trunk is already weak, too. it takes more energy to breathe for me. So what he suggested was for me to go on a BI-PAP [bi-level, positive airway pressure, which pushes oxygen into the lungs through a tube in the nose] at night with an oximeter so that I can breathe better at night, get some sleep, and maybe gain some weight. So that's that right now.

I did go to school today!!! YAYYYYY!!!!!! I did everything, too! I didn't even tell my mom this yet, but I did P.E. today. Now, i know what your thinking...ohhhh running...oh boy! No, that's not what i did. we played kickball outside (i was freezing!). the only thing I did was stretch and throw the kickball (pitch). So it really wasn't P.E., and my TA's totally knew that, if I had to take a break, i could and i would tell them. But, since I had my lipids last night, i bet you all know that i didn't take a break. But I did conserve my energy by getting to the bus in my wheelchair...how's that?..lol. I really enjoy school, and every minute is soooo precious to me just to be there.

This week is also Mito Awareness Week, so please pass on some information about Mito to a friend, neighbor, or even a stranger. I did today!

Erik is finally home from the hospital along with Malisa, so let's give them a YAYYYY!!!!!! I'm glad you guys are home, and let's try to stay home...lol

Amanda :-)

FRIDAY, SEPTEMBER 21, 2007
Hey!

Amanda Perrotta

So I'm still waiting on my Bi-Pap. I can't WAIT until it comes!

Thursday, i didn't get to go to school because of all of my breathing episodes. On Wed. night, I wasn't hooked up to my lipids (not that it makes a difference with my breathing) or D-5. That night, I had four breathing episodes, and, each time i woke up I, couldn't get back to sleep for a hour. That's four times, so i only got about four hours sleep. So the next morning, I woke up with only four hours of sleep, no lipids, and feeling like I just ran three marathons in a row. I tried to get myself together for school, but I knew I couldn't go, so I told my mom, and she said just to go back to bed. I slept until 9:30AM, woke up stayed awake for about three hours, then went back to sleep until the evening. When I woke up, I couldn't believe I let the day pass me by, but I knew I needed that sleep if I wanted to go to school Friday and to get some strength. Tony also came Thursday (while I was awake) and when he took my BP, it was so low he knew I was dehydrated, but my mom and I didn't because I was drinking all day. So my mom hung an extra bag of IV fluids to spruce me up a little. And it did because, later on that night, I actually got myself to go out and see Abby's trainer, Maria, and her Husband, Matt. I've missed them a lot, so it was good to see them. My mom and dad got something to eat, and I got a Diet Pepsi.

Today was such a GREAT day! I had my lipids run last night, and my D-5, so i was rearing to go! I went to school. the funny thing is, I've been dreading to wear a mask on the bus, but today, when i got on the bus, everyone was coughing and hacking, and I was like, ohhh. Why didn't i bring a mask? So I told myself to get a mask at the Nurse's office for the bus ride home, and I did! It seems the Fall weather is coming on quickly! Some kids in my class are sick, too. So I stayed away from them today (nothing personal...lol). But, all in all, I had a GREAT day today in school. I got to paint the walls on the new Art classroom, have my first private music lesson, and work on a new song for Family night (and this year, i'm not telling what it is until after Family Night is over). the wheelchair lift for the stage is all done, so it looks so nice, and i can't wait to be the first to try it out! And i had my first fire alarm [drill] of the year today...how annoying was that?...we had to stay outside for half an hour until the Firemen came and checked out everything..lol. So it was a pretty good day.

Tomorrow, i'm helping my mom work a garage sale...we have sooo much to get rid of, so, if you want to come out, come on out! Sunday, I have no idea if there's anything that's going on. I want to go to my Grandma's and try to finish a purse i've been knitting because the next thing i'm working on is a blanket for my dad for Christmas, and it takes a long time to do that.

Amanda :-)

MONDAY, SEPTEMBER 24, 2007
Hi!

So, Saturday's garage sale went pretty well. we sold some stuff on Saturday but not enough, so we decided to do it Sunday as well. We sold almost EVERYTHING on Sunday! Our basement and living room look so much cleaner and just so much better! I'm getting so excited about my new room.

Yesterday was just really a relaxing day. I gave Abby a bath along with every other animal we have. We also went to the Polish Fest to get some food (i forgot what the name of the food we got was, but i guess it was good from what my mom, dad, and sisters told me). I also got another sea salt lamp for my new room. But its not just one of those regular ones. it's like a turtle. It's really cool! Yesterday was an eating day for me. i ate one of Carolyn's pancakes she got from McDonald's, and i had to put literally the whole thing of syrup on it to get it down, but boy was it yummy and worth it. And the only good thing about this time of year is that my favorite ice cream comes out because Winter gets closer. it's the peppermint ice cream, so i bought that yesterday (I was sooo excited to see that!), and i ate half a cup of that. Then I ate some steamed broccoli and rice for dinner. Today, i don't think is an eating day because my stomach is just like, "whatever," to food.

I had to change my Dr. appt. today due to female difficulties...lol. So, I'm just relaxing. I got weighed today, and I am proud to say i am at least maintaining my weight! I weighed 97.0 with sweatpants on, a shirt, sweatshirt, (female items), and two pairs of socks. But my mom also had to take off two pounds because I just drank, and i had so much clothing on because it's freezing (well to me anyways!), so 95.0...but it's the same as last week!

OK, well, Thursday I'm going apple picking at school, and that's pretty much it for the week. I'll update sometime soon.

Amanda :-)

WEDNESDAY, SEPTEMBER 26, 2007
OK....

This is going to be a very quick update(medically).

My mom told me this evening when I got home that, if I had another breathing episode, again i'm going to the ER (via 911). Now, I usually have a breathing episode every night, so tonight i'll probably be in the ER. I just wanted to tell you guys in case you tried to email me or anything else. Other than that, everything seems to be going well. I made it to school today and was a little tired due to the night before with the breathing episodes (can you tell they're beginning to become a real issue?), so i laid down later in the day because of that, and i had a headache from the lights in the gym. But we went apple picking today instead of tomorrow (God works in mysterious ways!). I had a FANTASTIC time and couldn't ask for a better first field trip!

Amanda :-)

THURSDAY, SEPTEMBER 27, 2007
New Update!
Cheryl [Dr. Adams' nurse] called about 1½ hrs. ago and said to go to the ER because i feel so wicked tired today...i feel like a mummy because i only got about four hours of sleep last night because of the breathing episodes. So, when my dad gets home around 2-2:30-ish, were leaving or calling 911, i'm not sure which one yet, but were going.

Last night was TERRIBLLE! I was up about four to five times with the breathing, and i couldn't get back to sleep three times because, sometimes when I have them, i get so worn out from catching my breath that after it goes away i need to take deep breaths because of the struggling. it's like a shock or something, i'm not sure exactly how to explain it. it's really hard to explain it. But I just can't keep going like this every night with school and my Make-A-Wish trip coming up and other stuff. I want to be rested and have energy still for that excitement coming up. So that's where we are right now. When i'm settled in, because i'm pretty sure i'm going to be admitted, i'll update. Let's hope this doesn't take long.

Amanda :-)

FRIDAY, SEPTEMBER 28, 2007
Hey!
OK, very quick update. I'm admitted on the 7th floor, C-7, bed B. Last night they hooked me up to those heart monitors to monitor my oxygen and heart. So I went to sleep, and i guess, right when I went to sleep, my heart rate, pulse, and etc. dropped very low. So they had to call the resident that was on last night. He came and checked on me a couple times. My poor mom hasn't slept, so who knows what kind of mood she'll be in...lol.

This morning, the Dr. came in and said i'll definitely have to be on some kind of respiratory machine at night. That's really all for now. i'll update when i have more info.

Amanda :-)

SATURDAY, SEPTEMBER 29, 2007
Hey!

So, last night was the best night's rest I have gotten in about 6 months! For my mom and me! They put the monitor on me without the Bi-Pap for four hours (for insurance reasons) to monitor my breathing again. Then finally, at 2:30 AM, they put the Bi-Pap on, and I was able to breathe and sleep well. The only problem I had with it during the night was, after an hour or two after they put it on me, i had a hard time breathing, and I didn't know why, so I tried to tell my mom, but then i remembered i can't talk with it on, and my mom wasn't awake for me to sign to her. so i laid in bed so the monitor wouldn't go crazy and the beeping noise would go off and luckily it did. The nurse came in, and she got the gesture and called the person who was on call for the Bi-Pap. She fixed it. There was some kind of problem where a part came off or something, so i guess that's what happened. But other than that, it felt so GREAT to breathe again at night. I just hate how I can't talk if i need to go to the bathroom or something...lol. But I guess i'll figure that out.

OK, onto the next news. They didn't start TPN's yet because they're still not sure if they want to do them, so we'll see about that. This Resident came in today (I hate Residents, they always make mistakes!) and told me that they're discharging me today! So I was like, what?!?! They can't because, first of all, Anthem, who delivers all my medical equipment, doesn't deliver on weekends. And, second, my pulmonologist didn't come up yet, and they said the earliest i would be released is Monday. So my mom talked to the nurse, and she said i'm not being discharged today...ughh. stupid Residents! He spoke a different accent, too, so it was also hard to understand him...lol.

Oh, today I started getting the sniffles....i'm not sure yet whether it's allergies or if i'm starting to get a cold (hopefully its allergies!),

but we'll see, so let's pray that i don't have a cold. One more thing, i need a special prayer request for my roommate, Sean Robert. he has A LOT going on and is really having a tuff time. he's only 3 and is going to be having blood transfusions. And has to have three surgeries, if i'm correct. So please pray for him and his soon-to-be mom. Thanks! I'll update once I know more.
Amanda :-)

SATURDAY, SEPTEMBER 29, 2007 07:37 PM,
Hi!

I'M HOME!!!!!!!!!!!!!!

Yes, I say that with such enthusiasm! I'm going to let my mom update this one because there's a lot to put on here, but you know how slow she types so....here she is.

Hi all!!! Manda is HOME YAAAAAAAAY!!!!!!!

Manda is now on her bi-pap/ventilator and O2 during the day when needed. Her white cell count is very low, and she now has to wear a mask everywhere!!!   She has anemia and is on iron twice per day. Then, you know the problem that comes next???? You guessed it. I won't say it, so we have meds for that, too. Also, two other machines to monitor O_2 and heart rate. She is now getting most meds through her port. I'm just happy to be home with the family!!!! More going on, but, like Manda said, I'm slow at typing. Will update soon. Thank you sooooo much for everyone's support. We love you all!!! Jacki

SATURDAY, SEPTEMBER 29, 2007
I'M HOME!!!!!!

This is the third time i'm doing this because, for some reason, my site isn't working right...lol. So here's a quick update. I came home on my Bi-Pap. it worked wonders last night! I'll get more into that in my next entry. My white blood cells [which help to fight infection] are VERY low, so my Drs. tell me i have to start wearing a mask everywhere I go, which i'm not happy about, but, if it helps keep me out of the hospital, i'm all for it. If my white blood cells continue to drop or stay the same, i'm going to have to get a blood transfusion. I also came home on more pumps and more IV's. My nurse came out today, and everything seemed OK. They weighed me at the hospital, and i lost a pound, but hopefully with the Bi-Pap i'll gain that pound back, or at l;east maintain my weight. On Monday, i have my orthotic appt. to get fitted for new AFO's! And on Wed., i have an appt. with Drs. Adams and Dr. Schroder. OK, so that's what's up for the week. I'm going to try to make at least one or two days of school this week. let's hope for the best!

Amanda :-)

PS: please pray for my roommate that i had in the hospital. his name is Sean Robert, and he is going through a ruff time. He is having blood transfusions and has to have three surgeries.

SUNDAY, SEPTEMBER 30, 2007
OK, I'm home! I got home last night around 7:00PM. I came home with the Bi-Pap machine and more IV's, pills, and machines. My white blood cells are VERY low, so i'm taking pills for that,

and my Dr. told me i have to wear a mask EVERYWHERE I go. if my white blood cells don't come up within a month, i have to have a blood transfusion done. So i'm hoping these pills will work! I also have anemia i found out...so, yesterday, before i came home, i was de-accessed, and i got to take a shower. well, i shaved my legs, and i cut myself by accident and started to bleed like i had an operation or something. I bled through three washcloths! My blood went in my shoes that i was showering in and everything. My mom told the nurse and she stopped it a little after going through two more wash clothes and paper towels and then putting two bandages on it. So now i'm wondering if i have what my mom has (a blood disease called VonWilibrans (sp?) Disease) [Von Willebrand Disease is the most common blood clotting disorder. Though slightly less serious than Hemophilia, it is also a deficiency in one of the clotting factors.] I want to get tested again because i was tested two years ago, but the lady who tested me said it can always change. After i took a shower, my mom let a nurse try to access me, which was, ummm, a new experience. It hurt so much! I never felt so much pain where my port is. It still hurts today. She couldn't get it. so finally my mom put it in. When I got home, I slept so well last night! The Bi-Pap really makes a difference! I didn't wake up once!!!! And even though i didn't get lipids last night, i still have a little bit of energy in me. I think everyone should get a Bi-pap...lol.

Amanda :-)

MONDAY, OCTOBER 01, 2007
Hi!

OK, so first of all, i'm sorry for the long extended update of my being in the hospital...lol. The year sure does go by fast! Anyways, my spelling might be a little off because i'm wearing my pulse oxygen [measures the pulse from the fingertip]...yep that came today! Along with other things that came this week. So, as most of you know, the Bi-Pap is working GREAT!!!!!! I've been sleeping like a baby! I haven't woken up once, and it feels great in the morning not to be tried.

SO TODAY I guess either my school called or the Dr. called and said i can only go to school two days a week for half days. Which really stinks!!!! Because most of you know, i LOVE school!!!! School is the most important thing in the world to me besides my family. So, going twice a week feels like part of my freedom is being taken away. But, as long as i can see school, i guess that's what [I'm] going to have to do at this point.

I guess tonight I got a trial with my Bi-Pap, and my pulse ox machine. I had a breathing episode before I put my Bi-Pap on, and i was watching my oxygen, and it went down to 83%, and i told my mom, and she put my Bi-Pap on, and it went right back up to 100%, and i felt fine again, so they both work i guess...lol.

Amanda :-)

THURSDAY, OCTOBER 04, 2007
Hey!

So I got to see Dr. Adams yesterday. My dad went as he usually does, and he's always nervous at my Dr. appts., which I don't understand because he doesn't get nervous when i'm in the ER or when i'm admitted. but when i have a Dr. appt., he gets so nervous that he starts tapping his toes and babbling and just weird stuff. So i was getting annoyed by that. But anyways, I got weighed, and this is funny. i weighed in at 96.0 lbs. (don't get excited yet...sorry). I knew there was something wrong because I weighed myself that morning knowing they were going to weigh me later on to make sure it was correct. So, I went with it. Cheryl came in and asked about the feedings and lipids and everything else. When she got to how my bowel movement was, i told her I haven't gone since Saturday. So she was like, that's why there's a pound on you. So my mom was like, "Darn it!" But that's OK because i'm maintaining my weight, and that's all i care about right now. And i think i grew more, too! So, I guess what we're going to do is try school three full days a week. my days picked out are Monday, Wed., and Fri. And i have reasons for those days. But I can always sub [one day for another] if i have an important field trip or something going on. I'm going to start IV Carnitine (sp?) [L-Carnitine is a naturally-occurring amino acid that helps in the transport of fatty acids across the mitochondrial membrane inside the cell.] They want me to do IV Carnitine and D-5 at school, and my mom and dad have a meeting about today, but, if my school won't allow it...which i don't know why they won't because i know how to stop it if it comes to that, and i'll already be hooked up before i get on the bus....

If i can't do that, then i'm going to do a small feed at school just to get some fluid running through me, and nutrition. Because some days, when i have my lipids, i walk the halls because i have so much energy, and i guess i need that nutrition. There wasn't really all that much else that we talked about. I'm doing everything correctly, and that's it really. I'm on a new med. to help my bowels move more, not that you really want to hear that, but just in case...lol.

Today, i'm going with my mom and dad to my school. While my mom and dad are in their meeting, i'm going to hang out with my old teacher, Kim, and, if some of my teachers are there, i'll hang out with them, too.

I have such a busy week ahead of me (thank goodness tonight is a lipid night!). Tomorrow we're going to Sam's Club to get all the pasta for the party on Sunday (which I didn't even mention). The Walton Cruisers are coming just to say hi. So we have about 90 people coming over on Sunday...yea. So we have to bake a lot of macaroni for everyone! I made a sheet cake yesterday at the bakery, and i'll frost it Saturday. And Saturday, were making all the macaroni! So I'll leave you with that.

Amanda :-)

FRIDAY, OCTOBER 05, 2007
Hey!

So, I went to school today, D-5, mask, and all. It was such a rush, rush morning gettting all of my stuff together for school. I was hooked up last night to my lipids and D-5, so i had to disconnect, flush, then connect again. But the hard part was, i had to get it in a backpack (well, actually my mom did), but it was so hard...it took like 15-20 minutes to get it right so that the tubing wouldn't fall and i wouldn't step on it. I also woke up late, which didn't help, so i had less then an hour to get ready. Everyday I have to bring my D-5 in my backpack and my Bi-Pap and Pulse Ox machine. So, I have three bags on the bus...lol. But my bus driver says, even if I have to bring the kitchen sink, it's fine. I've had my bus driver for five years now, so she knows me very well!

When I got to school, Mark (one of my TA's) was waiting for me with my wheelchair so I wouldn't have to lug all that stuff with me to the nurses. I dropped the Bi-Pap and Pulse Ox machine off at the nurses and then went off to class. Now, remember, none of my classmates knew that i was going to be wearing a mask everyday now and a backpack with D-5 in it, so they asked, but i told them i would explain at Morning Announcements. I got so nervous because I had a flashback of last year when I had to tell them about my wheelchair, but now, when i think about it, that's nothing compared to what i had to tell them about today. I just told them that I have to wear a mask everyday so that i won't get sick if they have a cold or something, and I have a backpack on everyday that had IV fluids in it because I don't drink enough. They understood completely i think. Nina (one of my classmates) loves Mickey Mouse, and my masks are of Mickey and Disney characters (i'm always creative with that stuff), so, when she saw my mask, all she could talk about was Mickey and my trip and if she could go. So that made me feel better.

It was a little strange walking around the school being the only one with a mask on, but i'll get used to it just like i got used to the wheelchair last year. Other than that, my first day back went GREAT! I couldn't ask for more! A ventriliquest (sp?) came today, and i thought it was the most amazing thing i've ever seen, and i've seen ventriliquests (sp?) on TV, and this one was MUCH better! I just stared at him the whole time and his mouth didn't move at all! I was shocked! That was the best part of the day, that and going to Dunkin' Donuts with Joan and Corrine (two of my TA's) for lunch. Since I don't eat lunch, and everybody else was, they decided to take me to Dunkin' Donuts to pick up coffee for the rest of the teachers and even treated me to a Diet Pepsi. It was so nice of them.

Tonight, I went to Sam's Club, and I'm glad I used my electric wheelchair, let me tell you. we were in there for an hour! Even though the electric wheelchair weighs down the car, it's worth it! It was so much easier to steer and more comfortable for my bottom. We got stuff for the party on Sunday and just snacks and candy (he-he). I get a craving every once in a while for a piece of candy.

Oh, Tony (my nurse) came tonight and finally showed my mom and dad how to work the portable pump for my D-5. so now, for school, i can use my small backpack and not worry about blood backing up, and I can get all of it into me! So that's good.

Amanda :-)

The Cheyenne Kimball Guitar

SUNDAY, OCTOBER 07, 2007
Oh my gosh!

What a day! It was such a tiring, surprising, exhausting day! I hope that explained it all. I'm sorry. first of all, if i misspell a lot of words, it's because i'm so wiped out from today that my hands are going to flop all OVER!!! OK, so let's start with this morning.

I woke up at 7:00AM and was rearing to go from my lipids. So i got changed, did meds, feeds, and cleaned. Then I went over to the bakery where my dad was since 5:00AM that morning cooking pasta...lol. My mom and I just checked up on him, and i asked what time am i going to frost my cake. He said i had better do it when he's done with the pasta, so i did. So, once we got all the cleaning and getting set up and cooking done, that was good! Everyone started to come around 12:00PM. My grandparents came, and people who really surprised me next were my old teacher, Diae, whom i miss A LOT! I ran up to her and hugged her. Michele (my Speech Therapist) and Beth (my Music Therapist) [also came]. I talked to them a lot. My other teacher, Kim, also came, which i LOVED because i just love hanging out with Kim, and I just love her in general...lol. So most of my family came, and friends. When the Walton Cruisers came around 1:00PM, i went in the front yard and sat in a chair. It was GREAT seeing all the old cars come up the hill. When i saw Erik's car, though, it put the icing on the cake!

So, i saw Erik, and i thought that was my surprise, but when i saw Wayne (one of the Walton Cruisers) bring up two boxes wrapped, i was like, 'huh?' So he told me to open them, and you'll never guess what it was?! I got an autographed guitar signed by Cheyenne Kimball (the singer i re-wrote my lyrics to from my music video), and the other box was an autographed picture of her in a frame, a T-shirt signed by her, a CD signed by her, and pins. I was in shock (literally)!!!! I thought i was dreaming! Everyone was like, 'What do you think?' And i was like, 'ugh, uh.' So they could probably tell i was in shock...right?

So, once i settled down, i went back to the backyard with everyone and talked with Erik for a while and then with other people and other people and other people. So you can tell just by that that anyone could get wiped out. So finally, Erik and I were so drained, we went inside and reclined on the couch for a little while and watched TV. I finally caught my breath, and then i went back outside after everyone was gone...lol. So it was a LONGGGG day!!!! If i explained everything, this journal entry would be ten pages long...lol. Let's just say, it was a dream day! But back to reality now right?

Amanda :-D

WEDNESDAY, OCTOBER 10, 2007
Hey!

Ughh what an exhausting couple of days! I had so much fun on Sunday, but i got payday for two whole days...lol. But it was so worth it! OK, let's get down to business..lol

So, yesterday I slept in until 9:00 and stayed awake until 1:00PM then went back to sleep until 2:00PM probably. I needed the rest, though. I had my lipids, but they didn't really help. So Cheryl called yesterday, and i guess they're changing my formula (once again!) They're changing it because it has 20 more calories (i know, not a lot), but it will also build me up (so they say) for my trip that's only 18 days away!!!! So, i'm good with whatever will build me up and get me stronger for my trip so i can spend a whole day in Disney without getting wiped out! They're also taking some blood tomorrow when Tony comes for something I forgot. They're trying their best to build me up for my trip. They really want me to get up to 100lbs. I do, too...we'll see! My mom had to weigh me yesterday, and I was 97.0, but I also had some extra clothes on...lol. So, we'll see what my real weight is tomorrow. Tony i'm not sure if i told you this—I taught my mom how to use my portable pump for my D-5 for school, so now I don't have to worry about blood backing up and me watching my port every 15 minutes for blood. So, that's such a relief! And it actually fits in my small Eyore backpack! So i'm sooooo happy! The only problem is that it actually flows at the rate its supposed to, so i have to go pee every half an hour, so, when i go to school, my classmates will probably think i'm nuts...lol. Oh, the happiness of having D-5!

Tomorrow, I get to go to school, and i'm happy because my best friend that i miss sooooo much, Mike, will be there (he called me last night and told me he got a cold[5]), so i'm debating whether i should stay away from him or see if he's still sick and give him a hug. I might be safe and wait until he's fully recovered...lol. But i'm just glad i'll get to see him because i've missed him sooo much!!!! I'm also going to school Friday!!! two days...YAYYY!!!!! I'm making good progress this week. And i'm going to make my schedule for next week over the weekend...lol. I try to go to school on lipid days, so well see.

I have NO Dr. appts. this next weekend (that i know of). if i don't, i think i might sing Hallelujah!!! I'm so sick of going to the hospital.
OK, well I'll update soon.

---

[5]Mike Silvia, for various reasons, never spoke publicly until he met Amanda.

Amanda :-)

FRIDAY, OCTOBER 12, 2007
Hey!

Home today, but it wasn't a lipid night last night, and last night on my part was a little hectic, and, with my trip coming up, i need all the rest I can get, and i need to conserve the energy for what I want to do.

So, I didn't get to see Mike yesterday because the Apple Fun Run got rescheduled due to a lack of [good] weather, but I kind of see that in a good way because he was sick still, and by next week he should be OK to get near. So, I figure it was good that it got rescheduled.

Remember the guitar I got from Cheyenne? Well, since I got it, my music teacher, Beth, has started teaching me lessons on how to play. I started yesterday, and my fingers still hurt...lol. But i'm sure it will be worth it. Beth said that i'll eventually get calluses (sp?) on my fingers, so i'm soooo looking forward to that (wink, wink).

Yesterday, as soon as I stepped off that bus, my mom was like, "the guy is here with your portable O2." I'm like, "ughh, this is going to be a nice calm night (NOT!)" So, he was there for about 15 minutes showing my mom how to do everything because, instead of bringing my Bi-Pap to school everyday, i'll be bringing a mini oxygen tank. It will be sooo much easier, i think at least.

Then, after that, Denice, my Service Coordinator, came, and she was here for about 1 ½ hrs. I just sat and listened and said some things, told her how i was. Then, not even two hours after she left, Tony, my nurse, came, and he had to take blood, BP, weight, all that fun stuff! He was here until about 8:30, 9-ish. So i was up for that long. So, as you can see, i'm saving my energy for the weekend and for school next week.

OK, well i'll update when i have news. Have A great Weekend!

Amanda :-)

SATURDAY, OCTOBER 13, 2007
ughhh. So, yesterday i got a late delivery for my testing formula. Supposedly it has more calories and iron in it. So, I waited until this morning to try it, and, well, get to that later...lol

Last night [at Wal-Mart] was a BLAST (except for the whole wheelchair ordeal...lol). OK, we didn't bring my electric wheelchair because we went in my dad's delivery van, so we decided that i'll go in one of Wal-Mart's wheelchairs (which is disgusting to me! but whatever). so, once we got there, i got in the wheelchair and my mom started pushing me, and it went, 'clump, clump, clump.' i was so embarrassed! I just wanted to get out of the darn thing. i mean, it was loud enough that you could hear it from three aisles away! But i held in there. so, first I got my stickers to put on my AFO's for Halloween. When I was in the hospital, the person that works in the playroom put a Halloween sticker on my AFO, and that gave me a really good idea to start decorating my AFO's for each holiday with stickers, so i decided to get Disney Halloween stickers to put on them. So I got those, then I got a new Cloud robe, which is so warm, and i'm wearing it right now...lol. I found my Boo-berry cereal! I was so happy when i saw that because i've been looking for it in every store and couldn't find it, but I found it there. Then we had to go to the little kids' section and get my underwear...yea, i had to get the little kid underwear and bras with flowers and butterflies on them. The only good thing that came out of that was that i got to get High School Musical underwear...lol. And they only sell that in kids' sizes...lol. S o that was our nice trip to Wal-Mart last night.

So, this morning, i tested out my new formula. I did my regular feed, and about 10-15 minutes later, i got the worst stomachache ever! I was like, "OK, it will pass" at first, but when it didn't go away and i couldn't eat, think, or look at food, i knew this wasn't a good thing. So i just sat in my chair most of the day with my O$_2$ on and Pulse Ox because i could hardly get up because i didn't feel well. I felt every second that i stood up i was going to throw up! I tried my afternoon feeding, too, but it made it worse, so i'm now back to my normal formula, and my stomach still cannot even think about food, but we'll see tomorrow.

OK, well, Mon., Wed., and Fri. i'm planning on going to school. Wed. is also Family Night, so my mom and dad actually get to meet my new teacher! I'll update if anything changes.

Amanda :-)

SUNDAY, OCTOBER 14, 2007 ,
Hi,

lol...I just updated last night, and i'm already updating again this morning...how sad. just kidding. So, I felt sick last night, and I was hoping it was just allergies because I was sniffing and my chest felt kinda tight. So i thought i would wait until the morning to see if I was really sick. This morning, I woke up with a runny nose and coughing up stuff (nothing green or anything like that...yet). I always know when i'm getting sick. I'm just glad i'm getting sick now and not next week before my trip. My mom called Cheryl, and she said just to take an Aspirin (because i also have a headache on top of that) and cold medicine (i forgot the name of it) 4x's a day. Also to leave my O_2 on and just rest as much as i can. All i've been doing all day is sitting, and my bottom really hurts! So i thought i would just get up for a while and walk around the house. I have no fever yet, which is good, and I'm hoping not to get a fever. So let's cross our fingers on that!

If I feel better on Wed., i'm planning on going to school, but i'm not pushing it. usually i would because everyone that knows me knows i would try to push the school thing right now, even if I was sick, but this trip means more to me then anything, and all i want on this trip is to not worry about my being sick or anything else of that sort. So i just have to get through this and hopefully i'll be home free for a while. I'll update if anything changes.

Amanda :-)

MONDAY, OCTOBER 15, 2007
OK! This is going to be a exciting update!

But first let's get down to business,

So i have a low grade fever of 99.3° right now. I could feel it though, too, because i felt on fire! But it's not anything really serious right now, but i'm still watching it. So i'll still keep you updated on that. I feel a little bit worse today (my cough), and my nose really is starting to run today, but I have this motto: 'Things sometimes get worse before they can get better'. So i'm holding onto that for either my goal for school Wed. or for a haunted corn maze for my other goal this weekend.

This afternoon after I made my new bath of formula, Cheryl asked my mom to do a test on me. she asked to try another can of that new testing formula and put it in with my RCF® [Ross Carbohydrate-Free soy-based formula] and Isocource® [high-protein formula]. So she did, and i took my formula around 5:15-ish, and, like 20 minutes after that, i started to get cramps (but i'm kinda due for my monthly)...lol, so i thought it had something to do with that. I ate a bowl of salad, and my stomach really started to hurt, and i told my mom, and she told me what she did, and she said I had to do it to make sure it really hurt your stomach last time. So, needless to say, my stomach does not agree with that formula.

So here we go with the exciting news! Maria (Abby's formal trainer), her husband, and her dog, Maggie, came over for dinner tonight. they brought over dinner to make for us, which was VERY nice! So Matt had to leave early and Maria stayed and ate dinner with us. After dinner, Maria told me to pull up the papers she sent me for the Service Dog thing, so i did, and i printed them out. Maria told me were going to fill out the papers and send them in so Abby can become a Service Dog soon. I got so excited, I wanted to jump! I had to fill out all the things she does for me and all her info. It was just so exciting for me because it felt real now. So I just wanted to share that with you because all of you have been on this 'Abby to be a Service Dog' journey with me, and now it's finally going to become true! So that was my excitement and medicine that made me feel better for tonight.

This week, i'm just resting up, and that's pretty much it. I'm going to try to make it to school Wed. and, if not, it's fine because i've been doing schoolwork through home. My GREAT teachers have been sending it to me through email, and i thank them so much for doing that for me!!! So I'm not that worried anymore about schoolwork and what I missed! And my other goal, as i mentioned, was a haunted corn maze Sat. So that's pretty much it! I'll update soon!

Amanda :-D

WEDNESDAY, OCTOBER 17, 2007
Hi,

I'm still not feeling great. I think i'm actually feeling worse than i did a few days ago but that comes with the territory of having Mito. I feel like my body doesn't want to cooperate with me. I feel like i've been hit by a truck and haven't gotten any sleep, but i'm not tired.

The nutritionist (that i HATE!) called this morning and asked how everything was going, and my mom told her about my sinus infection (i don't have a cold, i have a really bad sinus infection). i'm on antibiotics for it and nose spray. And she also told her about my low grade fever of between 99-99.5° and how i'm not moving, only from one couch to another. So the nutritionist is going to talk to Cheryl to see if they (once again) can put me in the hospital to start TPN's to boost me up for my trip and get me better. I hate that I have to go to the hospital just to get my body ready for a trip, but i need to go on this trip. i've been looking forward to this, and that's what's been keeping my body fighting from getting sick (well it was working), so whatever it takes, i'll get there! My mom is still waiting on a phone call from Cheryl to be positive that we're going to the hospital, but when she gets the call, i'll update again.

I guess if I get admitted, my Wish Makers are making a trip to the hospital on Sunday!

Amanda :-/

WEDNESDAY, OCTOBER 17, 2007
Hey!

So, Cheryl called back and said she didn't want me exposed to any other germs in the hospital, so she said just keep doing what we're doing here at home. I'm on antibiotics. Cheryl told me to stay on my O2 24/7 until this passes and just to rest. I can't go back to school until after I get home because she doesn't want me pushing myself. I haven't been out of this house in three or four days. Since Saturday. But I really don't feel like going out either but know if I don't get myself out, i'll go into this being a couch potato thing. Maybe tomorrow, if i'm feeling up to it, i'll try to get myself out, but today is not even questionable. OK, well, i just wanted to

let you know.
Amanda :-)

FRIDAY, OCTOBER 19, 2007
Hey!

Wheww! so I think this sinus infection is almost starting to clear up, thank goodness because, if it got any worse, I don't think Dr. Adams would discharge me for the trip. Those antibiotics and nose spray are really helping!!! Yesterday, I went on deliveries with my dad to get some fresh air, and it felt so good just to get out of the house! I came home around 12:00 and took a nap. i'm still a little tired and need some rest. Last night Tony, my primary nurse, was supposed to come out, but he had a situation, so he's coming out tonight. My fever is still here. during the night it usually comes back. It's between 99.3-99.5°, which, to 'normal' kids/teens isn't a fever, but to me and maybe some other Mito kids, that's a fever. My regular temp is usually 97° because i'm always soooo cold! But last night I was so hot!

Last night was an unsleepable night (i think i just made up a new word!). Anthem delivered a new pump for my lipids because the other one wouldn't hold a charge, so they delivered the same one, but hopefully this one will hold a charge, and supposedly it's brand new, but i never trust pumps! So I connected myself last night to my lipids and D-5, and I went and sat down and watched my shows. During my show, which i was so much enjoying, the pump started to do that 'beep-beep' thing. yea you know that sound! So i looked at the pump, and it said to start it over and turn it off. Well, obviously i figured out that i have to turn it on and off every hour or two. So, I decided it was worth getting my lipids and I would do it. So I did until about 1:30 AM, then it beeped again, and it said 'air flow'. Well, my mom at that point had no patience hearing the beeping noise. So I didn't want to stop them especially since I was halfway through them, but my mom said we'll finish them in the morning since I have nothing better to do...lol. And at that point, when my mom was yelling, I did not want to dare talk back! So right now, i'm hooked up again to my lipids, and am really mad at this pump but thanking God that Tony is coming tonight and can fix it.

OK, well, tomorrow, Kim, my old teacher from class 6, is coming to visit and bring me schoolwork from my teachers in my class. And Sunday, my Wish Makers are coming!!!! I'm so excited. I'm trying not to get to excited until Sunday, otherwise I can go into a seizure, and I really don't want to do that right now...lol. So i'm trying to play it cool....he-he. OK, well, that's my busy week...lol. Amanda :-)

MONDAY, OCTOBER 22, 2007
Hi!

SIX MORE DAYS!!!!!
Yes I let my excitement out yesterday, not too much though. My Wish Makers came yesterday to give my mom my itinerary (sp?), flight tickets, and money. They also gave my sisters and me presents! I got a Make-A-Wish T-Shirt, a Mickey Mouse hat, candy, pens, a crossword puzzle, and lots of other things for the plane. It was nice to hear what was going to happen Sunday morning. And to actually hear that it was FINALLY coming!

The construction for my handicapped-accessible bathroom and room started, which means my house is a mess! and dusty! Friday wasn't so bad with the dust, but today it's like dust city in here, so my mom decided what's best for me if I want to stay healthy for this trip is, I'm going to stay overnight and days at my grandparents' house until we leave and maybe until this construction is over. It's so dusty here, and i don't want to get sick right before my trip. So I just packed clothes for six days, and one day i'll come over and pack for my trip. The only thing i hate is, I won't have Abby sleeping with me at night. :-(I'm not sure if i'll know how to get their laptop working right away, but, if i do, i'll update. OK, well, that's about it for now.

Please pray for one of my friends, Erik, who has Mito. He's not doing too good. So please keep him in your thoughts and prayers.

Amanda :-)

WEDNESDAY, OCTOBER 24, 2007
Hey! FOUR MORE DAYS!!!!!!!
Can you believe that?! I certainly can't. I'm just waiting for that release on Friday, and then i'll be off the walls with excitement!
Nothing much medical-wise has been going on (i think that's actually a first!...WOW!). My sinus infection is still here, but I don't have a fever anymore, and my antibiotic sure is helping. But what I figured out is that, if I put it in my tube, it doesn't help as much as if I swallow the liquid. So, even though it tastes like poison, I still swallow it because it works better if I do.

I've been soooo bored lately! The only thing that's kept me going is thinking about my trip every day. Every day I have a routine, and its getting old. I wake up around 6:30-ish, watch some TV, and do my meds and feeds, then I watch my show Charmed, get on my grandma's laptop to check my email, get some schoolwork done, take a nap, get up and do the rest of my schoolwork, take a bath, and the rest of the day is usually resting. Tonight, though, my Speech teacher, Michele, is coming over to visit me and bring me some things. And tonight, my grandparents will actually be home, so my grandma said she will help me with finishing my pocketbook, and then help me start my sister's lap quilt for Christmas. So there's something new on my schedule. And tomorrow my primary nurse, Tony, is coming for his annual visit to weigh me, take blood cultures and all that nice stuff.

There are an awful lot of prayers I need right now. For my friend, Erik, who is in the hospital and still not doing great; my friend, Carrie, who has been in and out of the hospital and been through so much; for the people who have lost their homes in those bad fires in California, that those fires will go out and no one else will die or get hurt. One of my counselors from Double H lives in California, and I emailed her last night to make sure she was OK. she emailed me this morning and said she was fine but said her aunt and grandma had to be evacuated, so please pray for them.
I'll try to update Friday to let you know if I get released, which it is looking good right now. And if my blood cultures came back good. Have a GREAT rest of the week!
Amanda :-)

FRIDAY, OCTOBER 26, 2007
Hey! TWO MORE DAYS!!!!!!!

And guess what else?! I've been released!!!! Cheryl must have called because the Respiratory people came out today to give me my portable oxygen for the plane. I'm so relived and now so excited!!!! I got so excited, I looked up all the rides in Disney and the rest of the parks. I'm still at my grandparents' house (which kinda stinks), because i'm beginning to get homesick. I miss Abby, my sisters, and my dad. I mean, I see them everyday, but it's still not the same. but, hopefully, tomorrow, if they get all that dust out of the room today, I can go home. I mean, I kinda have to, since the limo is going to be picking me up so early...lol. I haven't even packed yet...ahhhh so much to do in so little time. I'll get it done, though. Tonight, I get to spend a whole night with my sisters, though, because my mom and dad have to go to a wedding, so i'm looking forward to spending some quality time with them. :-) OK, well, I just wanted to give you the good news!

Prayer requests: For my friend, Erik, who is getting surgery to get his port out today, and they're putting in a PICC line [a Peripherally Inserted Central Catheter, which is a thin tube inserted into a vein in an extremity and advanced internally to near the heart for easier access to blood]. So please pray for him; for the California people who lost their houses, that they find a place to sleep, and for a safe trip!
Amanda :-D

SATURDAY, OCTOBER 27, 2007
Hi,
This isn't so much as a medical journal entry. it's more of a personal emotional journey i find myself just going through. No, don't worry. everything is still GREAT with my trip.

I've been staying at my grandparents' house since Monday morning. it hasn't been bad at all. they treat me GREAT here, like i'm some royal princess...like every grandparent does. But, last night and today, I found myself getting more homesick than I do in the hospital. Last night, my sisters came over to stay with me for a while while my parents and grandparents went to a wedding reception. It was sooo GREAT to spend some time with them (even though Dahea fell asleep right after she ate...lol). But Carolyn stayed up with me almost until mom and dad came home, and we just talked about the trip. it was nice to spend some quality time with her because I haven't seen her in four days. Well, when my mom and dad came back, I got excited because I thought I was going home tomorrow. My dad left, and I only saw him that day for three seconds maybe. Once my mom changed, she told me that we're spending Saturday night here. I got so mad, sad, frustrated. But I just fell asleep hoping that tomorrow i would feel better.

I woke up at 6:00AM the next morning and then went back to sleep. When I woke up, my dad came over. I hugged him, and I started to get that tightness in my throat before you cry. My grandpa was trying to ask me questions, and I was trying to answer him, but all i could say was, "mm-hm." I don't know if anyone noticed, but I was so upset that he came, I think it would have been better maybe if he hadn't. You know how people always ask, "Who do you think you're closer to, your mom or your dad?" I'm closer to my dad, but when it comes to when I get sick, i'm closer to my mom. I'm a Daddy's Girl. I kinda had to calm myself down because my grandpa kept asking me questions, so i went in the bathroom and brushed my teeth. I still have that urge where I need to cry because I miss my dad (more than anyone else besides Abby) and my sisters. I'm just grateful that tomorrow morning I'll see them for a whole week! I think that the best part of my trip, more then anything, is making up for the time I didn't see my dad. :-)

Today is going to be quite busy! My mom and I are going to run to Hannaford [Supermarket] to get some quick things, then we have to stop at the laundromat because our dumb washer isn't working from the construction, and sometime later on we have to pack. Tomorrow morning is going to be chaos until I get into the limo. Then I'll be relaxed. Thank you all for your messages and emails. I LOVED each one of them and love reading them every day. that's one thing that keeps things off my mind.

Prayer Requests: My Friend, Erik, is supposed to leave the hospital today. his surgery went well, I guess, but please continue to pray for him. Also Carrie, my friend, is still going through a ruff patch. and Natalie, that her breathing problems will get better. and for Rina, that she will continue to make it to school four and maybe five days a week. And for my new friend, Abby, that she stays strong and keeps that smile on her face! this will probably be my last journal entry until I get back or until I get to Give Kids the World. So, pray that I don't have a bumpy ride because supposedly it's windy for takeoff tomorrow.
Amanda :-)

The Make—A—Wish Trip

SATURDAY, NOVEMBER 03, 2007
I'M HOOOOME!!!!

I'm really not that enthusiastic about it here, but i'm kinda happy in one way...[my dog] ABBY!!!! I think that's the only thing i'm happy to be home about...lol. OK, so I really cannot explain everything because it's almost 12:00AM in the morning, and i just got back, but since i can't get to sleep and i'm on the computer, i'll tell ya some things!

OK, so the Limo ride was FANTASTIC!!!!! It felt like my family and I were movie stars for a minute. On Sunday, we got in around 12:30PM, so my mom had to go to a meeting, and so my dad, sisters, and I just hung out and explored our new home for the week. On Monday, we went to Disney and Epcot. I went on Space Mountain and all these other rides. I think it was Monday night when I went to GKTW (Give Kids the World) Double Dare game. I got to pie my dad in the face and then pie myself! It was so much fun! On Tuesday, we woke up and ate breakfast at the Gingerbread House and then we went to MGM. I had fun there. I saw High School Musical Pep Rally (I actually heard it more than saw it, but i was craving for HSM, so songs would due...lol.) Tuesday night I can't even remember if we did anything...lol. Wed., WOW! Wed. was Halloween, and, let me tell you, Halloween is HUGE over there! First, in the morning, we went to Universal and rode all the roller coasters we could find. then, when I got home, I got some lipids into me and got into my costume and headed down to where the parade was going to be and trick or treating. It was so BIG, Halloween was! I went trick-or-treating and, between my sisters and me, we all got three HUGE plastic bags of candy. And we brought all of it back on the plane...lol. Thursday, we just relaxed because of a medical issue, which i'll get to later because then i'll realize i'm talking about reality soon...lol. But it was nice that we went shopping. I got some TinkerBell stuff. OK, a lot of Tinkerbell stuff...lol. Friday, we decided to go back to Universal because were going to Disney World in January, but we're not going to be able to go to Universal, so another day would do good we thought. We rode all the same roller coasters again, and i just had a BLAST!

Oh, ha, I forgot. Thursday night was Christmas! For Christmas, they decorated it, like, all Christmas-y (if that's a word), and they had snow, and i got to get presents! Friday night, I was crowned a Princess. I have an official certificate saying I am one...hehe. I had so much fun dancing with one of Shamu's friends (Shamu and his friends came for the ceremony). I danced with one of his friends to one of the songs from High School Musical, "All For One." We did the dance, and he knew all the moves like me! I was so surprised! I had a blast with him! I think that was the highlight of Friday night. Saturday was our departure day. we checked out and then went to Animal Kingdom. We didn't do a lot there because we didn't have a lot of time, but we did do this one roller coater that was so cool! Then we went on that safari thing where you go in one of those jeeps and look at real animals. That was pretty neat, and the people were really good about getting my wheelchair into the jeep. Then, right from animal Kingdom, we went to the airport, where we had to wait three hours...ughh.

So this is what i did all week...eat ice cream, eat ice cream, and eat ice cream. OK, so i thought eating a lot of ice cream would put LOTS of weight on me, so I was excited! And I tried when i could to eat some breakfast and dinner, too. So I did that, so I thought i would gain weight. I came home today. i did gain an ounce!!!! I was so ticked at myself, i wanted to scream! Between my eating like a pig with ice cream and salad and candy. Jeez, how else can a girl gain weight?! I mean, how do others do it?!

I'm not going to worry about it for now. i'm so tired, and i know, if I don't get my rest, my body is going to be beat for another five days. You can probably tell by my typing i'm tired...lol.

So now to reality and medical stuff. My heart rate has been SUPER high!!! It started around Monday or Tuesday, so my mom put me on my O2 24/7. She called my nurse (because my oxygen was down a little, too) and asked if I could still go on the rides, and he said yeah, as long as my heart rate and oxygen are fine before I go on. So that's what's up medically so far, and hopefully it will stay that way! OK, well, I'm going to go get some sleep. I'm still at my grandparents' house because of the construction, so sorry. And i'm not sure when i'll be able to make everyone's CaringBridge sites, so sorry if i don't visit for a while. I have to rest.
Amanda :-D

MONDAY, NOVEMBER 05, 2007
Hi! I don't know if I'm getting my rest or not? Hopefully I am. I've been going to bed VERY early and waking up pretty late...later than normal anyways. Today, i'm going to try to take another nap during the day. My goal for school, if I catch up on my rest and feel like I have enough energy, is for Wed. So we'll see. I'll keep you updated on that.

I have a pretty busy week ahead of me. Tomorrow, I go and see Dr. Adams. I just saw him less then a month ago, and I usually just see him once a month, but he wanted to see me, I guess, after my trip to make sure I was OK. And my mom, aunt, sisters, and I were planning on going to Maine this Thursday or Friday, so he has to release me for that. I would be so excited if I was able to go because one of my counselors from Double H, the camp I went to during the summer, goes to college up there, and said she would love to visit me, so i would love to see her. She was the one that tucked all of us in at night and acted like our mother (which made me feel more like I was at home when I was there). So, let's hope I get released and that those lipids kick in tonight.

Wed., if I feel up to it, I'm going to try to go to school, which I hope I can because I have so much I want to tell all of my friends and teachers about my trip and show them pictures and give them their presents. so let's hope i'm up for that but not push it. Also, I'm looking forward to Wed. because i'm still living at my grandparents' house right now because the dust from the construction is still at my house, and my sisters are, too, and I miss Abby because, well, i was gone for a week, and then I came back and had to go straight to my grandparents' house. so I miss sleeping with her at night, so my dad and mom are going to bring her over Wed' for a sleepover...lol. So, i'm excited about that! Friday, if I get released, i'm going to Maine. i'll update more on that once I go to Dr. Adams tomorrow.

My Heart Rate thingy is still going berserk! I have no idea what's going on with that, but i guess we'll figure that out tomorrow. I also have to ask Dr. Adams something, or Cheryl, whoever can answer it. I'm going to ask my parents tonight about it. don't worry. it's nothing serious...but i've been noticing it more and more lately, and i just want to point it out now before next month with the Holidays and all...oh my gosh! Can you believe the Holidays are coming up already?! It feels like summer just ended. I've been hearing Christmas songs and all of that. But i LOVE Christmas! It's my favorite Holiday because the rest of my

family comes home, and i LOVE Christmas songs, so yeah.   I'll update more tomorrow, probably after my Dr. appt.
Amanda :-)

Abby Becomes A Service Dog

MONDAY, NOVEMBER 05, 2007
Hi!
OK, quick but exciting update!
Today, I received something VERY special!   About a month ago, I sent in for Abby's Service Dog papers for her to become an official Service Dog.   Well, today they came!   My mom went home for a while to get some stuff, and i guess it came first class, and she came back with it, and I just am so overwhelmed with just looking at it!   I can't believe that she's actually my official Service Dog now!   I mean, I can bring her everywhere now, and she can help me wherever i am.   I just wanted to share that with you because most of you have been with me on this adventure since when she just started her training when I got her.   I can't believe I actually accomplished my goal for her.   It took a year, but it was worth going to those classes and everyday going over and over the 'stays' and 'downs,' it was worth every penny now.

Today, my mom and I decided my body isn't ready to go on another trip right now.   I'm still tired from Florida.   I mean, if i go to Maine, who knows how tired I'll be?!   I don't want to wear myself out especially since I want to make three days of school every week for the next couple of weeks at least.   It kinda upsets me in a way because I was looking forward to seeing my counselor from Double HH, but I guess i'll see her maybe this winter or, if not in the winter, this summer.

My mom messed up my Dr. appt. with Dr. Adams. It's in two weeks, not tomorrow. But tomorrow will be a busy day. I'm going to try to take Abby out for her first official trip to the market. it's not big, but i don't want to start her out big. Dr Adams, I guess, wanted my mom to run another bag of lipids tomorrow because i'm going to try to go to school Wed., so i'm going to need them. That's my plan.

Amanda :-)

WEDNESDAY, NOVEMBER 07, 2007

Hi!

I went to school today! Sorry I had to say that first because I'm so happy I was able to go! I enjoyed myself a lot today. I got to see all of my teachers and friends and just do my schoolwork there! I made three of my teachers crazy hats for Crazy Hat Day, which was fun (trust me, i'm a little sneaky inside when it comes to that stuff...hehe) So I had fun, and i'm not going tomorrow but Friday.

I took Abby out shopping yesterday to Hannaford, Price Chopper, and then Movie Gallery. She did AWESOME! She didn't bark, did everything on command, didn't go up to anyone, didn't pee (which i was worried about even though she never goes inside a place she's not familiar with), and she was just all around GREAT! The only thing she did yesterday in Price Chopper was, we were in the seafood section, and she took a step forward when she was in a stay position and sniffed a little...lol. But, other then that, she was

FANTASTIC! Today, I took her into Target and Subway. she did AWESOME! So I have a feeling she's just going to get better as she gets older.

My heart rate is so much better today. When I went to school, I asked the nurse during the day if she could listen to my heart rate, and she did, and it was normal, 75. So I was relived because I was afraid I was going to have to carry around that small oxygen tank for the rest of the day (that would really stink!).

Tomorrow I have a lot going on (schoolwork wise). I have math work my math teacher, Chris, sent home with me. then, when I got home I got a very nice email for literacy saying I have to write a short, persuasive essay about why I shouldn't have to read the Harry Potter series. It's a long story how we got into that subject, but let's just say, I was looking up Harry Potter spells today. when I don't read the books, I just watch the movies, so then the whole discussion came on, so that's what i guess i'm going to be doing tomorrow, that and scrapbooking my Florida pictures.
Amanda :-)

About How Disgusting I Look

FRIDAY, NOVEMBER 09, 2007
Hi!
This entry is more of a personal entry than anything but i'm going to put some medical stuff at the end.

The past few days i've really been noticing my weight and how disgusting I look without clothes on. Before I get in the tub/shower, I look at myself, and I just think I look disgusting because all i see is a girl that looks like a skeleton. I look at my sister, Carolyn, and see how healthy she is and wonder if i'll ever be like that again. I want that so bad! She complains every once in a while about her weight and [whether or not] if she eats too much she'll gain, but she's perfectly healthy. I remember this time last year I weighed 130. I was a perfect weight for my age, and i looked FANTASTIC! Now, I look like something's wrong with me (so to speak), and I try to hide it with layers and layers of clothes, which seems to help every once in a while, but I can't stand it any more. I want to go back to my old weight of 115-130. I was asking my mom and dad tonight at dinner if I'll ever gain that weight back, and they said, "not as much as you used to".... It scares me because I don't look my age any more. I look younger, and I hate how all my family talks about is my weight some days. I don't know... Anyways, I started a new diet. TRYING to gain some weight, which hasn't helped (YET!), but maybe it will? On the days that I can eat, I eat my cereal and try some salad, and my mom bought these soft brownies, so i've been eating those. Hopefully this diet will work!

Medical terms: I think I'm getting a cold (which isn't good), but i'm staying clear of the fever. My heart rate has been normal, which is good. Tony came by Thursday and is trying to get me this machine, which I think Erik has. it takes your weight, BP, heart rate and i think everything (except blood) and then can send it to anywhere, like the hospital if they need my weight, or to [the insurance company] Anthem the days that they need my weight and all that stuff. So i'm kinda excited about that.

MONDAY, NOVEMBER 12, 2007
HIIIII!!!!
Oh, am I happy right now! It's such a different update than the last one. OK, so i'm going to get right to it, since i'm so proud of myself and so happy! My mom wanted a weight on me today for Anthem so that they could put it in my chart. I told her 'No' at first because I was scared to weigh myself (like always), but I got on the scale, and guess what?!?!? I weighed 99.8 pounds!!!!!!! My mom took off two pounds because i had on some layers, but do you know how proud i was of myself!! I think i actually am about 100.0 because, if you weigh yourself with clothes on a Dr's. scale, it would come out the same, so i'm about 100.0!!! Oh my gosh, i'm actually getting somewhere now. I think my brownie, cereal, and salad diet is so working. But i'm kinda getting sick of chocolate and brownies all together, so i might have to switch to ice cream or something soon, sugar free ice cream that is. I just wanted to share the good news with you because, from my last journal entry, you all knew how frustrated i was, but I think God heard my prayers before I went to bed, and I think i'm going on a good path now. Now I get to worry about all the cool things now —clothes, etc. So excited!!!!

Oh, I had a bit of a scare yesterday. I was sleeping yesterday morning when my Bi-Pap machine started beeping. I was still asleep, but when it beeps it means I'm not breathing. And i think it beeps for how many breaths I don't breathe or something like that. So, I guess I saw the light for a minute until my mom shook me...lol (I really didn't see any light. i was just joking). So, when Tony comes, he might have to adjust the Bi-Pap's beeping sound so that, even if i miss a breath or something, it won't automatically beep. Tomorrow, i have a dentist appt. (can't wait to see if I have a cavity or not, seeing how i've been eating brownies for two

weeks). Wed., i'm going to school. I'll update you when something else happens!
Amanda :-D

THURSDAY, NOVEMBER 15, 2007
Hi!
I don't know where to start, but, we'll start off with good news. I'm maintaining my 98.0 weight! I LOVE to hear that...that number, just love to hear it! I'm trying to eat like a hog and do my feeds at the same time so that i can keep gaining weight. I'm feeling really good lately, and i think it's because i'm gaining weight and i'm eating! But there's still some holes, but we'll get to that.

I've been going to school twice a week, and right now I think i'll stick to two days a week. It seems to be working for my body, and my energy isn't so bad the next day, so i think i'll stick with that right now because i'm heading down a GREAT path and i don't want to ruin it.

Tony my nurse came today. I've been having some problems swallowing carbonated liquids. He gave me some techniques on how i won't cough after I drink. But it seems to me that, if I drink with a straw, it helps, so maybe i'll just start drinking with straws. My port looks good. My Mickey (or as i call her, Minnie) seems to have a little more of that red stuff in it, but next week when Tony comes out, he says he can burn it for me. Yeah, sounds disgusting, but it helps. My back still has been killing me! I told my mom where it hurt, and she said it was right where my right lung is, so next week when I go to Dr. Adams, i'm going to definitely ask him about that, and i'm thinking he might have to take an X-Ray. Hopefully it's nothing serious and it's just the change of weather.

Tomorrow, I FINALLY get to move back into my own house! I'm so excited. I get to sleep with Abby and just be in my own house! Awww, it's going to feel so good. I'm going to try to go to school tomorrow, resting up right now. This weekend, my family is going to a church breakfast. i'm going to see if I can eat a waffle or omelet (sp??) or something that will beef me up. Maybe Thanksgiving next week, with all my pumpkin pie, will, though? I'm bringing Abby to the breakfast, so we'll see how she does. I got her patches today that I ordered. they're so cute! I just need to sew them on her backpack now.

Please pray for my friend, Malisa, who is in the hospital right now and going through an emotional and ruff road. Also for my friend, Abby, who is having a biopsy done in a few weeks.

SATURDAY, NOVEMBER 17, 2007
Hi!
I just want to update you on a quick thing (well, two things). I've been feeling GREAT lately (food-wise), and i've really been eating like every meal. Breakfast, lunch, and dinner. Well, I haven't quite gotten to lunch yet, but i think I might try today. Yesterday, I got to go to school, and we had hot lunch, and we had grilled cheese and tomato soup. Well, I was like drooling over the grilled cheese, but I can't eat it, so I think I'm going to start bringing a lunch to school again. Since i'm eating again, my Dr. put me on a fat free diet because, if i eat a lot of fats, it won't break up in my

body. So, last night, I went shopping for all fat free cereals and milks...lol.

I have to start drinking through a straw now because i've been having a harder time drinking everything, not just carbonated drinks.

I'm still at my grandparents' house because our house is so small with all the boxes all over, and we only have one bed downstairs to sleep in right now, and I need to sleep in a bed when i'm on my IV's, so, until it's most likely finished, we'll be here. Before we leave, i'll let you know. If someone has been trying to call us on my home phone, it's disconnected right now, so....
OK, well, that's the brief update.
Amanda :-)

Swallowing Problems Continue

MONDAY, NOVEMBER 19, 2007
Hi!
So I had a very interesting night last night. I went over to my other grandparents' house to see my dad's ucle and aunt (I don't know how to process the whole 2nd uncle thingy), but anyway they had dinner there... I wasn't that hungry then, so i just drank some soda. So after a while, Nana (my grandma) brought out dessert, and i tried a bite of the pumpkin ice cream, which was good . There was also apple pie, and I was being dumb and tried a bite.... well, i kinda choked on it and threw up in the sink everything i ate within the last three or four hours. It was disgusting! And i learned my lesson. After that, though, my

stomach felt sooooo empty, like I haven't eaten in three days, so i went back to my grandma's and had a bowl of Rice Crispies.

I'm still having a REALLY hard time swallowing liquids. My grandma and grampa have no straws at their house, so i decided to try out a sippy cup today (don't ask!), and it worked!... it actually worked better than a straw, so i am now drinking from sippy cups and feel like a three-year old again. But, I guess whatever it takes, at least I can still drink from my mouth and taste it. I'm grateful for that.

I went to the mall the other night with Abby, and she did GREAT! We went shopping in LL Bean, Bath and Body Works, and Boscov's. She just looked at everything and did her tasks. I was shocked she did that well! But, by the time we left, she was in my wheelchair with me, she was so tired!

This week, hmm, OK, tomorrow is the only day i'm going to make it to school (but i'm happy i'm making it at least one day). Wed., I'm going to be cooking like i'm Rachel Ray, and Thursday is Thanksgiving! Friday, Tony is coming. he usually comes Thursday, but, since Thursday is Thanksgiving, he can't, so he's coming Friday. OK, well, if I don't update before Thanksgiving, I hope EVERYONE has a Happy Thanksgiving, and, if you watch the Macy's Parade, enjoy because that's my favorite part of Thanksgiving!

TUESDAY, NOVEMBER 20, 2007
Hi!
I just wanted to tell everyone what's going on since I probably won't be on until a couple days after Thanksgiving, but who

knows? Anyways, first let's start with, I had a WONDERFUL day at school today! It wasn't the day really, it was the one person who made my day special. I've been having a tuff time adjusting this year to the new classroom. I'm in the same class (well kinda). I have all the same teachers (except for one), but my best friend went to another school, and I had and have been having a REALLY hard time adjusting. It's just weird not having someone to talk to all the time during recess. So, today I had my private music lesson for guitar/piano with Beth in the music room. I was just getting ready to play the guitar when my old teacher knocked on the door and said, "there's a surprise here for you." I looked over and saw my best friend that moved to a different school...Mike! I was so excited I just went up to him and hugged him. he got so tall that he's almost taller then me, and he actually lifted me up! I was like, "Woahhh. where did those mules come from?"....lol. It literally made my day, maybe my year! I think it might have been my Christmas present. And it came exactly in time because I didn't know if I could take much more school without seeing or talking to Mike, so it felt like I was on cloud 9 when i got to talk to him in person. Then he found out my phone lines were disconnected, and that's why he hasn't called me...lol. Oh how i miss him! I also found out he comes every Tuesday for gym, so I'm going to try to schedule my days for Tuesdays so I can see him once a week. Sorry, I just had to share that because it made my year!

So when I got home, my smile didn't last very long...just kidding. But anyways, my mom told me I have to go to the Cardiologist, Dr. Spoon. Cheryl says my heart is beating way too fast for a girl who is just sitting and her heart rate is over 100 beats per minute, and I can feel it when it is over 100. I'm not sure when i'm going, but i'll let you know when I find out.

So, tomorrow, I'm taking it easy for Thanksgiving. it seems like everyone in my family is sick or getting sick or i'm going to try really hard to not get to close to anyone on Thanksgiving even though I haven't seen most of my family in ages! So, hope everyone has a Happy Thanksgiving! Make sure you watch the Macy's Day Parade!
Oh, wanted to share this good news with you too! I made my goal.....i'm 100 pounds!!!!!!!!
Amanda :-)

THURSDAY, NOVEMBER 22, 2007
Happy Thanksgiving everyone!
I got a minute to get on the computer, so i thought i would update you and just say Happy Thanksgiving!

I did pretty well tonight. I aspirated [breathed in] two times with the liquids, but, other then that, i did pretty good. I ran a bag of Carnitor [an IV drip of carnitine, an amino acid beneficial to the building and strength of cells] while I was eating. My back hurts a little, though, right now because I think I was on my feet too much today, or maybe that wasn't it. It's been hurting, though.

I think the best part about Thanksgiving this year was that I wasn't in the hospital (like one year). I got to see my uncle, aunt, and cousins whom I only get to see once a year (this year twice because of Disney). it was so nice, and I was so grateful! I got a little disappointed at one time because i looked at our annual Thanksgiving family picture we take each year, and last year i looked so...healthy? This year, I had IV's in me and a mask on, O_2, vitals every minute. I had maybe two things on my plate, while last year I could eat almost everything! It's amazing how fast your body can change in a year, isn't it?

Please continue to pray for my friend, Abby, and for my other friend, Carrie, who is in the Hospital this Thanksgiving, and yet she still can feel the thankfulness (if that's a word). Also for my friend Malisa.

Amanda :-)

More Aspirating and Tremors

SATURDAY, NOVEMBER 24, 2007

I'm FINALLY rested up from Thanksgiving on Thursday. Boy, on Thursday, i looked like I got hit by a truck! Even my mom said so. Well, I have some good news and bad (comes with the territory, I guess). today we're FINALLY going to start moving some of our furniture back into our family room because, yesterday, the rest of the floor was put in. So, tonight, I'm going to try to spend the night just one night because the painting guy isn't finished, so I wouldn't want to breathe in the fumes from him at night, but tonight it won't smell like paint because he hasn't been there in three days. So i'm really excited I get to spend a night with my Abby girl! She's going to have like a party tonight because I'm bringing her to Walmart tonight with me as well (she'll be in all her glory!). So we're moving right along with the house. still looks a mess, but it's getting there slowly but surely.

I was having a fit yesterday because i see everyone putting up there Christmas decorations outside, and usually my mom, sisters, dad, and I have our outside lights and blow up decorations out on the lawn before Thanksgiving, so it's kinda weird for us. I guess we'll be decorating a little late this year.

OK, onto the bad news: I aspirated twice again yesterday. it was kinda my fault, though, because I forgot to use a straw (I certainly need to get used to some adjustments). So, the first time that I aspirated, my mom was not here, and i threw up my drink and my lunch in my grandma's bathroom sink! I was so mortified, and it smelled, so i washed it out good and sprayed some perfume she has in her bathroom (which sorta stinks...lol, so it didn't really make a difference!). The second time I aspirated, I didn't throw up (thank goodness!) I just coughed until my nice throat was content and hurt. So now, before I get a drink, i'm like, WAIT!!!! Let's get either a straw or a sippy cup...hehe.

The other thing i've been noticing is, the days I don't have my lipids, I have more tremors than normal in my right hand. I noticed it yesterday when I was typing on the computer. i was typing every wrong letter! I was getting so frustrated at my hand. So I'm going to have to see what that's all about.

Today, my dad, mom, and I are moving furniture in the family room like I said, then we're going to Walmart to get me some sippy cups of my own instead of using my cousin's...lol and to get my hair cut. And I have a feeling we're going out to dinner...just a feeling, but I don't know. This week for school, I'm deciding whether I want to switch my lipid days around so that I can go to an all-school breakfast and be there for my teacher's birthday, but then I won't be able to go Tuesday (the day before) to see my friend Mike. It's hard calling these decisions because usually my days are Tuesdays and Thursdays, but I HATE missing birthdays and special things going on school-wise. So, i might have to flip for it. I have to decide soon, though, because, if I decide to go Wed., i have to skip Monday's lipid day? I don't know. I might have those two days mixed up, actually I do...lol.

Please continue to pray for my friend's Carrie, Abby, Natalie, Malisa, Erik, and Rina!
Amanda :-)

TUESDAY, NOVEMBER 27, 2007
Hi!
Oh, lots to tell. Let's start with this morning. So, this morning, I was thirsty for some orange juice, so I went to the fridge and got some and started pouring it in my sippy cup (haha, laugh!). anyway, it spilled all over! I had a tremor in the hand i was pouring the juice into. I was shocked it got that bad! then, I spilled water all over because of my tremors. There's something not right about these tremors, but who knows, i'm just going with it! My mom said she's either going to call Cheryl and ask about it or ask about it next time we go to see Dr. Adams. I guess well see, won't we?

My heart has been beating fast as a bullet still. it's like i'm running a marathon when i'm sitting and relaxing, so that's another thing we have to adjust...hmm. My back is still killing me lately. it's weird because some days it doesn't bother me and some days just when i'm like relaxing it starts to bug me! I'm like ughhhh! Why can't you bug me when i'm not relaxing at least...lol. One more thing we need to adjust....oh goodness! You have to love this don't ya!

So, I was going to go to school tomorrow, but my mom and dad came home telling me we have a meeting with the overnight nurses who are going to be watching me once a week during the nights. And they have to see me, i guess, so there goes my Wed. and one of my teacher's birthdays, my teacher's yummy cake, all-school breakfast! There will be another one, though! I'm planning on goofing with my lipid days and going Thursday now and Friday! Well see, though.

Today is my mom's birthday (I won't say how old...lol), but Happy Birthday, mommy! Today is also a sad day for my family because a friend of my family died over the weekend. Her name was Stephanie, and she has been battling cancer for 11½ years! I think she fought her fight...and won! My mom and dad went to the wake today. not such a good present for my mom on her birthday, but I guess it was hard for some people. one week ago she was shopping for her Christmas dress and jewelry, and today she's gone. So please keep her family in your prayers, and also my friends Abby (that her birthday goes well!), Rina, Erik, Natalie, Malisa, and Carrie.

Amanda :-)

FRIDAY, NOVEMBER 30, 2007
Hi!
Well, I actually got some time to update...yay!
Tony, my nurse, came last night, and it's always great to see him. Tony + my dad = me laughing too hard! Anyway, you know the

pain in my back that i've been having right below my left lung? Well, Tony looked at that, and he made me do the E test to make sure I had no cancerous stuff down there, which all came back great! He's really thinking it's a kidney stone. And the reason he thinks I have one is that I get dehydrated very easily, and dehydration can cause kidney stones. And, when a kidney stone moves, it hurts your back. So, I have to go see a Urologist to get some tests done and see where we have to go from there.

I'm still waiting on the Cardiologist appt. because I'm not sure whether i'm going to Albany Med. or St. Peter's, so well see. Tony also burned my skin that was coming up from my G-Tube, and later on I thought it was infected because it got all blue and white...lol. And my mom was like, "This has happened before!" It never happened before, but I guess it happens with smaller amounts of skin, i'm guessing because the other times that i've had my skin burned around my G-Tube, the skin was HUGE! But it's clear now, and it has to get burned one or two more times. I forgot to ask Tony about this pimple that has been on my nose for months! It's like a small pimple, and it won't leave. it's not really a ball, though. it's more flat. My mom thinks it's because my nose doesn't get enough air at night because of my Bi-Pap and the pores get all icky. I'll make sure I ask him next time.

I'm 105 lbs!!!!!! Wanted to let you know that one because I don't think i've announced my weight in two weeks! I did make it to school yesterday, and did it tire me out! I felt it as soon as I came home. I slept all the way home on the bus, which is like a 35-minute ride back. But I was still tired when I got home, but I had to stay awake for Tony and I did. then I was hungry, so we ordered Chinese food. Then, I felt like i got hit by a truck! I didn't make it to school today because I didn't get lipids last night, but i'm hoping i'll make it two days next week. I'm not sure, though, because the urology appt. needs to be scheduled ASAP. We'll see, though.

I've started "Harry Potter and the Half Blood Prince," and there's a lot to that book, understanding it, vocab. words. and i have more schoolwork that comes along with that. But I promise I'll get to them soon.

Tonight, Alicia is coming over to stay with me. I can't WAIT! We always have a GREAT time! We play loads of games and watch High School Musical too many times...lol. Tomorrow, my family is going to a jewelry store for this Make-A-Wish thing. My mom has to speak about our trip and etc. I'm going to bring Abby, so that will be fun...lol. And were planning on moving back into the house Saturday before the snow comes. My new room is all painted, and the house is all painted also! I'll have to post pictures when i can. I don't think my sister likes it, but everyone else does. I think she gets embarrassed from it because of my FANTASTIC colors!

Please continue to pray for my friends Carrie, Abby, Natalie, Malisa, Rina, Erik, and Bayla!
Amanda :-)

TUESDAY, DECEMBER 04, 2007

I'm sorry I haven't been on anyone's CaringBridge site. our computer has been down, and we moved in back to our house over last weekend, so our computer JUST got hooked up again.

So, this is going to be a short update, and i'll update more tomorrow. I've been having tremors like NUTS! It's mostly on days when I don't get my lipids, but I do have some on days when I do, too. My mom said she was going to ask Cheryl and Dr. Adams, but I'm not sure if she did yet. I HATE tremors because i literally have to hold my hand if I want to hold a spoon or something straight. The other day when I was eating cereal, I held my spoon up, and i felt my hand go, and it tilted the spoon! I was like, "OK, well, just hold it if it becomes a problem." So that's what i've been doing, holding it. I also noticed i'm having tremors when I go to sleep, too...lol. I think I always have them when i sleep, but not as bad.

I still have the back pain from my believed kidney stones (i'm still not 100% sure if they're kidney stones, but i think they are).

I'm maintaining my weight of 105lbs, so i'm definitely happy with that! I really can't believe that i'm actually at a weight i like, i mean, i never get a weight that i kinda like, and i kinda like this weight...lol.

I didn't make it to school at all yet this week, but hoping to go tomorrow and Fri. I was sooooo exhausted yesterday, and I forgot I had a half day, too, today, so that didn't help that I got up at 6:30 and forgot I had a half day and went back to sleep. Today, i slept in until 10:00! Yesterday, I felt like a zombie...lol.

Keep in your payers these special friends:
Abby :-), Natalie :-), Carrie :-) , Erik :-), Malisa :-), Rina:-)

Amanda :-D

Continuing Back Problems

THURSDAY, DECEMBER 06, 2007
Hi!
So i'm updating more....lol

Tony came by today for my regular Thursday checkup (that's what I call it anyways). I slept through most of it i think, but when i woke up, my mom and he were talking about this system (i forgot the name) where you can weigh, check BP, pulse and etc. on it and send it to my Dr. and to Tony. So I guess we're going to be getting that. Probably Monday because I have to be here for it, and i'm going to school tomorrow.

We mentioned to Tony about my newest back problem. I have an ache up near my shoulders now. It started yesterday on the bus ride to school and lasted almost the whole ride to school. I couldn't even listen to my iPod, that's how much pain i was in (and that's not often!). He still thinks it's a kidney stone because I still have the pain near my left lung. But my mom called Cheryl, and there's a four-month waiting list to go see the Urologist, and, face it, I really can't do that pain when i'm going to Disney in January again! Well, I can handle it, but only to a certain degree. So Tony suggested that, the next time I have that pain, my mom and dad bring me to the ER (nice Holiday isn't it?). So, well see what happens... hopefully this pain will go away! It's funny how one thing stops and more things worse start to come (not worse. i should say not much better).

We also told Tony about my tremors, and he suggested I put a 1 lb. weight on the side that's having tremors when I eat so i don't spill cereal or whatever all over the place. Or I could but two of the 1 lb. weights so, when I type, it won't be all sloppy like last time...lol. Could you tell i was having tremors? I also told him i was having them at night, and he said they were ticks. But i always have them at night. I just didn't know they were ticks!

I weighed myself today.... 103. I lost almost 2 lbs. It's not that's bad, it could be worse. But I kinda have a goal to get to my sister's weight, and it's not going good so far. In my opinion, I don't think I'll ever get back to my old weight again. But you never know. I believe in miracles!

Please continue to pray for all my friends... Carrie, Malisa, Abby, Natalie, Rina, and Erik!

Have a GREAT rest of the week!

Amanda :-)

FRIDAY, DECEMBER 07, 2007
Quick Update:

So, Cheryl called back last night, and, just as i thought, when things were 'kinda' going well, the nice, splendid news comes out. The pain in my back moved up the other day near my shoulders, so my mom talked to Cheryl about that, and Cheryl seems to think its my gall bladder. Yeah...from the nice lipids that i love so much and help me, but i'm starting to think i don't love them so much anymore!...lol. So Monday, i'm going to the Dr's. to get a script for a CT [computerized tomography] scan, and i think on Tuesday i'm going to get a CT or it's a Neuro appt. (i'm not sure. i'll have to double check). I have so many Dr. appts coming up, it's unbelievable! But, hey, i say better get it all done in one shot than tons...right?

I made it to school today and LOVED it! I got to go to my piano lesson, and i played Christmas songs on the piano. I also participated in Hot Lunch. We made lasagna! And I got to make one of my CB [Caring Bridge] friends a present in art! Gotta love school! OK, this weekend i actually do have plans now because, guess what?! My sister, Carolyn, got her license!!!!! So she's taking Dahea and me shopping! So i'm excited about that!

Please continue to pray for my friends:
Abby, Rina, Carrie, Malisa, Erik, Natalie, and Bayla!

Have a GREAT weekend and enjoy the snow!
Amanda :-)

SATURDAY, DECEMBER 08, 2007
QUICK UPDATE AGAIN!!! :
So my mom and dad decided to try to hold off on taking me to the ER unless it gets bad until Monday because the ER tends to be a bit more busy during the weekend (and i'm sure most of you know that!). Today was a painful but exciting day for me. I was in pain most of the day with my back, slept for half of the day. But, when I woke up, my mom and sisters were decorating the

Christmas tree! So that was a nice surprise. I didn't get to go shopping with my sisters today because i was so weak and couldn't move because of the fatigue and back.

I probably won't be on the computer much because the Tylenol® only lasts for like 1½ hours, so...

Please continue to pray for my friends: Rina, Abby, Natalie, Malisa, Carrie, and Erik!

Have a GREAT rest of the weekend!
Amanda :-)

Continuing Back Pain

TUESDAY, DECEMBER 11, 2007
Hi!
WELL, I really don't know where to start. I made it through the weekend with the HORRIBLE pain in my back. Sunday night I didn't sleep at all, the most sleep i got was five hours, which isn't like my kind of sleep. So the next morning was even worse! I couldn't get out of bed, didn't move, was pale, and just felt all blahh! So, later that day, guess where we headed? Off to the ER! Yes the ER! I really didn't want to go, but my back was literally killing me! They had me in triage right away and in a private room right after that. We got there around 4:00PM, and, yes, i got admitted around 12:00AM the next day. I was so tired because I haven't slept in two days almost.

Now, getting to the good stuff: THEY have no idea what's going on with me right now. They're either thinking [it's] my left kidney from the damage my urinary tracts have or just plain old Mito and my muscles getting weaker in my back. I'm on Morphine and Tegradol (sp?) [Tramadol, for moderate to severe pain] every 4-6 hours. Yesterday, when I was in the ER, they did an ultrasound, and nothing showed up unusual. they also did blood work, and there was nothing there, so tomorrow they're going to do a CT to try to rule out my left kidney. The worst part of this whole thing is, something made me weak that i can't sit up on my own or walk on my own. I feel like i'm half dead. I was thinking today before I went to sleep, "I think I kinda have an idea of what Malisa went through last year and every day now." The thing is, the Dr. won't let me out until I can at least walk to the bathroom door by myself (and that without holding on to the IV pole). So, That's my goal for this week.

There's one good thing about this whole situation. I get to see my friend, Kiki, from camp again. When they were transferring me last night, i saw her walking the halls, and she was waving, and i didn't notice who she was at first, and then i was like, oh my gosh! So, i'm pretty excited about that.

This is my Case Manager's laptop, so I'm not sure how often i'll be able to update because i can't get to the computers right now, and my mom is computer illiterate. So, that's it for now. i'll try to update ASAP, but for now here are my prayer requests...i have A LOT of them this week!

Please continue to pray for my friends: Malisa, Carrie, Abby, Natalie, Erik, and Rina. And please say a special prayer for these two special friends, Bobby, a friend in my class whose house caught on fire last night, and he lost a lot in his room, and a friend in the hospital, Sean.

Have a GREAT week everyone!
Amanda :-)

PS: I'm on floor 7D-North, room 722 [D7-North].

WEDNESDAY, DECEMBER 12, 2007
Quick Update:
My CT scan came back clear from what the DR said, so it's muscle. Cheryl came up today with Dr. Sanchez to see how my walking and sitting up were. She said i'm starting PT and OT [physical and occupational therapy] right away. So the nurse sent the script right away and she said i might start tonight. My left foot is all puffy and has a callous on it from i think not moving it for three days. So i think they're going to give me some cream for that. Later on today, my mom is going to try to get me out in the wheelchair to go to the Ronald McDonald house to see Santa (it's not really an outdoor favorite to see Santa for me, but i think of it for a good laugh). Also, my mom said there's a beautiful tree in there, so i kinda want to see that. I miss my Christmas tree at home, so i think it will be nice to see another one. Later on tonight, my dad, grandparents, and Speech Teacher are coming to visit. So i'm going to be busy, busy, busy! Dr. Adams is supposed to stop by tonight or tomorrow to see if I have to go on TPNs or up my lipids. The nurse put me on O_2 because of my heart rate. I think that's it.

I'm getting some Christmas presents done while i'm here (so that's a good thing!). I'm sorry if some of you get them late (it's this big road block i'm in right now).

Please continue to pray for my CB friends: Carrie, Malisa, Erik, Abby, Natalie, and Rina! And two special prayer requests for my friends Bobby and Sean.
Have a GREAT week!
Amanda :-)

THURSDAY, DECEMBER 13, 2007
Hey!
4th day in the hospital and still i'm finding no light at the end of the tunnel. It seems like this pain and fatigue are never going to end! I wish it was just a dream and i could wake up in my own bed at home and walk into the living room and see my beautiful Christmas tree, but I guess that's not going to happen quiet yet...at least not until I walk and can sit up on my own.

I never made it to see the Christmas tree last night, but Santa did stop by last night to see me and give me a present. He gave me a HUGE snoopy plush animal and an MP3 player! also got a candy cane (even though i can't eat it i enjoyed seeing it!). My old teacher came by last night and surprised me. She was very kind and brought me a balloon and a cute little penguin..hehe. My grandma, aunt, and cousins also stopped by last night and brought me an eggnog latte (so yummy!) we just chatted for a while my mom and dad got out for a bit. My teachers came by also yesterday afternoon and brought cards and stuffed animals. You should see my wall of cards already! Today Yogi (my favorite

Therapy Dog) came by and gave me a stuffed animal; I also got his picture taken with him.

Medical-wise I'm still in a LOT of pain!   Every two hours or less i'm taking pain meds.   Tomorrow, they have to switch one pain me because you can't stay on it for more then five days.

I started PT today, and let me tell you, and i think some of you understand where i'm coming from, this is going to be a LONG road for me!   This is the worst my body has ever gotten, and i can hardly hold my head up to recover from that. i think it might take a while, but i AM determined to get home by Christmas or before!!!!!

I am so close to finishing everyone's presents!   Today, i got everyone's cards done, so all that is left is presents!   And they're all handmade!   I'm hoping to ship them out by Monday.

That's really it for now. I'll definitely keep you updated! Please continue to pray for my friends: Malisa, Carrie, Rina, Abby, Natalie, and Erik! And please say a special prayer for my sister who is traveling back from Pennsylvania this weekend.
Amanda :-)

"Always keep a positive attitude!"

FRIDAY, DECEMBER 14, 2007
Hi Again!
This is hopefully going to be a quick update. Last night I made it to The Ronald McDonald House to see the BEAUTIFUL tree!

My wonderful nurse, who i think is the best nurse around here, found a Barker Lounger for my mom to push me in to go see the tree. It felt so nice getting out of that bed and seeing the snow out the window. I used to hate seeing the snow, but i think now i will appreciate it more. i think I actually already do.

So, something funny for a change. Last night, when I got back from my nice ride, I accessed myself, and my nurse (by the way, her name is Bridget) and my mom decided to give me a sponge bath and wash my hair. Well, I can't walk to the bathroom yet, so they had to do it in my bed, so doing my body was fine, but when it came to doing my hair, that was a MESS! Poor Bridget had to change my sheets again when she just changed them earlier...lol. I felt bad, but i felt clean!

I am still so sore from PT yesterday! It feels like I got run over by a truck! Especially since late last night I started to run a fever, which now is 102! How lovely, but there's always a risk when you come to the hospital right? One minute i'm so cold and the next i'm sweating like a pig! And i was really nausiated (sp?) this morning, so i didn't eat my breakfast. I also am having some very bad migraines!

Later on today, my [in-home] nurse, Tony, is coming up to visit, and my dad is coming, and i'm not sure who else. Have a GREAT week and weekend! I'll keep you updated.

Please continue to pray for my friends: Malisa, Carrie, Erik, Rina, Abby, and Natalie. And please say a special prayer for my sisters who are traveling home tomorrow on these slippery weather roads.
Amanda :-)

SATURDAY, DECEMBER 15, 2007
Hi!
Well, the Drs. finally figured out a plan for me! They started me on Nerotin (a muscle relaxer for my back) [Neurontin is used to treat pain caused by shingles and as an anti-epileptic], and they said maybe that will help, and, if it does, then they're going to transfer me via Ambulance to Sunnyview Rehabilitation Center. It's not a definite thing yet, but its like a 90% plan.

I broke my fever late last night. I had sweat all over me! My mom also got me out for another ride in the lounger with Kim. We just did some laps around the floor then went to the Ronald McDonald House. It kinda felt nice to get out. My dad also came up last night and brought me some more clothes and a picture of Abby (I miss her so much!).

Thank you everyone for the prayers and wonderful messages. They mean a lot to me! Please continue to pray for my friends: Carrie, Malisa, Erik, Abby, Natalie, and Rina. And please say a special prayer for my sisters who are traveling home from Pennsylvania in this weather.
Amanda :-)

SATURDAY, DECEMBER 15, 2007
Hey!
I learn so much in one day! So I'll give you the good news at the end of the entry, but first the medical news. I'm going for another

CT to make sure it's not my kidneys (they are just double checking). So i'll be leaving for that soon. OT came in today and tested me on what I can and cannot do. She said I have a long road ahead of me, but i'll get there. She said it's good that I can bathe my arms and belly by myself, so that's a start. She also made me sit up, but, every time i sat up, she let go, and i went back, and she had to catch me. She will be coming every Monday and Friday. Joan, one of my teachers, stopped by today and surprised me with two books she bought about dogs. It was nice talking to her and seeing her in general. The pain in my back seems to be getting a little better. Like I don't need the pain meds as much. So hopefully, if my temp stays down, i'll be moving to Sunnyview on Monday.

Now for the good news! Abby is coming up today!!!! My nurse told me earlier this morning, and later on my dad is going to bring her up! I'm super excited because I haven't seen her in six days! It's her first time in a hospital, so let's hope for a good visit.

Thank you to all who have been praying for me. it means A LOT! Please continue to pray for m CB friends: Malisa, Carrie, Erik, Abby, Natalie, and Rina!
Have a GREAT weekend!
Amanda :-)

SUNDAY, DECEMBER 16, 2007
Hello!
Well, I went for another ultrasound today to make sure my left kidney was extra A-OK. You all know how Mito Drs. can be. they want to make sure you don't come back, not because they

don't want to see you. just not in this condition...lol. So, everything on the ultrasound turned out perfect as it was.

Today was mostly just a relaxing day. my 2nd roommate went home, so now i have the whole room to myself! My sisters and dad came up to visit with Abby today (and, by the way, Abby did GREAT yesterday, and today she just lays on the bed...lol and makes sure nobody touches me...lol). It was the last time i'm going to see my sisters for one month! It's kinda sad to me if you think about it. I mean, to me, it doesn't feel like Christmas this year because, #1 I'm in the hospital, and #2 Carolyn and Dahea are gone in another country! It just isn't the same. It will just feel like a normal day on Christmas.

My pain is going away slowly, which is good because that means going home faster and me walking sooner! I guess i'm just waiting for a bed at Sunnyview.

I found another skin clump (well, at least that's what i call it) around my mickey (or as i call it, Minnie). So Surgery will have to burn it...a couple of times.

Tomorrow, Kim (my old teacher), and her daughters are coming to visit, and my grandparents and maybe my dad. So, tomorrow will be a busy day for me. And Brenna will be here.

Please continue to pray for: Malisa, Carrie, Natalie, Abby, Erik, and Rina! And PLEASE say a special prayer for my sisters who are traveling on a plane to Korea on Tuesday Morning.
Have a GREAT week!
Amanda :-)

MONDAY, DECEMBER 17, 2007
Hello Again!
It seems like i'm updating ever hour! Anyways i'm going to try to make this a REALLY short update, but that's a small possibility because my updates always seem to become more than needed. I'm a talker! So, a man from Sunnyview came today, and he said i'll be leaving AMC [Albany Medical Center] on Wed. to go to Sunnyview. Well, unless i get a fever or something (which i hope i don't!). He told my mom and me a lot about Sunnyview. You have to do three hours of therapy a day (broken up). You get your own room. You don't do therapy on Sundays and have a half day of therapy on Saturday. There's also a child life specialist there, so i won't be bored all the time, too! Sunnyview is a Pediatric and Adult Rehab center, so i'll be with children...so nice! So, that's what he told me. I just can't wait until i start walking again.

A Dr. came today and looked at my Mickey Button. he said it's a weird place to have it. You know how all the skin is coming up? Well, he put this stuff around it to make it heal a little bit, and, if that works, i won't have to have surgery to get a mickey in another place. So I'm hoping this works!

I decorated my room today (not that i'm staying here much longer!). But i'm going to bring the decorations over to Sunnyview. I think my dad might buy me a Christmas tree too...lol.

The Dr. took me off the IV pain meds and put me on pill pain meds (crushed up, then through the G-tube). My pain really is doing well! I took pain meds this morning at 6:00, and i just took it right now at 3:10!!!!!! So i think that pill is working.

Thank you to everyone who's been praying for me, I really appreciate it! But i have some prayer requests of my own. Malisa, Carrie, Erik, Abby, Rina, and Natalie!
I hope everyone has a GREAT week!
Amanda :-)

TUESDAY, DECEMBER 18, 2007
Hello!
So the transporter came in a minute ago and told my mom and me we're leaving tomorrow to go to Sunnyview! We're leaving at 10:00 AM via ambulance. So I'm kinda excited about that. I'm not sure about the whole computer thing, so i'll update tomorrow when i get a chance. I'll probably start therapy tomorrow right away, maybe not...i'm not sure. I guess we'll see.

The Dr. who took a look at my Mickey yesterday and put some gauze stuff around it to see if the skin [is] coming up around it was here today to see if the skin was shrinking. it is slowly but surely.

I think last night was the most fun i had since i came here, which was nine days ago. Kim's daughters came, and they took me in the lounger after my bath to the Ronald McDonald house to play some air hockey. Let me say, they don't know how to drive that buggy! I had so much fun playing air hockey with Brittany and watching Brianna get kicked in the head by the swinging monkey from the tree....lol. Then we headed to the playroom to get a game, and we picked Pictionary and Kim, Brittany, Brianna, and I played in teams. That didn't go so well because we kept guessing each other's pictures on the teams we were on.

Tonight is going to be busy because Sunnyview is an hour and a half away from my house, so my dad is going to bring everything we need up here so he doesn't have to drive back and forth. My mom also has to do like two loads of wash, pack, and help me with a sponge bath. So that's a really busy night.

Carolyn and Dahea got off all right this morning, so thank you for your prayers for them. now I just need one more prayer—please pray that they get to Korea safely. Also, these few prayers: Malisa, Carrie, Abby, Natalie, Rina, and Erik!
Have a GREAT week everyone!
Amanda :-)

TUESDAY, DECEMBER 18, 2007
Heyy!!!!
I have to post this because i'm extremely excited!!! And I know it's probably one of the few things that will keep me going. This summer, if some of you remember, i went to Double HH Camp. I became very close to one special counselor; her name was Tess. She sometimes writes in my guest book. Well, we've kept in touch, and i've missed her more then anyone can imagine since last summer. So I checked my email today, and she said she was coming to Albany in January! I got so excited! So were going to try to hook up during January. And i'm going to try to do something special for when she comes. my mission for when she

comes is to stand up and hug her.... actually hold my head up and stand! So, that's something i'm GOING to do!

Today, Abby came, and it was quite an interesting visit...lol. Santa came and gave me an early present, and, well, it was her first time seeing Santa, so she growled and barked at him and just didn't like him at all! So let's just say Santa did a VERY quick pose for the picture...lol.

My nurses started this thing on my bed [sheet]. My Care Partner, Kristi, started to show me how to draw a Christmas tree. when she was done, she wrote a note, and then another nurse did the same thing, and then a chain happened, so guess my mom and I are going to cut the sheet and hang it in my room at Sunnyview.

I want to give a HUGE thank you to Erik who sent me a beautiful bracelet and an ornament with Abby on it (which i'm going to hang up on my mini tree in Sunnyview), so Thank You VERY much Erik! Please continue to pray for my sisters who are still in the air flying to Korea. also please pray for my mito friends: Carrie, Malisa, Erik, Abby, Natalie, and Rina!
Have a GREAT week!
Amanda :-)

First Time at Sunnyview

FRIDAY, DECEMBER 21, 2007
YAYYYYY!!!!!!!
I finally got a computer to update on...lol. Oh my gosh so much to update and so little time. So, we got to Sunnyview safely, a little

bumpy ride and exhausting, but safely. When we arrived, I really didn't like the place at all, to be honest with you. But you know what, i LOVE this place, and it's really starting to help me. Yesterday, i held my head up for about two seconds, today almost a minute!!!!!!!!! Can you believe that?! I mean, i know that's not much, but to me it's a miracle! I have such a busy schedule here, so i'm not sure when i'll get to update, but know that i am getting better VERY slowly but surely! I want to thank soooooo MANY PEOPLE because a lot of people have done so much for my family and me. First, I want to thank Abby and Joey for their package that they sent. I LOVE the ornament. i'm going to hang it up on my tree when my dad brings it up on Sat. I want to thank everyone who sent cards. i can't remember everyone because there's to many people, but what keep me going are the cards and letters. Some people are also asking me which room i'm in. i'm on floor 3, room 365, bed 1. Oh, i forgot something funny that i did in the ambulance...lol. I guess i was falling asleep, and i D stated [destabilized?]....TWICE!!!! My mom didn't get a kick out of it, but i sure did. OK, well, anyways, i have LOADS of visitors coming up, so i better go! I'll try to update when i ever get a chance.

PLEASE CONTINUE TO PRAY FOR MY FRIENDS: Malisa, Carrie, Erik, Abby, Natalie, and Rina! And, please say a special prayer for my sisters who are in Korea.

Have a GREAT weekend, and, if i don't update before Christmas, have a GREAT and MERRY CHRISTMAS!!!!

(Hugs) Amanda :-)

In The Hospital for Christmas

TUESDAY, DECEMBER 25, 2007
OK!
I can finally update as often as i like thanks to my grandparents
who bought me a laptop for Christmas with more other nice gifts.
Before I get to all the medical stuff and how my Christmas was, I
want to say a few Thank You's: First of all, thank you to ALL of
you who have been sending me messages through the Sunnyview
email. everyday when i get back from therapy, there's always an
envelope on my bed with all of your messages, and i read each one
of them, and they go straight to my heart.

Second, I want to thank EVERYONE who has sent me stuff for
my tree—cards, anything...you have no idea how excited i get
when i see them and how beautiful the ornament or what else it is
looks. my family and I are extremely Grateful for all of you.

Now getting to the medical stuff, then Christmas. I've been
having a problem with my heart rate. it's been really low! So,
when I do PT and OT, my mom always has to bring the Pulse Ox.
A couple days ago, it got so low, they had to lift my head up and
make me drink. So, hopefully, that won't become a HUGE
problem.

PT and OT have been going pretty good, I would say. Yesterday in
PT, I stood up with A LOT of assistance but for three mins!
Then, the second time, I did the same, but my heart rate got so
high, i couldn't do any more standing, so we did leg movements.
In OT, we just did leg movements. I did this cool thing in OT
also, because I get OT, PT, and Speech 2x's a day, where i went
down to a living apt., and she had me go into all the rooms to see
if i could with my electric wheelchair without bumping into

anything, and i did it perfectly, and then i baked muffins...lol. Last night was hard because usually on Christmas Eve I go to my grandparents' house for dinner with my family, and my sisters are in Korea (of which they called, and i got to speak to them!), and my dad was home, so it was just my mom and I. So I was really upset, so I just went to bed early to try to get the next day started.

Well, I woke up at 7:30 and cleaned up, watched the Disney Parade, and then my dad came! He brought me my eggnog coffee and eggnog (can you tell i LOVE eggnog?!). I opened some of my gifts, and then Kim and her family came and brought me presents, and, let me tell you, one of them is REALLY soft and comfy. Briana (Kim's daughter) and Brittany (Kim's other daughter...lol) made me a Tinkerbell blanket!!!! It's so soft and comfy! I LOVE it so much that my dad took my horse one [that I had with me] home...lol. When Kim's family left, my dad's side of the grandparents came and just visited for a while, then my other grandparents came and brought pumpkin pie, whipped cream, and presents. It was all like a roller coaster today! Then, Aunt Dawny and Uncle Jim came by, and we gave her present, which i think she LOVED!

It was a nice night. But some people were a little too generous this Christmas, and I won't say who, but I was a little too spoiled, in my opinion, this Christmas. For being in the hospital on Christmas, i think i made the best of it and enjoyed it.

Please continue to send the letters through Sunnyview because i'm not sure when i will have time, with all this therapy, to go on laptop. I hope everyone had a GREAT Christmas and continue to have a GREAT week! Please continue to pray for my friends: Malisa, Carrie, Abby, Natalie, Rina, and Erik, and my sisters!

Amanda Perrotta

Amanda :-)

THURSDAY, DECEMBER 27, 2007
Hi!
Oh, what an exhausting day yesterday! I'll tell you more about that later. first i want to thank all of you who are sending in my Sunnyview mail. i really don't get a chance to check my guest book as often, so Sunnyview mail is more convenient. And it really sparks up my day (especially with PT!).

So, yesterday morning was easy. usually my mornings start our with an OT session of bathing, where they watch me get dressed and see where I need help and if I have progressed anywhere. So i did that yesterday. Then I had an hour break, which was nice, seeing that i didn't know what i had ahead...lol. I got to talk to my sisters in Korea over MySpace in my hour break. They're doing pretty good, i guess. I had Speech after my hour break, and mostly we just talked because Dee is usually always late, as she says (yes, Aunt Kim Dee is my Speech Therapist). I had a half hour break after that, then it was full blown.

I don't have my usually physical therapist, Chrissy, until next week sometime, so for this week i have subs, so what they had me do yesterday in PT was, they put me in a harness and had me put weight on my legs for 20 minutes!!!! I thought literally my legs were going to fall off!!! And with that, they were like, "Amanda, try to hold your head up." I was almost going to say, "OK, you try to do this with this disease and hold your head up together!" Ugh. sometimes it's so frustrating when therapists don't understand you!

Luckily my usual one is coming back next week, and she does [understand me], and she knows my limits and doesn't over push me like that. I thought i got hit by three trucks.

Right after that, I had OT....yes OT! I had to do stuff with my arms, so it wasn't that bad, but my body was just drained. As soon as i got back to my room, i ate quickly and went to bed. I slept for about 45 mins, then i had Speech again. We played In a Pickle (Thanks, Chris. i LOVE that game!). then Dr. Hess came in, and we talked, and, right after that, i had Recreation, which is my FAVORITE! We played on the Wii (I got it for Christmas from my nurse), and we had so much fun! So that was my day! And i have the same exact schedule today.

Yesterday, they were trying to come up with a plan to see when i can go home because some of this is part of the Mito, but some of this isn't, so Dr. Smio is going to call Dr. Adams and come up with a figurative plan.

I got to everyone's site, right? I tried to make my rounds yesterday. it was kinda hard with my being tired, but i felt guilty because i haven't been to anyone's site in a while.

Thank you Mark and M&M for visiting last night. i LOVE the pink cow. Tonight I'm getting my hair cut downstairs...lol. Hey, better than letting it grow out, right?

OK, so my birthday is coming up, my sweet 16th birthday, and the only thing i want for my birthday is cards from all my CaringBridge friends. My birthday is January 10th. Please don't feel like you need to give a card. you could just email me a

Sunnyview letter. I just love cards and would love cards from all my friends from CB.

Please Keep These special people in your prayers: Malisa, Carrie, Abby, Natalie, Rina, and Erik! Also please keep my sisters in your prayers as they are in Korea....thank you!
I hope everyone has a GREAT week!
Amanda :-)

FRIDAY, DECEMBER 28, 2007
Hi All!
I'm very talkative (well, to the computer) and energized today, so WATCH OUT!

Yesterday went VERY well!   My Physical Therapist was a very nice man.   He actually let me take breaks on the standing machines.   But that's not my whole day, is it? I have to say, yesterday was the smoothest day i've had since i've been here. PT in the morning yesterday.   i did the standing machine, and i probably held my head up for about four to five seconds? But I say better than nothing, right? I got really tired like five minutes before i was finished and couldn't hold my head up, so he put me back in my wheelchair, and i went back to my room and collapsed in bed and slept for a good solid 20 minutes, and by then, i was woken up by the sound of my lovely speech teacher, Michele, whom i kinda miss teaching me speech. I have learned...lol. I talked for a minute or two with Michele   then headed down to the gym for OT. OT was good. yesterday we worked on upper strength in the arms and control in my head again (which i think we're going to do today). I LOVED Rec. yesterday, and i'm really looking forward to it today! Yesterday, we played Trouble, but today we're going to work on this Tinkerbell thing I got for Christmas. it's a coloring thing. Rec. is the one downtime therapy i have...lol. Last night, Kim came up, and we got out for a while without mom and went to get my annual Chipwich. then, by the time we came back, it was time for my haircut. Yes, I got a haircut last night! It's so cute, too! I LOVE it!!!!!! I'll have to take pictures.

My schedule today is so wacky! I had and OT dressing at 8AM, then Speech at 10:00, and we just talked about knitting really, then i had PT at 10:30, and i did the Standing machine again, and then i came back and collapsed for about 35 minutes. And I don't have anything until 1:00!!!! And I don't end today until 4:00, and i end with PT!!! Isn't that NUTS!!!! I call that a wacky schedule! Tonight, Abby, daddy, and my grandparents are coming up to visit. i'm really not sure if anyone else is coming, but, if they are, YAY!!! I LOVE visitors as long as they all don't come at the same time...lol because then i get so tired after.

Tomorrow is only a half a day of therapy, so i'm so excited! Did i mention we rented out an appt. at Sunnyview for New Years? It's so my dad, Abby, Uncle, and aunt can spend the night.

I really want to thank you, Aunt Kim, for sending me my daily letters. they really keep me going! I also want to thank everyone else for sending me letters. Thank you guys sooo much!

I forgot to mention one more thing. i was supposed to mention it in yesterday's post but forgot. Dr Smio saw me yesterday, and i guess he talked to my mom and said i might be here for a while. I'm really trying to think of different ways to decorate my room now that most of the Christmas decorations are down. i don't know what to put up. I have some HSM [High School Musical] posters up (that's for you, Rina!), and my class made a banner for me that i WON'T take down. But that's really all i have up. So, if you guys have any ideas send them away! I'm all for it. when i have time to make them i will. i just need ideas!

Please continue to pray for my friends: Malisa, Carrie, Natalie, Rina, Abby, and Erik! And a special prayer for my sisters who are in Korea. I hope everyone's week is going well!
Amanda :-)

SATURDAY, DECEMBER 29, 2007
Hi All!
It's Saturday, so i only had a half a day of therapy...YAY in a way! The rest of yesterday went well. I slept after PT, and the rest of my therapy went well. In Rec., I went to see the therapy pool. My OT and PT say if my head gets stronger, i might be able to go in the pool! So that's something to look forward to. Last night, my mom and dad got to go out, and i got some time to myself. I went down to the gym and colored, then came back and went out of my way to get the phone, and i did and called Mike, and we chatted for a while, then, once i hung up, my grandparents were walking in, so it was, like, PERFECT timing! Then, when my parents got back, my grandparents, parents, and I walked to Ellis [Hospital, accessible through a walkway] and back, and when my grandparents left, my dad washed my hair and helped me get ready for bed. I stayed up late last night!

Today was really easy. I woke up, ate breakfast, got washed, and then it was time for OT. In OT, we practiced getting up from my wheelchair on the parralell (sp?) bars and standing. i did it three times, i was really shaky!!!! but i did it and didn't give up, which i know some people do, so i gave myself some credit! Right after that, i had PT, and I was SOOOOO proud of myself in PT. we practiced head control, and you will never believe how long i held me head up for! I held it up by MYSELF for about 10-20 seconds!!!!!!!!!!!!!!!! Yesterday, I only did like five, i'm up to that long! If i keep doing baby steps, i'll be in that pool in no time and walking in no time with my head held high! I'm so excited to show my dad tonight what i accomplished today! He's going to be so proud!

I had Speech at 12:00, and we played Trouble. While i was playing, i received a package from Heather. Thank you so much, Heather, for my socks, stickers, and my ornament. It's actually hanging on the front of my door to show everyone!...hehe. Right now i'm watching Hairspray while i type...lol. I LOVE this movie! I LOVE any movie with singing (and Zack Efron)

I wish I could call every single one of you and thank you personally for all that you have done. You have no idea how much it means to my family and me. Thank you so much to each one of you who send me messages everyday to raise my spirits, emails, letters, and just ANYTHING!!!!!! I LOVE you all!

Please pray for all my CB friends, but especially Abby, who had Seizures yesterday. And for my sisters who are still in Korea. I talk to them everyday almost. Carolyn is getting a GREAT experience!

I'll try to get to everyone's site later to see how everyone is doing. I'm sorry I've been slacking a little bit.

I hope everyone has a GREAT weekend!

Amanda :-)

SUNDAY, DECEMBER 30, 2007

Hi all!

I wanted to update when i got a chance because tomorrow it's back to reality with therapy...lol. Today was so NICE! It was relaxing in the morning into the afternoon. I woke up, ate, bathed, then watched my Harry Potter. Then it was afternoon, and visitors started coming. My aunt and uncle came with my cousins, and we went to the Ellis cafeteria to get something to eat and just fooled around with my wheelchair for a while. then, when they left, my other uncle (he's not my real uncle, but we call him my uncle because he's my dad's best friend), came with his two kids, and we played Wii for like an hour. That was SOOO much fun because i actually got to play Wii with kids my own age...lol. We finally figured out the way to play boxing, and i think i got my workout for the day..lol. I hit them at the TV like i never did before! It was so funny!

But anyways, a little while after that, Kim came with her daughter and her daughter's boyfriend. Then, like two seconds after that, Beth, my music teacher, came, and two seconds after that, MIKE CAME!!!!!! I flipped out on the inside, i was sooooo happy! Like, i don't think anyone had any idea how happy i was. I was so sweaty, and my mom was like, "i think we better check her temp," and i was thinking it may be because i got too excited! He brought me a Build-A-Bear (It's Harry Potter...hehe), and his brother came. It was nice because we just walked around for a while and talked just some random and silly things. But it was like my perfect birthday present! I was kinda sad when he left because i thought, "When am i going to see him again because i don't get to see him much?!" But his mom said she'll bring him back soon. So i'm looking forward to that! I'll try to put pictures up, but, for some reason, my dumb camera won't let me put pictures up on this website. it will on my MySpace and Facebook.

Guess what I did today when everyone left? I was on the toilet (nice, right?) and held my head up for like a minute! I'm telling you, by the time my birthday hits, i'll be able to hold my head up for three hours at least! I know i'm going to walk again. My mom keeps telling me to prepare myself, but guess what, i'm not, because she's not me, and doesn't know my body like I do, so she doesn't know how my body feels every second of the day. I have a goal (it's for Carolyn) for Carolyn's birthday on February 12th. i want to walk at least two steps. That's my goal. Maybe once i get in the pool, all my muscles will relax!

I don't get Sunnyview emails during the weekend (i forgot to tell you all that), so, if you sent some during the weekend, i'll get them tomorrow.
Natalie -- I did get your present, thank you soooooo much!!!!!!!!!
I LOVE the watch and the lanyard! All my therapists compliment me on my watch..lol. Please continue to pray for my CB friends!
I hope everyone has a HAPPY NEW YEAR!!!!
Amanda :-)

TUESDAY, JANUARY 01, 2008

Amanda Perrotta

HAPPY NEW YEAR!!!!!!!!!
I hope everyone partied like a rock star last night...ha-ha. I don't think all of you caught onto that, but anyways, we have a lot of catching up to do, so let's get started!

I have some good news to report! Yesterday in OT, I held my head for three mins.!!!!! I keep getting better at it every day; actually i think today in OT i held it for at least five! My goal for my 16th birthday next Thursday is to hold my head up for 16 minutes (isn't that clever?). My head kinda looks like a bobble head, though, the way it moves side to side or all around, so my OT is going to suggest to the Dr. about a neck brace when i eat or just try to do things without a head rest for a while and see if that makes a difference, so i guess we'll see what the Dr. says as he makes his rounds tomorrow.

Now you better calm yourself down for this one, OK? In PT yesterday, Chrissy thought, since i was doing pretty well with the head, we should try standing up. well i stood up!!!! (with a lot of help!!), but that's a really nice start. that's not all, OK. sit back down. I walked three baby steps with about three people holding me up!!!!! LOL, I was like so excited for myself yesterday!!!!!! I proved to the Drs. and everybody else that my legs work, and they can walk, so all you have to do is give them a chance to work now, like you did my head. So PT was pretty exhausting yesterday, let's leave it at that! Chrissy is going to ask the Dr. about my going in the pool. the only thing is the oxygen, but i can go without it for 20 minutes. It's not like i'm going to die! So hopefully the Dr. will see it the same way also.

Today's therapy went good. i didn't have my normal therapists, so the subs didn't quite know what to do with me. In OT, I reached for things and threw them with weight on my arms, and in PT i did the standing frame for 15 minutes, which i thought was AWESOME!!!

Last night was soooo much fun! The appt. was perfect for all of us! Aunt Dawny and Uncle Jim brought WAYYY too much food for us!!! I thought the King and Queen were coming for dinner!!! We had Lobster, broccoli casserole, salad, mashed potatoes, steak, and cheesecake for dessert (couldn't eat all of it because of my swallowing, but the stuff that i could tasted sooo good!). Uncle Jim and I played the Wii, and he beat me so badly at Bowling! I need a rematch! I stayed up to late last night, 10:00 PM! Way past my bedtime...lol. Oh, and guess who else spent the night last night? Abby! She snuggled with me most of the night...lol. Daddy, Uncle Jim, and Aunt Dawny went home around 10:00.

I know a lot of people want me to send emails to them right now, I'm really sorry, but I can't. i wish i could, but i don't have enough time with therapy and trying to rest up also. I try to answer as many questions as i can on here.

Emily: Thank you soooo much for the New Year Card! My mom has to put it up on my wall.
Natalie: It was so nice talking to you the other night. I hope we can do it again sometime.
Thank you all for your emails! I love each one of them. I keep them in one envelope so that one day I'll remember how much support i had.

Please continue to pray for my CB friends. And for my sisters who are in Korea.
Hope everyone has a GREAT 2008!
Amanda :-)

WEDNESDAY, JANUARY 02, 2008

Hi!
Awww, what an exhausting day!!!! I'm telling you, if these therapists don't kill me...lol. This morning, i had my regular dress in. i did that in i think 15 minutes, which is the same. But hopefully i'll get that 15 minutes down to maybe 10? Anyways, let's start with last night. i didn't have lipids, so keep that in mind. I did my dress in and was exhausted! But luckily i had a half hour break until Dee came (Speech), and we played a game. Then i had PT, for which...hold yourself down!...I walked about ten steps (with a lot of help from my mom and Chrissy), but ten steps is getting somewhere. After that, i thought i was like hit by a train two times back to back. I had Recreation straight after that, and usually i look forward to Rec. because it's the only therapy that's relaxing, but i didn't even want to do it, and i didn't enjoy it at all! Once i was done with that, i ate a quick lunch and slept for about 45 mins. I must have been in a sound sleep because i was drooling...lol. Woke up and it was time for OT....

OK, OT i officially hate now! It literally killed the rest of my body. I was on one of the mats, and my therapist, Elena, had me pull my chest up and spin the spinner (we were playing chutes and ladders) and then switch hands to move my person. I thought i was done after that, but, oh no! After that, she had me hold my chest and head up for 21 seconds, which i know doesn't seem a lot to you, but for me, holding half of my body up was like running a marathon!!!! Luckily, i was done after that (with OT anyways). After that, i had speech again, and Dee and I are going to decorate my room for my birthday with balloons all on top of the ceiling and streamers hanging down, cool eh? Then, i had half an hour break. then i had PT again, and i had to do the standing frame. Literally killed me. I couldn't hold my head up for long, only two mins., and then i was done. I think Chrissy knew it, too. Then, after that, i was done! I have some pain in my back right now, i think because i pushed myself a little too hard today, and i can feel it!!!

My body is like, ughhh!!! It's not going to be good tomorrow, i can tell. And they think they're going to push me harder! Can you believe that?! I mean, i'm seriously not a complainer, BUT, when it comes to my body, and they try to push more just when i'm starting to get there, i think i have a right to complain. But i guess they'll see if i'm too tired tomorrow or not. I can already tell by my typing! Anyways enough of that.

So, it's only a week until Carolyn and Dahea come home!!! It feels like they just left. i can't believe i've been in a hospital for a month! I've never been in this long (i don't think so anyways). When they get off the plane, they're coming straight here. So, it will be like around 5:00 [PM], i think by the time they get here, so we'll have time to spend.

My dad and Abby are coming up in a little while, so i better get going. I hope everyone has a GREAT week! Please continue to pray for my CB friends! And please say a special prayer for my sisters, Carolyn and Dahea.

Amanda Perrotta

Amanda :-)

FRIDAY, JANUARY 04, 2008

Hi!
Sorry I haven't updated. My mom went home last night (FINALLY..haha, just kidding...lol) to get some nice rest. My mom (from now on) is going to go home on nights and sleep at home and come back up in the evening, except on Saturdays she'll sleep over. So, what's going on? Well, Chrissy and Elana are working me hard (as always!) Last night was my first night without my mom with me, so it was kind of a challenge. But i got through it. When i woke up this morning, it was DEFINITELY a challenge because i had to bathe, eat, and get ready for my dressing for OT. But I did it with help. Once i was unhooked from my IV's and in my wheelchair, i got A LOT picked up and done. During the night, the nurses threw everything all around, so i had to pick everything up in the morning! So i did it in my wheelchair, and, [for] the stuff that i couldn't, i asked for help. I faced the fact today that i might have to get used to that, asking for more help with reaching for things and stuff like that.

My mom had a meeting with the social worker yesterday, and the main goal for me is that they want me to be able to transfer to my wheelchair on my own before i go home. So, once i can do that, then i can go home and be an outpatient!

Today in therapy PT, I did some standing and noticed that I can stand for much longer than i did when i first came here, which is good because that means i'm making progress! Then i did some sitting. i needed a little help with that (OK, a little more than a little), but i did good!   In my second session of OT, it was REALLY hard!   Elana had another therapist help her get me in to a kneeling position, and i didn't last long until i fell. then she just helped me sit up, and we played Yatzee. she said i did a GREAT job, though, and she gave me a high five!   I did some homonyms in my second session of Speech. So it was a long day!

Right now, Brittany (Kim's daughter) just dyed some parts of my hair pink!   I hope it comes out good!   We also did the tip of Abby's tail...lol. I hope she doesn't mind!   Thank you so much, Rina, for the posters and the Happy Birthday!   I put the posters up!

Bobby- I did have a GREAT Christmas!   I miss you and class 8 A LOT!   I got a Wii from my nurse. What did you get?

Ted- Thanks. i'm feeling a little bit better. how are you doing?

Thank, you EVEYERONE who is sending the Sunnyview email. i look forward to them every day!!!!!

Please continue to pray for my CB friends.

And for my sisters, who are in Korea.

I'll try to keep you more updated...sorry

Amanda :-)

SATURDAY, JANUARY 05, 2008
Hi!
I LOVE Saturdays here...lol. Only half a day of therapy, and i can check my CaringBridge...hehe. I did really well in PT today!!!   My therapist had me try to sit up on my own, and i think i did (slouchy) but for about one second...lol. But it counts, right? He said i did WONDERFUL!!!!   The same progress in OT. i wish i could say more, but maybe tomorrow i can!   I did some

homonyms in Speech, and that was it for today! Then i just relaxed and watched Hairspray in my bed. It was a nice relaxing day. My mom and dad are just heading up with Abby. My Speech teacher, Michele, just stopped by and brought me a Tinkerbell poster to hang in my room!! I think, when my birthday is over, i'll hang it on my door. Tomorrow, it's probably going to be a relaxing day.

So my pink streaks of hair came out AWESOME! It's more of a reddish, but it looks AMAZING! Abby's look pretty good, too...lol. The nurse, while we were doing it, came in and looked at us like we were NUTS!...haha.
Tammy-I don't want anything for my birthday, just a card will do. And don't give me a fuss!!!!!!!!
Please continue to pray for my CaringBridge friends. And please say a special prayer for my sisters who are in Korea and will be traveling home soon.
Amanda :-)

SUNDAY, JANUARY 06, 2008
Hi everyone!
This isn't much of an update. just wanted to tell everyone how excited i was last night and Thank You's. last night, my counselor from Double H camp, Tess, came!!! I was getting so anxious by 4:00PM because that's when she said she would be coming...lol. That's how i am when i don't see people in a while. i get really anxious, and then, when they come, i can't stop talking...lol. So anyways, Tess and her boyfriend (ughh, i already forgot his name, but he worked at camp as well, i guess) [came by], and i wanted to jump right out of my chair, and, of course, i can't do that (yet!)

but wanted to. She brought me all these magazines and hair clips, which i didn't even notice until she left...haha. Thank you Tess!!!

I was telling her about Abby, therapy, C.B., and camp. We have a plan—i'm going to fill out my paperwork for camp and see what session i get into, then i'll email her, and, i guess, she'll apply for that one? I think that's how it goes. It was funny seeing her in jeans because the last time i saw her she was wearing shorts 24/7. I didn't want her to leave!!! I wish Tess lived closer so then we could see each other more. But hopefully we will get to spend a WHOLE week together this summer.

So my dad spent the night last night, hilarious, i tell you!!! He was the one who had to help get me on the toilet, and he was like, "three blind mice." He cracks me up! After i washed up this morning, my dad and I went down to Ellis and got some breakfast to eat. I have to tell you, my appetite hasn't been that crazy lately. Yesterday I ate half a bowl of cereal for breakfast (i usually eat two [of the small] boxes!). i ate one of those small boxes of cereal for lunch and half a bowl of oatmeal for dinner last night. And i wasn't even in the mood for my regular Chipwich. This morning, i only had half a bowl of cereal also, so i'm getting a little nervous. i'm hoping this is going to pass because, right now, i really don't want to worry about losing weight AGAIN, with all this other stuff going on. Today is weigh-in day. i hate weigh-in day because i hate scales...lol. Most teenage girls weigh themselves, like, everyday. me, well, i'd rather not know my weight and know that i'm eating healthy, which i am.

Joan-Sorry i didn't get a chance much to talk to you last night. i don't see Tess very much, so i had a lot to tell her!!! I'm sorry!!!

Thanks everyone for sending me Sunnyview email, especially Aunt Kim and Nikki for daily updates (even if your blabbing...haha) Please keep my CB friends in your prayers
Also my sisters, as they will be traveling back to Albany in four days!!!!! That's going to be my favorite birthday present (i say that now...lol).
Amanda :-)

MONDAY, JANUARY 07, 2008
Hi!
Ughh. today was a long and exhausting day! So, i think most of you know, i went in the therapy pool for my first time today, and i think that was the most that [they] took out of me. But anyways, last night my mom spent the night with Abby! Abby was so well behaved. she just laid next to my mom all night and slept! And, when i woke up, i called her, and she came over to my bed and jumped up and cuddled with me...lol. So she was really well behaved!

This morning, I had OT, and i'm really independent now with dressing myself, so i don't need to do OT dressings, so Elena (my OT) is just going to start my regular OT sessions in the morning. This morning for OT, i had to put weights on my arms and do the pegboard, then play catch with a basketball. I had speech after that. Dee and I worked on strategies for reading. Then I had PT. Chrissy and I practiced standing (which i did OK on), and then we worked on my sitting posture. I have to say myself, my sitting is getting better. I can't hold myself up (yet), but my goal for this week is to sit up by myself. I'm getting there one step by one. I had an hour and a half break, but they needed to weigh me, so that took about half an hour, and, by the way, i'm maintaining my weight. I had to be down by the pool 10 minutes before PT started, so let's say i only slept for 15 mins. today.

The pool was nice. i wasn't ready for it, but my mom took it...lol. We worked on my walking and leg exercises in the pool. It was a lot easier in the pool!!! I guess Chrissy and i are going to the pool Mon., Wed., and Fri. The only thing that i hated was, half way through the session, i started to get really cold and turned blue and purple, so, when i got out, Chrissy put, like, five blankets and towels on me, and, when i got back to my room, the nurses put me under hot water and gave me a bath. So that made my warmth go up. I had OT right after that, and, let me tell you, i was no good at OT. i think swimming takes a lot out of you even if you're not technically swimming. I couldn't even hold my trunk up for one second. My body was like Jell-O, but Elena made me push, and i knew i had to push it a little, so i did (hopefully it won't show up tomorrow...lol). I had Rec. after OT, and we made a banner for my door for my birthday. i have to take a picture!!! My door looks soooo good!!!! I think everyone knows it's my birthday...haha.

Thank you Jenn Stacey for my birthday card i LOVE it! Did you make the little things inside it?
Niki and Aunt Kim, you don't blab too much..lol. I was joking! Anyways thanks for letting me know what's going on!
Please continue to pray for my CB friends, also please say a special prayer for my sisters who are traveling home on Thursday.
Amanda :-)

TUESDAY, JANUARY 08, 2008

Amanda Perrotta

Hi all!
This is going to be an extremely quick update because it's already way past my bedtime, and i'm tired, but i wanted to make sure i updated you all on how things went today!   So my regular PT therapist went away i think i told you that though, so i had so many subs today! But all of them were extremely nice! I started using a sliding board in PT today to see if it was easier for me to transfer that way or the stand pivot. it was so much easier with the sliding board because i didn't have to worry about my legs at all but i did have to worry about my trunk, so it was kinda a win-win situation. But i did it, so that's good!

This morning i had a new nurse (she was new to the floor) and she apparently didn't know anything about my meds, so it took her 30 mins. to get my meds into me!!! It was just a cup of liquid (meds crushed up and water) and she spilled it all over me and my bed. she had to change the bed 2x's!!!! And she forgot all about my Koquten (sp?) and Kolonopin [Klonopin, generically clonazepam, used to treat panic disorders and control seizures], so i was not happy with her at all! I let my mom know, and she marched right up to the nurses station tonight and the already knew.

Tonight i put more pink/red streaks into my hair, I told Kim earlier to call me Tonks (from Harry Potter) because i look like her...lol. I think it looks good though. My mom took the dye home so she can do Abby's ears tomorrow night after she gets home from her grooming appt. I can't wait to see what Carolyn and Dahea think!

Tomorrow, i hope is going to be an easy day of therapy!   I'm looking forward to baking brownies in OT, and i'm kinda (a little

kinda) looking forward to swimming. I get so cold after just 15 minutes of being in the pool that i just want to be in a heater! Then the nurses have to put hot water on me. it's nuts! Please continue to pray for my CB friends! Also please say a special prayer for my sisters who are traveling home tonight!
Amanda :-)

I CAN GO HOME!

WEDNESDAY, JANUARY 09, 2008
HIIIII!!!!!!!
OH MY GOSH!!!! OK my hands are shaking because you have no idea what news i'm bringing to you today. OK. I'm going to start with my day (sorry, your gonna have to wait...lol).

So everything went fine this morning with Speech and PT. Dee and I started decorating my room for my birthday in Speech, and, in PT, i did the standing frame and some leg excercises. After that i put on my bathing suit because i had swimming today, ate, and took a 40-minute nap. I woke up and waited for someone to take me down to the pool. It was like 1:05 [PM] when someone came and asked if anyone got me, and they took me down, and i was so confused because it was only going to be my second time in the pool, so we went in, and they already lowered the [level of the water in the] pool. So i didn't get to go in the pool today. I went back upstairs, changed, and had a regular PT session. I did some sitting, and the sub PT said i was doing good! I had Rec. after that, and i made Dahea's birthday present and card.

Amanda Perrotta

Then i had OT with Elena, and i made brownies and frosting to go on them and, let me tell you, it was challenging to get around the kitchen in my wheelchair and get things (especially when Elena took my head rest off!). After that, i had Speech again with Dee. we finished decorating my room, and, at the end of it, i saw my sisters walking in!!!!!! I started to cry, and Carolyn started to cry. Carolyn gave me a huge hug, so did Dahea, and they brought me a balloon. They weren't supposed to come home until tomorrow!!!! They knew they were coming home today, though...lol. We went to Ellis and got a bite to eat and talked, and talked, and talked! We have soooo much catching up to do!!!! I missed hem so much!!!!! I have to say, no one can out beat that birthday present!

My other big news is that the Drs. decided that i'm ready to go home!!! And do an outpatient program. but the down side is, we don't have the ramp for me to get in the house, so that's the only thing holding me back right now. So, when that's in, i'm good to go!!!! Isn't that wonderful?!??!?!?!

I have sooo many people to thank for cards and presents (which they shouldn't have gotten).
Rina-Thank you for my singing card. i open it every hour...lol. It's hanging on my birthday card wall.
Heather-Thank you for my card and my puppy. i love him! He's so cute when he cries...lol.
Kelly Boltz-Thank you sooooooo much for my card. i LOVE my cards, and it's hanging up with all my beautiful cards on my "cards wall." If i forgot anyone, i'm sorry. i'm kinda tired and overwhelmed with the surprise of my sisters!

So tomorrow i turn 16! But it doesn't mean i don't have to do the same amount of work as normal...lol. Please continue to pray for my CB friends.
Amanda :-)

My 16th Birthday

THURSDAY, JANUARY 10, 2008
Hi!
Oh boy, this is going to be VERY short because its 9:30 [PM] and i'm VERY tired, but i wanted to tell you all what an exciting day i had (so it may not be that short....lol). I had a regular therapy schedule today (no i didn't get any special arrangements because it's my birthday...lol), i have to tell you, some exciting news of what i did in OT and PT today. I've been working VERY hard on sitting up by myself, and my goal for this week (every week i have a goal) is to sit up by myself. So this morning in OT, i told Elena (my OT) to let go of me. she did, and i went back a couple of times, but after like three x's, i sat up by myself and just sat there!!!!!! I was sitting up!!!!!! And no one was helping me!!!! I reached my goal before i needed to reach it!!!!! I was so proud of myself!!! I also did some standing in the standing frame and the parallel bars, and i got up (almost) by myself!!! I amazed myself today. now if i could just walk i would make myself a miracle.

Today, i also learned how to transfer onto a regular toilet (instead of a commode) off of my wheelchair. It was hard because i had to use my trunk, but it was worth going on a regular toilet....lol. So that's my exciting news for today!!!!

After my therapy was done, I came back and Michele, Dianna, Corinne, and Dianna's friend were there. They surprised me with gifts. Michele brought over Dianna and told me she is my new speech teacher!!!! I thought that was the BEST gift from them that i could ever ask for!!! Thanks Michele, Dianna, and Corinne for EVERYTHING!!!!

After they left, my dad came up with my sisters and brought loads of presents and cake. My sisters brought back presents for me from Korea, so i opened a few and LOVED them... THANKS Carolyn and Dahea! Right after that, everyone started pioloing (sp?) [piling] in!!! My grandparents came, Kim and her husband came, and Aunt Dawny and Uncle Jim came. We had cake and the opened presents. Thank you Kim for my High School Musical game. I LOVE it!!! Thank you mom and pop for my clothes....you sure know my style! And thank you Aunt Dawny for my bracelet and my Tinkerbell stickers and croc decoration (i can't wait to wear my crocs now!).

Carolyn and I FINALLY got to play some Wii. It was sooo much fun! Oh, one more fun fact before i go on to the thank you's, we received a little note today that we might be going home Tuesday!!!!!

I have a lot of thank you's, so, if i missed you, i'm sooo sorry!!!
Elsbeth-Thank you for my CD and the hair band!
Aunt Kim, Uncle Billbo, Liam, and Belle-Thank you for my UNBELIVABLE autographed High School Musical picture! My dad is going to hang it up in my bedroom!

Heather-Thank you for my card and my little dog, he's sooo cute! He's right on my dresser...lol

Thank you to everyone who called and wished me a Happy Birthday. you have no idea how much that meant, and to everyone who sent a Sunnyview email. I know your names i just can't type them all.

Ted-I had ice cream cake for my birthday. I didn't have any friends over, i just had family. How are you doing?

Bobby-I feel better than i did when i got here...thank you for asking! How is school going for you?

Please keep my CB friends in your prayers!

Amanda :-)

FRIDAY, JANUARY 11, 2008

Hey!

I have a little break right now, so i thought i would update you on some more exciting news today and just progress! So, today was kinda back-to-back because all of my therapists had meetings, so i really didn't get my hour nap into me. I woke up this morning with a bad headache because last night i went to sleep at 11:00 PM because i made it to watch ER...lol. That was one of my goals...hehe. It was worth it too, i was screaming at the TV when Sam walked out on Abby. Anyways, this morning, my mom left for meetings to get the ramp going for my house. So i had the day to myself. I had OT first, and i sat up by myself for 20 minutes (i did a little bobbling, but that's pretty good!). I had Speech after that, and we played In a Pickle. I had a half hour break after that.

Then, I had PT, and I WALKED!!!!!! Now hold on, i didn't just walk like five steps, OK. i walked about 15!!!!!!! I had some help, but only with one person!!!! I was soooo proud of myself because now i know for sure i can walk again! If i keep this up, i'll be walking like i used to in no time! I mean, i know i can't push it, but i can do what i know i can do. I gave it my all today in OT and PT!

I had about an hour break after that. i ate my lunch then got into my bathing suit then went to sleep while listening to the movie Hairspray...lol. I took like about a half hour break, woke up, and went down to the pool. In the pool, i did some more walking and leg exercises! I liked it until i turned blue again...lol. The nurse brought me up and put me under hot water, and i bathed myself because of the chlorine...there's soooo much!!!! Right now i'm relaxing and waiting for my mom to come. My dad and sisters can't come tonight because Carolyn and Dahea have to study and stuff.

Please continue to pray for my CB friends especially Erik, who is in the Hospital.
Amanda :-)

Finally Getting Some Air

SATURDAY, JANUARY 12, 2008
Hi all!
I always say this, but maybe this time it will be true? "This is going t be a short entry"....lol.

So today was kind of slow, as normal Saturdays are at Sunny Sunnyview (hehe). I had my first therapy at 9:00AM. i slept in until 8 this morning because i was so tired last night! So, this morning was kind of hectic for me. I got up, ate breakfast quick, washed up, and, right after that, my CP had to help me transfer into my wheelchair for OT while my nurse had to start my IV. it was NUTS! And i didn't even brush my teeth or get my braces on yet. I was unplugging the IV pole so i could kind of pick up the room (because the nurses in the middle of the night make a mess) when my mom walked in. Then my PT came in, and we went to the therapy Room, and i did the parallel bars again...i walked 15 steps! By the 13th i was like, "ughh, OK, i'm glad it's Saturday!" But i can tell my legs are getting stronger. it may take a month or so to get the full effect back, or i might not even get what i had back, but at least i know i can do a little bit of stepping, and i'm progressing in that area! I had Speech at 12:30PM, and we played a game. I had OT right after that, and i was so tired she just did the therapy in my room with me. i did some weight barring [bearing] on my arms. If my arms aren't like Popeye's when get home, then something's wrong because the way i've been using my arms...wheww! I went to sleep right after that and slept for about half an hour when my mom woke me up and Intek (my dad's friend who works at the bakery with him) and his wife and daughter came to visit me. They brought some sort of yummy Korean food that i LOVE! I don't know how they knew i loved it, but they knew. they also brought me a bear. he's so cute! I forgot to take a picture! I was so tired i forgot...lol.

So, once they left, my dad and mom decided to go out to dinner (with Carolyn and Dahea of course), so i got kinda mad because i haven't been outside these walls in almost two months! So my mom asked the nurse if i could have a pass (Saturdays and Sundays people who are getting better get passes to either go visit home or go out and see a movie or do whatever!...but only for a limited time—Saturdays are 4:00-8:00PM, and Sundays are 8:00AM-

8:00PM.) So the nurse gave me a pass, and off we all went as a family out to dinner like five minutes away, but it was soooo nice to breathe in the fresh air and just see houses and people...lol. It was just nice! I mean, you really don't notice how much you appreciate the little things like restaurants and trees until you're in somewhere for almost two months. So, i have to say that that was the highlight of my day!

I can't wait to go home! My mom went home with my sisters, and my dad is spending tonight with me...lol. I showed my dad that i could take steps, and he was like, "now all you have to do is jump over a table"...lol.

Tomorrow morning is weigh-in day. i'm kinda interested to see how much i am because i look like i'm more then 112....but whatever it says, right?
Emilie-Thank you for my birthday card, and thank your sister's friend for making it for me, please.
Please pray for all of my CB friends, especially Erik.
Amanda :-)

SUNDAY, JANUARY 13, 2008
Hi!
Today wasn't a normal relaxed Sunday (which i guess in one way was good) because, sometimes on Sundays when nothing is happening, i go basurk (sp?), and i just get sooooo bored!!!! But, luckily, today i had lots of visitors, and i had nothing to worry about being bored. I woke my dad up around 7:45 AM. i guess he didn't sleep that well last night because the nurses kept coming in to check on my IVs and check my BP and vital signs. And, when

they did that, they turned on the lights, so i guess that kinda woke him up (i'm a heavy sleeper...lol). So i got washed up and we went to Ellis to get some breakfast. when we got back, Aunt Valerie and my Uncle came, and they brought me some awesome scrap booking stuff for my birthday (Thanks Uncle Tomorrowy and Aunt Valerie and my new cousins!) After they left, my other aunt and uncle came with my cousins, and they brought me my birthday present. i got a Tinkerbell sweatshirt and Tinkerbell body wash (Thank you Aunt Mimi, Ed, Woody, and Sarah!). Like two minutes after they left, my mom, sisters, and Alicia came to visit with Abby, too...lol. It was nice talking to Alicia (she's my respite worker) I LOVE hanging out with her! Thanks Alicia for my Tinkerbell coloring set! Half an hour went by, and like six of Carolyn's friends from her school came in and brought ice cream cake, cupcakes, chocolates, presents (it was all High School Musical themed!) It was a surprise birthday party for Dahea and me. It was very nice.

Did i mention it was all High School Musical themed?! It was AWESOME!!!!!! Thank you guys sooo much for doing that for Dahea and me. I'm sure she really appreciated it as well. when they left, my mom and I got my clothes out for tomorrow and got everything set that i needed. My mom needed to go home because she has to get Dahea set up for school. let's pray that she's able to visit tomorrow with the snowstorm on the way!

My dad had a sore throat this morning, and i'm starting to get one, so i hope this isn't going into anything!
Please continue to pray for my CB friends especially Erik!
Amanda :-)

Amanda Perrotta

MONDAY, JANUARY 14, 2008

Hi!

Today was a non-stop day for me in therapy (my therapy was. since it was my last day of therapy, they wanted to work me harder...lol). I only had a 45 minute break today, but some days i like when they keep me going because if i have a two hour nap and wake up. i don't want to get up in my wheelchair. In PT today, I took some steps on the parallel bars (Elena actually got to watch this time...Elena's my OT). And, for my second session, i went in the pool. I turned blue (AGAIN!) after about 15-20 minutes. It was funny because, each time i go in the pool, i get a new PT that goes in with me. this time it was a guy that was sooo funny and nice, and, when i told him i turned blue, he didn't believe me, so after 25 minutes when we started to come up, he asked me, "So you didn't turn blue?" And i had towels all over me, so i took my hand out and showed him my hand, and he was like, ohhh. My hand was all blue and purple...lol.

Anyways, OT today was just testing to see if i improved from when i first came here to when i left, and i guess i did with my arm strength. Then Elena and I worked on my sitting, and i have to say, i am getting sooo much better with that! I sat for about 20 minutes then took a break and then got back on the saddle again! In Rec., i made thank you cards for all of my therapists and nurses. I'm super excited to be leaving!!!!! My mom came up today around 2:00PM and we started packing up some things. let me tell you, i'm going to have A LOT of unpacking to do!!!! It's going to take at least three days...lol. My mom had a lot of paperwork to get done today, too, with all of the STAR program and the wheelchair business and ramping. AHHH, all that yucky stuff that HAS to get done that we don't want to do.

I'm going to miss a lot of people here, though. I gained a lot of friendships while i was here (even though i'm only 16, i guess you can always have a friendship with an adult). I learned that while i was here. It's going to be sad to leave, but i'll see them again with outpatient therapy (well, i'll visit!).

Darcie-Thank you VERY much for my decoration. I'm not sure where i'm going to hang it yet, but i'll see when i get everything together...lol.

Thank you everyone who has been on this roller coaster ride with me. I know there have been some ruff patches, but we finally made it back! THANK YOU!!!!

Please continue to pray for my CB friends! Especially Erik, who is in the hospital, and my other little friend, Sean Robert, who is also in the hospital.

Amanda :-)

I'M HOME!!!!

WEDNESDAY, JANUARY 16, 2008

WOW!!! It has been a long night last night, and so far it has been a long day (and i'm sure i'm going to have a long day ahead of me). I came home around 11:00AM yesterday. My dad had to carry me inside and put me in my wheelchair because we don't have a ramp yet and will not be getting one for another two to three months!! How lovely, huh? So, it's a bit of a struggle on that part, but we're dealing with it the best way we can. Yesterday, thank goodness Dahea was home! She hasn't started Catholic High yet, so she helped me unpack the hundreds of bags of stuff i had from the hospital, like Christmas presents and cards, birthday presents, and, if i get any more clothes!!!! I mean, before i was like, "mom, i need more clothes!" Now, i really don't even want to look at them...lol. They don't even all fit in my dresser, so Dahea took some upstairs and put some in the closet.

We finished unpacking today, and i'm going to get washed up in a bit because my mom has to take Dahea to get everything ready for her first day of school tomorrow, and i'm going to the bakery.

Last night, we were watching American Idol, and there was this one young woman who had a little girl who had a similar disease like Mito. She had to wear AFO's, had seizures, all of that stuff. So my dad started talking about me making progress in therapy, and i was telling him i was making HUGE progress, and i'll be walking in no time! Drs. tell you different things like, oh, it might take a couple months (i'm already taking about 15 steps!) I know i have a problem with low energy and that i'm different than a 'normal' kid, but i also know my body and know what it can do and handle. And i know when it's ready for a challenge or not. My goal to be walking like I used to is March...i don't have a certain date, just anytime in March! That's my goal. I've reached all of my goals so far, and i'm going to reach this one.

We have A LOT going on this week and weekend, but i'm really glad! Tomorrow is Dahea's 17th birthday, so she's still deciding what she wants for dinner, but she wants carrot cake for her cake, and Alicia i think is coming over.

In two weeks, i'll return to Sunnyview for therapy. for now, i'm getting home therapy. I can't wait to go back to Sunnyview to see all my nurses, and some other people, of course! And, as soon as all this bus stuff is taken care of, i'll be going back to school two days a week! I'm getting soooo excited (especially because i have a whole new wardrobe...lol).

Please keep my CB friends in your prayers, especially Erik and Sean.

Amanda :-D

THURSDAY, JANUARY 17, 2008
Hi Everyone!
Things are getting better (in the house). When I first came home, it felt like so much had to get done (i don't want to imagine what my mom went through!). But it's my 3rd day home, and i'm finally catching up to things.

Last night, Tony (my nurse) and Denise (my Service Coordinator) came at kinda the same time, so i was trying to watch my show, talk, move, all that jazz at the same time...lol. It was nice to see Tony again. i usually see him every week, but i haven't seen him since Christmas!!!! So i guess we're right back on track (fingers crossed and knock on wood). After they left, my family watched American Idol, which always gets me laughing at this time of year anyways. I was super tired last night and went to bed right after that. I woke up this morning with a VERY sore throat (yeah!), but it could be worse right? I got in my wheelchair, went into the kitchen, and kinda did my normal routine but with a little help, and in 45 minutes instead of 20.

I took another nap after Charmed because i didn't get my lipids last night because, i guess, my company, Anthem, didn't expect me home so soon. So, i've been yawning all day, but i took a good 45-minute nap. I bathed when i woke up and got ready for Dahea's Birthday, which, by the way, HAPPY BIRTHDAY DAHEA!!!!!! Alicia came over for dinner tonight, and we had fatode (sp?) and my dad just went to get Carolyn so we can have dessert.

I guess tomorrow they're going to deliver all my stuff. Commode, sliding board [for inclined exercise], bar. I have therapy starting next week, so WATCH OUT!! Amanda is going to be stronger than Supergirl herself...haha. I'm telling you, my arms are like metal....hehe. I have OT and PT 3x's a week, and i think Speech 3x's a week, too much, i'm not sure. Tomorrow, if it doesn't snow and ice too much, i might take a surprise visit somewhere...hmmm, i know people will guess, but i'm not going to tell...secretive!!!!

So, tomorrow night, Alicia is coming over. Sat., i'm shopping till i drop!! (even though i don't really like it that much...lol). Hey, it's an outing. i'll take it! Please keep [praying for] my CB friends. Amanda :-)

SATURDAY, JANUARY 19, 2008
Hi!
This is a REALLY short update tonight because it's almost 11:00PM, and i'm getting tired...hehe.

So the throat thing turned out to be a little something. I can't remember exactly what it was, but the Dr. gave me a nasal spray for it and a pill. She also gave me a prescription if it got worse, which it isn't getting any better right now (but it's only the second day). I'll keep watching out for that. I haven't had lipids in about four days, so my hands are shaking like there's no tomorrow, and, every morning, i feel like i've been hit by a truck!!! Tomorrow, i bet it will be a train, maybe a plane?!...haha.

Today was kinda low key until 2:00PM. my family went out shopping (we haven't been out shopping since, like, September!). It felt soooo awesome to get to a mall and to a store! And to buy things was even better (even if it was just cereal or a CD). My sisters had a heyday with their extra money from Korea...lol. Oh my gosh! I never saw my sister in that much shopping action. I also returned [bought?] my High School Musical Sing It game, so i'm super excited to play it tomorrow. I wanted to play it tonight, but my dad wouldn't set my WII up in the living room.

Tomorrow is just a low-key day. I'm going to be playing my game all day..haha. Please continue to pray for my CB friends, especially Darcie, Rina, and Natalie.
Amanda :-)

TUESDAY, JANUARY 22, 2008
Hey!
So the sore throat FINALLY went away, but now i'm getting post nasal drip (sp?) and, as you know, that could turn into broncidous (sp?), so i think my mom is going to turn that prescription in, and i'll start taking the medicine my Dr. ordered for me if i got worse. So i'll keep you updated on that.

I got the High School Musical game up and running on Sunday and, let me tell you, it's addicting!!!! My sister and I started playing it around 11:00AM, and we only took one break for lunch, and we played until 4:00 or 5:00PM. It was sooooo addicting because, each time we sang a song, we earned so many points and, after we earned so many points, we unlocked a new song or a new outfit for our character, a new character or a new location. I didn't think my sister would get that into it, but she was like, 'oh just one more song, then it will be your turn.' I finally gave up because my throat was getting more sore.

Kim and Phil came, and they had to listen to me sing (poor them!)...lol. I also felt bad because i've been kinda quiet because i haven't had my lipids in a week, and i just don't have enough energy to talk, like i have so much, then, when i'm done, that's it! I'm done for the rest of the day, so i should have kinda saved some of my energy from the game to talk to Kim and Phil. Poor Phil and Kim brought me Chipwiches, and the only place Phil could find them was at Ellis, and he searched about six places to find them...lol. Thank you Kim and Phil...i think i already ate about five!!!!!

Yesterday, Carolyn and Dahea had off [from school] because of Martin Luther King Day. So, guess what Carolyn and I did? We played High School Musical Sing It!!! We played for about an hour and a half. Carolyn had to get ready for her ring dinner. she got her ring this year. She bought a light blue crystal to go in the middle, a basketball on one side and a Bible on the other side. It's really pretty!!!! So, Alicia stayed with me last night while my mom and dad went to the dinner, which also happened to be a benefit for me! I guess it was nice. Alicia and I ordered out dinner then played the game.

I've been dying to start therapy!! All I want to do is see myself walk again (even if it is just one step). I want to see myself walk by myself!!!! I'm dying to get my feet moving. I have to tell you something, the first thing I want to do when i can walk more is dance a little bit...lol. Isn't that funny? I used to hate going to my dance lessons, but now i miss them!!!

I guess my family and I are going to Disney in August. it's not for sure yet, but it's something to look forward too!!!! I'll be doing a countdown now...haha.

WEDNESDAY, JANUARY 23, 2008
Hi!
So I think my sore throat is finally going away!!!!! I have no clue how, but it is (no questions asked!). I started therapy yesterday. I had PT at the last minute. Joan and I did some stretches and some leg and arm exercises (i guessed correctly!). She understood about how I just want to get up on the parallel bars, and I should probably get to Sunnyview ASAP! And I felt the same way! I had OT today, and Charlie and I worked on arm exercises, and guess what?! He showed me how to transfer by myself, and i can do it! I transfer by myself now! I go to the bathroom by myself now and transfer to the toilet. It feels so good that no one's watching me or anything. It may take about ten minutes, but i'm doing it myself! So, we're making progress slowly but surely!
The whole nursing thing is soooo slow! My mom is trying to get it set up so my dad and she can get away for a night out or something like that, but they're just soooo slow!

It's been over a week since i've had my lipids, and i feel like i'm in a bubble and like i'm here but not really here (do you know what i mean?). I can't concentrate on anything for over ten minutes, and i can't remember much. I'm getting lipids in me tonight, so i'm thrilled!!!!!

My mom also got the bus thing for school rolling so that when I decide and my parents decide i'm ready to go back (which we're heading for February 11th!), it will be all set...hopefully! Isn't my mom the best!

I think that's pretty much it for now.
Please continue to pray for my CB friends!
Amanda :-)

THURSDAY, JANUARY 24, 2008
Hey!
Wheww! i only have 20 minutes until my Smallville returns (at least i think it does...lol). So today, I had PT. I did my leg exercises on my own with some help from my PT, Joan. I'm telling you, leg exercises are tiring!!!! I wanted to fall asleep after that (actually during PT i thought i was going to fall asleep!) Joan said maybe next week, since i'm starting to bear a little bit of weight, I can try a walker!! Because my upper body strength is VERY strong!!!! I bet I could do about 100 push-ups...lol. No, i'm not joking, that's how strong i think it is. But it's depending on the day as well. I had my lipids last night (can you tell?) I feel so much better! I feel like a new person...almost. i just need my legs back! I know my legs want to move. they're just giving me a

hard time, and i need to know how to discipline them. I'm learning. you learn something new everyday!

I've been having this weird feeling every day (i think it's a neuro problem. that's what my mom thinks as well). it's like i'm here but i'm not here. It happens, i think, every day. I'm going to ask Dr. Adams about it next week when i go and see him and see what he says. But i'm guessing what he's going to say is, its probably Neuro. Tomorrow, I have OT and maybe Speech. I haven't had Speech yet, so we'll see how it goes! Tomorrow, if i'm up to it, i might also be going to one of Carolyn's games, then go out for a bite to eat. It will be nice because i'm inside all day, so it's kind of a change in pace.

I forgot to tell you, I got my Double H application two weeks ago!!!!!!! I'm getting super excited about going again and seeing Tess!!!!!!!!! And going for Open House. It's just one of those weeks where you can forget about Dr. appts. and all that jazz...lol. OK, well, i better get going!

Malisa-Can you please thank your friend, Niki, for me? please tell her i LOVED the card! Please continue to pray for my CB friends, especially Natalie and Darcie.
Amanda :-)

SUNDAY, JANUARY 27, 2008
Hey!
I've been meaning to update, but i've been a little busy and not feeling well. So, Friday night was lots of fun. I decided to live life a little and go to my sister's basketball game. I'm usually the one who stays home while my parents and Dahea go to her game

(because i HATE the loud noise), but i said to myself, Carolyn only has 1½ years left of playing basketball. how many more games am i actually going to see her play in and win? So I went, and she did AWESOME!!! She wasn't in for a whole quarter, but she was in for about eight minutes, and she scored two points and made some rebounds. I was proud of her!

We got a bite to eat after that at Red Robin. (it was like 9:00PM when we ate!!! so we all ate very little.) I came back, and I couldn't get back to sleep, so My dad brought me into bed and gave me my laptop, and i did some emails because my brain wouldn't shut off. I have some things that are running through my head lately, and all I have to say is, Thank goodness I have my friend Nikki to email! Thanks Nikki!!!!!

Yesterday was a relaxing day. My mom and dad FINALLY got a night out to themselves while Carolyn and Dahea got to watch none other but me! We made Carolyn go and get us McDonald's and Subway subs.

I woke up this morning and had a scare. I started not to feel that well in the bathroom. I got that feeling the one i was telling you about, and all of a sudden i turned very white and pale. And my hands were shaking, and i was very weak! My mom got me out of the bathroom and to the couch and laid me down, put a cold cloth on my head, and gave me my oxygen and some orange juice because sometimes my sugar drops. After like five to ten minutes, my color started to come back, and i felt a lot better! I'm just getting very scared that i'll get these feelings all the time now. But i'm going to See Dr. Adams this Thursday, so i'll ask him.

Later on were going to Target because i have some Target certificates i still haven't spent from my birthday/Christmas. I'm gong to see if i collected enough change also for Guitar Hero, and, if i put all of my money and certificates together, maybe i can get it? If not, i'll save my certificates and money and keep working towards it because i really want that game!

Tomorrow i have a Cardiologist appt. So the STAR bus is picking me up around 9:30-ish. I'll tell you what's going on there. Please continue to pray for my CB friends!
Amanda :-)

TUESDAY, JANUARY 29, 2008
Hi all!
So, yesterday was funny! I woke up at 9:00am, and, you know how the bus was supposed to pick my mom and me up at 9:30AM? i got very panicky and yelled to my mom, and she was like, "oh, Sunnyview messed up your appt. for January and February." I guess they mixed up the month thing, so that was a nice way to wake up, so my real appt. (hopefully) is February 12th (my sister's birthday).

Yesterday I had Speech for the first time since the summer. It was kinda weird since I don't really care for the Speech Therapist. I'd rather have Dianna or Michelle 100%!!!!!! Gosh, I want to get back to school so bad!!!!!

So, i'm not sure if i have PT today. (you never know with the visiting therapists!) Tomorrow I have speech again, and somewhere between tomorrow and Friday (except Thursday) I have OT. busy week. I have an appt. with Dr. Adams on Thursday, so we'll see how i'm doing in that appt....lol.

Tammy just called, and it was soooo nice to hear from her! I'm sorry i haven't talked to you in a while. Tammy, Erik, My mom, and I are going to try to meet up on the 5th because we both have appts. at Albany Med., i think? I have to start getting stuff ready for the prom i'm going to with Erik. I think it's in March (please correct me if i'm wrong!!!!!!) I know i have to wear a blue dress. I have all my jewelry, so i'm set with that. the only thing is, i really want to wear nice shoes (not sneakers for once), so i'm going to have to search around to find nice shoes to fit my AFO's.,
OK, well, that's pretty much it.

Please continue to pray for my CB friends! And please say a special prayer for one of my teacher's parents who are sick.
Amanda :-)

WEDNESDAY, JANUARY 30, 2008
Hi all!
Today was a busy day....busier then i expected! Last night, I didn't get to sleep until 1am. I had a stomach ache last night, and, after it went away, my head wouldn't shut off, so i just laid there, pet Abby, and watched TV. I woke up this morning really early for some reason. Usually I get up around 9:00AM. this morning, I got up around 8:20AM. I didn't even get seven hours of sleep i bet. I woke up, did my meds, ate breakfast, then my mom told me my grandma is coming over for lunch. I was excited because i'm knitting a blanket for my sister or her birthday (it probably won't be ready for her birthday, but it will...maybe a month after

it...lol), so Minnie (my grandma) came over and brought lunch and fixed my knitting, and she stayed for about and hour.

Then Speech came... ohh, [at] home, exciting!   She was sooo rude!   She came in with snow up to her ankles (because it was snowing so bad today) and went right across the floor and sat down. meanwhile, the snow was melting on our floor...lol. It was funny but rude. I mean, she could have wiped them at least!   So after Speech, i took an hour nap, then i had PT. I tried standing today, and, on the second try, I did most of it by myself with a walker!   My right foot doesn't seem to want to go down, but Joan (PT) says it's from not stretching it enough. So we're going to try standing again on Friday. I know when I get back to Outpatient Sunnyview, things can only get better.

Tomorrow is my appt. with Dr. Adams. I'm curious to see what he has to say and just what he, Cheryl, and Kate are planning for me. I really want to discuss a diet plan with Kate because i'm getting into eating soft foods, and I don't want to gain any more weight. i like the weight i am right now. i think i look good, and it's a perfect weight for me and my age. Right now i'm just doing a low fat, fat-free diet because i get my lipids every other night, and that's almost all fat, so that's enough fat for me...lol.

So I have my dad buying two different kinds of milk for me and my sisters. then i'm eating frozen yogurt instead of real ice cream = kiss Chipwiches bye bye... :-(So that's what i'm doing right now. I'll discuss more things with Kate tomorrow. The bus (supposedly) is going to pick my mom and me up. my Grandma is going to meet us there because she wants to come, and my Aunt Dawny is going to meet us there after, just to have lunch...lol
Please continue to pray for my CB friends!

Amanda Perrotta

Amanda :-)

THURSDAY, JANUARY 31, 2008
Hi everyone!
It was such a long day today! I woke up at 8:00AM. I usually
don't wake up that early, but I also went to bed around 12:00AM
(which is early for me), and i had lipids last night (energy!). I got
dressed sooo quickly because my mom was on a roll. you could
tell she didn't want to miss this appt...lol. I think my therapists at
Sunnyview would be so proud of me! It would be a world
record! The van came right on the dot, 9:00! I have to tell you,
the vans are AWESOME!!!! I love how you just go up to the lift
and they just lift you right up into the van.... it's very cool.

It was a little strange at first riding in a van in my wheelchair, but i
got used to it. I reminded myself to bring my iPod next time
because it was too quiet for me (i'm used to my sisters
yacking...lol). We got to Albany Med., and we were there a little
bit early, so we decided to go up to the 7th floor, which is the peds
[pediatric] unit where i usually am. I wanted to visit Bridget,
Eldrid, and everyone else. I went to Dr. Adams' office, and my
grandma beat us there...lol. We were only sitting for about five
minutes when the lady called us. When we went into the room,
Kate saw us, and she was so excited to hear that I was eating a
little and that i gained weight, and she couldn't get over my red
hair! She thought i should put purple in with it...lol. Maybe! I
told her all about the night sweats (which i haven't told all of
you...lol) and the hotness on my hands, but they're still cold. She
said she'll tell Dr. Adams.

My mom brought my Double H paperwork so Dr. Adams can fill it out. I know how much they LOVE to fill that out! I saw Cheryl, and she was thinking for a minute about maybe TPN's, but wasn't sure. She's going to boost me up to Carnitor 3x's a day. And I guess you can mix it with my lipids, so that's what we're going to do! Also, we talked about my diet, and i'm doing the opposite! I'm supposed to be on a high fat, low carb and low sugar diet. So I guess i'm starting that! Cheryl was talking about the prom and everything...lol. Dr. Adams came in, and he explained how I shouldn't go to TPN's yet. that should be the last resort just because of the metabolic strokes, and TPN's are really only for people who don't eat and for extra nutrition. So, for right now, i'm good with the lipids and Carnitor. He explained the night sweats and the finger hotness...lol. I can't really explain it...its hard.

After the appt., we went back to the 7th floor, and I saw Eldrid. it was nice to see him just by stopping by. he was talking about the prom, too. how do these nurses know these things?! Then my mom and I went down to the cafeteria with my Godmother and ate lunch. It was a nice day, but it was also pretty exhausting. if i didn't have my lipids, i probably wouldn't make it through the day. The ride back was kinda bumpy. the guy put my wheelchair right on the window, so it kept banging on the glass...lol. Kim is supposed to be coming over later to drop my homework off. Then, it's pretty much going to be a relaxing night. The season premiere of "LOST" is on tonight, so i'm excited about that!

Please continue to pray for my CB friends, especially Sean Robert, who is back in the hospital.
Amanda :-)

Amanda Perrotta

SATURDAY, FEBRUARY 02, 2008
Hi all!
So, I'm going to start out with a funny story this morning to get everyone in a good mood! Thursday night, when Kim and Phil were here, this guy from this health [supply] company came. He was supposed to deliver my mattress, to stop me from getting bedsores, and my bed rail. So he came in, and he pulled out a single bed mattress thingy. I was thinking, "am i seriously going to sleep on that?" It was plastic, smelled, and was too small for my bed. So, he was telling my mom and supposedly my dad...lol (don't ask) how he could get me a full mattress that would stop my bed sores, but I really don't want a new mattress because I'm sleeping very comfortably on my mattress right now without getting any bed sores, so why should I change anything if i'm doing fine? So, I slept with my mom that night because she had to wash my sheets. then, the next morning, my mom took the mattress off and put my new sheets on.

Yesterday was kinda crazy! I woke up, and Dahea was home..lol. I guess her school was closed. she also gets Monday off....lucky her! So, she did some cleaning, and I tried to help with the vacuuming. i did about a quarter of the rug. It was kinda hard because the vacuum is sooo heavy, and, even when i put my breaks on, it would like pull me forward. I was supposed to have PT and OT yesterday, but I have no idea where that went....lol. That's what I don't like about home therapy.

Carolyn's game was canceled last night (and no one told me until the last minute, so I had no idea what was going on!). So, instead, we went out to dinner with Minnie and Poppy (my grandparents).

I'm really trying hard on my new diet, but it's hard when it's an Italian place and you can't have pasta but only once a week. I had eggplant (without the cheese!) and a salad. Tomorrow is Sunday, which means I can cheat a little. Dr. Adams and Cheryl said I could once a week.

Today, I'm just relaxing and resting up for all these appts. coming up this week. I might do some homework, too. I have to get hooked up to my Carnitor in a minute, and I haven't been drinking much yesterday or today, so my mom is going to hook me up to a bag of D-5.

Please continue to pray for my CB friends.
Amanda :-)

Shopping For Special Foods and Splurging on Carbs

SUNDAY, FEBRUARY 03, 2008
Hi!

Is everyone watching the SuperBall [Super Bowl]? I was, but I had to do some stuff on my iPod so I could actually not bore myself on the transfer bus tomorrow...lol.

So, this morning, my mom, dad and I went shopping for some sugar free and low carb foods. I only found a couple of things, but i'm sure if i look around i'll find more. I found a great looking pumpkin pie...lol. I was going to eat it tonight, but we'll get to that later..lol. It was soooo hard finding dinners for me because, some nights, my family eats dinners that I can't swallow or eat (diet wise), so i have to pick something out in the market in the frozen section. So my dad and I tried to find some dinners today with no sugar and low carbs, and we found zip! It was sooo hard! But i'm sure we'll either find something or I'll Google some recipes and bake...thank goodness i LOVE to bake!

After shopping, we went out to a brunch sorta thing. I ate an omelet (did good there because i was saving myself for tonight....lol). When we came home, I walked a little (rode to be exact) to get some fresh air. I don't get out a lot because my dad works during the week, and he's the only one who can get me outside....OK him and Tony. We went up to Mr. and Mrs. Dujack's tonight, which was fun. I mostly just hung out with my sisters. This was where the eating started...lol. I ate a gooey brownie. When we got home, I ate my waffle (we ordered it from the diner we went to this morning) covered in syrup and butter. TERRIBLE!!!!! I KNOW!!!!!!! But tomorrow i'm back on track, and i'm being good. No worries.

I think my sister might be getting a touch of a cold, so i'm trying to stay a distance away from her (even though I share the same germs with her, i want to be extra cautious!)

OK, well i'm off to watch more of the game! GO GIANTS!!!

PLEASE CONTINUE TO PRAY for my CB friends, especially Erik, who is in the Hospital.

Amanda :-)

MONDAY, FEBRUARY 04, 2008
Hi!
OK, so Last night I guess those waffles caught up with me, but I knew that was coming, but not this hard! Last night around 9:00PM, I was watching the game, and all of a sudden, it hit me. I felt so tired and weak, and i couldn't move. I knew it was because of the waffles and the brownie. Ughh. but it was soo good! So at least now I know what is coming once a week, and I can decide if I want to eat a carb and be run down like that or maybe skip a week and eat a carb the next week. My mom hooked me up to my lipids (thank goodness i was due for my lipids!), and I asked her for some D-5. So, that ran all night. This morning I felt a little better, but I was still tired. I had a Neuro appt. at 10:00AM. The bus came at 9:00AM. I was waiting outside. The Neuro appt. went well. When they checked my reflexes, though, in my legs I guess i only had a little in my right, so they're going to do the MRI sooner, like in April.

After the Neuro appt. we went up to visit Erik. It was nice to see him and Tammy. The bus wasn't coming for another half hour, I guess, so we had lunch downstairs. When I got home, I hooked myself up to a bag of D-5 and went right to sleep. I hope this all goes away by tomorrow! My body is tired, but i'm not, so we'll see how i am tomorrow.

Tonight, I'm just going to relax and watch my shows...lol. Tomorrow, I think I might have Speech and maybe PT (i'm not sure for PT because Joan calls before she comes).

Please continue to pray for my CB friends, Especially Erik and Abby's brother, Joey. And a special prayer for my Teacher's parents.
Amanda :-)

WEDNESDAY, FEBRUARY 06, 2008
Hi everyone!
So, yesterday I was still dehydrated. My mom hooked me up to a bag of D-5 on Monday night, then, when I woke up yesterday morning, she hooked me up to another bag of D-5. I still felt a little bit icky yesterday. I just flopped around and didn't do much. I had PT yesterday, though. Joan brought in the walker and had me try standing again. On my first try, I did pretty good. I stood for a minute and 30 seconds! It wasn't with much help from Joan or my mom either. I was using half of my upper body strength, though, so I have to work on putting more weight on my legs. But I thought I did GREAT for my second time with a walker. I didn't do as good the second time because i didn't stand as long. But she said, instead as standing as long, try picking up my feet, so i picked them up about two to three inches off the ground!! I'm really getting there slowly but surely. It really hurt my body later. But I know it will be worth it!

Last night (Thanks to Mindy), I was browsing some of the recipes on the computer, and i have a weird thing of having breakfast for dinner. So i found my waffles!!!!!! So my dad said the recipe is pretty simple, so we're going to make them either tomorrow or the next night! I'm soooo excited (and i have sugar free syrup to go with them!). Today i'm pretty awake. I had my lipids last night. I'm drinking more today too. So i think i'll stay away from the waffles for a while (well, the carb ones anyways). I have speech, i think, later, and that's it. i'm going to try to get some schoolwork done. I always say that, and something else ends up happening (which i don't like!). So, after my shower, before i sit down for my shows, I'm going to do a little of my schoolwork. i'm setting it on my desk to remind myself. I might even put a note! Tomorrow I have OT. Charlie works me harder than any therapist, so i better be prepared!

My mickey is driving me NUTS! It's draining like there's no tomorrow, and it's all bloody, and there're those things coming out of it, which are getting bigger. Tony is coming tomorrow, so hopefully he can burn it a little.
Please continue to pray for my CB friends, especially Erik and Carrie, and please say an extra special prayer for Abby.
Amanda :-)

Food Issues and Being Backed Up

THURSDAY, FEBRUARY 07, 2008
Hi!
So, today was a little overwhelming. This morning I woke up very early because, last night, my mom told me I was going to have to get up early because Charlie (OT) was coming. So, I guess I worried about that, and I woke up a little before 7:00AM. So I went back to sleep and woke up at 8:30AM. My mom called Tony (my nurse) the night before, too, and he was supposed to be coming this morning also. Speech is rescheduled for next week because of the weather i guess. After breakfast, I saw Tony and

Charlie both walking up the driveway!!! I was like, oh, this is going to be funny, doing OT while Tony checks me over.

So they both came in. Tony started. Poor Charlie only got to do arm exercises with weights and transfers, and then he left, but he said he's going to come one night because my dad and mom have been putting me in the shower (when i'm de-accessed), and he's going to show me how to do it myself. Tony didn't have any silver nytrae [nitrate] sticks to burn some of the stuff around of mickey site, so another nurse is going to come tomorrow and burn it. He said it looked HORRIBLE! And it does. it has blood coming out of it, and the big skin pallops [polyps]. It's a mess right now. He ordered a bigger mickey button to put in.

Now on to the bigger stuff. For the past month, I've been having a problem where, when I eat, the food digests so slowly. Usually when a person [in my condition] eats around 8:30AM and checks to see if it digested at 10:00AM by pulling back, usually you wouldn't get any residulance [residual], but i am. I'm getting about 80 cc's [about 3 ounces] of my food back. We checked today when Tony was here. I ate around 8:30AM, and Tony checked around 11:00AM, and we got back 60 cc's of my breakfast still, and we could probably get more. So Tony called Cheryl because my stomach has been expanded, too. Even with my Miralix [Miralax, a stool softener], I don't move my bowels every day.

So, Cheryl talked to Dr. Adams, and he said it's probably something with my stools being backed up, and I have to up the Miralax and go until i'm dead...lol. For some reason, I have this hunch it's not that, even though I want it to be that. Tony said to give it a week and we'll see. I'm just praying that I don't have to have another surgery, because that's what it would come down to, i think, having either a J-tube or a G-J-Tube. So i'm trying to not think about that right now.

Carolyn was home today, so it was kinda nice to have her home because usually it's so quiet, so it was a nice change. Tomorrow I have PT. Joan is going to help me to walk a little... thank goodness i get my lipids tonight!

Jenn Stacey-Thank you for my Valentine's Day card! It was so cute!

Please continue to pray for my CB friends, especially Erik, Abby, and Carrie

Amanda :-)

SATURDAY, FEBRUARY 09, 2008
Hi!

So PT was cancelled yesterday. I was kinda disappointed in a way...but then again, in a way i wasn't because I wasn't feeling so hot yesterday for a while. For the past three days i've been taking my Miralax like CRAZY! And, of course, i've been moving my bowels like crazy...lol. This morning, i had diarrhea. that's when Cheryl said i can go back to doing my normal dose of Miralax. I'm still getting all of my food that's in my stomach when i pull back. Yesterday I waited four hours after my breakfast to see if it would still be there (because i wasn't hungry for my lunch yet), and, when i pulled back around 12:00PM, i got a tubful of my breakfast.

I kinda have a theory, and i told my mom, and i think she agrees. I've been having these spells like auras, which I told you all about. I take my meds in the morning when I wake up. if my breakfast doesn't digest within four hours, then that means my meds must not digest for about three to four hours, so that, i think, kinda explains the spells. I don't know, it's just a theory. I'm just concerned because I hate the spells that i'm getting, and i don't really want them to continue, and, if they're from the slow stomach, well, something has to be done. I can't keep having these spells where I get all sweaty and i drench through my clothes, my hands won't stop shaking, and sometimes i get dizzy.

Yesterday was a nice relaxing day/night. My mom had to bring my sister to the Dr., so my Grandma stayed with me. We just watched TV. I wanted to play my Wii, but I didn't want to be rude, so, for three hours, I watched TV...lol. Last night Dahea, mom, dad, and I went out to dinner and then to PetSmart. I had to get a couple things for Abby. Her collar is all yucky, so i got her a new red collar with bones on it, a new bone, a couple new balls to play with, and a new dish and a mat, so we went all out...haha. I saw my friend, Jade, from school there. I think she was kinda surprised/scared to see me especially since she never saw me in an electric wheelchair before. She always saw me in a manual one. So i think she was kinda frightened a little bit because she wasn't used to it, but it was REALLY nice to see someone from school, especially a friend.

Today is my Aunt's baby's, or should i say, babies' (she's having TWIN GIRLS!) shower. I'm kinda looking forward to it. I usually like to relax on Saturdays, but it's nice to get out when I can. I had my lipids last night, so i should be OK! Oh, I wore jeans last night again for the first time! It felt soooo good!
Please continue to pray for my CB friends, especially Erik and Carrie.
Amanda :-)

PS: I'm seriously trying to get my mom or dad to get my camera so that I can take pictures of my room. hopefully this weekend someone will get it!

MONDAY, FEBRUARY 11, 2008

Hi!

The last couple of days haven't been going so well. Yesterday went pretty well. I felt pretty good (energy wise), but I knew I was crashing. Yesterday was mostly a relaxing day. I slept in until 9:00AM, and my dad made me eggs while my sister and I watched a movie (I LOVE when just me and my sister watch movies). Later on that day, we went to my aunt's house for dinner. it was my grandparents' anniversary, so we celebrated there. It was nice to see my cousins because i don't get to see them often, so, once in a while, it's nice to see them. I ate a little bit, but not much. So, when i got home, i ate a bowl of cereal. This morning, I woke up and felt like I got hit by a train. My body felt all out of whack. I had some auras, and I have hardly any energy. I ate some cereal and stayed up for about two hours, then i went back to bed for 2 ½ hours. When i got up, i checked my residualance for breakfast, and i got about 30 CC's of bial (like stomach juice) [bile] and blood. So my mom was concerned about the low energy and bile and blood, so she called Cheryl, and Cheryl made and appt. with Dr. Sanchez for tomorrow at 12:30PM to see what we're going to do. I don't know if he's going to admit me or do tests. Right now all i'm doing is just resting. I'm soooo tired and feel like i've been running and running!

Amanda Perrotta

Last night was a lipid night, so the lipids apparently aren't working. I don't know if they're going to put me on TPN's or not, now that the lipids aren't working.
Please continue to pray for my CB friends, especially Erik and Carrie.
Amanda :-)

No Energy Even To Say Happy Birthday

TUESDAY, FEBRUARY 12, 2008
Hi,
This right now is taking every ounce of energy out of me, so i'm going to make this as short and simple as i can. I went to the GI [gastro-intestinal] Dr. today with my mom and grandma. He said my small intestine is squirting bile back into my stomach. my stomach is not emptying. they're going to try a medicine that is off the market, but, if you use it properly, it won't hurt you. they have to do a stomach-emptying test to see further results, and, if nothing comes from that, they might have to do surgery. I'm not sure what kind. i'm thinking J-tube or G-j tube. So, that's what went on today. I was so happy that I didn't get admitted. I was scared the way i looked that he would admit me or do something. I have such a lack of energy right now, i don't know what to do! I haven't felt this way since before i started my lipids. I told the GI Dr. about it today, and i think he ran through it with Dr. Adams (they share the same office), and i guess he didn't want to do anything. I feel soooooooooo desperate that i want TPN's! I know TPN's come with side effects for me, but they would help so much right now.

My sister's birthday is today. I tried saying Happy Birthday to her. she couldn't hear me (i said it five times) my voice is that soft. I try to make it louder, but i have no energy for it. My Best friend called tonight. we usually talk about the most random things. i couldn't talk to him. he had to just talk to me.... my mom had to hold the phone up to my ear. I'll see where we go tonight. tonight, i get lipids. I've been on D-5 all day because i have hardly drunk one thing. If I still feel this way tomorrow, I have to get my mom to call Cheryl again. I can't stay this weak for another day. My mom is doing EVERYTHING for me!

I'll try to update tomorrow if i have enough "energy".

Please continue to pray for my CB friends, especially Erik and Carrie.

Happy Birthday, Carolyn!

Amanda :-)

THURSDAY, FEBRUARY 14, 2008

Happy Valentines Day Everyone!

Well, I'm starting to feel a tad bit stronger, which i'll take over nothing. Yesterday, I woke up around 9:30AM and was awake for about 30 mins. then I was asleep again for another two hours. I woke up, and I was awake for a good three hours, and then I went back to sleep for another 2½ hours. Then my body finally made up its mind to stay awake for the rest of the day....or was it night? I've been on the couch since three days ago. I haven't been off it. My body right now is going through a big loop, and, in a way, i'm so grateful it's happening right now instead of in June or May when i'm getting ready for Double H because that's the only thing i'm looking forward to this summer, that and Disney. OK, Double H a little more.

I still can't talk that much. if you get close to me, I can whisper, and then you can hear me really well. Last night was funny. my dad tried playing schrades (sp?) with me. I wanted to turn the volume up on the TV, but obviously he didn't get it.

Did anyone ever hear of the saying when one door closes, another door opens? Well, that's what's kinda happening to me, but in a bad way (maybe?). My back is starting to hurt again. And not in the same spot. It's starting to hurt on the right side from the lower part up into the shoulder blade. So i'm not sure if my back is getting worse or if it's just a temporary thing (which i'm hoping!)

Today and tonight are all booked solid! My Grandma is coming over in a bit to bring me coffee and just talk i think. my Godmother is coming over later to just hang out, and then, later tonight, a visiting nurse is coming over maybe to burn my access pullops (sp?) [polyps] finally. Cheryl also called yesterday to tell my mom to run the lipids every day until i get over this big hump. I'm not drinking right now either, so my mom's been running the D-5 like nuts, which is making me go to the bathroom every five minutes!

I hope everyone has a GREAT Valentine's Day! I'm not sure i will be able to stop by your sites, but, if i don't, Happy Valentine's Day Abby, Natalie, Rina, Carrie, Malisa, Erik, Penelope, Gina, Emilie, and Sean Robert

Please continue to pray for my CB friends, especially Erik and Carrie.

Amanda :-)

FRIDAY, FEBRUARY 15, 2008
Hi!
Still feeling the same as yesterday. I thought I would be able to move around a little by myself by now, but I guess it's just going to take a little longer. My body is not behaving! Anyways, last night, the visiting nurse Cheryl came, and she checked everything out. everything was great except i had a low grade fever. It kept going on and off all night. It's gone now, but usually with my fevers they appear during the night. So, we're still keeping an eye on that. Aunt Dawny stopped by yesterday and brought WAY too much!!!!!! She brought me a supposedly late Christmas present, and I can't stop looking at it. it's a blanket with a HUGE blown up picture of Abby on it. Like, her face is right on the blanket. It's sooo cool and cute! I have it laid out on the couch. She also brought lunch for my mom and me. It was nice to see her because I don't get to see her often, only in the hospital, which is not where I would like to see her...lol.

This morning, I woke up, ate my breakfast, and went right back to sleep. I took, i think, two to three naps today. I don't know why i was so exhausted! My grandma is coming over later to just hang out with me while my mom and dad go to Carolyn's last home basketball game. I was planning on going because I wanted to be there to cheer her on, but this got the best of me, but i'm cheering for her at home on the inside! I know she'll do GREAT! Dahea is also staying home. My grandma picked up a movie i wanted to see (Game Plan). it looks too funny not to see. After Carolyn's game, my grampa is coming over because Carolyn, mom, and dad have to stay for the guy's game because my dad is the scorekeeper. I'm really looking forward to this weekend because my Speech Teacher, Dianna (i LOVE saying that...sorry Michele...you'll always be my first Class 8 Speech Teacher!) is supposed to be coming over to watch a movie, hang out, talk, stuff like that.

I haven't seen anyone from school (well, except Kim, but she's like my second mom) since my birthday, so i'm really looking forward to it! My mission for when I get better is to go see Step Up 2. I have a free movie ticket, and i REALLY want to see that movie!!! So, when i get better, i'm there!

I found out when i'm going for my emptying study: next Friday at 7:00AM!!!! Can you believe that?! I'll have to wake up at like 5:30AM! I'm not going to make it! My mom will have to bring my Bi-Pap...lol.

I'm sorry i didn't get around to everyone's guest books yesterday to say Happy Valentines Day. I'll definitely get around to them this weekend. All i've been doing is sleeping.
Please continue to pray for my CB friends, especially Erik and Carrie.
Amanda :-)

SUNDAY, FEBRUARY 17, 2008

Hi,
This is not so much a positive entry. I'm still feeling very weak and tired mostly all the time, and my voice is very low. I thought i was getting better myself, but i'm not. My mom called Cheryl this morning because she was kind of worried that I am still like this. Cheryl called back and said to bring me to the ER. So, we're off to the ER in three hours. I already know what they're going to say:

"You're dehydrated and not getting enough nutrition." so my guess is, i'm going to be admitted and possibly put on TPN's because my lipids aren't working right now. This year is turning out to be a mess for me. I remember before the beginning of the year saying, "I know this year will be better".... where did that go?! But i'll tell you the good part of yesterday....at least my hair looks good....haha!

Yesterday, I went to Wal-Mart to get my haircut and get a couple little things. I saw Rose again (my favorite hairdresser). It was funny because she said if I was ever in the hospital again to let her know so she can stop by and visit me. little did i know she might be seeing me soon!...lol. I got a new Wii game, which i didn't get to enjoy yet, but i will soon! I got some sugar free chocolate syrup so i can FINALLY make my chocolate shakes. It was nice to get out, but it took SUCH a HUGE toll on me. I was beat, and all i did was lay back in the wheelchair. I felt like a little kid in a stroller sleeping.

I feel bad about Carolyn's birthday dinner tonight. I ruined it (again!). I'm not sure if she was looking forward to it much, but i feel bad anyways because it's her birthday dinner. OK, i'm getting tired from typing. I'll update soon.
Please continue to pray for my CB friends, especially Darcie.
Amanda :-)

Admitted to the Hospital Again

MONDAY, FEBRUARY 18, 2008
Hi,

It was a long night. We were in the ER for about 10½ hours. They admitted me...just like i thought they would. They took about all of my blood out because they were worried I had the Flu because Tony (my nurse) has it, and they were worried I caught it from him, so they still have a precaution thing on the door, so, before you come in, you have to wear a gown, mask, and gloves....weird. I still feel the same....sleep almost all day. i really don't have a voice, and my stomach overall isn't emptying. I'll give you all my room number later.

They finally found a bed for me around 12:00AM, and i was soooo tired (usual). They hooked me up to my D-5 and lipids. When we woke up this morning, the floor [that I'm on] had a scare. a boy stopped breathing, and all the nurses had to rush to the room. So, all my IV's were on hold for a while. I've pretty much been sleeping all day. they took more blood today (i'm not going to have any left!). Then my mom helped me take a bath, and i went back to sleep. Cheryl stopped by right before i woke up and said i should be here if i'm not drinking and if i feel like this and sleep all the time. She said i have to have formula now that i'm not drinking. They're going to try to do the emptying study earlier, too. So, that's what's going on right now.

Have to tell you a quick story. Last night, my mom went to get a coffee, and my dad was with me. They came to take me for X-rays (for a port), and it was a really cute guy!!!! Well, he was the one who did the X-rays, and he was soooooo nice, and i think that was the best part of the hospital so far, and that's the only good part....haha.

Please continue to pray for my CB friends and the little boy who crashed this morning who is now doing fine and will hopefully continue to do fine.
Amanda :-)

TUESDAY, FEBRUARY 19, 2008
Hi,
Well, Dr. Adams stopped by yesterday when I was sleeping on my 10th maybe 11th nap of the day...lol. He said all of my cultures were good except something to do with my emune (sp?) system and that this all probably has something to do with a "bug". He said the best thing for me now is to rest, be on D-5 24 hours a day, lipids 24 hours a day, and some other IV's....and we'll see where we go from there.

I had my emptying study this morning, and I hope I never have to do that again!   The "eggs" i had to eat tasted like they were ten years old!   I thought I was going to puke, so I asked my mom if she could leave the room while i ate.   When I finally shoved them down, they took me into the room, and i had to lay there for two to three hours while the guy took pictures.   I fell asleep on and off while watching "Finding Nemo".   My bottom was hurting like CRAZY, though, because i have that breakdown.   The guy said from looking at the pictures, my stomach seems like it doesn't empty at all within two hours and starts to empty at three hours. When the test was done, i came back up and slept!   Later on, Kim and her daughters are coming to visit.   Dianna and Michele also, and my dad and Abby.
Please continue to pray for my CaringBridge friends.
I'll update tomorrow.
Amanda :-)

Amanda Perrotta

WEDNESDAY, FEBRUARY 20, 2008
Hi,
Ughh. I still feel (and i think I have a right to say this word during this period) like cr-p! I can only stay awake for, like, a maximum of 45-50 minutes. my eyes i can't hold up. my body feels sooo fatigued. Let's hope this all blows over soon.

So, yesterday I had a very nice 3rd year Resident from Neuro come and visit me while I was asleep. She shook me until I woke up and yelled my name......what a NICE doctor!!!! I was so ticked off with her. But anyways, she told my mom about another test for another kind of myopathy. It's a needle sticking test. I guess it will determine if I have another kind of myopathy. That's all I need...lol.

Michele, Diane, and Aunt Dawny came to visit yesterday. I LOVED seeing them all (even though i only got to see them for like ten minutes). OT and PT stopped by to evaluate me, and I just wasn't up for PT yesterday, so she just did range of motion. I'm sorry Aunt Dawny, I didn't get to spend that much time with you! I had a really bad day yesterday, too. My color was pitiful. I had a temp of 99.8, and that's really high because usually i run 97.

Carolyn, Dahea, my Grandma, and Alicia (my Respite Worker) are coming in a minute. I didn't get to see Carolyn last night, so i'm glad i get to see her today. I don't know what i'm going to do when she goes to College...i'm going to have to move with her! I'll update tomorrow about everything.

Please continue to pray for my CB friends!

Sorry I haven't been able to get to your sites. I haven't been answering emails much either....i just don't have any energy hardly to type.....sorry! :-(

Aunt Dawny-Thank you for my balloon. it brightens up my room!

Diane and Michele-Thank you for my Q-20 [20 questions game] Harry Potter edition...i played it again today....i stumped it!

Amanda :-)

THURSDAY, FEBRUARY 21, 2008

Hi,

So, I still feel the same...I can't really talk, very fatigued, having HA's [head aches] and back pain a lot. Last night was a hit, though. Aunt Dawny came to visit me, and, at that time, I was running a high temp (101.1°), so I've been having these breathing episodes where i feel as though I can't catch my breath, but my stats are fine. I had one while Aunt Dawny was here, and, at the same time, the little girl [in the bed] next door was having really bad pain, so she was groaning, so all the nurses and Drs. were in our room...it was quite funny (not at the time, though).

My Flu culture came back negative, which we already knew. I had more blood drawn from my poor port last night, just to make sure i don't have an infection brewing somewhere in my line. Today I also had more blood drawn for something...lol. They're taking care of everything! I also had to go down for X-Rays for the episodes i've been having....that wore me right out!

I was supposed to have PT today down in the gym, but Dr. Adams and Cheryl refused, so the PT came up, and she's going to try to come up every day....i'm not sure about the OT, though. So, Dr. Adams wrote the script today for TPN's! Ughh, how I don't want them because all of the side effects, but, in another way, i do because of the energy I get out of them. Dr. Adams stopped by my room just when i woke up, and he was really talking about, once i get strong enough with the TPN's, going in for surgery for either a G-J tube or a J-tube. This is going to be a long road, but i'll get through it just like i do every time.

Thank you Brittany for showing me how to work my Webkinz. Please continue to pray for my CB friends.
Amanda :-)

Back on the TPN's

FRIDAY, FEBRUARY 22, 2008
Hi,
They moved us into a private room last night because, I guess we're going to be here a while. They're starting the TPN's today to see if it will perk me up a little...i'm hoping they will. My breathing episodes have been going on constantly, so today they're putting me on a respirator to help me breathe 24/7. I'm .not to sure about that, and i'm not sure if I will like it, but, if it helps, i'm all for it.

Yesterday, Dr. Adams and Dr. Betzel told my mom and me that I will be having surgery next week sometime for a G-J tube and, if that doesn't help afterwards, then they will have to bypass the stomach and do the J-tube....but the G-J tube should help. I'm still very sleepy and fatigued and can't talk at all really. I have to either type or sign to my mom or anyone who visits for them to understand me. I'm really only awake for 30-40 mins. I'm hoping the TPN's and the surgery will get me out of here and perk me right up to being myself again.

Thank you everyone for praying and signing my guest book. i'm so sorry i haven't gotten around to signing yours. But know that i'm praying for all of my CB friends....and i will keep praying!
Amanda :-)

SATURDAY, FEBRUARY 23, 2008

Hi, it's Jacki, Manda's mom. She is too weak to update today. Believe it or not, she asked me to. Manda is still very weak and not awake too much. Her stomach no longer is working. The doctors are trying to build her up for her surgery on either Thur. or Fri. this coming week. Manda is still running a fever and not able to speak very loud—it is so hard to understand what she wants and needs!!! We will try to keep you all updated. From Manda's Father and me, we wish we could thank you all enough for all you do every day by stopping by to check on her. Do not EVER think we do not know that you all have things going on in your own/child's life, but you still take the time. For that, we are EXTREMELY GRATEFUL!! To each of you, may God bless you all and your families!!!! With much thanks and love, The Perrotta Family!!!

MONDAY, FEBRUARY 25, 2008
Hi Everyone!

I'm back! Miss me? As you can see, i'm feeling a little bit more perky this morning. Obviously the TPN's are starting to kick in. I can now stay awake for about 1½ to 2 hours! I'm so happy by that. may not seem like much, but i'm getting there slowly but surely. I still can't talk, and i'm not drinking, but that will come in time. Yesterday was a rest day. i slept soooo much yesterday. I actually took a 2½ hour nap (i never take that long of a nap!). Kim and Phil came yesterday and brought me my "real" Chipwiches. I think I have so much ice cream in the freezer the rest of the floor will probably think i'm nuts! But i eat it! Michele also stopped by (i was hit back-to-back with visitors, so i was kinda going to bed when she came), so sorry Michele! Michele brought my mom, dad and sisters snacks and stuff, my parents really appreciated it!

Today I feel pretty good, I just got done with PT (which wore me out!) My PT thought I was ready to stand when Dr Adams said I can't even go down to the gym yet. She's one of those pusher PT's, and i really don't like those kind because they're like an energizer bunny. The Peds. [pediatric] Dr came in today. she said i looked much better, and we're going to keep the TPN's going. I had a burst of energy earlier in PT. i suddenly sprang up. i don't know where that came from, but then i got dizzy and kinda fell down a little. My mom told me last night the Drs. are talking about transferring me back to Sunnyview after I heal after surgery. I'm not to fond about that, but i think it might be reasonable in a way because i don't have enough energy to get up everyday and get on a bus. They didn't say yes or no yet.

I'm still running a low-grade fever,so the bug must still be in me. I hope it gets out soon!   The surgery is heading for Friday....I hope i'm more hungry after that.

I'm still sweating like anything. it's from the fever though, so i've been wearing a hospital gown (i hate it!) That's really all that's been going on. I finally was awake enough to see what's been going on with all of my friends. OK i'll update tomorrow. Please continue to pray for my CB friends!
Amanda :-)

My First Missed Goal

TUESDAY, FEBRUARY 26, 2008
Hi!
Oh the love of TPN's! (lol). The TPN's are doing wonders each day. I can now stay awake for about 2½ to 3 hours, which is AWESOME!   I'm making progress. I am finally getting a little of my voice back (not much), just a little peep, but it's something to work with.   I'm hoping each day my voice will get stronger. I'm still not drinking, and i'm not eating that much. last night, i didn't eat dinner, but around 8:30 i had a Chipwich...lol. So that counts somewhere...hehe.

My inflammation in my back is killing me. the Tylenol® hasn't been helping at all, so the Peds Dr. up here is going to see if she can find a pain med that's not [administered via my] IV so i won't get addicted. Last night, it hurt so bad, i couldn't get to sleep, and then, all of a sudden, i was so tired, i just fell asleep. I've also been getting AWFUL breakdown on my bottom, so Steve came up and is trying to get me an air mattress...gotta love him!

They now have a permanent date for my surgery. it's definitely on Friday, but i'm not sure what time yet. My mom asked this morning, when do they think i can go home, and they said, maybe Monday or Tuesday. But they're still thinking about Sunnyview also. I wasn't too fond when I heard Sunnyview at first, but the more i've been thinking about it, the more i want to go back. I was just starting to make progress with taking steps when they pulled me out. I haven't made ANY kind of progress at home because my home therapists hardly ever come because they're either sick or cancel. And, if I do outpatient, the bus ride will take more energy out of me than when i get there. i won't have any. It's just, i had a goal, and i didn't reach it, and the only way i'm going to get to that goal now is to work extra hard but not tire myself out to put my body back in the hospital.

Corrine came by yesterday (one of my teachers). she was nice enough to help me put back my destroyed flowers...lol. And she helped my mom get me out for a walk. It was really nice to see her. thanks, Corrine, for Visiting!
OK, well, that's it for today!
Please continue to pray for my CB friends!
Amanda :-)

WEDNESDAY, FEBRUARY 27, 2008
Hi!
What an awful weather day. I so dislike this kind of weather. So, last night was a lot of fun! (not!). The Peds Dr. started me on pain medicine, and it's really working. it stops the pain from the myopathy [disease of the muscles not caused by any nerve

disorders] for about four to five hours. So i'm loving that! It also is helping my HA's [head aches], which i think my HA's are related to my auras.

I got my new bed yesterday. it's VERY comfortable, and it helps a lot with my breakdown on my bottom. my bottom still hurts every once in a while, but not 24/7. The neurologist came down yesterday also, and i'm really not sure what she had to say because I was half asleep, but something about one of my medicine levels being low, and she wanted to up the medicine, but, since it's just sitting there in my stomach, it will be low, so, we'll wait and see until after the surgery, and, if it's still low, we'll have to up it. I'm still not eating very much. I didn't eat dinner at all again last night...I did have a Chipwich. But my grandma today brought up my carb bars, so i'm being good now!

Last night, my nurses and I had a party! I was watching American Idol because it was guys' night last night, and who doesn't like the 17-year old, i think his name is David [Archuleta]. I was pretty much drooling over the TV while my nurse was just sitting here laughing at me. It was such a quiet night here last night that she watched the whole hour with us. Then, another nurse came in with a baby and started to hang out. it was pretty much a party! The party didn't last too long, though, because ten minutes after i went to sleep, I felt sick to my stomach and felt like i was going to throw up. And, of course, being on my Bi-Pap, i have to take it off or i'll aspirate [breath back in], so the nurse brought in a bucket, and my mom put a cold cloth on my head. I felt better ten minutes later. I think it might have been a reaction to the pain meds because that was one of the side effects. So, needless to say, i didn't get much sleep. that and my [in-home] nurse spilled my pain meds on me in the middle of the night, but there could always be something worse to wake you up...besides it was VERY funny!!!!!

This morning i feel a little bit better. I only took one nap so far, and it's 12:00PM! So, i'm getting closer. The nurses weighed me today with the hover lift, and i was 126.8 lbs.... yes, i know it's very exciting! I guess the TPN's have been giving me all the right calories, so that's why i'm, like, the exact weight i should be, but they have to keep an eye on it. I'm very excited about it! They're still thinking about Sunnyview. we won't know until after surgery. The Drs.' only concern is my fatigue right now and how often i nap. I know i need to go back there! That's the only way i'm going to walk again, and no matter what any Dr. or whoever says that my muscles are gone, i flex them, and i feel the muscles, so i know i can walk! They just have to give me a chance. OK, well, i'll keep you updated.

Please continue to pray for my CB friends!
Amanda :-)

THURSDAY, FEBRUARY 28, 2008
Hi!
not a lot to talk about today (which is good!).
Surgery's on for tomorrow! Dr. Adams isn't putting me with the regular Peds surgery dept., it's with some other dept. So i'm excited!!!!! I'm feeling much better today as you can tell, and i'm going to put up a picture, too, so you can see!

Yesterday was pretty much the same with the HA's and the back pain. I've been awake for a while now and only taken one nap,

and its 3:00PM!!!! I got to meet Gina today for the first time. Thank you Gina for my Teddy Bear! Gina helped me with my mobile, and every Dr who comes in here now is complimenting it...lol. Dr. Pretty P/Neela (aka my Peds Dr.) kept playing with it and complimenting it. I LOVE Dr. Pretty P/Neela!!!!! That's pretty much it. My mom or someone will update you tomorrow. Please continue to pray for my CB friends!
Amanda :-)

FRIDAY, FEBRUARY 29, 2008
Hi!
Yep it's me! OK, well, i'm going to explain before i start rambling. I get very hyper sometimes after i get the woozy medicine, so i'm VERY hyper right now, so don't mind my talking...lol. So the surgery was a success (YAY!). I was awake because they couldn't get me to sleep...lol. Well, i was asleep like the last five minutes of it. They gave me three to four injections of the woozy medicine, so i thought i would go to sleep considering what i did before... i'll tell you that story later.

Anyways, they had one complication, and that was that they stuck the tube in way far and they had to pull it back out and put it back in, which hurt soooo bad because i was awake first of all and wasn't sedated fully, but all was well. But other than that, it only took 45 mins. to an hour for my surgery. seemed shorter probably because i thought i was on a roller coater. i thought the table kept moving around and in and out, and i kept seeing clouds!...lol.

Oh, and you have to hear this story. My mom, before they put the woozy medicine into me, she told me to think of David the cute 16-year old on American Idol, so i was like, "OK." So, like, it must have been in the middle of the surgery when i fell asleep for a couple minutes and was dreaming that i went to one of the concerts and met him, and he asked me out...lol. It felt so real to me, though, because of the medicine. Anyway, the tube feels weird right now, but i'll get used to it because its just like my G-tube before i got my mickey. Anyways, before i went into surgery, they came early because i was supposed to have my surgery around 3:00-4:00PM. They came and got me at 1:00PM, and i was just getting ready for my bath because Erik and Tammy came to visit me (thanks for visiting and the balloon Erik and Tammy!). so i was just getting the water, and the guy walked in and he asked for me, and he said, OK, i have to get the nurse quick so that you can take your bath, but take it quickly. So you should have seen me. i have never moved so fast in my entire life because i wanted to be clean because i can't take a bath until tomorrow night. So that was my entertaining day.

Later, my sisters are coming up and bringing me a yogurt shake because i'm on a soft liquidy diet until further notice. I'm running a fever right now of 99.6, but hopefully that's just post-op. I'll update tomorrow!
Please continue to pray for my CB friends, especially Darcie and Malisa.
Amanda :-D

The Clogged G-J Tube

SATURDAY, MARCH 01, 2008
Hi!

So i'm still a little bit woozy. not much, but i'm really hyper still. not as much as last night, trust me! So, last night was very exciting!!!! My mom and I were up until about 12:30AM because the nurse that did my 4:00PM meds must have clogged my G-J tube with something, and, when we did my 9:00PM meds, the nurse couldn't get anything in. the tube wouldn't let it. So, she had to call the head nurse, and she came down and came up with a solution....hot water!!!! Why couldn't I think of that?...lol. So that was only one part of my night.

Before the nurse left for the night and changed 7:00PM shifts, she started my TPN's, lipids, and Carnitor. So, about half an hour later, i felt my bed all wet, and i told my mom, and my mom thought it was from the anesthesia, so she looked, and my lipids and Carnitor were dripping in my bed. she never connected my lipids and Carnitor to my port!!!!! So, we had to change my sheets and pillowcases. It was just a funny night.

Today, i feel a lot better and more with it. I was so excited today to see Liam and Belle and my uncle and aunt from out of town. I don't get to see them much, and it was VERY nice just to spend time with them. They did the most amazing thing any aunt or uncle could do! They made purple bracelets (the flexible plastic ones), and they say on them, "For Amanda." I was so thankful that they did that. My whole family has them on. Thank you Aunt Kim for making them!!!!

A special package came for me today from Dianna (thank you, Dianna, for doing that for me!) It was a DVD, and it had all of my teachers, friends, and just everyone on there leaving me a message saying 'feel better.' I wanted to cry when i watched it for the first time, especially since i saw one of my favorite teachers cry when he was saying 'Feel Better.' They had to blur the picture (he must have been crying hard...aww. i kinda felt bad! But it made my day because Dianna showed me my new desk, my cubby....it was AWESOME! Thank you for everyone who participated in it! Kim and Phil are here right now. they took my mom and dad out for dinner, or my mom and dad took them out for dinner...which one?!

My stomach is so expanded that i look about five to six months pregnant. did i mention that? I'm starting tube feeds tonight. Yes, i'm starting up on the pump again so that i can get off these TPN's!!!!! I'm running a fever of about 100.0. Other than that, i'm doing GREAT! We're shooting for Friday or Saturday to move to Sunnyview.
Dianna-A HUGE thanks for that DVD. it's unbelievable, and i'm going to watch it every day until i get back to school. THANK YOU!
Please continue to pray for my CB friends, especially Darcie and Malisa.
Amanda :-)

Getting Overfed

MONDAY, MARCH 03, 2008
Hi!
Oh, what a night i had (my mom had a better one though!....lol)
I'll tell you more about that later.

Yesterday, I didn't update because nothing really went on, so it would be like two sentences...lol. But, I definitely have some stories for you today!   So, the Drs. started me on feeds through the kangaroo pump [an automated feeding pump].   right now, i'm at a 30 pace, but, every two hours, were going to try to go a little higher.   Cheryl stopped in today and said not to go too far with the feeds, though, because of my stomach. I'm not eating much, maybe a Carbsmart® ice cream bar at night or some strawberries, but that's it, so i'm really relying on my feeds right now and the TPN to keep me at this weight.

This morning, when I woke up, I smelled the weirdest smell i ever smelled before. it smelled like rotten grapes, sour-ish. The head Dr. of the PICU [pediatric intensive care unit] came in this morning and said that the dressing around my G-J tube probably needs to be changed because there's so much fluid around it, so i can't wait for this smell to go away!   Last night, we had a kinda big problem: one of my nurses who is one of my favorites, she started my lipids and TPN's for me around 5-ish. Well, my mom and I were woken up at 12:00AM by another nurse saying my lipids were finished!   Well they were not supposed to run out until 3:00PM today!   So they had all the Drs. and nurses flying in here because they had to worry about my liver now. They put me on a machine that watches my heart rate and O_2 level. My poor mom just sat in the rocking chair all night and watched me because i could have stopped breathing for all i know!

But anyways, they're going to check my liver levels today to make sure that no more damage is done. i have some damage done i think already on my liver, but they're going to see if anymore was done from this. I'm still running tacky from it all, but let's hope that goes away!   So, that was my exciting night!...lol. I'm still running a fever between 99-101.

One of my nurses checked my pee today and said it was really cloudy, so she's going to keep her eye on it to make sure i'm not getting a urinary infection. Last night, I got to see one of my friends from Double H. she's here on the other side of the hospital, so she came and saw me last night. she doesn't look so good, so please pray for her. i really want to see her at HH this summer!

Please pray for my CB friends, especially Darcie, Erik, and Malisa
Amanda :-)
B+
["Be positive," Amanda's first use of this symbolism in her journals.]

TUESDAY, MARCH 04, 2008
Hi!
I wish I could say I'm doing GREAT! But it's always something, right?..lol. Well, last night, i started a high temp of 101 and had diarrhea. I thought the diarrhea was from an ice cream i had. This morning, I woke up with the same high fever and went diarrhea again. The nurse told my mom to stop the feeds for now, so you know what that probably means: a bit of a hold off on Sunnyview for a few days. My stomach hurts every once in a while, so the PICU Dr. is wondering if I have the stomach bug that is going around. I also have weird fluids coming from my stomach when i'm not eating anything, so i have a pholie (sp?) [Foley, or tubed] bag on right now, and its about 1/3 full. I see it keep emptying, which isn't good, but we'll see what all the Drs, have to say about all of this tomorrow. I feel as if i have less energy than i did in the past few days. I still can stay up for a whole day, but i just feel

blah. i know i'm brewing something, i just don't know what! My nurse just gave me some Tylenol® for my fever, so i think i'm a little cooler. My liver test came back low, actually lower than last time. i know, weird right?! Don't ask me how that happened! But, thank goodness that some good news came in today!

That's it, medical-wise so far. I was supposed to be going to Sunnyview Thursday or Friday, but i don't think that's going to be happening, the way i'm feeling today.

Today, I didn't do much. I got out of my room once and went to the playroom to help the childlife specialists make pictures to decorate the room for spring. I think it will look nice. Tomorrow, if I feel better, i'm going to try to get down there again because they're doing something with pillowcases. sounds fun!

OK, well, i'm just out of energy, and my sisters are coming up. Please continue to pray for my CB friends, especially Darcie, Erik, and Malisa.

Amanda :-)

WEDNESDAY, MARCH 05, 2008
Good Evening!
I thought I would begin with a new phrase today...lol. So, today was quite a colorful day. no, seriously colorful! This morning, I woke up around 4:30 and found purple stuff from my J-tube. My nurse told my mom about it last night and told her she flushed it, but it came back up. So my mom showed my nurse this morning, and she was just speechless because everyone kept saying, "I've never seen anything like this before!" Has anyone ever seen the

color of G2 [Gatorade 2]? Well, it's like that color. Meanwhile, I still have stuff draining from my G-tube when i haven't eaten anything. I'm still having diarrhea, and my stomach hurts in two places, kinda where my G-J tube is and, like, right in the middle of my stomach. I also spit thick green mucus stuff up this morning, so the amazing Dr. Pretty P/Neela called the VIR [Vascular and Interventional Radiology] team and GI, and they didn't get up here until 4:ooPM. tomorrow, they're going in to fix the tube or replace it. they're not sure yet because they didn't do any tests. So, i guess we'll see tomorrow!

Meanwhile, i've been TPO [probably NPO, which stands for Nil Per Os in Latin and means nothing by mouth] for two days now, but i'm not that hungry anyways because my stomach hurts! My voice is back down and so is my energy level. Dr Pretty P was planning on taking me off TPN's today and upping my feeds, but she had to reorder TPN's and stop the feeds because i've been getting naucious (sp?), too! So, we're kinda in a tunnel right now, but we'll be out soon! I'm going into surgery tomorrow at 7:ooAM, and i'm not sure for how long because it depends on the tubes and me. But i assure you all, i'll be nice and hyper after (as always after anesthesia). So, that was today's update!
Please continue to pray for my CB friends, especially Darcie, Erik, Malisa, and Carrie!
Amanda :-) B+

THURSDAY, MARCH 06, 2008 03:44 PM,
Hello!
So, I didn't get the woozy medicine because they only wanted to look at my tubes and do a dye test, which made me feel like i was

going to puke on them (which would be sooo funny!, but they were too sweet for me to do that to them). I'm very just blah today. i haven't eaten in three days, and i'm living off of TPN's. i'm not taking in my feeds because, when the nurses put my meds in my J-tube, it makes me nauseous!   Last night I even had this weird sharp burn in my stomach.   OK, so last night, well this morning at 1:30..lol, I had a CT scan to make sure my tubes weren't out of place!   There was nothing on the CT scan (thankfully in a way). I woke up this morning at 7:00AM, and they took me down to VAR [radiology] around 9:00AM. They did the dye test, and the tube was fine. the only thing they could see was that my bowels are now shutting down, and that means nothing's working down there!   So really there's no point for my feedings or anything else.

The Dr. is coming up later to talk about options and tests (yea more tests.) the one thing a Resident mentioned was going to Boston (Boston is known for treating Mitochondrial kids), but i really don't want to go!   But, if it helps, i'm all for it. So that's what went on today!

My big thing today was going scrub shopping downstairs today!   I bought Strawberry Shortcake scrubs!   I can't wait to put them on!   The nurses probably thought we were nuts!! Yogi [the therapy dog] also came to visit me again. he brought me some rocks from Maine and a picture of him...lol. His owner, John, offered to bring Yogi to visit me whenever i go back to Sunnyview. I'll tell you what happens tomorrow!
Please continue to pray for my CB friends, especially Erik, Darcie, Carrie, and Malisa
Amanda :-) B+

Amanda Perrotta

Both of My Tubes Replaced

FRIDAY, MARCH 07, 2008
Hi!
Last night my J-tube got clogged, so i didn't get any of my seizure meds. the Dr. had to call the surgeon, and all she had to say was, "Put an NG [naso-gastric intubation] tube in!!!!!"   Well, that didn't help because i already have a G-tube, and they do the same thing, and putting meds in my stomach, well my meds don't digest in my stomach....nothing does!   So i had headaches and auras all night, so i didn't get much sleep. i was tossing and turning all night. But it was a lot more sleep than i got the previous night before!   This morning, Dr. Pretty P/Neela came in and said we have to replace this tube because it's faulty!!!   I'm the lucky one who gets a faulty tube..lol.

So, sometime today, they're replacing both G and J tubes!   I'm sooooo happy!   I'm hoping some of my nausea will go away so that i can EAT!   Also, for a little more excitement this morning, my G-tube clogged, so i didn't get my morning seizure meds, so i'm hoping VAR better move fast, but i don't think i'll be in surgery until later on today because i'm an add-on. I'm hoping i get general anesthesia this time because i wasn't asleep at all last time, and i hurt a little, but nothing bad. but this time, they're replacing both because they're both clogged. Well see. you all know i'm hyper after any anesthesia, so i'll update! (hopefully).

The GI Dr. came in last night. he was a new and younger one. He told us about Boston, and thank goodness we're not going! We're really thinking about this medicine. it's from Canada, but we're not going to go there until after all this is done. I guess we're switching over to him because he was VERY good!!!! He had more medical knowledge.

I'm just hanging in there for right now. Honor, the dog that prayed for me last week at this time, is coming up later, so he'll probably pray again...he's too cute![6] I can't seem to email or get that picture up on any website! It's bugging me! I'm also making birthday presents for my cousins. they're little backpacks, and i'm putting their names on them with glitter and then making like hearts, flowers, crowns, and stars. Whatever fits the description of their personalities...lol. OK, well, hopefully i'll update you guys later or tomorrow.

Please continue to pray for my CB friends, especially Darcie, Erik, Carrie, and Malisa

Amanda :-)

B+

SATURDAY, MARCH 08, 2008

Hi everyone!

Well, my surgery went GREAT yesterday! It took a little longer than last week's because they had to take both tubes out and replace them. plus, while they were in there, i guess it was a little messy, so they cleaned me out! They tried putting me to sleep (AGAIN!) with the same medicine, but it didn't work..lol. I was just woozy and felt GREAT! Sometimes i wish i could have that medicine more...haha. I have to tell you, even though i was a little

---

[6]Honor hops his paws up onto the bed and rests his head down in a prayerful posture when others pray.

woozy, those VIR nurses are too funny! They made me do like a fire drill with rolling onto the table and everthing...lol.

Last night was soooo hectic!! I had, like, 20 visitors, and i enjoyed each one of them, but it paid off later on into the night. Diane and Michele came and insisted that i put their picture up of both of them with me, so i'll do that later on just for you guys! Today isn't such a great day. I've been nauseous most of the day because of the nurse putting my meds in my tube, and i wanted to try to eat something, but then my stomach got a hold of it, and i got nauseous again! I'm hoping that will pass soon so i can eat again without any pain. I have medicine for the nausea, but it's only helping a little bit.

This morning, i also woke up with a new problem (whoopee!). when i went pee, it burned and hurt, and i haven't been putting out that much, so i'm not sure what's going on there. I was supposed to start my feeds today, but i'm so nauseous, i would probably puke if I did. So, that's the medical update for today....

I can't believe that tomorrow it's going to be four weeks since i've been here! It's crazy! But i know i have a lot more to sort out before i can go to Sunnyview and go home, so it's just a slow progress. Everyone's been asking if i'm answering emails. i'm not right now, but i do read them!!!!

Please continue to pray for my CB friends, especially Darcie, Malisa, Carrie, and Erik!
Amanda :-) B+

MONDAY, MARCH 10, 2008

Hi!

OK, I just got my pain medicine, so i'm feeling good right now...lol. I was going to have my mom update again because i'm not feeling good at all today, but the pain meds just kicked in (thank goodness!). So, all i'm on right now for my seizures is Kepra, so i'm in withdrawl, and i'm really having bad HA's [headaches], and my hands are a bit shaky today. Did anyone wonder why i'm typing in purple? Yes my tube is purple again!!!! I thought i would throw a bit of funny in there.

I haven't moved my bowels in a week, so they were thinking about giving me an enema, but Dr. Adams saved me and said i'll move at my own pace. Dr. Adams came in earlier and told us he didn't want me catching anything else, so he's going to try to get me home later this week or next week. He's sending me home on TPN's and my regular lipids. They're going to be mixed, though, at home. My mom has to go for training with them again probably tomorrow. I'm still running a low-grade fever, not talking much. my stomach hurts right now, but that's nothing! So, that's basically what's going on. We're putting Sunnyview on hold for a bit because i'm worn out, but, when i get better, i'm going back in-patient. I'm really looking forward to that! Thank you everyone for all the prayers! They were very much appreciated.

Michele came today and walked a little with me (my mom dragged me to get me out). She and Jacob made me a B+ shirt!!!! She said she kept seeing it...lol. Thank you, Michele!

Aunt Dawny and Uncle Jim came earlier too. i always enjoy their visits! Thank you!

My dad is coming up with Abby later. I miss her so much and can't wait to sleep in bed with her again.

Please continue to pray for my CB friends, especially Darcie, Erik, Carrie, and Malisa, and a new Mito friend I met whose name is Jaden.

Amanda :-) B+

More Seizures

WEDNESDAY, MARCH 12, 2008

Hi!

Well, yesterday was quite an eventful day! I had seven or eight seizures within 24 hours. I guess each time, though, the Atavan helped. I've been quite tired, though, because the Atavan makes me really drowsy, so i've been sleeping a little more than usual. This morning, I only had one seizure, but thank goodness didn't go full blown into it. Dr. Pretty P/Neela stopped by and told my mom and me that we have to love the Kepra (because the Kepra's not working), and we don't have many other choices with IV seizure meds.

So, each time someone walks in the room, we have to feel the love of my Kepra. Dr. Pretty P bumped up my Kepra and put me on Atavan, one in the morning and one at night and whenever i need it for a seizure (which i'm hoping no more today!) We're supposed to be going home Friday, but now with all the seizures, we're not sure, but my mom and I are still hoping for Friday (that means spending time with the family on the weekend!). My voice is still very weak, and i'm not really eating or drinking anything orally. But hopefully we'll get that back! So, that's what's going on today medical-wise.

Sarah (my cousin) is coming up today because it's her birthday... HAPPY BIRTHDAY, SARAH! I made a present and card for her, and Brenna is bringing me wrapping paper so that i can wrap her gift.

PS [Pastor] Jim came up yesterday, so thank you, PS Jim, for visiting and praying with my family.

I just had a Karate session in my room to get some of my nerves out of me..lol. I kinda liked it! I wonder if there's any way i can take up karate?
Please continue to pray for my CB friends, especially Erik, Carrie, Malisa, and my new Mito friend, Jaden.
Amanda :-) B+

THURSDAY, MARCH 13, 2008
Hi!
I'm not feeling too great today. I've been sleeping most of the day because the Atavan that they give me when i seize makes me very drowsy! So i've probably slept most of the day. They hooked me up to an EEG [electroencephalograph, for measuring brain waves] a few minutes ago. I seized right when they got them all on i guess. I've had three seizures today (that's good!) The EEG is only going until tomorrow at 7:00AM. Thank goodness because my hair didn't even get washed today! Dr Pretty P/Neela put me on a new HA patch; you put it on your skin and it absorbs, i guess. My HA's are bad today! I think I only had one moment where i had no pain, felt so good! I'm not going home Friday. our new

goal for getting out of here? Monday. We're not sure whether all my seizure meds can be controlled by then or if everything else will be controlled, even if we have to take some Atavan home. So i'll update you tomorrow of what's going on with that. That's my medical update!

Yogi [the therapy dog] came today and brought me an Easter Basket! It had socks, candy, and Easter bunny and stickers in it. He also brought me a HUGE picture of him, and on it it says, "Amanda and Yogi." He also brought me a cupcake that was like a dog kinda. It's really cool! I wish i could eat it!

I finally made a bowel movement today!!!! It kinda eased my stomach. Hopefully it will just get better.

Please continue to pray for my CB friends, especially Erik, Darcie, Carrie, and Malisa, and my new Mito friend, Jaden.
Amanda :-) B+

FRIDAY, MARCH 14, 2008
Hi all!
What a day it has been. So, the overnight EEG went well. they caught some footage on there, which was exactly what they wanted. They didn't see anything different (which is good!). So, all is clear now with Neuro. I woke up this morning very pale and just hurt all over. My stomach was the most hurtful thing, though. Last night my stomach got HUGE! So, Dr. Pretty P/Neela put me on a NO FOOD DIET FOR A LITTLE BIT, JUST until my tube is all healed inside. So i'm just drinking liquids. It didn't help, though, that i got my monthly on top of all of this.

So far today I had three or four seizures. i cannot remember because i've just been plain tired today. The Drs. are thinking now later next week for me to go home! YAY! I miss my bed and everything else home so bad! So that's what's going on medical-wise right now.

I received a package in the mail today from my Aunt Kim. It was a B+ [Be Positive] shirt with Andrew's logo on the back. Thank you Aunt Kim. And thank you Andrews family for helping my Aunt Kim send it. it means so much!

My hair is all gook right now because of the glue they put in, so later on my dad said he's going to wash it twice...lol.
Please continue to pray for my CB friends! Especially Erik, Darcie, Malisa, Carrie, and Jaden.
Amanda :-) B+

SATURDAY, MARCH 15, 2008 05:15 PM,
Hi!
Today i am VERY exhausted and tired, so this entry most likely will be short. Last night I had a total of four seizures (we're getting there!). They started me on a patch for pain yesterday. it's working really well. every now and then i still get a HA. Last night, my mom, dad, and Dahea went out to dinner while Kim and Phil stayed with me. It was kinda nice to have time to spend with Kim and Phil. They helped me make my St. Patty's day hat. When my dad got back, he washed my hair like three times to get all that glue out. I was finally too exhausted to stay up any later, so i went to bed and slept right through the night and woke up today at 11:00AM.

I had only three seizures today (and let's keep it that way). I'm still very tired and fatigued. I was unhooked from all my IV's today for an hour so my mom took me out in the Barker Lounger just to get out. I've been getting really itchy. i'm not sure why, so we'll see what that is all about. My mom talked to one of the Drs. today, and he said he might try to put me back on my Colonzepin (sp?) [Clonazepam—an anti-convulsive and relaxant], but it will turn into water, so you just put the pill under your tongue. So hopefully, if he decides to do that, it will help. That's my medical news today!

Aunt Kim, Uncle Bilbo, and my cousins came to visit me today. Sarah's birthday party was today, so they came here before they went to the party. Thank you guys for visiting!

So i have a lot of visitors coming up later, so i'm gonna rest i think. But here's a new picture for you guys for Saint Patty's day.
Please continue to pray for my CB friends, especially Darcie, Erik, Malisa, Carrie, and Gina.
Amanda :-) B+

TUESDAY, MARCH 18, 2008
Hi!
So, my seizure status from yesterday was four (pretty good, eh?). Today, i've only had three seizures, and it's already 4:00PM! I'm hoping these seizures stop soon so i can go home! Dr. Adams stopped by today, and he walked in while i had a seizure, i guess. He was telling us how, if my intestines and bowels were [going] to turn back on, they would have by now, so he's not really upbeat

on that. Dr. Adams is lowering my Carnitor to 2x's a day again because he said that it might have something to do with my seizures. It might be interrupting with my other meds. He also might test me for another specific type of Mitochondrial thingy. Dr. Adams just said i might be here for a while because he wants me to go home when i'm seizure free again. my body has some kind of energy and just basically when i feel i'm ready (which, i would say, i am right now, but that's not the truth!). So that's my update for today.

The most fun i had yesterday was the Chair Race i had with some of the nurses. It was really fun! I won both races (of course!..lol). Today, i got out and played Bingo and won a little something for my cousin, Belle, for her birthday coming up. It was fun because one of my friends from HH camp is in, so we sat next to each other and played.
Emilie-Thank you for my card! You're too cute!
Please continue to pray for my CB friends. Especially Darcie, Erik, Malisa, Carrie, and Jaden.
Amanda :-) B+

WEDNESDAY, MARCH 19, 2008
Hi!
Ugh, it's been an exhausting day! So far, i've had three seizures and am hoping to have no more. I've been sleeping most of the day. My mom went home to get some new clothes and shower while my grandma stayed with me. Poor Minnie (my grandma). i had a seizure while she was watching me..lol. Last night they tried giving me an antibiotic through my J-G tube, but let's say that didn't work out so well. My stomach blew up like i was pregnant with Baby David [Archuleta] again, and i got very nauseous! OK,

and i cried, too, which i usually don't. So my mom refused the 12:00AM dose, and we tried again this afternoon, and my stomach did the same thing—blew up, and i got very nauseous. So, from now on, we're doing the antibiotic through an IV, but it probably won't get the best results as it would through my G-J tube. It's an antibiotic, so i won't get septic.

My HA's are still here, so Misty had to give me Tylenol® through my bottom!!! It hurt so bad and brought back so many bad memories of when i was little and had seizures. So that's my medical update for today.

I went down to the playroom today to make a Princess Hat (not that i'm ever really going to wear it). But it was fun making it! Right after i was finished, i started not to feel so well, and we were downstairs, so my mom had to rush upstairs to get me on my floor. Then i had a seizure...lol.

Right now, since the pain meds didn't work, my HA's [are bad]. My nurse and my mom are tying to figure out something they can give me.
Please continue to pray for my CB friends. Especially Erik, Sheldon, Carrie, Malisa, Darcie, and Jaden.
Amanda :-) B+

THURSDAY, MARCH 20, 2008
Hi!
So today is turning out pretty well! I think all of your prayers are finally coming in! Last night was VERY hard for me. I've been very homesick, and i cried a lot last night because i miss

everything! But i think I mostly cried because, after i have a seizure, i get very emotional! I had five seizures yesterday total. Today, i've only had two or three so far!!!! Can you believe that? Anyways, i got emotional again this morning after i had a seizure and cried because i wanted to go home. well, needless to say, Cheryl came up and decided to have a meeting with my mom and dad. My grandma stayed with me while they had their meeting. I guess we're going to find another seizure drug (like Atavan, but something that will last longer), and, if it works, then i'll be able to go home within two weeks with nursing care around the clock. That wasn't my ideal idea, but, anyway i can go home is fine with me! Dr. Pretty P/Neela put me back on my HA medicine again because i've been getting VERY bad HA's 24/7. So, that's my medical update for today (good one, huh?)

I decorated for Easter today. My room is quite colorful! I have a Happy Easter sign on my door with flowers around it also. And i have a Bunny hanging up on one of the curtain hooks...lol.
My sisters are coming up later with my grandparents, and Zack is coming to visit. I'm excited!

Belle and Liam-Thank you for my Tinkerbell picture. it's so cute!
Beth-Thank you for my purple bear, the other one definitely needed a friend.
Please continue to pray for my CB friends, especially Erik, Carrie, Malisa, Jaden, and Sheldon.
Amanda :-) B+

FRIDAY, MARCH 21, 2008
Hi!

So, we're doing better with the seizures. I've only had three today!!! I'm hoping i get my 9:00PM Atavan early so i won't have another seizure. I'm really tired today. i slept in until 11:00AM. Then i woke up for a while, then went back to sleep and slept until 1:30PM. Dr. Adams came in today and lowered my Carnitor level down. I think i'm taking half of what i used to. The only thing is, i'm more tired because i'm not getting my regular Carnitor dose. Dr. Pretty P/Neela stopped by, too, and has a goal for herself and me. She's rotating to another floor in two weeks, so that's when she wants me out of here...lol. There's really nothing else medical-wise going on (which is good!).

Gem (therapy dog) visited me today. He napped with me in bed! I have so many pictures. i'll have to put up one! I decorated an egg today and finished wrapping Belle's birthday presents. So that's really all. just tired and sleeping almost 24/7.

Please continue to pray for my CB friends, especially Darcie, Erik, Malisa, Carrie, Jaden, and Sheldon.

Amanda :-) B+

SATURDAY, MARCH 22, 2008
Hi!
Today was a GREAT day for me!!! I've only had three seizures so far, and it's almost time for my seizure meds!! Today, I felt more like my old self and got to giggle and just play around. I even tried some ice cream (i know!), and that didn't really agree with me, but the taste at first was TOTALLY worth it! I just paid after...lol. There's nothing medical really going on except for seizures, and i'm brewing a temp right now of almost 101. But let's hope that's just a one-day thing!

My cousins visited today, which was really fun! We went down to the Ronald McDonald house and played air hockey. so that took my mind off of not going home.

Jaden is in again, and he made me a picture, so thank you, Jaden. he also bought me a stuffed doggy with bunny ears...lol. Thanks Jaden.

Malisa-Thank you for your card and butterfly. And for the talk last night. it really made me understand more.

Happy Birthday, Belle! I hope you liked your present.

I hope everyone has a Happy Easter!

Please continue to pray for my CB friends. Especially Malisa, Darcie, Jaden, Carrie, and Sheldon.

Amanda :-) B+

SUNDAY, MARCH 23, 2008
HAPPY EASTER EVERYONE!!!!!!!
I hope everyone got a visit from the Easter Bunny and enjoyed their Easter Day!

So, i'll tell you about my Easter later. first things first. I've only had two seizures so far!!!!!! I'm very excited. I'm awake more now because i'm having less seizures. I'm still running a low grade fever, which my mom and I think is from all these polyps coming up around my G-J tube site, so someone is going to look at my site in the AM. I go into cellulitis [inflammation of the skin and tissues, often surrounding an organ or site of an operation] very easily, so that's probably what's brewing. Other than that, i'm doing GREAT!

I had a GREAT Easter Day! I woke up around 9:00AM and found an Easter basket on my table. The Easter Bunny must have stopped by here. My Uncle Jim came early and brought me an Easter gift from him and Aunt Dawny. Thank you, Uncle Jim and Aunt Dawny for my beautiful Tinkerbell necklace. i'm going to wear it the first day i get to go out and shop! My dad and sisters came after church and brought me bundles of stuff. I got a High School Musical basket filled with all HSM stuff; i loved it! Kim and Phil came and brought me an Easter gift from them and Brittany and Brianna (Thank you Kim, Phil, Brittany, and Brianna for my cow..lol, and my bunny). My other aunt and uncle came with my cousins and brought me a Tinkerbell balloon and their love! Thank you guys for stopping by! Then, my other Aunt came by with my cousin and brought me a bear (thank you!). My grandma and grampa came and left just a minute ago. Thank you, Minnie and Poppy, for my Easter gifts!

I'm hoping to stop by everyone's site later. i'm sorry that i haven't been too good lately about saying hi! So, i'm sorry. I'll make sure i stop by everyone's site by tonight (that's my goal!).
Please continue to pray for my CB friends, especially Darcie, Erik, Carrie, Jaden, and Malisa.
Amanda :-) B+

TUESDAY, MARCH 25, 2008
Hi!
So only three seizures yesterday (YAY!). Today is a little different, though :-(I've already had three seizures, and the day's not over. let's hope that i get my seizure meds before i really need them! The past two or three days, when i go pee, it's brown, so

the Dr. said i was probably dehydrated, so they're starting me on some IV fluids to get my hydration up to par. So, that's really all of my medical news. My mom had a meeting with my new nurses, and everything is slowly coming!

Today i slept a lot, and, when i was off my IV's, my mom took me to get HSM so i can watch it. See, Rina, i'm with you everywhere! So, i've just been sleeping most of the day.

I have a VERY special prayer request for tonight. The month and a half i've been in here, i met a little boy named Jaden who has Mito and just found out today he has cancer. Please don't worry about praying for me. just please pray for Jaden and the long road he has in front of him.
Please also continue to pray for my CB friends, especially Erik, Malisa, Carrie, and Jaden!
Amanda :-) B+

WEDNESDAY, MARCH 26, 2008
Hi!
Oh what a day! It's been crazy around here, i tell ya! So, today i've only had two seizures so far (and let's hope for no more!). This morning, I woke up around 10:00AM, and i was VERY pale!!!! When i woke up, PT was here, and she had me do sitting up (which made me more tired, but it will be worth it someday). I didn't try any weight bearing because i knew how i looked, and i didn't want to push myself. I slept most of the day. i finally got some color back and felt better by 12:00PM.

Dr. Adams just stopped in, and he's starting me on Dilantin [an anti-epileptic drug]. He's hoping that that will take care of all my seizures so either my mom or the nurse at home won't have to give me Atavan. I think i'm starting it tomorrow. Dr. Adams also said we should be out of here by sometime next week!!!!! I'm so excited!!!! They started me on IV fluids today, and i can already tell it's making a difference because my lips aren't as dry. So, that's my medical news for today!

Thank you to everyone who has been praying for my friend, Jaden. those prayers must have gotten to him fast because I found out today that it was a medical mistake!!!!! So his mom is very happy! Thank you again for praying for him, and please continue to pray for him because he still needs it!
Please also continue to pray for my CB friends, especially Erik, Gina, Malisa, Carrie.
Rina-This is a special note for you! Yesterday, my nurse ordered me a singing HSM balloon, and came in with four of them all singing. I'm going to post my picture of it later! I wish you were here yesterday to see them all!
Amanda :-) B+
PS: Right now my email isn't working, so please leave me a note on here...THANKS!

THURSDAY, MARCH 27, 2008
Hi!
OK, so right now i'm feeling pretty good, so just WATCH OUT!!!...lol. They started the Dilantin [an anti-seizure medication] today, and whoa, that stuff makes you feel good! I'm liking this stuff so far...lol. They're only doing one dose today, and tomorrow they start three doses. I've only had one seizure!!! we still have the night ahead, but i'm thinking positive! Last night,

around my tubes, it started to hurt and itch, so i think we're going to have to burn them really soon! My pee is still brown when i go, which means i'm still dehydrated. I think Dr. Adams said we're upping the fluids, which means i'm going to have to go pee every minute! So, that's my medical news for today. Oh, I'm running a really low BP [blood pressure], but my fever is gone for right now.

Please also continue to pray for my CB friends, especially Carrie, Erik, Malisa, and Jaden!
Amanda :-) B+

My Shrinking Stomach

SATURDAY, MARCH 29, 2008
Hi everyone!
So, i have GREAT news to report today (i sound like i'm some weather man..lol). anyways, i didn't have ANY seizures yesterday or today so far, so those prayers worked. I guess the new and fascinating Dilantin is working, and i'm glad it is because, if it didn't, i would have to go home on Atavan. Last night was kinda tuff for me for a little while. I get really hungry sometimes, and i can't eat anything right now because my bowels and stomach are shut down. So, last night, it felt like i was starved or in jail. My stomach had that shrinking feeling, so there's no doubt that i'm either losing more weight or my stomach is shrinking.

Oh, and i forgot to mention, i lost three pounds in one week. I had a pity party for myself last night, and, after half an hour, i got over it and played some Guitar Hero. You have to have a pity party for yourself every once in a while. i think it's good for you as long as you don't have one every day. Last night, after i put my Bi-Pap on, i started having these terrible, sharp pains right near my tubes. My mom called the nurse because i was in so much pain, so she called the Dr., and Dr. Pretty P came in and told us we'll give pain medicine a try, but the problem is with that. the pain medicine makes bigger problems with my GI tract. But i had to have it, and, after like five minutes, it helped a lot! We found out my muscles are cramping inside, so this might happen every onCe in a while. My BP is running very low!

Kim and Phil-Thank you for coming last night and for my Butterflies! I'm sorry you had to be here when i had my Pity Party.

Please pray for my CB friends, especially, Erik, Jaden, Carrie, and Darcie

Amanda :-) B+

SUNDAY, MARCH 30, 2008

Hi!

God is definitely watching over me 24/7! I didn't have any seizures yesterday!!!! I'm on a good path for going home! We are having other issues, though, which i hope won't go any further. YESTERDAY, we had a small problem with my port for a moment. It didn't flush, and we didn't get any blood return, so poor Peggy (my nurse) had to re-access me, actually my mom did, and then we got blood return, but it still flushes very hard. So, we're just keeping an eye out on that, and hopefully it won't do anything else!

I think my mom found out why my G-J tube hurt the other night. Today we looked at the number it was on, and it seemed shorter, so we called a Dr., and they have the number on file and are looking for it, so, when they find out, my Tubes will probably have to be pushed in a little. I'm still running a low-grade fever. the highest it went yesterday was 101.5°. It was really high, and i was so sweaty. So, that's most of my medical news for right now.

Last night i had a GREAT amount of quality time with my sisters. It was very fun, and i think i needed some alone time with both of them (even though Dahea slept for two hours..lol). I still had fun with Carolyn. we played Guitar Hero and she got sooo addicted to it!! Once Dahea got up, she played, too, and became addicted..lol. I think i just need more quality time with both of my sisters because i miss them like CRAZY, and Carolyn and Dahea only have one more year until they go to college, and who knows if their college is going to be near where i am.

Please continue to pray for my CB friends, especially, Erik, Jaden, Carrie, and Darcie.

I'll try to get around to everyone's site either today or tomorrow because today i'm dying my hair purple!!!!!
Amanda :-) B+

MONDAY, MARCH 31, 2008
Hi everyone!
There's some good news: i don't have a lot of medical news today (YAY!)!!!! The pain around my G-J tube started hurting again today, and my nurse took a look at it, and she said that Steve (who specializes in all the tube stuff) will have to come and look at it. She gave me a hot pack to put on it an that made it feel a little less painful, but i really think, before we leave, it really should be

looked at because i don't want to get home and have to come back.

No seizures today!!!!! I'm loving this Dilantin (no, really i am!). So that's pretty much my medical news for today (yipee!). I had PT today, and i really worked hard, and i'm trying to get my legs strong for when i walk again (which i hope is going to be soon). My legs really want to move and walk. I had another Karate lesson today, and i'm doing full lessons. i can't wait until i get home and settled so i can sign up! The Drs. gave me a date they're reaching for...... FRIDAY!!!!! So, on Friday, i'm going to be saying "TGIF!"

Please continue to pray for my CB friends, especially, Darcie, Erik, Carrie, and especially Jaden. he had to go into surgery today, and he's still not back.
Amanda :-) B+ (means "Be Positive!")

WEDNESDAY, APRIL 02, 2008
Hi everyone!
So i have some bad news to report: i'm not leaving for another TWO weeks!!!!! Can you believe that?! Ugh, i'm so mad!.....APRIL FOOLS (ONE day late). Did I get ya? It was the best i could think of. OK, so here's the real medical news: I'm definitely going home Friday (unless something goes wrong, which won't!). There won't be any nurses around me 24/7 because supposedly they don't handle all of my meds. So, my nurse is going to be my mom! And i'm going to have a care partner around me during the day to help my mom so that she can get some rest because she's going to be up all night.

Last night, I had a lot of pain where my inflammation is. i think it's moving to the other side of my back. They gave me a hot pack (well a hot cloth). My G-J tube still hasn't calmed down. Steve was supposed to come and look at it yesterday, but something must have happened. Hopefully he will stop in today. That's really it!

To get my boredom away from me, i'm a rock star on Guitar Hero (i beat a volunteer yesterday). I'm making stuff for floor C-7, too. When my dad comes, he's going to start bringing stuff home (YAY!). It'll probably take two trucks to get my stuff home.

Please continue to pray for my CB friends, especially Erik, Gina, Carrie, Malisa, and Jaden. He's still on pain meds and sleeping all the time.
Have a GREAT week and remember TGIF!!!
Amanda :-) B+

FRIDAY, APRIL 04, 2008 09:25 AM,
Hi everyone!
Well i was going to update when i got home, but i forgot it's going to be so chaotic, so i decided to do an early update before i leave. My back and head continued to hurt all through last night. I hate taking the pain medicine, but it gets to a certain point when you have to. I've been nauseous lately. i'm really not sure whether they're going to put me back on the medicine that calms my tummy down. oh, we'll see! My ambulance is arriving around 2-2:30PM. I usually don't like to ride in an ambulance, but i think this time i'll be OK with it...lol. My room is so empty and looking sad because my dad brought almost all of my stuff home

yesterday. I only have my pillow and blanket! When i get home, Tony (my nurse) and Anthem are coming to deliver a LOT of stuff! So, it's going to be hectic, but we have to get through this part.

It was so sad the past few days of saying bye to my nurses (especially the ones i always have!). But i know i'm here a lot, and they are too, so i'll see them again soon when i have a Drs. appt!
So that's really it for now.
Please continue to pray for my CB friends, especially Darcie, Malisa, Rina, Jaden, Carrie, and Erik
Amanda :-) B+
PS: I'm glad you all fell for my April Fool's joke. i thought i would get you all! ....lol

SATURDAY, APRIL 05, 2008
YEAAAA, I'M HOME!
Oh, i'm so excited i'm home. it feels GREAT! The ambulance ride was very smooth, and i'm just enjoying being home. OK now for the medical stuff (i always hate doing the medical part..lol). So, my mom, i think, is finally getting the hang of doing my TPN's and all of my meds through my port. I'll definitely say i hate getting up at 5:00AM, but it's worth it just to help my mom. she's doing a GREAT job (and she's not grumpy. OK, well kinda). This morning, I woke up, and, after about an hour and a half, went back to sleep...IN MY OWN BED! I'm still having some pain in my back and HA's, but that's no problem. I'm moving to a smaller needle because i'm still having problems with my port.

The day I left, we had to re -access again, so just pray that we need a smaller needle and nothing else! Tony came by last night and did everything. he showed my mom how to do some stuff. Oh yea, Gina, Tony said hi! Anthem came yesterday, too, and, boy, we had a HUGE delivery! We had four or five bags and a box...lol. oh, that was a lot to put away! Other than that, i'm just getting used to being home again (maybe this time i can stay home a little over two weeks...lol.)

Please continue to pray for my CB friends, especially Erik, Gina, Jaden, Carrie, and Malisa!

Amanda :-) B+

MONDAY, APRIL 07, 2008
Hi!

Sorry I didn't update yesterday. i was really enjoying just being home and stuff i haven't done in a while. Let's start with the normal "medical news"..lol. I think we're FINALLY getting down a schedule. It's sometimes hard for me to wake up at 5:00AM, but you do what you have to do! This morning, i hardly was awake. It was pretty funny. My back is still hurting every day. my mom has been giving me Toradol [a non-steroidal, anti-inflammatory drug for short-term, moderate pain control], but, about five to six hours later, i get that pain again. Last night was the worst i think. Today, I had a different sort of pain. I had sharp pain in my stomach. i've never had it before, but it felt kinda funny! My mom gave me some Toradol and went back to sleep, and, about an hour later,. it helped! I'm just hoping that that pain is nothing and it goes away.

My G-J looks icky around it. Tony was supposed to come today, but he got busy. I wash around it every day, but it's still all goopy and disgusting. This morning, all of my nurses from AMC called (of course, i wasn't awake, but my mom answered). they just said hi and made sure i was taking my seizure meds and wasn't causing trouble (me, causing trouble....yea right!). So that's pretty much all the medical news (i love it when there's not much!).

I got out yesterday in the air and turned blue. i was super cold! It's supposed to be 70 degrees on Thursday, so maybe (maybe!) i'll go outside.

Kim came yesterday and delivered stuff from my class (card and a balloon). It was so nice of them. Thank you Class 8 and Kim!
Before i'm done, my sister wanted me to mention that she has been doing my flushes. Thank you, Carolyn, you're such a good Care Partner!

Please continue to pray for my CaringBridge friends, especially Darcie, Erik, Gina, Carrie, Jaden, and Malisa!
Amanda :-) B+

A Little Movement, A Big Polyp, and a Bad CP

TUESDAY, APRIL 08, 2008
Hi All!
So i have some GREAT news to report today. This morning, I had a VERY, VERY small bowel movement. It was very small and real soft (am i disgusting any one out yet?..lol), but it's good news because i haven't had any bowel movements in almost two

months!   That doesn't mean my bowels are coming all the way back, but they're trying to work.   My Drs. said they'll probably never come back all the way, but they might work once in a while, so i'm doing good!

Last night, Tony came and burned around my site. he said it was the biggest polyp yet (quarter sized!), and he put new bags on me, and they finally aren't falling off!!!!!   My new care partner [CP], the supposedly permanent CP, came last night, and let's say she wasn't that good..lol. She was talking on her phone while she was supposed to be helping me. So, we kinda go rid of her, and now my mom and dad have an extra job, they're CP's too!   So pretty much that's all the medical news i have (GOOD!)

Last night, PS Jim and Mrs. DuJack came and visited with their puppy!!!!!! Oh my gosh, I couldn't let him go. he was too cute. I tried to convince my mom and dad it would be great if we got another puppy, but they didn't fall for it!...lol. Thank you PS Jim and Mrs. Dujack!
Please continue to pray for my CB friends, especially Jaden, Malisa, Erik, Carrie, and Darcie!
Amanda :-) B+

WEDNESDAY, APRIL 09, 2008
HI!
OK, so, before i get to the medical news, i need three special prayers, really extra special prayers. My grandma just called and told my mom that my aunt is going into labor (C-section) in a hour so please pray that my cousins (twins!) and my aunt get through the surgery fine. Thank you!

OK, on to the medical stuff! Tony came by today and burned my polyp and it shrank half size (it was like quarter-sized), so i'm sure in a few days it will be gone. it really hurts, though! My pressure was low today, i think 90 over 50 something? It wasn't the lowest i've ever gone, but it's low for me. Tony ordered me a teleheath [a machine for remote sensing]. That will monitor my BP, pulse, and weight. I can't stand up by myself right now, but when i do, i can use that part. My mom talked to my Service Coordinator today (Denise) and told her that Lourna, my first CP was AMAZING! She can come to the house four to five nights a week. So i'm very happy about that. That's pretty much it. I got out for a walk today, and i have to admit, it was very nice out! I got cold when we were coming back, but the temperature was so much higher than a few months ago (not that i got out much this year..lol).
Please continue to pray for my CB friend, especially Darcie, Malisa, Carrie, Erik, and Jaden.
And please pray for my twin cousins and my Aunt.
Thank you!
Amanda :-) B+

THURSDAY, APRIL 10, 2008
Hi!
I'm not feeling so well today, so i'm going to make this short. Last night i started a low grade fever of 99 point something. I felt sooooo hot and wanted all the windows open. In that case most of you should know i don't feel good because i'm always cold! I had bad pain in my back and around my GJ tube. It feels like sharp and burning pain. I went to sleep last night pretty early for me. I woke up this morning and felt OK, but around noon was when i didn't feel good again and ran a low grade temp. I had the

same pain, but i was tired, too. I never usually take a nap in the afternoon, since i started TPN's anyway. I woke up, and my voice is a little weak, not that bad where you can't hear me, but just a little softer than usual. I'm OK right now, so i'm going up to Albany Med to see my new baby cousins. So, we'll see what happens tomorrow. i just waned to update.

Thank you all for the prayers for my new cousins and my Aunt. They sure did work because my cousins are now coming off oxygen/Intubation machines, and my Aunt is being moved to the normal floor. she didn't have any strokes last night, and her BP is starting to come down. So I wanted to thank you all.
Please pray for my CB friends, especially Darcie, Malisa, Erik, Jaden, and Carrie.
I might go up and see Jaden tonight if he's still there (of course with a mask on!), and to say hi to my nurses. Let's hope i don't get jinxed this time.
Amanda :-) B+

SATURDAY, APRIL 12, 2008
Hi!
Sorry I didn't update yesterday. It was my big day of shopping and going out to eat (even though i can't really eat anything). My fever is gone, and around my tube site isn't hurting as much. a little bit, but not much. Tony came yesterday and unclogged the tube (yes, it was clogged!). He got orders so he can do that if he has to again. He also accessed my smaller needle yesterday. it's now flushing so easily. I'm so thankful it was that! Nothing really else is medically going on right now. i'm just a little dehydrated, but that's because i took a break today (which i know isn't good) and paid for it. So that's about it.

Last night, I had too much fun shopping and going out to dinner. We went to Walmart, and i bought Guitar Hero 3 and a new outfit, leggings, and a new top! I paid with my own money, so i was excited i had enough for my outfit and the game. Then we went to McDonald's to get me some ice cream. I think last night was pretty fun. Today, i WENT back to Walmart to get my hair cut (that's what we were going to do last night, but it was closed). Let's just say i really dislike my haircut. i feel like a guy with a woman's body......lol. I really wish i never got this haircut!!!! But i'll just let it grow out again and try to deal with it the best way i can.

That's pretty much what's going on.
Please pray for my CB friends, especially for Jaden, Malisa, Darcie, Carrie, and Erik!   and a special prayer for my new cousins, and for my Aunt and Uncle.
Amanda :-) B+

SUNDAY, APRIL 13, 2008
Hi!
I'm so excited right now, but i'll tell you why after all the medical news (you know i have to leave you hanging (or for those of you that are going to scroll down to hear the good news, DON'T TELL!)). OK, well, I got rehydrated, and my lips are no longer white as a ghost. My site around my tubes still really doesn't hurt, just every once in a while. You know what i think, that's pretty much it, very odd, but GOOD!

I went to my cousin's birthday party today, and my uncle, aunt, and cousins came in from out of town. I don't get to see them much (sadly), but i'm going to! Tomorrow i'm going up to Utica to spend the night, and Friday night, when we pick my sisters up, we're going to spend the night again (i think?). But i'm so excited about tomorrow. i don't think i've ever been this excited in my life! Maybe for my MAW [Make-A-Wish] trip, but that's normal. I'm going to charge my camera up tonight so that i can take lots of pictures and post them. I can't bring Abby because they just got a new puppy. Abby can handle it without me for one night. So, that's where i'll be tomorrow.

I don't know how my mom and I are going to pack all my medical stuff. I have my Bi-PAP, oxygen, IV pole, wheelchair, meds...the list goes on, but at least i have one night of going to my aunt and uncle's house and have fun! That's all i care about.
Please continue to pray for my CB friends, especially Darcie, Malisa, Carrie, Erik, and Jaden.
Amanda :-D B+

MONDAY, APRIL 14, 2008
Hi everyone!
Last night, my mom decided to start my TPN's in the morning (it would be easier, and it was thoughts from everyone). Need to remind you that i didn't get TPN's the night before either because i was VERY dehydrated, so Tony (my nurse) called and told my mom to stop the TPN's and run D-5 all night. So, last night, when Lanora came, i was OK, pretty beat, but wanted to stay up to help her build her own town on my game (My SIMS game). So i went to bed around 12:30AM. I didn't wake up at all last night, which is odd for me because i usually wake up two to three X's at night.

So i knew there was something wrong there. I woke up this morning, and i felt pale, beat, run over. I knew it was because i didn't get my TPN's. I woke up at 10:00AM and was up for about an hour, then felt even worse, so i went back to sleep and slept for a good 2½ hours. I didn't even know that my mom started my TPN's....that's how wiped out i was/am. I woke up a little more energized. hopefully i will make more progress during the day and into the night. My bottom is very sore today. i hope i don't get a level two bedsore again!

My J-G tube is leaking! I felt something wet last night and felt around my bag, and it was leaking. very small, but we don't have any extra bags i don't think right now, so Lanora put a towel in my bed last night so that it didn't leak into my bed (Thank you!). I think that's all the medical news. goodness! it goes from one day being NOTHING and the next is like on and on.

So, I'm guessing all of you are like "you're in Utica already!?" No, i'm not, and i'm not going to be until Friday (for one day to spend the night). My mom didn't know when she said yes that she has a nurse meeting with her today, so that's what landed me here still. So my mom is going to meet my aunt on an exit tomorrow and drop Carolyn off, and when we go to pick her up on Friday, we're all going to spend the night (except for my dad). I have to admit i was pretty mad/sad because i hated to disappoint my cousins again. I told Belle (the youngest) back in November that, when we go to Disney World (in which they already went, and i was supposed to go), we're going to go on the teacups together and spin round and round until we're dizzy. that didn't happen because i was in the darn hospital. I missed Belle's birthday party that i told her i was going to be at, and where was i? yes the

hospital! It seems like i'm always in the hospital, or something to
do with hospital stuff, when i promise people i'll be there. But
that's part of my life and will always be. I'm just very thankful i
got to go to my other cousin's party yesterday. I hope i can make
it to Liam's, too. i know how excited they get when their cousins
are coming. So i'm looking forward to Friday and praying to God
soooo hard that nothing will get in my way.

Beth-Thank you for donating to the March of Dimes!
Please continue to pray for my CB friends, especially Darcie, Erik,
Malisa, and Erik. And an extra special prayer for Carrie. she's
supposed to go home today, and i know how much she wants to
leave that hospital, so please say an extra prayer for Carrie that she
has no infections or fevers!
Amanda :-) B+

WEDNESDAY, APRIL 16, 2008
Hi everyone!
I wasn't feeling that well yesterday, so i decided to skip a day of
updating. Yesterday, i started PT and OT again [at home]. OT
was nothing!   All Charlie had me do was transfer from my bed,
couch, and toilet. Then, when i had PT, that was work! I did all
my leg excersises, and she had to evaluate me, and Joan said my
legs have gotten a bit stronger, so tomorrow, Joan's bringing the
walker!!!!! I'm too excited! I had a good point yesterday where i
got outside (winter coat and all) and stayed outside in my electric
wheelchair for about 2½ hours. Last night, Lanora came, and i got
some very good sleep (i always sleep better when she is here for
some odd reason). My pump was being bad last night, so i only
got a couple drips of my TPN's. so, needless to say, today i was
very tired, and my BP is pretty low. Tony came this morning and

fixed the one leak on my bags. my J-tube was clogged again, so it wasn't draining. now it's like a fountain! On Friday morning, he's going to show my mom and me how to unclog it so that if it gets cogged in Utica, were all set! He had to burn around my site again because there was extra skin around it still. Anthem is coming later with a new pump and new TPN's. Dr. Adams had to make a new formula for my TPN's because it was a bit thick for the pump we think. So that's what's mostly going on.

My mom and I are still on for Utica Friday afternoon. My mom, aunt, and I are going to the movies tonight to see Prom Night. it looks a little scary, but i like getting scared...lol. I'll have nightmares, but, hey, you play, you pay! So that's pretty much it! Please continue to pray for my CB friends, especially Erik, Darcie, Malisa, Jaden, and Carrie.
Amanda :-) B+

Scary Movie After Effects

THURSDAY, APRIL 17, 2008
Hi everyone!
Yea, color today! [Amanda originally typed this into CaringBridge in a colored font.] I'm doing so much better and feeling better. Yesterday was a pretty exhausting day, so i slept in a little, and i'm just taking it easy today for my trip tomorrow to see my cousins! Yesterday, I pretty much slept all day and woke up in time for dinner and a chance to bathe before i went to the movies. I didn't have PT today because i told Joan i'm going to skip because of the trip tomorrow. The new formula for my TPN's i.s working GREAT! There's no beeping in the middle of the night. it

beeped this morning. but at least i got a little over half of the bag of TPN's in me. There's not much medical news today. i haven't checked my BP today, so, when i do, let's hope it's high and not low. So, that's pretty much it.

The movie last night was crazy scary! Oh my gosh! I never thought i would make it through the movie without having a seizure or something. It was worse than any Halloween movie, and it was only 1½ hours! My mom and aunt said the movie was short, and i replied, "It seemed like it would never end!" The only part i enjoyed...there were a couple of cute/hot guys in it....lol. Let's say i was up all night and didn't go to sleep until 4:00AM! I stayed up watching Full House to get the nightmare i had out of my head [which I had when] i first went to sleep for half an hour. I told my mom i'm never going to see a scary movie again until i'm like 90 and can't hear or see....lol.

Today, Phil (Kim's husband) is coming over to look at our front lawn so that they can start building the ramp. Mrs. Dujack is coming over later with the puppy (i think)!!!!! I absolutely love that puppy and just any dog. I would have 100 if i could take care of them all and give each enough attention. Abby, i guess, right now needs all my attention, though.

I got a present today from my grandparents for making my confirmation: a web cam!!! I'm so excited to use it, i have it all hooked up and everything! I've been trying to test it out all day, but no one's on during the day, so it's hard.
Please continue to pray for my CB friends, especially Carrie and Jaden.
Amanda :-) B+

Amanda Perrotta

SATURDAY, APRIL 19, 2008
Hi!
Well, i'm not feeling so hot today (yeah, i was hoping for a good entry, too). I woke up with a cold sore on my lip the other morning, and i knew something was brewing then. I did GREAT in Utica and had lots of fun! I didn't have one problem there (yes!), and i was so excited to see my cousins, aunt and uncle, and, of course, their new puppy that i want and love so much! THE MORNING I woke up in Utica i felt so, so, soooo not energized and just down. That's because i didn't get my TPN's through the night. So, hopefully, we'll get that straighten out, too. When i had breakfast this morning, everyone was talking to me, and i was like, "ugh, when are we going home, and when can i get some sleep?!" I was just like ughh all day today. All i wanted to do was sleep and have no pain.

Of course I had some of the worst pain i have ever felt when we were traveling back. I got my monthly, and i had such a hard time breathing when we were in the car on the way home, so my mom had to turn my O$_2$ up a lot, and she pulled over to a stop. I was sweating, and i NEVER want to have that feeling again. My mom asked me if i needed an ambulance, and i just didn't know what to say, so i just said no. It was really that bad. So i'm praying this whole week i don't have that kind of pain ever again!

When we got home, my dad helped me onto the couch, and i fell asleep for two hours, and my sugar dropped when i woke up, so my sister left OJ on the table before i went to sleep, so i took a sip of that. Right now, i'm doing OK. not enough energy to take a bath (and you all know how particular i am with my baths), so tomorrow morning i'm taking one. So, that's my medical update.

I started Karate the other morning! I got my whole uniform and i got badges to put on them. I guess my Karate teacher's going to be coming every Friday?

Rina-You have no idea how much your CD made my day! It made me have a little more energy, and all the songs you picked were DEFINITELY all our songs. Thank you for drawing the picture. i look GREAT! I hope one day we can actually meet each other, though :-)

Please continue to pray for my CB friends, especially Darcie, Erik, and Malisa

Amanda :-) B+

MONDAY, APRIL 21, 2008

Hi all!

Well, my pain finally went away (yes!). I'm up and moving today thanks to my lovely TPN's! Yesterday, i had some needed good fun, so that's why i didn't update—because i didn't get in the house until 8:00PM, and a new movie was on (Princess) last night, so i decided to watch that. No news medically is really going on. I'm doing pretty good today. So well leave it at that.

Last night, my cousins (they really aren't my cousins, but we've been together since we were babies, so we call them our cousins) came to have a cookout with us, and after played basketball. Playing basketball was so much fun. I haven't had a chance to shoot hoops in a long time, probably last summer, so i was excited that i could even make a hoop being in a wheelchair. What can i say i have some nice strong arms, he-he!!!! So that was a lot of fun, and i'm putting up pictures. :-)

Tomorrow is my confirmation. it's really late, and i have a med. [appointment] schedule, so i think the Bishop is going to do me first and then, if we have some time to stay, we will, but probably won't, and then we're coming back and having my favorite Coldstone ice cream while my family is having cake. Personally, i think ice cream is better than cake...lol. So, i'll be pretty busy tomorrow, and i'll be taking lots of pictures, so watch for those either tomorrow or Wed.
Please continue to pray for my CB friends, especially Erik and Darcie.
Amanda :-) B+

A Confirmation Miracle?

WEDNESDAY, APRIL 23, 2008
Hi!
I think today there's more good news than bad (which is excellent!). Well, yesterday in PT...are you ready for this?!?! I STOOD UP FOR FOUR MINUTES!!!!! And here's a plus, i stood up with my PT only helping me with one finger!!!! Now, how will you reply to that?!?!...lol. So, that's only part of the good news. For the past three days i've been having bowel movements!!!!!! I haven't had a normal BM since February, and i think it's finally starting to come back (my bowels anyway!) This morning, i woke up with not even 50 cc's in my bag, amazing! I think the Bishop did something else besides confirm me...lol. Not much medical news is really going on. THAT'S GREAT!

Yesterday was so hectic! I woke up very late because i think i just had to make up that time from going to Utica. And, when i woke up, i had to bathe, get dressed, etc. It was soooo crazy! But afterwards i felt good and not rushed. I'm going to tell you, i'm not used to dresses, so i felt kinda weird in a dress and stockings. When we got there [at Confirmation], there was a rose waiting for me on my seat, and everyone was there! It was nice, and when it was my turn to be confirmed, i think the Bishop talked to me for like five minutes. I felt kinda weird going up, and there wasn't anyone else around me (except for my wonderful BGM), so i think it felt like everyone was watching me, which i think would feel weird to everyone! When we got home, i ate some of my Coldstone ice cream, and i got some gifts (and i didn't know you get gifts when you make your Confirmation). Thank you everyone for my gifts. i really can't name all the gifts and who they're from, but THANK YOU!

Nicole (my CP) spent the night last night, and we had so much fun. we played H.S.M [High School Musical] and Karaoke on the Wii. It was quite funny and fun!
This morning i feel GREAT! So pray that it doesn't go away for a very long time.
Please continue to pray for my CB friends.
Amanda :-) B+

FRIDAY, APRIL 25, 2008 12:13 PM,
Hi!
Sorry i didn't update yesterday. i was quite busy, and i'll let you know what went on yesterday in a second.

Amanda Perrotta

Medical News first as always!   My Dilantin levels are low, so i have an appt. with Neuro in June. Last night, when i went to pull back for blood return, i didn't get any!   So my mom put some of that blood clotting med in me (i do know what it's called. i just can't think of it...lol), and then she tried pulling back, and it was fine. it was a little bit hard to push, but we're ALL thinking it's NOTHING!   I've been having some bowel movements and A LOT of gas (lol). When i get gas, it's a good thing because that means something's working down there in my empty stomach. We tried to plug my G and J tubes the other day, and i felt fine, and i probably could go longer without my bags on if Cheryl didn't call and tell my mom to put the bags back on because she doesn't want the icky stuff in my system. Last night, Nicole (my regular CP) was sick, so her sister came. It was a bit different, but i like her!

OK, so, i saved the best for last!!!!   Yesterday, I had PT, and Joan gave me a choice if i wanted to stand or go walking. I told her i wanted to try walking since i haven't walked since October i think. it would feel good. So, she had the walker, and i stood, and i WALKED...not just one foot but five FEET!!!!!   Can you believe that?!?   I was super excited and it felt incredibly great to get my whole body up and walk!   So that's one good sign, and i think i walked because, since October, i've known i would be able to walk again, even though some people said differently.   And look at me now.... i didn't give up and had a goal, and i achieved it! I'm super proud of myself, and i'm going to keep going!
Tonight, i'm just going to relax because i had Karate today, and i worked hard and had to wake up at 9:00AM, which is sooo early for me.
Please continue to pray for my CB friends.

Uncle Bilbo-Happy Birthday!

Amanda :-) B+

SUNDAY, APRIL 27, 2008

Hi!

I'm doing pretty good. I had a burst out yesterday, which i'll tell you about later. I had another bowel movement yesterday (which is good). I'm beginning to have BM's at least three to four times a week. Which means i'm getting there, slowly but surely. My port is doing good right now (knock on wood). I think that's pretty much all the medical news i have (which is GREAT!).

Yesterday, for some odd reason, i woke up feeling sad/mad. I'm usually not a person who is mad or sad. So all day i sat on the couch and was on the computer still feeling that way. My mom and dad finally convinced me to go outside and get some fresh air. We took a walk over to my neighbor's, and we were there for about 45 minutes. When I was there, my throat was getting all crunched up (that crying feeling but you're holding it back). When I got back, i asked to go inside and begin crying...lol. I had no idea what I was crying about. I was sick of everyone just talking about medical stuff, but i doubt that was it. I think just FINALLY i broke and needed a day to cry. So, when i stopped crying, i took my bath, and my family and my uncle and Abby went to PetSmart to pick out some toys for Abby, and then we went to Walmart so i could get somebody special a birthday present, and, of course, i needed to get a game for my Wii. Then, of course, my sister wanted to go to Target, so there we went. We got home at 9:00PM, and i didn't feel like updating. I wanted to play my game...lol.

Amanda Perrotta

Today, i feel GREAT! I was a little pale this morning and just felt like i had to rest, so i did. I was going to do the Walk this morning, but i just couldn't get up, and i know the day before i had to choose either going out shopping or the walk. I needed a little fun after yesterday, so i chose shopping. It's like one of Malisa's journal entries, sometimes you have to choose over two things you really want to do. But thank you to everyone who either donated or walked this morning. I really appreciate it! And a special thanks to Beth for occupying my sister...lol.

Please continue to pray for my CB friends.
Natalie-Your present and card should be coming to you this week.

I thought i would start a new thing by putting a new quote i like everyday. So here it is.

"Be glad of Life because it gives you the chance to love and to work and to play and to look up at the stars" --Henry Van Dyke
Amanda :-) B+

TUESDAY, APRIL 29, 2008
Hi!
First of all, my typing is really off today, so i'm just warning you! Last night was FUN! (NOT!). When I woke up yesterday morning, I saw that there was no fluid in my bags. Well, that's not normal for me right now, but i just didn't think anything of it. By nighttime, there still was no fluid in my bags, so i started having stomach aches, and then i knew that my tubes were clogged. My mom attempted to unclog them with warm water 3X's, and, by

the third time, she finally got it unclogged. It hurt so bad, though, pushing the water in, and she had to pull back, so that hurt even worse. My BP is still a little low, but, other than that exciting night, i'm feeling fine. I have a lot of plans this week, so i'll get you going on that.

Last night, i felt the urge to walk or stand, so my mom let me try to stand with the wheelchair in front of me so i would have something to hold onto. I got up and stood with the help of my wheelchair, and then i decided to take a hand off the WC. I did, and a couple seconds after that, i just stood without holding onto anything (for like five to seven seconds). It was nice just to see how tall i was compared to my dad (boy i got taller!). So, then i took the next leap to see if i could take some steps. I had a little help from my mom, but i took about five to seven steps! Without a walker. I had my mom hold onto me a little, but, other than that, i pretty much did the rest. Today, while Minnie is here, i'm going to try it again.

My mom called Cheryl today because i wanted to talk to her about Double H camp. I know i can go, but my mom doesn't think it's a good idea, and it will take a lot of energy out of me, and it will, but i'd rather end up in the hospital knowing i took a chance by having the best summer ever, just by the one week of being there. So, i'm just waiting for Cheryl to call back to see if we see eye to eye.

This week i have a LOT going on. Tomorrow night, i'm going to try to make it to my school's family night. I remember last year, i signed the song my "Wish." This year i was supposed to sing with my sister, "On the Ride," by Ally and AJ. But I decided not to because it was hard enough getting me to go because i thought i wasn't ready to go back, but i know i have to go back sometimes, why not now? And, plus, it will be nice to see my teachers again. Friday, some friends and family are coming to our house for our meeting for my fundraiser.

Sat. or Sun., I really want to go to Double H's Open House. I've been waiting to see my personal Heaven since i left last summer. So, i'm also going to talk to Cheryl about going this weekend. I know all this might wear me out, but it's stuff i have and need to do.

Please continue to pray for my CB friends.

"No one has the right to feel hopeless. There's too much work to do"   --Dorothy Day
Amanda :-) B+

WEDNESDAY, APRIL 30, 2008
Hi all!
First of all, i really want to say sorry about [not] getting around to everyone's journals. Everyday i have the intention to go and see how everyone's doing, but then something happens. So i'm going to try to sign everyone's by the end of this week. So, Tony came over today to get my blood level for my seizure meds He weighed me (i stood up for that!), and i'm maintaining my weight!   124 lbs.!!!!!! I actually lost since i've been in the hospital, but it's only three pounds. My BP is good today. My tubes have been acting up a lot lately, so Tony unclogged them and put new bags on them. They're getting all yucky, so i'm having my tubes replaced

in June or sooner if the plastic breaks off. So that's all my medical news.

I got to go to my school's Family Night tonight! It was soooo much fun getting to see all my friends and teachers. I thought i wouldn't be able to do it, but i got through it! It was just plain nice to see how the school looks. The only part i didn't get to see was my classroom and my new desk, but i'm sure i'll be able to see it soon enough.

Please continue to pray for my CB friends. And please say and extra prayer for Jaden as he is in the Hospital again.

"There is nothing like returning to a place that remains unchanged to find how you yourself have altered." --Nelson Mandela
Amanda :-) B+

FRIDAY, MAY 02, 2008 01:01 PM,
Hey!
So, last night, I was a little busy, so i didn't get to update. So, yesterday was a bit of a down day for me. I was paying back for going to Family Night, but it didn't matter because i enjoyed it. My BP was down yesterday, and i slept until 12:00PM and then just laid on the couch the rest of the day. Last night, i did some practicing taking steps and just standing by myself. Today, I feel much better. i feel all rested up for the weekend, and my BP is back up. Tony came today and re-accessed my port and flushed my tubes so that they won't clog as much. We had a bit of a problem putting my G-tube bag back in because the tube is stretched now because of the bags, but we finally got it in. My J-tube is on its last legs; it's torn because my dad put the clamp on

too tight, so hopefully it will hold out until June. That's really all medically that's going on.

My mom had a meeting with my school today about my IEP [Individualized Educational Program]. I guess i'm getting a tutor and doing schoolwork through a web cam. They told my mom that, if I was able medically to go to school next year, i would be going to Latham Wildwood and would be in Class 9. Now, that wouldn't regularly bother me, but my best friend is there, and we haven't seen each other since January, and we haven't been classmates since last year. I miss him a lot, so it's hard to think that i would be going to the same school as him next year if i didn't have any medical problems. I'm not sure whether i should tell him or not. in one way, i don't think i should because he would be really mad and sad [if told him and then ended up not going], but in another way, I think i should. I don't know!

I made brownies this morning for my Fundraiser meeting tonight. My sister made another dessert, and I promised Michele i would have our bakery's cookies, so hopefully my dad will remember the cookies (probably won't, but...). I'll be busy tonight watching the premiere of Chasing Zoey (i've been waiting for this movie for two week now, so i'm VERY excited!)

Tomorrow is my cousin's First Communion, so i'll be going to the party. not Church, but i'll make the party. On Sunday, we're supposed to be going up to my personal Heaven, Double H. I told my grandma, when i'm 100 and i die, my Heaven will be watching over Double H....lol.

So that's all that's going on. I'm gonna try to videotape myself walking later so that i can put it up on here.

Please continue to pray for my CB friends, especially Jaden who's still in the hospital.

"Friendship is one mind in two bodies"   --Mencius
Amanda :-) B+

MONDAY, MAY 05, 2008
Hi!

Sorry I haven't updated in a few days. to tell you the truth, i've been very busy! Which is good. The other day, I was supposed to go to my cousin's First Communion party, but, instead, my body slept in until 1:00PM!!!!! The night before, though, I didn't get to sleep until 3:00AM, so my body probably needed a little rest. I was fine that day except for having the worst stomachache in the world later on that night. I went diarrhea like two times and then just laid on the couch for a while.

Yesterday was VERY nice!!! It was the day i've been waiting for and enjoyed it as much as i could. My family and I went up to my personal Heaven (Double H) for open house. I didn't know when i got there that my counselor from last year was going to be there, and it was super nice to see her again and know that she's going to be at HH this summer along with three of my other counselors from last year!!!! Tara told my mom and me what session i'm going to be in. It's either session 3 or 5. Session 3 is still in July, so i'm hoping i get that one because my family is planning a trip to Philadelphia in August. So that would take a toll on my body like Florida did last year. i went to Florida the day after i got home from camp!! I saw my cabin and the barn and the high ropes course. it was just a good day. I can't WAIT to go back!

We got home around 3:30PM and had some dinner. Lanora came last night and stayed up with me for a while. I was scared last night because i watched The Mist (DON'T WATCH IT!), so i was glad to hear that Lanora was coming. This morning, I feel good. my BP is pretty good, so i'm doing good. Nothing much exciting today!

Please continue to pray for my CaringBridge friends. Especially Jaden. Thank you to everyone who's leaving a message. i'm sure he enjoys reading them!

"Time is what we want most, but what we use worst."   --William Penn
Amanda :-)   B+

My New Quote: The Cure for Mito is Living Life

WEDNESDAY, MAY 07, 2008 04:43 PM,
Hi!
Oh, what a day! Yesterday was a great day! Nothing much went on yesterday, so that's why i didn't update. Today, now i think i'll have to update today. This morning, i woke up and i felt fine! My aunt was here, and i talked to her for a bit while doing my meds. Tony came about an hour after i woke up. He made me a Tinkerbell bag to go over my [tubes'] bags so they won't show! It's very cool! We did my weight. i gained a pound (yeah, not so happy about that, but i know i need it at the same time.. I

decided i'm going to cut down on the ice cream because of the sugar. even though it's not really going in me, i'm still gonna cut down. So, my new diet is ice cream for lunch/breakfast, and then dinner is my regular broth.

I did my blood again today for my liver count (yes, did i tell you i draw my own blood?!). I kinda like to do it...lol. Then i started feeling very nauseous, and my breathing started to get faster. I couldn't lay down and try to go to sleep because i felt to nauseous. Tony called Cheryl because i felt like i couldn't breath right. Cheryl told him to give me an extra dose of my stomach medicine, and he did, and it helped a little bit for my stomach but not for my breathing. Cheryl said, if it didn't slow down in a few hours, then i would have to go in. Luckily i wasn't as nauseous, and i put my Bi-Pap on, and, after like 20 minutes, my breathing slowed down. I'm OK now. a little tired because i used a lot of energy with my breathing, but OK. I felt bad that Alicia (my respite worker) came to visit, and she walked in on me breathing like i ran a marathon. So, that was my exciting day! I'm just glad it slowed down so i wouldn't have to go to the ER.

My BP was a bit low today, and my blood sugar was a bit low, but i can understand why...lol. So that's what's going on medically...lol. I'm just relaxing tonight and tomorrow. I'm really excited about American Idol since my boy David A. did really well last night. he was the best! So, i'm excited to see if he goes tonight, which he won't! lol.

I have to tell you something. I just thought of my own quote today! It will be on the bottom for my quote of the day. I don't know where it came from, but it just appeared in my brain. So i'm quite excited to share it.

Please continue to pray for my CB friends, especially Jaden, who just went back home a couple of days ago.

"The Cure for Mito is living life" --Amanda Perrotta
Amanda :-) B+

THURSDAY, MAY 08, 2008
Hey!
So, I normally don't update everyday, but i thought you might want to know this info. This morning, my mom had a hard time getting my meds into me because my port wasn't working right. She's been flushing it two times in between meds, so my mom called Cheryl, and Cheryl said we have to go in tomorrow and have a port check and put some of that TPA(?) [Tissue Plasminogen Activator—abbreviated tPA—a substance that breaks down blood clots] stuff into it. But if that doesn't help, then we MIGHT have to change my port. I'm hoping everything is good and we won't be there for a night or two. So, I just wanted to let everyone know about that. A new Bi-Pap is coming for me so i can put my oxygen into it. it's a weird but cool machine! Nothing else is really going on medically-wise, but hopefully i'll be home tomorrow and can update you all.

I have a small favor for all my Mito friends. I'm having a fundraiser for UMDF [United Mitochondrial Disease Foundation] and myself. Well, since mostly all of you can't be here for it (unless you didn't tell me something), i thought of an idea. I'm going to get a HUGE poster board, and if every Mito friend of mine could email me a picture of themself with their name, how old they are and favorite color, that would be much appreciated!

I'm going to make a Mito Friend poster and put it somewhere for my fundraiser. Please, this would mean sooooo much to me! Even if you don't know me that well, i would love to get to know you and have you be a part on my poster board. This is the only thing i can be in charge of.

Please continue to pray for my CB friends!
I watched RENT last night on TV, and i just couldn't get this song out of my head allll night last night, so here it is!
"The heart may freeze, or it can burn. The pain can ease, if I can learn. There is no future, there is no path. I live this moment as my last." --From RENT[7]
Amanda :-) B+

SATURDAY, MAY 10, 2008 09:39 AM,
Hi all!
I'm sooo sorry I didn't update yesterday. i was extremely tired from the morning, and i had to wake up at 7:00. All went good there. They put some dye in my port, and, when they put the camera under, all looked well. So, we went back home (need to remind you that my grandparents came with me). We don't have a ramp built yet for my wheelchair, so someone has to always carry me in. Well, my grampa decided he could do it, so he did! Once we got to the door, he didn't know there was a step there, so he kinda fell (with me in his arms!). So now i have a little bump on my head. at first i thought that i needed to go to the ER because i was kinda dizzy and my head hurt. But all is well. Thank you, Minnie and Poppy, for coming with me!

---

[7]Music and Lyrics © 1993, Jonathan Larson

Tony called last night and disagreed with VIR [Vascular and Interventional Radiology]. He told my mom that the port's tilted, and VIR wouldn't know anything because they're not the ones who operated on me for the port. So on Monday, i'm back up to the hospital to see what's going on for real!

I have a feeling my BP is gonna be low today. It's just one of those days. I had to take some pain medicine that helps me with my stomach. My stomach has been hurting every morning for the past four to five days, and i hate the feeling because it's like a vomiting feeling.

Today, i'm just relaxing, and my dad is coming home early to set up my mom's new swing for Mother's Day (I LOVE SWINGS!), so i think i'm more excited than she is...lol.

Please continue to pray for my CB friends.
Jaden-I want to hear all about the circus.

"Faith is to believe what you do not see. The reward of this faith is to see what you believe."   --Saint Augustine
Amanda :-) B+

SUNDAY, MAY 11, 2008
Hi!
Just wanted to give you a quick update. I've been having a bad time with my port (again!). I didn't get a blood return on it all day yesterday. My mom has a meeting with my surgeon on the phone tomorrow, so i guess we will see what she says. Tony and my

mom really think it's tipped, so it might just be coming out? That's really all that been going on medical-wise.

I hope everyone had a happy Mother's Day today. I sure did! Yes, i'm a mom to my dog, Abby. I even got a "Mother" pin...lol. Please continue to pray for my CB friends!

"Go with the flow"   --Amanda Perrotta
Amanda :-) B+

MONDAY, MAY 12, 2008

ATTENTION ALL MITO FRIENDS!!!!!!
I'm working on the poster for my fundraiser, and i'm going this week to print all my friends' pictures out. If you haven't sent me a picture of yourself with your name, age, and favorite color on it, please do!   I'm so excited about this project, and I want ALL of you to celebrate the fundraiser with me. You can either email me your picture or leave me a message. I appreciate all of your support.

I'm not really going to update today because there's not much going on. My surgeon called this morning, and she talked to my mom about my port issue, and she's going to call back later and think of an idea. I have an appt. with Dr. Adams June 9th, and the replacement of my tube will be on June 10th.

Please continue to pray for my CB friends.
"And though I cannot see You
and I can't explain why,
Such a deep, deep reassurance
You've placed in my life, oh

We cannot separate
'Cause You're part of me
and though You're invisible,
I'll trust the unseen"
[from the song: "Never Alone," by Barlowgirl][8]
Amanda :-)

WEDNESDAY, MAY 14, 2008

Hi!

Sorry i didn't update yesterday. I wanted to know everything before i gave you the scoop. So, my port is still getting blood return on and off. my IV's are running super slow and etc. The surgeon finally made up her mind today, and i'm going back in to Albany Med. on the 28th. I'm not getting a new port. i'm getting something like a port, but it's a triple line [inserted directly into a large vein in the neck, chest, or groin with one lumen for injections, one for blood removal, and one for blood feeding]. And the down side of it is, usually with Mito kids, it gets infected a lot. So that's the only down side of it. Adding to my scar right now from my port, i'm going to have like two more. They're going to cut above my port and around the side. The procedure is like 1½ hours. It's a bit longer than [it was for] my port, but they have to cut more of me...lol. so.... The other thing is, while I am there, they won't be able to replace my tubes at the same time because, for my port thingy, it'll be in the real OR, and i have to get my tubes replaced in VIR. So, i'll have to go back on the 10th of June for that, so it's kinda like a back-to-back stay.

---

[8] © 2006 Word Entertainment LLC, A Warner/Curb Company

Nothing much is going on other than that for medical news. I'm still continuing to take steps/walk. I think I have the right to call it walking now. I have a path every night i walk. It's only really to the kitchen and back, but that's all i can do and probably will ever be able to do (because of the energy problem). But i'm happy with just walking around my house. I haven't done that in about 5½ months! So it felt and looked kinda weird to me...lol.

Maria, Abby's old trainer, is coming later on to teach her to stay out on the front lawn without going into the woods. So i'm really excited for her to learn and just to see Maria. I've been working on a puzzle with Yulanda (my CP). It's a picture of two Cairn Terriers (which Abby is) laying on a pillow. It's too cute. I'll make sure i take a picture of it when i'm done.
Friday, Prince Caspian is coming out, so two of my CP's are taking me to see it. I'm so excited!
Please continue to pray for my CB friends, especially Jaden as he is back in the hospital for a GJ tube...   ...and for Audrey who earned her wings a couple days ago. and for her family.

"All life is an experiment" --Ralph Waldo Emerson
Amanda :-) B+

THURSDAY, MAY 15, 2008 03:03 PM,
Hi All!
I just woke up from a nap, so my typing might be a little off. Tony came this morning and did a checkup (that's what i call it) on me. My BP is pretty good today. He unclogged my bags because they were super clogged! So, they're back to their job. I took some blood for my levels and weighed myself. I lost about four to five pounds in one week. Tony seems to think it's all the

fluid in me that it finally came out. I had a BM yesterday, so that might have been what was weighing me down also. I haven't had a BW in like 2–2½ weeks, so it was good that i had one. My meds are still running super slow, and it takes like 1½ hours to get one medicine in!!! I get super tired from waiting up from my meds some nights. I'm getting excited about my new catheter. It's going to have a triplet thing, too! So I can do my D-5 with some of my meds. nothing else medical-wise is going on today. I just woke up from a nap.

Tomorrow, i'm going to see Prince Caspian!!!! Yulanda and I are super excited.
Please continue to pray for my CB friends and my Aunt Dawny, and please say an extra special prayer for Audrey and her family.

"I arise in the morning torn between a desire to improve the world and a desire to enjoy the world. This makes it hard to plan my day." --E.B White
Amanda :-) B+

SATURDAY, MAY 17, 2008
Hey!
Whew. I just got home! I actually went out tonight to go shopping with my gift certificates i got for my birthday (which was in January!..lol). Today was a pretty good day. I woke up and went outside on the swing and just sat there for a while. We then decided to go to Walmart and Target because i had gift certificates, and i had to do a couple things there. I wanted to print out everybody's pictures for my poster but forgot the computer chip for it. So hopefully i'll get to that soon.

I got a couple crafts i can do this week when i'm bored, and then maybe save them as birthday presents for people. I actually wore a skirt out today, it was so nice. I didn't think it was going to fit me anymore because i gained weight, but it fits me perfectly! Yesterday was an okay day. I was a little low on energy for the morning but came around just in time for the movie (which was GREAT!). If you have no plans to go see it, i would rethink that. I loved the music in it, too. I had karate yesterday morning, and i bruised up my knuckles a little. I was bleeding on my uniform...lol. I'm almost done with all my white belt learning, so i'm getting excited!!!! Yolanda came yesterday (she went to the movies with us), and, after we came home from the movies, she gave me a bath. My mom had two interviews [for home nurses] this week. We have no luck finding good ones. the only good ones are Yolanda and Nicole. We lucked out with them! We might be taking a trip to Maine this summer, so they might come with us! Medical news-wise, my Dilantin levels are a bit low. But i'm not worrying about that yet since i'm not having a funny feeling like an aura. my liver function came back good. And i guess the rest is good.

My port is getting worse and worse, i tell ya! The other night, we waited about two hours for one med. to go through. It was supposed to run in a hour. i'm getting excited about my new catheter (yeah, who ever thought i would be super excited about a catheter).

That's really all that's going on. Tomorrow, i'm planning on just chilling and watching the first Narnia movie with my dad (he hasn't seen it before. i know it's a tragedy!)

I've been getting a lot of inspiration from songs lately by listening to my iPod. You really never know how much inspiration is in a song unless you really listen to the words. So, tonight I'm leaving you with one of my favorite inspirational songs.

Please continue to pray for my CB friends. Especially Jaden and for Audrey and her family.

"Feel the rain on your skin.
No one else can feel it for you.
Only you can let it in.
No one else, no one else
Can speak the words on your lips.
Drench yourself in words unspoken.
Live your life with arms wide open.
Today is where your book begins.
The rest is still unwritten."

--"Unwritten," by Natasha Bedingfield [9]

Amanda :-) B+
HAVE A GREAT WEEKEND!

MONDAY, MAY 19, 2008
Hi All!
Oh what a day! This morning, I didn't feel so well when i woke up, so I decided to go back to sleep for two more hours. I had a HUGE stomachache when I woke up, so that knocked me down for a loop this morning. When I finally decided to wake up, my mom had to weigh me for Tony since he's away fishing. I lost another pound and a half. I'm getting tired of losing, then gaining,

---

[9] © 2004 Gator Baby; EMI Music Publishers, Ltd. EMI Blackwood Music, Inc. Gracenote

then losing, then gaining. Why can't my weight just stay in the three same numbers? My grandma came over and watched Firehouse Dog with me. It's a really cute movie! Tomorrow, I might watch Dr. Dolittle 3. i begin to watch it in the hospital and then fell asleep, so i might finish it tomorrow. I had tutoring today. We really didn't do much except talk. work begins tomorrow (hopefully?).

Sunday was a really relaxing day. I just watched movies all day, which is good in a way. I saved some energy there. We watched the rest of Narnia. my dad didn't get the movie, how Aslyn represented Jesus, and the White Witch represented the Devil and temptation. So i might not even bother showing him the 2nd one..lol. I 'm doing pretty good medical-wise, just the weight loss, and that's pretty much it.

Please continue to pray for my CB friends, especially Jaden

"You will never be happy if you continue to search for what happiness consists of. You will never live if you are looking for the meaning of life." --Albert Camus
Amanda :-) B+

PS: My Fundraiser web page is up. here's the link if you want to check it out: www.amandasjourney.org

WEDNESDAY, MAY 21, 2008
Hi!
Ugh, what a ruff two days it has been. Yesterday morning, I woke up with cramps. (all girls know what that means!) I was in wicked pain all day and slept until 2:00PM yesterday. When I

woke up, i did a bit of my puzzle and watched some TV. Yolanda came last night and brought me a HUGE coloring book full of Tinkerbell and her friends. I colored two for two special people i'm going to see soon. Today, I feel OK. a bit better than yesterday, but i'm still feeling ugh. I needed some pain medicine this morning for my stomach. i felt like i was going to throw up. luckily my stomach meds kicked in after that. My grandma and aunt came over today and just hung out with me for a while. I had tutoring today, too. I took two tests and did some math. I'm glad it's only an hour because i'm not sure if i would be able to handle more time. it would probably put me into a seizure. At school, we only do a half an hour of math, so that's probably why i get stressed out so easily with work that lasts over a half an hour.

I weighed myself today and went back up to 122.8. I want to admit to myself that i'm really that much, but i had to tell myself i have extra clothing on than i did last time, so i'm not sure what my real weight is right now. That's all really that's going on medical-wise.

So, all you American Idol fans out there, what did you think about last night?! Archuletta won it all! He's going to be the next American Idol! I also have some pretty cool news to share with you all. My sister, dad, mom, and i (with a bunch of other family) are going to the American Idol concert!!!!!!!! I'm so excited! We even got really cool seats!!! So, watch A.I. tonight, and i'll post tomorrow about it.

Please continue to pray for my CB friends.
"Always remember, the future comes one day at a time"
--Dean Acheson

Amanda :-) B+

FRIDAY, MAY 23, 2008
Hi All!
I was going to update yesterday, but i had a so-so day. Let's start off by saying CONGRATULATIONS DAVID COOK!!!!! I really wanted David A. to win, but i think David Cook earned it. Yesterday was a so-so day. I had tutoring, and that went OK. Yesterday was just an off day. we'll leave it at that. My BP is doing good lately, but i also lost another 1½ pounds. Right now, i'm maintaining the 121 lbs., and i'm gonna try to keep that up! My bags from my G-and J-tube haven't been emptying like they usually do. The nurse unclogged them and everything, so i think that's a good sign for my stomach anyways. There's nothing much going on medical-wise except what i told you.

Tomorrow my family and I are going to try to make it up to Elmira for a fundraiser for UMDF!!!! My friends are doing it all! So give a huge clap for them! I'm going to be spending the night, so were going to be traveling with a lot of baggage...lol. My mom tried getting this oxygen thing, but i guess you have to reserve it, so my mom is going to try to reserve it for Double H this summer. I won't be able to update until Sunday or Monday because i know this trip will take a lot out of me, but it's something i've been looking forward to, so its worth it!

I got done with karate ½ hour ago, and my aunt and grandma are over to visit, so i'm going to go visit with them.
Have a nice Memorial Day everyone!
Please continue to pray for my CB friends.

"Faith is to believe what you do not see; the reward of this faith is to see what you believe."   --St. Augustine
Amanda :-) B+

Pain Control Classes and Morphine

SUNDAY, MAY 25, 2008
Hi Everyone!
Oh, this might be a VERY long journal entry because i have a lot to talk about. Let's do medical news first (ick!). So, Cheryl called my mom the other day and told her that i'm going to have to go to pain control class. What that means is, when i'm in a LOT of pain, my mom can start a morphine drip. But i can only use it if i can't handle any pain anymore. I'm not sure if I told you, my weight lately, it's 121. Yes, i'm trying to get it back up a couple more pounds. My BP has been pretty good.   I've been in a lot of pain with HA's and stuff. I think that's all the medical news for today!   Oh, also a reminder that i'm going in for surgery this Wed. Then, i'm back on June 10th for my tube replacements.

So i'm not sure all of you know but my two friends/sisters did a fundraiser for me and UMDF. I think they had to do it for some class? I'm not sure. It was really nice!   We woke up yesterday morning at 6:30AM. Yes, that's way too early for me. But i slept in the car (it was a three-hour drive). Kim and Phil (my friends' parents) led us up. When we got there, it was sooooo nice! They had green everywhere, and they had dancers, singers, tap dancers, a bake sale, raffles, the list went on. But what i liked about the whole thing was, when you donate $5.00, you get a free UMDF bracelet. I stayed there for about two hours, and then i was just getting tired and needed to do some IV's. We went back to the hotel (which was nice!). Oh, did i mention that Abby went?

I took a cat nap, and when i woke up, Kim, Phil, Brittany, and Brianna were there. We talked for a while (we went from one subject to the next...i think we did, like, 14 subjects in a matter of 15 minutes...lol). We went down to get something to eat. I had a bite of broth and later i had some ice cream. I wasn't feeling too well after i ate my ice cream, so i went back to the room and put on my pajamas and got into bed. When everyone came up, i was dozing on and off, and Kim's squeezies made me go to sleep faster..lol. I finally went to sleep, woke up the next morning, and we all had breakfast, and we left! It was such a nice fundraiser, and they made about $500.00 for UMDF, and a couple hundred they gave to us. I'm glad they raised money for Mito. So that was my mini vacation.

Please continue to pray for my CB friends. I really do care about what's going on with my CB friends. i'm just really resting up for my surgery on Wed. I know it's going to take a lot out of me.

Today, i'm going to use my friends Rachel's [favorite] qoute: "Disability is not a 'struggle' or 'courage in the face of adversity.' Disability is an art. It's an ingenious way to live." ~Neil Marcus
Amanda :-) B+

THURSDAY, MAY 29, 2008

Hi Everyone. This is Jacki, Manda's mom. Manda did well with surgery yesterday but is extremely weak. She came in under the eight ball anyway with a weight loss of eight pounds. I think we are going to LOVE the Hickman-catheter with triple lumens. Today is not a good day. Her two H's [hemoglobin and hematocrit, two measurements of her blood's volume and ability to carry oxygen] are very low, so I asked them to re-test before they consider transfusing. Let's pray they were just a fluke!!!! I want to thank you all for all your visits, thoughts, and prayers for our Manda. They mean more than you all know!!!!

This next part is from Amanda. She's too weak to speak, and you can hardly hear her, so she wrote it down for me to type. Message from Amanda: Extra prayers for Shawn Robert and Shannon. He went home on hospice. PLEASE, We Love them both!!!! Also for Jaden and all friends of CB. I will try to get to your sites soon, and I am praying for all my CB friends!!! B+

Quote of the Day: "We don't have Mitochondrial Disease. We have DREAMERS Disease." --Amanda Perrotta, B+

Thank you all. Love and prayers, The Perrotta Family xxoo

FRIDAY, MAY 30, 2008

Good Morning everyone. This is Jacki. Manda had a very rough day yesterday. She ended up having to have two transfusions. Her H's were very low. Her color this AM looks a little better, though. I think the blood helped. With her white count being so low, she is compromised to even more infection. Let's hope that will not happen!!!!! Manda was vomiting this morning. This yucchy green stuff. She was in tears because she is still in a lot of pain, and then the retching on top of it. Not good. Hopefully today will show some mercy on her. We can only hope. I don't have a quote from her today. Maybe later. Thanks to all for your prayers and thoughts. Please keep all CB friends in your prayers as Amanda would wish!!! Hope you all have a Great Day!!! I will try to keep you updated. Than you, and God Bless you all! Jacki

SATURDAY, MAY 31, 2008

Hi all. It's Jacki. Manda is still very weak and not feeling well at ALL!!! Yesterday, vomiting, and the same this AM. Last night, she had a clot behind her Hickman [catheter], so they had to TPA [tissue plasminogen activator] her [to dissolve the clot] twice. Tomorrow, they want her to on the telethon. They are coming to her room. The nurses said that they would get her all prettied up for the cameras. Other than that, nothing, just sleeping all the time, which is what she needs right now. Thank you ALL very much for all you do!!!! No quote for today. Hopefully soon. As Amanda would wish, please continue to pray for all of her CB friends and Families!!!! Just a quick little add on: Especially Sean Robert and Shannon. We love you both!!! Also Erik, who is going to his Senior Prom, that he has the time of his life, and ENERGY!!! And last, Manda wants to say happy belated birthday to her Godmother, Aunt Dawnie!!!!! Will update soon. May God Bless you all! Jacki

MONDAY, JUNE 02, 2008

Good Morning. Just a quick up date this AM. Manda is starting to feel a little stronger. We are going to try to get her up and out for a walk today. She might be having her tubes replaced today.

Amanda Perrotta

We will have to see. We had some sad news this morning. Sean Roberts went home to be with God early this morning. Please pray for his mom, Shannon, and all of their family at this most needed time. Amanda and I will miss him!!! Please also continue to pray for all of Manda's CB friends and family! Thank you to all!! Jacki

TUESDAY, JUNE 03, 2008

Hi Everyone!

It's Amanda here...YAY!! So, my mom has been keeping you posted i hear (Thank you, mom). As you know, i came into AMC [Albany Medical Center] for a new catheter for my TPNs and all my meds It's working GREAT now after some blocked transfusion, getting it unblocked, and me throwing up because of the blockages in my tubes. So i'm going home tomorrow....YAY!!! I'm super excited. Abby's birthday is on Friday, and i wanted to get her a present before her birthday, so now i have time! I had my tubes replaced today. it was quite painful. They gave me loopy medicine, but, trust me, that didn't help. My legs were shaking because part of it was, it hurt like nuts, and the other half was that i was having tremors..lol. And the girl was like, "you have to stay still now," and i was like, "How am i supposed to stay still when i can't control my body." but, hey, that's just the way they roll..lol. The procedure was an hour long because a student was doing it, and she pulled the wire back in and out about 20 times, so my stomach is a little fragile right now..lol. Nothing else is really going on right now.

I'm about to play a game of Wii with Jaden. Jaden is going home today!!!!! I'm so happy for him!!!! Jaden and I have spent a HUGE amount of time together in the past week, so it was nice just to hang out with him, and i hope to see him soon, but in a different circumstance. So, that's all the medical news for today. I'm glad i'm back and cannot wait to get around to everyone's CB sites to see what's going on. I wanted to thank you all for the encouraging messages and prayers. My mom reads them to me everyday.

Please continue to pray for my CB friends, and continue to pray for Shannon, Sean Roberts' mom as he passed away yesterday, and it's such a sad loss to me, his (our) nurses, and everyone!

Amanda :-) B+ (always!)

WEDNESDAY, JUNE 04, 2008

Hi all. This is Jacki. This is going to be quick. Manda is HOME!! YA-HOOOOO!!!!! She is VERY tired and sleeping right now. Manda did great yesterday for her tube change, but, at 5PM, her body had had enough. She went to sleep and never woke up until 10AM this morning. Thank you to everyone for thoughts and prayers! Also for ALL of Manda's CB friends and families. Please continue as Amanda would wish. One extra prayer, please: I met a mother next to our room. Her daughter is in EXTREME pain. I don't even know her name, but please pray for the family. I know what it is like to feel so helpless and watch your child in pain. Parents should not have to do this. So please pray for them. That's all for now. Please keep Shannon in your prayers (Sean Roberts' mom). Our thoughts and prayers are with them! Have a Great Day friends!!! Jacki

Amanda Perrotta

Home Again!

THURSDAY, JUNE 05, 2008

Hellooooo!!!!

Ahhh, it feels so GREAT to be home! I slept in my own bed last night, and i just woke up this morning around 11:30AM....lol. Yesterday was a bit overwhelming. Tony (my nurse) had to come. Anthem was delivering (and, may i point out, that i got my FAVORITE delivery guy yesterday!!!!!). Tony did the regular, checked my BP, changed my bags on my tubes and all that jazz!!! But through all that, i'm doing good. There's really not any medical news flashes, but i'm just happy to be home!

Tonight, everyone's coming over to my house for our fundraiser meeting. I'm excited because i get to hang out with Britany and Brianna!!!! Also, my old (not like old woman, just old...oh, you know what i mean) Speech Teacher might be bringing her son, Jacob. he's so cute, and i haven't seen him in, like, six months, so i'm excited to see him. We're going to celebrate Abby's birthday tonight with Frosty Paws ice cream, and tomorrow is her real birthday, so we're going to make a trip to PetSmart so that Abby can pick out her favorite toy or bone.

I'm making special cookies for the meeting tonight. One kind is all peanut butter, and the other is some kind of trail mix cookie. Hopefully they'll turn out well and everyone will like them. That's it for today (we should have a party because this entry was so short....YAY!!!!!!). Please continue to pray for my CB friends, especially Jaden, and extra special prayers for Shannon (Sean Roberts' mom)

346

"When humor goes, there goes civilization."   --Erma Bombeck
Amanda :-) B+

SATURDAY, JUNE 07, 2008
Helllooooo!!!
I thought I would do [this entry in] green because it's such a nice
HOT day out!   I'm loving this weather because i'm always cold,
so this week i don't need all the extra blankets. Medical stuff first
as always. Tony came yesterday and changed my dressing on my
catheter. We were having some minor trouble with my catheter
the day before, but now we finally have it under control. I've
been having some good movements in my stomach lately, which is
GREAT!   One step closer to eating actual food.   Nothing
otherwise. it's nice and short. I had some pain med. last night,
but, other then that, i'm doing good.

I had a GREAT time last night!!!! My whole family, Abby, and I
went to PetSmart for Abby to pick out her present. she picked
out three squeaky balls. oh, how she loves those balls!   I also got
her a portable bowl. It's like this little bowl I can take with me to
the hospital so, when she comes up, i actually have somewhere to
put her food besides my own hands...lol.   Then, we went to
Stewart's to get some ice cream. And we went to the lake where
i'm having my fundraiser. It's going to be a really nice fundraiser
just by looking at the lake and everything. When we got home,
we all sang happy birthday to Abby, and she FINALLY got her
Frosty Paws ice cream.

Today, i'm just going to relax, and later just me my mom and dad
are going out to eat, either at Friendly's, Applebee's, or the diner.
Nothing much is going on tomorrow.

I realize this entry was mostly about Abby, but what can i say? she's my baby!

Please continue to pray for my CB friends, especially Shannon.

"A person who has never owned a dog has missed a wonderful part of life." --Bob Barker

Amanda :-) B+

SUNDAY, JUNE 08, 2008

Hello All!

I kinda felt like a purple today...lol. Even though it doesn't match my background. So guess what?!   One of my port thingies is kinda blocked, so were going to have to TPA them sometime tomorrow. I might end up going to the hospital (hopefully not staying, though!). I haven't had my lipids/TPN's in like three days because of my catheter, so i'm lacking on energy right now. Hopefully when they TPA me tomorrow, i can get my TPN's/lipids ASAP!!!! I've been sleeping in until 11:30AM lately, so i must need the sleep somewhere in my body. OK, well that's really it with the medical terms.

Not much is going on in my life right now. Yolanda, my mom, and I are starting this healthy fitness thingy...lol. Every morning, all of us are going to go on a walk to McDonald's to get me my breakfast and for them to stay healthy...LOL!!!!!!! Plus, these days, i don't get out as much as i would like to or want to, so doing that every morning will get me some fresh air!   So just wanted to update you on that.

I've been watching a lot of movies, so i thought i might tell you what i'm planning to watch every week and then tell you a nice review, an Amanda review!...lol. So, this week, i'm planning on watching PS:I Love You and Step Up 2. Tonight, I'm watching The Circuit on ABC Family. What i'm really looking forward to is [the movie] CAMP ROCK!!!!!!

Please continue to keep all my CB friends in your prayers.

"Grief is like the ocean: It comes like waves, ebbing and flowing. Sometimes the water is calm, and sometimes it's overwhelming. All we can do is learn to swim" --Vicki Harrison

Amanda :-) B+

MONDAY, JUNE 09, 2008
Hi Everyone!
I just wanted to update you all. Right now we're packing to go to the ER. last night, another line clotted, and Dr. Adams wants me in right away. i haven't had my TPN's in four days, so my energy is seriously low. Please pray we're in and out.

And please continue to pray for my CB friends, especially Jaden, who is in the Hospital and isn't feeling well

Amanda :-) B+

TUESDAY, JUNE 10, 2008
Hi All!
Ohhh! So last night was the longest night of my life (OK, besides when i go to the haunted hayride..lol). So we didn't end up staying at AMC (THANK GOODNESS!). We found out that i

had a couple of blood clots in my catheter lines. It took four treatments to get them out!!! I had no energy last night, so it made that even more fun! I felt paralyzed from my stomach down because i was so out of energy. I told my mom i wasn't sure if i could get into the car. They were going to admit me, but they wouldn't be able to get my TPN's last night, so my mom and dad decided to take me home and start them. so i feel GREAT today! We had the STAT nurse do all my treatments for my clots, and she recommended that i see that blood Dr. that i went to a year ago. They think i have a blood disorder, i think (not sure on that, so...). The only GREAT thing about last night was that i had a HOT Resident Dr., and my mom and dad embarrassed me more than anything with him (ugh!). As soon as he came in the 2nd time, they were like, "Oh, Amanda, at least you got a cute Dr." I think my cheeks and his cheeks turned soooo red, but he was already married, so i guess i didn't have a chance...LOL!

Anyways, i'm back now and feel pretty good. my blood sugar was low last night, i think, because i felt like i was going to pass out, so i had a bit of orange juice, and that helped. So, that was my fun and exciting night!

I'm going to watch PS: I Love You today, so i hope i can get all of you a good review! My sister saw it in Korea, and she said it was pretty good, and Kelly left me a message in my guest book and said it was good, so we'll see.
Please keep all my CB friends in your prayers, especially Jaden. I saw his mom last night, and his right lung collapsed, and he hasn't moved. please leave him a message in his guest book for him to have a B+ day.

"Sometimes in our lives we all have pain
We all have sorrow
But if we are wise
We know that there's always tomorrow "
                   -- A lyric from Lean on Me by Bill Withers [10]
Amanda :-) B+

WEDNESDAY, JUNE 11, 2008
Hello There!
Not much medical news to report today. Tony came and did my blood, rebandaged my catheter, and changed my bags. I'm having a lot of icky stuff coming out of my bags today. more in the J than the G, but i have that once in a while. Tony's getting me a sugar tester so that when i know my sugar is low i have to have frosting or something to make it come back up again. Dr. Porter (the blood Dr.) ordered some more tests on my blood that Tony took today, and she wants more blood for other tests when Tony comes again. I lost another pound, but Tony said that i probably lost it because i haven't had my TPN's since when i had the blood clots, so it may take another day or so for me to gain back my weight. I think that's pretty much all the medical news for now.

So i watched three movies the past few days, and i'll tell you about all of them. first, let's start with "The Circuit." It was OK. If you're a HUGE race car fan, then it would be the perfect movie for you, and there was way too much R rated stuff in a family movie, so that's that one. I watched "PS: I Love You" today, and it was such a cute movie, so i'll give it four thumbs up. there was some R-rated stuff in there, so, kids, don't watch it!!! And last

---

[10] © 1972 EMI Publications

but not least, today i watched, "The Eye" with my grandma and OH MY GOSH!   I jumped so high i could probably touch the ceiling, it was too scary!!!! It made my heart skip a beat or two. I was like shaking through the whole thing and probably will have nightmares tonight.   But if you like scary/mystery movies, then five thumbs up it is, but in my case, i give it half of a thumb...lol. My movies for the next couple of days are going to be: "Over Her Dead Body." it's supposed to be really funny!!!   And I haven't seen "Shrek 3" yet, so i want to see that. So that's my review for today!

I also watched Oprah yesterday, and WOW!   what an inspirational episode. It was about the show "Crazy Sexy Cancer" and about a man who has been diagnosed with cancer and only has a few months to live, and he was such an inspiration! He did this lecture on how the people you're really not fond of...you should always see the good in every person, how you shouldn't complain about things because you're lucky to be alive, and just the most inspirational stuff i have ever heard before. So, please, if you didn't see that episode yesterday, PLEASE YouTube it because it will make you think more about what you do everyday and how you should appreciate every moment even if you're stuck in a house all day.

Please continue to pray for my CB friends, especially Jaden, who is getting his port taken out, that the surgery goes well.

"Life is either a daring adventure or nothing." --Helen Keller
Amanda :-) B+

Always Seeing the Positive

THURSDAY, JUNE 12, 2008
Hi ALL!

So, first i wanted to tell you why I put this picture up. This is of me and Abby right after i got diagnosed with Mito. I know I look soooo different (well, it was 2006!). I put this picture up, not just to remind me of our upstairs, but to remind me of never seeing the positive or seeing a different picture of things when i first got diagnosed. i was just a regular 14 year old. I didn't know this was going to be my future, but i'm thankful it is. I'm thankful I can teach other people and myself about living life. So that's why i put this picture up.

So, there's only a bit of medical news today. i wanted to post today so my short term memory loss wouldn't get to me...LOL! This morning, i didn't get any blood return from one of my cath lines, so i hope a blood clot isn't planning a stay. I lost another pound. don't ask me how, i just did. All i know is, i'm never letting myself get down to what i was at this time last year—92 pounds! I think that's really all. YAY!

Nothing much is going on otherwise. later, i'm going to do my patio garden with my dad. I usually do the garden with my dad in the backyard every summer, but, since i can't get into it, were going to do both a patio and grass garden. On Sat., the family is going to get some cool fireworks in Massachusetts i think?

Please continue to pray for my CB friends, especially Jaden, who is still in the hospital.

"Hold fast to dreams, for if dreams die, life is a broken winged bird that cannot fly." --Langston Hughes
Amanda :-) B+

SATURDAY, JUNE 14, 2008
Hi Everyone!
So, it's 1:16PM right now, and we haven't left for Massachusetts yet, and i'll tell you why later!   I didn't get to update last night because our family decided to go out and get something to eat, and then we went to Walmart for some stuff for Father's Day. I'm making my famous pasta salad for tomorrow.

I got my haircut last night. i decided i'm going to start growing it out (just for something new), and, today, i dyed my hair a little bit darker than my original color, but i LOVE it! So, onto the medial news.   I felt GREAT yesterday. there wasn't much going on medically yesterday.   This morning, I woke up and had a weird feeling, like i was going to throw up, and i did. I thought my tubes were clogged again because that's what happened when i was in the last time. I felt fine after i threw up and went back to bed, but, when i got up again, my stomach was all yucky, and i felt tired still and just not up to par. I feel fine now!   My mom called Cheryl, and Cheryl told her those are signs of septice [sepsis]. My mom took my temp, and i'm 99 i think. Cheryl said if it gets to 99.9 to bring me in. So, i'm praying it doesn't go up anymore.

I tried to take my blood sugar tests this morning when i felt yucky, but i forgot how to do the needle..lol. So i was like, ughh, whatever!   I can't eat or drink anything until further notice, which is killing me because i'm soooo thirsty, and the D-5 isn't helping at all! Just a little water would help. So, we'll see what happens when Cheryl calls back later or my mom calls her. In the meantime, please pray i don't have to make another trip to the ER. So that's why we're not going to get our stuff for the 4th of July yet. I can't go anywhere!!!

My sister, Dahea, just painted my toenails and nails to make me feel prettier...LOL. I didn't get a chance to watch Over Her Dead Body yesterday, but i have a feeling i'll get a chance today. I did watch part of Iron Man but didn't like it that much. Yolanda brought it, and i felt so bad that i wasn't getting into it.

At Walmart last night, i bought some more fabric to make another cover for my bags...lol. I might start making them for friends who have any kind of bag, but first i want to see how long it will take me. Please continue to pray for my CB friends, especially Mr. Jaden. he's still in the hospital.

"If you can imagine it, you can achieve it; if you can dream it, you can become it."   --William Arthur Ward
Amanda :-) B+

MONDAY, JUNE 16, 2008
Hi All!
Don't worry, i'm still here...lol. Yesterday just flew away from me, so i didn't get a chance to update. I'm doing much better today. i think the whole throwing up thing was just a tease or something. I was still a bit tired yesterday but feel fine today. My J-tube bag has stuff coming out of it like it's candy!   And, well, i can say for

myself, it doesn't look like candy...lol. There's not much going on medical-wise, so thankfully this will be a short update.

I hope you all had a nice Father's Day. Our family had a picnic and had steak and all different kinds of salad. I made my pasta salad, which i think turned out OK. It's always nice to see everyone. After the family left, i was hungry, so we went to this homemade ice cream stand which makes the BEST ice cream (let's just say, we only go once or twice a year), and i got the specialty blue moon...lol. It's actually blue!!! I also started my Mito poster, and you'll never guess what i did!!! OK, so i printed all of my friends' pictures out, and, when i got to Penelope's, it wouldn't print out, so i was like, "OK, i'll print it out separately," so i ended up forgetting all about Poor Penelope, and i thought i had everyone on my poster when i glued them yesterday, and this morning i was like, "where's Penelope?!?!" So, Penelope you're going to have to go in the middle of the poster with me because i'm definitely not leaving you out!!! But, other than that, the poster is coming along good. i'm thinking of ideas as i go, so we'll see.

Today, Minnie (my grandma) is going to come over, and i'm going to start my cover for my bags...LOL. I'm not sure how long it will take, so that's why i'm starting today. i really want to have it done by Thursday, which is Carolyn's school graduation (no, she's not graduating, just singing), but we'll see.
Please continue to pray for all my CB friends, especially Jaden.

"Life is like a library owned by an author: In it are a few books which he wrote himself, but most of them were written for him."
--Harry Emerson Fosdick

Have a GREAT day!
Amanda :-) B+

MONDAY, JUNE 16, 2008
Hi!
Quick update!
I'm going to the ER tomorrow because i have Dumping Syndrome [a condition where the contents of the stomach "dump" into the small intestine before being properly digested]. I'll update when my laptop is charged!
Prayers for all my CB friends!
Amanda :-) B+

Above: Lou, Amanda, and Jacki at the airport in Memphis
Below: Amanda and Carolyn and their dog, Buddi, Summer 1995

Amanda and Carolyn at Santa's Workshop,

Amanda Perrotta

Above: Amanda at the beach in New Jersey.
Below: Amanda in 4th grade at Oakwood Christian School, 2002

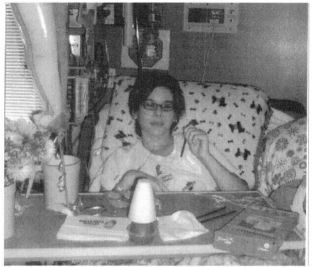

Above: Working on an art project at Albany Medical Center
Below: Christmas 2007 at AMC

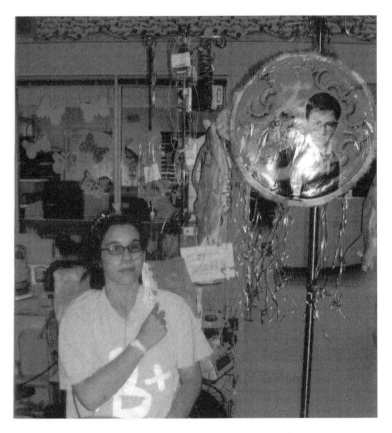

Having a Harry Potter and Tinkerbell party in the playroom at
Albany Medical Center.

Above: Chilling with Abby in Maine
Below: In Maine with Minnie working on her cousin Liam's
Christmas present.

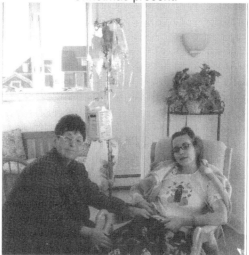

Above: Amanda and Carolyn at the Times Union Center for the
American Idol concert
Below: Pippy trying to keep Amanda awake because she
doesn't have her bi-pap on.

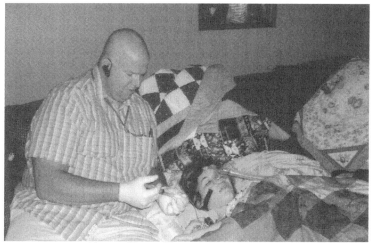

Above: Nurse Tony serving at home.
Below: Watching *Night at the Museum* at home with dad,
October 2008

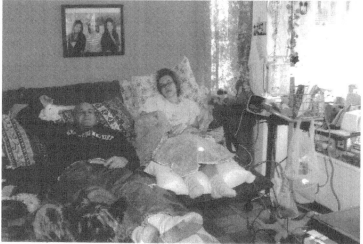

Above: Amanda and Abby
Below: Sleeping at home

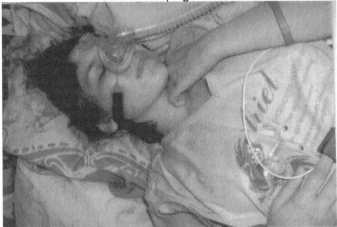

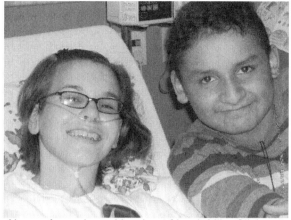

Above: Amanda and her best friend, Mike Silvia, at
Sunnyview Hospital, December 2007
Below: New Year's Eve at Sunnyview

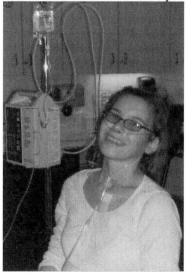

Amanda Perrotta

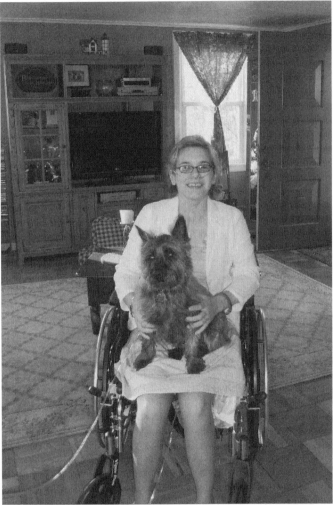

Amanda and Abby for her Confirmation, May 2008

Above: On the Albany Medical Center roof to watch
the fireworks, July 2008
Below: With mom and Maude after a Silly String fight

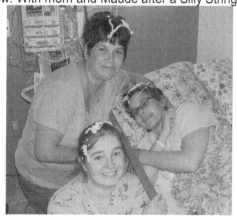

WARNING!!

This is my way of making money this summer!

All Medical Supplies dropped in Amanda's Bed Cost.

Flush syringes = 50¢
Caps of all types = 25¢
Gloves = 50¢ per glove
Tubing = 75¢
Alchohol wipes = 25¢

Any other syringe types = 50¢
Q-tips = 35¢
Guaze = 30¢
Masks = $1.00
Any type of personal iteams = 50¢ - $1.00

made by Amanda   Suggested by

Above: Amanda's "Warning Sign" at AMC
Below: At home with her birthday cake for dad

Above: Finishing the 3-D Cinderella's castle
puzzle with Dahea
Below: With Gem the therapy dog at AMC

Amanda Perrotta

Above: The family at the fundraiser, Snyder's Lake, August 2008
Below: Amanda's actual journal entry for "Lesson #15"

"You can either write or tell about it"
LESSON #15
16 yr.

September 17th 2008 When you have
an illness or if you just have
an issue you should always
either talk or write about it.
Thats one of the reasons I
started this journal, this reason
and a couple others. I dont
like talking to people much,
so I feel like writing in
this journal is like talking
to a person. When I write
about my feelings in here.
I dont get as mad, sad or
frustrated as much. This is
a very short lesson. But
it needed to be told.

♡, Amanda B+ F.R.O.G

At the beach in Maine, October 2008

Sometimes our life's road brings obstacles and setbacks that cause us to take three steps forward and then get thrown two steps back. For a season, the clouds never seem to break and the rain just pours and pours. But usually, with time, we find the strength to make that extra effort to regain our footing and reclaim our lost steps. In Amanda's case, however, instead of three steps forward and one or two steps back, she faced three steps back and only one or two forward. Sometimes she was only able to muster the energy to make one small step forward and conclude, in her ever-positive way, that it just required a little more time, another week, just a little more effort, to recover her lost two steps.

At this point in Amanda's life, her mounting problems and accumulating medical conditions resulted in increasingly backward steps at every turn. Her spirits remained high, though, and her outlook was so vigilantly focused on others that, backward steps and all, her life only radiated love and joy to all around her. In Amanda's unique way, she constantly turned every dark day into a beacon of life and gratitude.

TUESDAY, JUNE 17, 2008

Hi all. It's Jacki. Manda is back in Albany Medical Center, in our shared room with Jaden and Jess. We really don't know what is up yet other than she is vomiting and dumping through her J bag. The color is very gross. She is running a low-grade fever on and off. Also, we came in by ambulance because of chest pains. We don't know what's going on there either. They ran blood cultures and took some scans of her chest and stomach. No results as of yet. They have her back on morphine for pain. Will update soon. Please, as Manda would want, continue to pray for all CB friends and Families, especially Jaden and Jess, and The Lawton Family (Kylie). Thanks to all. God Bless!!! Jacki

WEDNESDAY, JUNE 18, 2008

Hi all. Manda is still in a lot of pain and still vomiting. They still don't know what is up. Not all the tests have come back. I am thinking a good stomach virus. I hope. We have another clot, too, so they have to address that. We did get some of the results from Dr. Porter. Manda's protein C and S are low [two of many proteins made in the liver that are essential to the normal clotting of blood], which is not great because that puts her at greater risk for clots. Do not know how or what they do for that yet. They did mention another med. Other than that, she is tired, but her spirits are wonderful as always!!!! Will update soon. Please continue to pray for all CB friends and families, esp: Jaden, Gina, Kylie. Thanks to all for thoughts and prayers. May God Bless you all!!!! Jacki

WEDNESDAY, JUNE 18, 2008

Hi all. It's Jacki again. Just a new update that we didn't expect. Not great news here. Dr. Adams came in earlier and told us that Manda has an enlarged liver. She has a pseudo obstruction, with barium still in the small intestines from the test done in March, and her G-J tube has migrated up the esophagus. Not what we expected or were prepared for!!! We are meeting with GI and surgery Drs. some time tomorrow. Manda's in a lot of pain. We are also requesting no more residents see her—ONLY her doctors. Please say extra prayers!!!! Also for ALL CB friends and Family!!! Thanks to all. May God Bless!!! Jacki
P.S. I almost forgot. She also has another blood clot :{

Amanda Perrotta

FRIDAY, JUNE 20, 2008

Hi all. Amanda wanted me to update in purple. Well, Manda is still in a lot of pain . They did repair her G-J tube yesterday. Both were migrating up the esophagus. She is still retching and very nauseous. Today brings a dye study down in VIR because she is still having many blood clots. If the test comes back that it is mechanical, she would need more Heparin [a blood thinner] added to IV's, not just put in her lumens. But if it is not mechanical, she will be moved to the PICU for IV's of Heparin or Coumadin [another blood thinner]. I will let you know. No word on what they can do for obstruction as of yet. Did say they are limited. Not Good! Please continue to pray for all CB friends especially Jaden, Kylie, Gina, Erik. Thanks to all. God Bless!!! Jacki

Just an add on. Please pray. Manda is going in for surgery. Her Hickman [catheter] snapped with ethanol in the lumen. They have to move the whole Hickman to another spot (they think the neck). Will try to update. Other test on hold now for clots!!

SATURDAY, JUNE 21, 2008

Hi all. Manda had a very rough day yesterday. They did not get to do any of the dye studies for her blood clots due to the fact that the lumen and tube snapped off with ethanol in it. They could not get access to place another Hickman catheter. Manda now has a pick line with triple lumen near the site of the old Hickman, which only lasted three weeks. Still have to watch for clots.

Manda woke up during [the operation] screaming in pain for thirty minutes because they couldn't find access to get a line in. Very sore and still retching and nauseous. Also added is a test for her gall bladder, which is common when using TPNs and lipids, so we will see. Then, some time soon, we will address the obstruction!!! One step at a time. Life Line first, then everything else. A thank you to all friends and family, for everything you all do!!! We are truly blessed and VERY GRATEFUL for you ALL!!!! Please continue to pray for all CB friends and families, as Manda would wish!!! Esp: Jaden, Kylie, Gina, Erik!!!! I will update soon. God Bless! Jacki

SUNDAY, JUNE 22, 2008

Hi all. Manda is still in pain, but I think they are getting a better grip on it. Today brings lots of rest and a visit with Abby and her father and sisters. Abby ALWAYS helps!!!! She is still retching and very nauseous. The Zofran [to prevent nausea after surgery] helps with that. Tomorrow brings a HIDA scan for the gall bladder [in which a radioactive material called hydroxy iminodiacetic acid is injected into the bloodstream to trace its route through the liver and bile ducts] (will let you know results). So far, PICC-line [a Peripherally Inserted Central Catheter inserted into the arm and run up into the vena cava near the heart] is doing its job. Will update when more news. Thanks to ALL for love and your support!!! Please continue as Manda wishes to pray for all CB families and friends, esp: Jaden, Kylie, Gina, Erik, Sharon, and the boys. God Bless!!! Jacki

MONDAY, JUNE 23, 2008

Hi All. Amanda is very weak this AM. Pain not good at all. They changed her meds for pain to Dilaudid and Morphine for breakthroughs. And no more Toradol because of her enlarged liver. We are just hanging out waiting for the HIDA scan. Manda's sleeping a lot. That's about all for now. Will update when more news. Please continue to pray, as Manda would want for all CB families and friends!! Esp: Jaden, Kylie, Sharon and the boys, Erik, Gina!!! Thank you All!!! God Bless! Jacki

TUESDAY, JUNE 24, 2008

Hi All. Manda's HIDA scan showed only 17% use of her gall bladder and reflux in the small intestines. That means the gall bladder has to come out, and they don't know yet what they are going to do about the small intestines! Manda's surgeon will not be here until Thursday! We don't have a scheduled time yet. Dr. Adams is concerned this will put more stress on her body (the surgery). Right now, she is sleeping a lot, and that's good. Manda's levels have been running a little low, too, so they are watching them. That's all for right now. Her sprits are good even though she keeps asking to go home!!! Abby was here last night, and that really HELPS!!! Thanks to all, and, as Manda wishes, please continue to pray for all CB families and friends. Especially Jaden, Kylie and Josh, Sharon and the boys, Gina and Erik, that he makes it home for graduation!!!! Will update soon. God Bless! Jacki

WEDNESDAY, JUNE 25, 2008 08:43 AM,

Hi All! Quick update. We don't know if they are going to remove Manda's gall bladder. Why? Manda has a disease of the gall bladder called Biliary Dyskinesia [which prevents it from functioning correctly during digestion whereby bile backs up and cause pain] due to the Mito. They don't promise surgery would or could help the pain because the nerves are involved, which they can't remove. Don't know yet what is going to happen. Will update soon. Manda is more comfortable now being on Dilauded and Morphine. Still retching and nauseous, but Zofran helps some. Thanks to all for everything!!! Esp: Diane for the wonderful basket of goodies and water. :-)

Please, as Manda would wish, continue to pray for all CB friends and families, esp. Jaden, Kylie and Josh, Cody, Gina, Sharon and the boys, Erik, who [was discharged and] went home, that he will be up for graduation!! Congrats Erik!!! God Bless ALL!! Jacki.

~~~~~

Hi ALL! It's me, Amanda. I haven't been able to update because of the pain i'm in, and i'm just sleeping a lot. I wanted to let you know i'm doing fine, and i appreciate the prayers and for everyone who signs my guest book. my mom reads them to me everyday. i look forward to them! Please continue to pray for my CB friends. Amanda :-) B+

There Are Worse Things That Could Happen

THURSDAY, JUNE 26, 2008
Hi Everyone!
I bet you all missed my colors huh?..lol. Anyways i'm back. still not feeling as good as i want to, but they finally have my pain

under control with meds so that i can update!   So, onto the medical stuff as always!   Dr. Weber can't do my surgery unless we want to wait two weeks, and we kinda want to get out of this joint, so were not waiting. So, Pretty P (Dr.) is setting up my surgery with the adult surgeon. She said they'll speak to us either tomorrow or Monday. i'm hoping tomorrow because that will give me a better chance of going home for the 4th of July! No much other medical news. still nauseous, retching, and in a lot of pain, but i'm not complaining. there's worse things that could happen!

I wanted to thank you all for being so supportive through the last week and half. i'm so blessed to have so many good friends and family. My mom and grandma are planning on getting me out [and around] in a second. i really don't like moving around because it makes the pain come faster i realized. But you have to get out once in a while. OK, well, i'll leave you with that.

Please continue to pray for all my CB friends and a special prayer for my buddy, Cody.

"There are no classes in life for beginners: right away you are always asked to deal with what is most difficult."
--Rainer Maria Rilke

Amanda :-) B+

THURSDAY, JUNE 26, 2008
Hi All. Manda's on her way to surgery now. Please say extra prayers!!! Will update soon!!! Please continue to pray for all CB friends and families!!! Thanks to All!!! God Bless. Jacki

FRIDAY, JUNE 27, 2008
Hi All. Manda had her surgery!!! She did OK. They had to sedate her afterward because she was in so much pain, and her heart rate was so high. Now, she is on the monitors. I am going to try to sleep a little. I will update a little later. Thanks to all!! Keep praying! And for all CB friends and families!! God Bless.
Jacki

SATURDAY, JUNE 28, 2008

Hi All. Manda is doing OK—still in a lot of pain from surgery but to be expected. They have her on a PCA [Patient-Controlled Analgesia—a system by which Amanda can push a button and medicate herself when she feels pain] of Dilaudid and are also pushing IV Dilaudid for a pain breakthrough. Manda's spirits are good, as always!!!! I don't know how she does it. She NEVER complains. The doctors said it's just going to take more time for recovery for her due to her condition and that she is not mobile, but she will do it!!! She hates the electric compressions on her legs as they squeeze too hard (to prevent blood clots). Today brings trying to move a little and maybe Cody's birthday party. We will see!!! I will update soon. Hopefully it will be Amanda next. Thanks to all for your messages. I read them to her every day; she loves them!!! Please continue to pray for ALL CB friends and families! God Bless, Jacki.

9:04 AM:

Amanda Perrotta

Hi All. I think we have the pain under control. They are using the PCA but with a basal and bolus of Dilaudid [whereby she is receiving a predetermined amount of pain medication, the basal level, while still able to press a button if she needs more, the bolus]. Manda is so VERY weak, but her body has been through some much. She gets frustrated with the weakness (my fighter, thank God). Of course, her spirits are good. She just sleeps mostly. She did want me to send a message to Natalie. She wanted to know if you got to meet her doctor (Dr. Adams). She told him you were going to be at the conference. Not much else going on. Still on monitors for heart and compressions for circulation (to prevent clots), which she hates but is tolerating. Will update soon. Thanks to all for everything you do!!! Please continue to pray for all CB friends and families as Manda wishes!!!!! God Bless!!!! Jacki

P.S. Manda misses you, Maude (RN).

MONDAY, JUNE 30, 2008

Hi all. Manda looks a little better today. She actually is awake right now. I tried to get her to update. Not ready yet. I can't wait. She does a much better job at this. Today, I am going to try to get her out in her chair for a small walk!!! Still on compressions and monitor. I think she is getting used to it.

Manda's liver is enlarged, and her enzymes are high. Not good. Her liver is now compromised, but expected (from the TPN's and lipids). It's a doubled-edged sword. We would not have her if we didn't use them, but they kill the liver. The doctors are watching this closely.

Enough of the medical. Manda's spirits are wonderful!!! She can't wait until the fourth of July. She LOVES fire works! That's all for now. Will update soon. Thank you to ALL!!! Your thoughts and prayers are Truly appreciated !!! Please continue to pray for all CB friends and families as Manda wishes, especially Jaden, whom she misses sooo much, Cody, Kylie and Josh, Gina, Erik, and Sharon and the boys. God Bless. Jacki.

TUESDAY, JULY 01, 2008

Hi all. I didn't get to update late yesterday or this AM because Manda had surgery again yesterday at 3PM. Not expected at all!! Manda's tubes migrated, and bile backed up into her system. Wonderful! The doctors replaced the tubes with larger and different ones. She did OK, very sore and tired. Today, I went home for a couple hours to see Carolyn Rose and the house. Minnie (my mom) stayed with Manda. They had fun. They watched a movie. Dr. Hoppins and Dr. Adams came in and said they could do no more for Manda than keep her comfortable. We already knew this, but it is still never easy to hear!! :(

But on the positive side, today brings her comfort, and she is out of her room, in her chair, and making a craft. Ye-Ha!!!!! She is one tough cookie! Thanks to all for everything! Please continue to pray, as Manda wishes, for ALL CB friends and families. Esp: Jaden, Cody, Kylie and Josh, Sharon and the boys, Gina, and Erik!!! God Bless. Jacki.

THURSDAY, JULY 03, 2008

Hi all. I haven't updated because we didn't have any new news. Manda's right, lower side has been very painful and tender. They think it could be her appendix. They did an ultrasound and are looking at it today. Don't know anything yet. Other than that, everything is still the same. Still on monitors and electric compressions (to prevent blood clots). Manda was a little more perky yesterday!!! Brit and Bree came and did her toe nails. :-) Thanks, Girls!!! I think Amanda loved it!!! Still on the PCA and sleeping a lot. That's it for now. Thanks to ALL for all you do!!! Please, as Manda wishes, continue to pray for ALL CB friends and families, esp: Jaden, Cody, Kylie and Josh, Gina, Erik, Sharon and the boys!!!! God Bless! Jacki.

FRIDAY, JULY 04, 2008

Hi all. Happy 4th of July! So, good news: not Amanda's appendix!!!!! But a new plan: Dr. Qualia (GI) is making arrangements for Manda to be transferred to Tuft's in Boston to see the motility specialist some time next week. Manda has to have a Manometry [a measure of the pressure within an organ] to tell us if she has neuropathy or myopathy in the GI system, or both. That is the news that yesterday brought. Today, hopefully, rest and some 4th fun.

Manda's Aunt Mimi and Woody (cousin) brought all kinds of 4th goodies for her!!! Thanks guys! Also, one of Carolyn's teachers, Miss Russell, did, too! Thanks! And Manda's teacher, Diane, brought her a Miss Liberty crown (lights up). Thank you, Diane! I think she will be set. I will keep you updated on our trip to Boston as soon as I know. For now that's all.

Manda is still the same: good spirits, sleeping a lot, good pain management. Manda wants to thank Rina for the CD. She LOVED it! And Natalie, for her cards and letters for her room. They are GREAT! Thanks to all for everything you do!!! We Love you all. Please continue to pray, as Manda wishes, for ALL CB friends and families. Esp: Jaden, Rina, who just came home from the hospital, Kylie and Josh, Gina, Sharon and the boys, and Erik. God Bless! Jacki.

SATURDAY, JULY 05, 2008
Hi All! Manda had a Great 4th!!! She slept ALL day then was ready. Manda's nurse, Peggy, took us out to the top of the parking garage to see the Albany fireworks!!! We didn't stay to long, but she did well! Manda loved them. Abby too! Carolyn Rose and Aunt Mimi and Sarah were there to celebrate with her, too. Oops, dad too! Don't want to forget dad. After that, the nurses and Manda came back to her room, and they did her poppers, from Miss Russell :). Also yesterday, Manda received a special delivery from Marybeth and the Lena Gang. BALLOONS!!!! She LOVED them, thank you guys. You are so sweet!!! Thanks also, Marybeth, for leaving Manda messages every day. :)

That's about all for now. I know it's not much news, but I try to keep you up, not only on the tough moments, but the good few and far between. We have to run with those when we are blessed to have them!!! Thanks to all. Please, as Manda wishes, continue to pray for ALL CB friends and families. Esp: Jaden, Erik, Kylie and Josh, Gina, Sharon and the boys, and Malisa, who, if it wasn't for her, I don't know what Manda would do, nor myself. She has been such a wonderful role model for all with Mito!!! And a friend!!! God Bless! Jacki.

SUNDAY, JULY 06, 2008
Hi Everyone!
It's me Amanda! I thought i would surprise you all today. my mom kinda got a break from typing..lol. I'm going to let you all know about my medical stuff like usual first, and then i'll get to the fun stuff! So, my pain management is good. i finally figured out that before i got the bathroom, i press the button on the PCA [patient-controlled analgesia], and i won't hurt as much. Today is when all the calls are being made for Boston. i think we're just waiting for an EMC [Emergency Management Coordinator] for the ride in the ambulance.

They tested my urine yesterday because it's been a really dark brown, and my lower back was hurting, so they wanted to make sure it wasn't my liver, and the test results came back this AM, and it's normal—everything's normal! I thanked God for that about 1,000 times! My H's [hemoglobin and hematocrit] are low once again. we did the boost of iron, but obviously that didn't work, so now they're thinking of giving me a blood transfusion before i leave. I think that's all the medical news for now!

So, I wasn't updating because i couldn't find a way to make myself comfortable while typing, so i finally found a way! I enjoyed myself on the 4th. we watched the fireworks from the top of the hospitals roof. i thought it was just going to be me and the other boy, but there were like 500 people up there. i got a pretty good view. It was a nice 4th, though, to be in the hospital. My aunt, uncle, and cousins are coming in from out of town today. i'm very excited about that! That's all that's going on. I have to tell you guys a funny story, though, because i just think it's funny.

So, when Dr. Qualia (GI Doc) came in, he mentioned CHOP [The Children's Hospital of Philadelphia] (where Darcie and Malisa go) and, after i heard that, i was like, "CHOP!!!! REALLY!!!???!!!" It was sooo funny because i thought i was going to CHOP for my surgery, so, when i heard i wasn't, i was like, "awwww!" But if you saw my face, it would have been funnier.

I wanted to thank you all for leaving me sooo many messages. my mom and sister tried reading them all to me. I'm very thankful i have so many good friends and family. My dad took my letters home, and, when i go home, i'll put them up. thank you for all the letters and notes.

Marybeth and Leena-Thank you for my colorful balloons! Balloons are my favorite when i'm in the hospital, so i was very excited when i got them.

Please continue to pray for all my CB friends!!!!! I'm sorry i haven't checked in on anyone in a while, but i've been sleeping a lot, but the first thing when i get better is to stop in on you all and see what's going on. I'm thinking of you all everyday and praying for you all at night.

"There are no classes in life for beginners: right away you are always asked to deal with what is most difficult."

--Rainer Maria Wilke

Amanda :-) B+

Amanda Perrotta

MONDAY, JULY 07, 2008
Hi All!
Not to much medical news to report today. They're starting all the papers today for Boston, and i think most of the phone calls start today as well for the trip. The Dr. came in earlier this morning and told my mom and me that I don't need a blood transfusion just yet. But, if they [my hepatic enzymes] continue to drop, then we'll start talking more about it. I made a mistake yesterday about the whole liver thing. My liver is slightly enlarged. I was talking about how they tested me for a UTI [urinary tract infection], but that test came back normal, so all is well there. That's pretty much all the medical news.

Yesterday, I had a lot of visitors, but there were three special people who came. My Respite Workers, Yolanda and Nicole, came with their mother, who is the sweetest person you could meet. It was an honor to meet her. she blessed me and prayed with me. Thank you for coming, Yolanda and Nicole and your mom.

Today i'm going to try to get out and take on Peggy with a Wheelchair/IV pole race...lol. It's going to be hard steering both an IV pole and a wheelchair, but we'll try our hardest. It will be good fun!

Last night, I started writing a children's book about Abby and how she works for me. I actually finished it! I would love to publish it, but I don't know how to go through the making a book thing. We'll see!
That's all for today!
Please continue to pray for my CB friends.

"Years teach us more then books"   --Berthold Auerbach
Have a GREAT, B+ Day!
Amanda :-) B+

TUESDAY, JULY 08, 2008
Hi guys. It's me Jacki. Manda is not feeling well enough and is
tired today, so she asked me to update. Lucky you. So, just
waiting to go to Boston and trying to keep her comfortable!!!
Today, she looks wiped out again! Yesterday was great. Well,
great to us. Any day Manda is with us and with it   is
WONDERFUL!!!!! Yesterday, she did a craft in her room and
started her book on Abby (which, I think is just so great). Manda
has such a way with writing. Today brings resting and waiting as
usual. Will keep you updated. Thanks to all for everything!!!
You are all so loving and amazing!!!

As Manda wishes, please continue to pray for ALL CB friends and
families, esp: Jaden, Kylie and Josh, Gina, Sharon and the boys,
Erik (that he enjoyed his Graduation Party with energy), and
Cody. Minnie, for Her visits every day. Kim and the clan, for
keeping me in line, and, of course, Aunt Dawnie, with her loving
way as always when she herself is not well!!!! Thanks from the
bottom of our hearts!!!! God Bless!   Jacki.

WEDNESDAY, JULY 09, 2008
Hi all. Manda is just back from the OR. They did a colonoscopy
in preparation for our trip to Boston. She has a build up of stool
from the TPN's and Lipids. She is now having problems with her
colon. They tried flushing, hoping to release some of the pressure

and stool, but they might have to repeat on Friday. Let's hope Not!!!! Manda is resting and very sleepy. Her color is not great, but she is one tough cookie!!!! Hope to make arrangements soon for Boston. Doctor is on vacation as of now. Will update soon.

Please, as Manda wishes, continue to pray for all CB friends and families! Esp: Jaden, who is now here in the hospital, Gina who is on her way in, Kylie and Josh, Sharon and the boys, Erik, Cody, And all who are at need at this time. Thanks to all for everything you do everyday!!! Special thanks to Aunt Pat F. and family for the card. Truly appreciated!!! I will update soon. God Bless. Jacki

THURSDAY, JULY 10, 2008
Hi all. Manda is doing OK this AM. She is still a little nauseous, but I think it's from all the probing they have done inside her. She is headed back to the OR tomorrow AM for another colonoscopy. She's not too happy about that, even though she is out when they do this. She wakes up a little cranky!!! I know I would, too!!!! Other than that, just quiet time and resting. We tried something different last night. I called Healing Touch to come in for Manda. It really helped her relax; she feel asleep!!!! The RN who did this was so sweet. It is wonderful. They offer some other alternatives for pain, not just meds. I will update soon. A quick message to Dahea and Carolyn (who are both away right now): your sister says she loves you both and misses you, too!!!

Thanks to all for everything you do!! Please, as Manda wishes, continue to pray for all CB friends and families, esp: Jaden, Gina,

Kylie and Josh, Sharon and the boys, Erik, and all who are in need at this time!! God Bless! Jacki.

FRIDAY, JULY 11, 2008

Hi All. It's me Amanda!

As you know, I haven't been feeling good the past few days, so that's why I haven't been updating. So, medical news first as always. I'm still feeling quite nauseous today. Dr. Adams upped my Zofran [for the treatment of nausea and vomiting] to 3x's a day. It helps a lot when I get it, but it wears off eventually. They took my blood the other day to see if my liver and etc. were OK. My liver enzymes are, I think, higher then last week's, so we're watching out for that. My sugar is a bit high, too. And everything else is pretty much the same.

They were going to make a new recipe for my TPN's, but, since some things are high, Dr. Adams suggested that they don't, so i'm on the same recipe. A rash started developing on my leg yesterday. Dr. Adams checked it out and told me it may be was probably a virus because i have little bumps in the back of my throat, and i totally forgot what they're called, but it's probably due to that. Dr. Qualia didn't end up doing another surgery today. we're not sure why. He's working hard on [getting me to] Boston right now. we're thinking i'm either shipping out of here Monday or Tuesday, but who knows with Drs., right? I'm not sure if they're doing another surgery in Boston to get my stool out now that Dr. Qualia didn't do it, so i'll let you know if that happens. That's pretty much all the medical news.

Today was a pretty just laying around day. I thought i was going down to the OR, so i had to stay in the room, but now that i'm not, my dad, mom, and I are going out for a walk later on. Brenna came in this morning and gave me [temporary] tattoos because she thought i was going down to the ER, too. I have like five tattoos on right now. there's one on my foot that i LOVE, and i might get one exactly like that in the future.

Tomorrow night, my dad is spending the night so that my mom can go home and spend a night in her own bed and pack for Boston. My sister comes home today, so my mom gets some special time with my sister tomorrow night while i get some special time with my dad! That works out GREAT!...lol.

Thank you for all the prayers. They're definitely working slowly but surely! I'm not really emailing right now but i check it.
Rina-Thank you for my Card. i actually just got it, and i LOVE the picture, and, yes, Abby does think she's human..lol.
Please continue to keep all my CB buddies in your prayers, especially Jaden, Gina, and Cody

"Ask yourself this question: Will this matter a year from now?"
                                                    --Richard Carlson
Have a GREAT night!
Amanda B+

SUNDAY, JULY 13, 2008
Hi All!
Sooo sorry I didn't update yesterday. I was having too much fun with my dad..lol. Anyways, there's not much medical news to report today, which is GREAT! Pretty much the same today: nauseous and in a bit of pain.

Last night was good fun. My dad and Carolyn came up and stayed for about 30 minutes. then my mom and Carolyn left and dad and I just hung out. We didn't do much because what is there really to do in a Hospital? I picked out a movie that we watched, Transformers. I think my dad liked it. he didn't fall asleep...lol. So, right now i'm just hanging out until Abby, mom, and Carolyn come up.

I still haven't heard any news from Boston, which is getting me mad because, the sooner i get in, the sooner i'll get out. I have sooo many places that I want to go to this summer (or whatever's left of it). My grandparents and my family are supposed to be going to Pennsylvania the end of August, and i'm supposed to be going to the "American Idol" concert August 6th with my family and friends. But we'll see how things go. let's take it one step at a time.

I just saw the coolest people pass by my room. they were true Amish people, one man and two little boys. WOW! did that make my day or what?! I LOVE seeing different cultures, so that's part of why i want to go to Pennsylvania and to see Malisa, Rina, and Darcie!

OK, well, today's was a short update. i'll update when i update. Please continue to pray for all my CB friends and their families. Especially Jaden, Cody, and Gina.

"Now you're feeling more and more frustrated and getting all kind of inpatient waiting. We live, and we learn to take one step at a time. There's no need to rush. It's like learning to fly or falling in love. It's gonna happen when its supposed to happen, and we find

the reason why it's one step at a time." --Jordan Sparks (One Step At A Time)
Have a B+ Day!
Amanda :-) B+

MONDAY, JULY 14, 2008

Hi all. Manda asked if I would update today (lucky you). I think Manda and dad had too much fun (I hope). Today brought very low Hepatic enzyme levels, and they have to give a blood transfusion but yet have to wait. They have to do some other blood work on her tomorrow AM. All of Manda's markers are either very, very low (not good), or they are very elevated, which is not good as well!!! Her liver enzymes are extremely high (from the TPN'S & lipids). We rob Peter to pay Paul. Not fair!!!! With all this, her spirit is so STRONG!!!

I took Manda out today, in the fresh air. She was freezing, but it was good for her. We are still waiting on news from Tuft's. The waiting is the hard part. That's it for today. Thanks to all for everything you do!!! I don't do as well as Manda, but she wanted me to let you know what was up. Please, as Manda wishes, continue to pray for all CB friends and families, esp: Jaden, Jaden's Nurse friend, Erik, who, I think, is on his way back in, Gina, who came in today, Kylie and Josh, Cody, who is here, Sharon and the boys, and all else who are at need.   Thanks Malisa for our chat last night. You are an angel on earth. We love you!!! God Bless. Jacki.

TUESDAY, JULY 15, 2008

Hi All!

I thought I would write kinda fancy today...lol. Yesterday was kind of a hard day for me because i was in a lot of pain. they decreased my pain medicine, so my stomach was a bit more uncomfortable than usual. Anyways, i'm back and doing OK. Today is a back-to-back day filled with surprises. Dr. Qualia came in this morning and told us that the only way we're going to get that test in Boston is if we can get all of my stool out. And that's exactly what they're going to do either today or tomorrow. I'm going to the OR for a four- to five-hour procedure. But, before all that happens, Dr. Qualia wrote for an X-ray and some other tests for my liver. my enzymes are extremely high, so they're just making sure it's not anything else. My H's [hemoglobin and hematocrit] also came back lower than the other day, so i think they might be doing a transfusion sometime soon.

So that's the latest medical update. please pray for me and my family so that I can get through this surgery. it's the longest one i've ever had, and i need all the prayers i can get. I didn't do much yesterday because i was in pain. I did manage to get out for a walk. My mom actually took me outside for a bit until i said it was cold. then we just went back in and walked all over.

Please continue to pray for all my CB friends especially Jaden, Cody, Erik, and Gina.

"It takes courage to grow up and turn out to be who you really are" -- e.e. cummings
Have a B+ Day!
Amanda :-) B+

THURSDAY, JULY 17, 2008

Hi all. Sorry I didn't update yesterday. Manda is headed in today @ 10:30AM for her procedure. Keep your fingers crossed and say a LOT of prayers!!!! Manda's spirits are great!!! She is TRULY AMAZING!!!! I know I am her mom, but she awes me every day. What a blessing she is. All my girls!! I will try to update later. Please continue to pray for all CB friends and families as Manda wishes!! Esp: Her Jaden, Cody, Erik, Gina, Kylie and Josh, Sharon and the boys, and all else in their time of need! God Bless! Jacki.

FRIDAY, JULY 18, 2008

Hi all. It's me, Jacki. Don't know where to begin. I guess first, the procedure yesterday did not help. OK, the Dr. came in yesterday and spoke with Louis and me. Not good news. Manda has beginning stages of liver disease from TPN's and lipids and all her seizure meds. They can't correct this, but they are going to try to slow it down. Unfortunately, they had to stop TPN's and lipids for one to two weeks (Manda's only nutrition). She is only on hydration [water]. Manda will get very weak and lose weight, and that along with all of her other health issues. Louis and I asked the Dr. to please explain this to Manda. Dr. Qualia did great!! He told Manda that Boston is off for now because her liver was sick. He explained everything to her. Also, he is testing her for medically-induced Hepatitis. This happens in chronic illness a lot of times. Manda was upset. She cried. We all did, but we will get through this. Just a bigger bump on the path of LIFE!!!

Manda is very quiet and very nauseous. Will update soon. Just wanted to let you know that Boston will have to wait for now.

Thanks to Michele for the Tinkerbell balloon and visit. Also to all, for your love and support. I know I don't call too much anymore, but I do think of you all, and CB friends and families, too!! As Manda wishes, please continue to pray for all CB friends and families!!! We love you all. God Bless!!! Jacki.

SATURDAY, JULY 19, 2008
Hi all. It's Jacki. Manda is doing okay but can't stay awake very long. Her body is just so weak and tired. She tries to talk and falls asleep. This is from not having her TPN's or lipids. mom and I did get her up in her chair yesterday for a short lap around :-). They had to put a catheter in yesterday. She is having trouble urinating, but I think it is helping. She hates it!!!! Not much else here. I am going to try to get home later, and Carolyn Rose is driving up to stay with Manda. Carolyn Rose needs some sister time, she said. She is going to do Amanda's nails and watch a movie. That's it for now. Just a quiet day and plenty of rest for Manda!!! Will update soon. Thank you, Father, for the visit yesterday, and to Jim and Karen, too!!! It means a lot to Louis and me. Please continue to pray for all CB friends and families as Manda wishes!!! Special little add on: Manda's twin cousins, Natalie and Sophie, are being baptized tomorrow. Even though she is not able to go, Manda is thinking of them!!! Just wanted Aunt Valerie and Uncle Tom to know. Also that Aunt Dawney feel better soon. And Oreo, too!!! Thanks to all for everything you do!!! God Bless. Jacki.

Amanda Perrotta

SUNDAY, JULY 20, 2008
Hi all. Manda had a rough night. They had to keep waking her up because her blood pressure was very low. Carolyn is so tired (my baby doll). What a wonderful sister she is!! She said they had all the lights on all night. The Dr. came in this AM and told us that Manda is getting too weak, so they have no choice but to start TPN's and lipids back up tonight. Also, another blood transfusion this afternoon. They were trying to give the liver a break, but they can't. There really isn't a choice.

They draw labs every AM, and her liver enzymes have not gone down at ALL!! Manda is sleeping now most of the time but did manage to watch a little of a movie with Carolyn Rose. I am so glad they had time together!!! They need that. They both miss their other sister Dahea, though! That's it for today. We are asking for no visitors for today, please. Manda is not up for it today. I will try to update soon. Please, some EXTRA prayers for Manda and us. It would be greatly appreciated right now. As Manda wishes, please continue to pray for all CB friends and families!! Thank you all for everything you do! We love you all. God Bless!!! Jacki.

MONDAY, JULY 21, 2008

Hi all. Manda had a better night last night. She had her transfusion, and TPN's and lipid's are running. I think she should be a little more with it today, I hope. The Drs. said the high liver enzymes also add to her being loopy. Manda had another blood clot in her PICC lumen.. They TPA-ed it [to dissolve the clot], and we are crossing are fingers the PICC won't have to go!!!!!

Other than that, not much. Manda is sleeping a lot, and quiet. Will update soon. Can't wait for Manda to be back updating (she adds so much more humor). :-) Thank you all for everything. Please, as Manda wishes, continue to pray for all CB friends and families. God Bless! Jacki.

TUESDAY, JULY 22, 2008
Hi all!
I haven't been feeling all that well lately, so i've been having my mom update. Medical stuff first, as usual. As you all might know (?)... I had my blood transfusion yesterday, along with my TPNs and lipids. I feel a lot better today and not as sleepy! Yesterday, Dr. Adams and Dr. Qualia decided we're going to hold off on Boston so that I can get stronger for that trip, and I'll go home when they can weine (sp?) [wean] me off my pain meds and everything else. The catheter is still in me, but I'm gonna tell the Drs. today i've had enough! I HATE it! I can kinda pee by myself. I had another blood clot yesterday in my PICC line; they TPA'd it, and it worked, so the PICC is working fine now. That's pretty much all the medical news for now.

So, we decided for the "American Idol" concert that a nurse from my hospital is going to take my dad's place so that they can be there if anything happens. I'm taking Pippi (Bethany!) if she's available that night. We're still aiming to go to Pennsylvania and to go to Hershey Park, and my mom said I can ride all the roller coasters i want.

Nothing really else is going on. I'm just looking forward to going home. There's only a month left of summer, and i want to enjoy it while it lasts because, in the winter, you don't really get to go out much.

Oh!   Today the Hospital is having a party for Erik and me.   It's Erik's birthday, and they're having a party for me just because i've been here for a month and a half.   I told Brenna (my Child Life Specialist) what we needed, and she went crazy with party stuff! Happy Birthday Erik!
Please continue to pray for all my CB friends.

"As I grow to understand life less and less, I learn to love it more and more."   --Jules Renard
Amanda :-) B+

Silly String and Tie Dye for Jaden's Birthday

WEDNESDAY, JULY 23, 2008
Hi all!
Where to begin?   The Drs. decided i'm going home on the machine for pain and straight catheters as needed.   Yesterday, they took out my Foley catheter, and, ahhhh, it felt soooo good!   I thought there was going to be a lot of pain, but it didn't hurt coming out.   I'm doing pretty good peeing right now.   i haven't had to have the straight catheter in yet, so i'm doing well!

Today was kinda a dopey day for me.   i've been sleeping since last night and just woke up at 1:30PM.   My TPN's are going to be going all week and then off during the weekends.   So, i'm going to be feeling icky all weekend, but it will at least give my liver a break.   My liver enzymes went up again, but Dr. Adams said they should do that and that they will eventually go down just a bit because they have to get used to my body with the TPN's. That's it for the medical news.

Erik's and my party went GREAT yesterday. i was glad i had it on his birthday. Some things just happen during the right time. Brenna got everything i wanted, especially the silly string. She gave me two cans of it to spray the nurses, and she also gave me one can for the nurses so we can have battles. We also tie dyed socks at the party. I'm only wearing them inside, though, because mine don't match at all because we ran out of the colors that i wanted. I also put all the goodie bags together for people, and Brenna got Erik and me a "Harry Potter" piñata. It was quite fun! Please continue to pray for all my CB friends. one day i will make it to all of your sites to see what's going on.

"The whole of life is like a moment of time. It is, therefore, our duty to use it, not misuse it." --Plutarch
Amanda :-) B+

THURSDAY, JULY 24, 2008

Hi all. It's me, Jacki. Manda is having a tough day, and she had a very tough night!! Manda has had some metabolic strokes— slurred speech, confusion, and a hard time staying awake. This is from taking her off her TPN's and lipids this past weekend. Robbing Peter to pay Paul again!! We are going to try to do TPN's and lipids five days on and Sat. and Sun. off. We are trying to give her liver a break. Manda's very tired but continues to fight. We take one day at a time and are grateful for every day!! Manda's best time of day seems to be late afternoon. Minnie and I try to get her out every day over to the craft room with a child life specialist. They are WONDERFUL!! Thank God for them.

That is all for today. Manda has asked for continual prayers for all CB friends and families. Also a special note to all Manda's nurses. Louis and I thank you all for the love and care you have for Manda and our family every day!! We love you all very much, and you will always be a special part of our family. Thank you all for all you do. God Bless!! Jacki.

FRIDAY, JULY 25, 2008
HI all!
It's me, Amanda. Sorry I didn't update yesterday or earlier this morning. yesterday was a hard day for me, and today is a LOT better! Yesterday, I jut slept most of the day. I did get a chance to get out for a walk and go to the playroom to do a craft, but [only because] my mom insisted i get out of the room. Not much medical news today. i'm not dumping as much as i usually do in my J and G bags. Tomorrow, my TPN's and lipids stop until Monday night. I'm sooo not looking forward to that because i hate how i am and act when i don't get my nutrition. That's about all, though. Through and through, i'm doing pretty good today.

Today, Minnie is coming up and hanging out, and my family later. I wanted to thank everyone for all the gifts and cards. they are appreciated much! I LOVED the HSM [High School Musical] set and the dog you gave me, Emilie. everyone is signing him!
I'll update if anything changes. Please keep all my CB friends who are like my little sisters and brothers in your prayers at night.

"A loving heart is the truest wisdom"   --Charles Dickens
Have a B+ day!
Amanda :-) B+

FRIDAY, JULY 25, 2008

Hi all. Manda had a good hour and a half this morning then was in extreme pain and nausea. It was a tough day and night. I am very grateful for that time but wish it could last. It is very hard to watch your child be in so much pain and not be able to help!! The only reason I am updating is because the day changed so quickly. Please, as Manda wishes, continue to pray for all her special CB friends and families! God Bless!! Jacki.

SUNDAY, JULY 27, 2008

Hi all. It's Jacki. Louis spent the night with Manda so that I could have some quality time with Carolyn Rose. Today brings rest for all (which is needed). Manda is sleeping a lot but in good spirits, and pain under control as of now. Her status changes often and quickly. We are asking that all visitors at this point please call ahead to see if she is okay. Sorry, but we have no choice. We truly appreciate you all VERY much but have to do this for her and us as a Family. Know that Louis and I will NEVER be able to express the true gratitude and love and support you have all given. We are BLESSED as a family to have you all on Manda's Journey with us. It will never be forgotten!! We are hoping to bring Manda home this Wed. That is pretty much it. Manda is having special time with dad, and I am sure she is glad to get rid of mom for a while (teenagers) :-). dad spoils her :-). Not too much else.

Just watching her closely. Off TPN'S and lipids until tomorrow night. Thank you all for all you do. Please, as Manda wishes, continue to pray for all CB friends and families. God Bless. Jacki.

MONDAY, JULY 28, 2008

Hi all. Plans are in the way for Wednesday to bring our Manda HOME!! Manda is very weak and sleepy, but home will be good for her, and all of us. Manda's color is not great today (jaundice), and her voice is so soft, but she still lets you know what she wants!! TPN's and lipids start again tonight. Thank God. That's it for today. Jaden, Manda misses you too, and loves ya lots!!

Please, as Manda wishes, continue to pray for all CB friends and families!! God Bless!! Jackie.

P.S. A very special thank you to Tony, for a beautiful letter he wrote to me about Amanda. What a wonderful young man!!! Thanks, Tony. You are a sweetheart. Like mom, like son. You are a blessed mom, Peggy, and should be very proud!!

Simply Remembering the Taste

TUESDAY, JULY 29, 2008

Hi All!

This is Amanda! I bet you all can tell now by the way i start off my journal entry. Anyways, medical news first as always. Yesterday i felt VERY weak, so i didn't do too much, mostly just sleep all day. I was very hungry, though, yesterday. The way i eat is unique. I can have just about anything in my mouth and then i spit it out, just to get the taste and remember what each food tasted like.

Tomorrow i get to go home, so i doubt i'll be updating because i'll be home enjoying the rest of the summer. I can't wait to sleep with my Abby. I think they unclotted my line this morning. I'm not sure if i have a cold thing going on lately, but every morning, i've been sniffling, and my eyes run all day! Not much else has been going on.

Minnie is hanging out with me right now because my mom is with my sister going to a college thing at Saint Rose. I'm trying to watch "Charmed" while i type, so sorry if i misspell.
Please continue to keep all my CB friends in your prayers. Soon enough, i'll get to all of your sites!
Have a B+ day!
Amanda :-) B+ :-)

WEDNESDAY, JULY 30, 2008
Hi everyone. It's Carolyn (Amanda's sister). Just a quick note to update because mom is busy getting Manda settled in. She's home. *YEA* Right now, Manda just started to fall asleep and is very tired and weak. Ambulance ride was very smooth. We just wanted to thank everyone especially Albany Medical Center C-7 nurses, for all the love and support they have given to Amanda and our family. We'll see some of you on Sunday when you visit. My mom or Amanda will be updating sometime tomorrow. Please, as Manda wished, continue to pray for all CB friends and families :-). Thanks and God bless all!
Love,
Carolyn :)

Amanda Perrotta

THURSDAY, JULY 31, 2008

Hi all!

WHEEW! My family and I finally got situated around 10-ish last night with Tony. Tony came to help my mom and dad with the three million boxes we had, all full of medical supplies. I went home via ambulance, and, once i got home, I was extremely tired. slept for three hours! My mom and I learned how to work my PCA [patient-controlled analgesia, or pain medicine] pump, so now, if i need an extra hit of it, i just press a small button instead of that big one at the hospital (no offense). We also got a schedule down and all that jazz. Unfortunately, I had to bring the pee rule home with me: "If you don't go after four to six hours, then we're going to catheterize you." And i HATE that, so i've been doing well right now, thank goodness. I pray to God every night that i won't have to be cathed. So far He's listening.

I have two ingrown toenails from when i had my seizures back in Jan-April, and my mom said i slammed both my toes in this hard part of the bed and they've been nagging me ever since. There's not much other medical news.

My family is going to take a vacation this summer somehow, but it might not be Pennsylvania. My [grandmother] Minnie is trying the hardest to get us there so i can ride all the roller coasters i want. But if we don't make it there, we'll most likely be going to Maine. Pippi (my nurse, whose name is really Bethany) is coming over this Sunday just to hang. OK, she might be cleaning up all the silly string i sprayed all over. (Thank you, Brenna, for everything in my book bag, and that board was a great idea.)

"American Idol" concert is next week, and Pippi is also coming with us to that. Pippi and I are going to be pumping up the party!!!

Please continue to pray for all my CB buddies.

"Every artist was first an amateur" --Ralph Waldo Emerson
Have a B+ day!
Amanda :-) B+

FRIDAY, AUGUST 01, 2008

Hi all!

Oh, what a lousy day it is here (well, for me!). I'm making myself bored...lol. I wanted to update you all before my big trip. Yes! I'm going on a road trip tomorrow! But first, i have to tell you all my medical news because that's the way it goes (and don't skip down!).

So, everything is going well with all my meds. Tony bumped up my basal rate on my PCA a bit because i was pushing my button a bit too much. it's helped a lot because i don't need as much as i did. I'm peeing, and i've not been catheterized yet (and i don't plan on being). I'm so proud of myself every time i go a lot (i'm like a toddler here). I've been really nauseous today, more than normal, i have no clue why, though. I told my mom that i know how it feels to be pregnant now—i'm nauseous all the time!! I'm really enjoying my new IV pole. It's a fun, bright colored one that my dad got for me. Rina, you would really like it. it's blue and has roller blade wheels!!! There's not much else going on. i'm resting a lot today for tomorrow (Abby, too!).

Amanda Perrotta

So, tomorrow, i'm going up to Lake Lazerne. We're going up for a night and going horseback riding. I LOVE horses and always wanted to take lessons but never got the chance because i got sick, so now's my chance. I know how to ride and all, but i usually never can because of my immune system. My mom originally wanted to take me to Double H, my camp (or, as i call it, my Personal Heaven), but, the thing is, if I went there, I wouldn't want to leave and would be VERY sad and mad that i didn't get a chance to go this summer, so i'm begging my mom NOT to go there. So, i'm just saving ALL my energy for tomorrow and Sunday because i don't get my TPNs on Saturday or Sunday because my liver gets a break then, but i'm hoping, if i save all my energy for tomorrow, i'll have enough energy to enjoy myself riding.

I started a 3-D puzzle today with Minnie, and its harder than expected. We didn't even get any done today. we just had to sort the pieces (and there're 400 of them). So, i'm hoping maybe on Monday we can start it.
Please continue to pray for all my CB friends.
Have a B+ Day!
Amanda :-) B+

SATURDAY, AUGUST 02, 2008

Hi all. It's Jacki. Today is not our day to take Manda's road trip. Manda is very tired and weak plus it is rainy out. Just a reminder to ALL, PLEASE read between the lines.... This site is set up for Manda to vent and share feelings and to keep family and friends updated. Sometimes it is confusing, but it is the way Manda

408

portrays her journey!!! Please try to understand, without anything else being said!!! So, today Manda will rest up for Pippi, her AMC nurse, coming tomorrow to visit.

Thank you Bethany!!! Also Maude, Peggy, Allie, Ashley, Elma, Deb, Steph, and Kathy!! I hope I didn't forget anyone. Oh, Maryanna, we love you all, and Manda misses you lots!!! Thank you all!!! Carolyn just left for her trip to Utica to visit with her cousins. Not much else going on, still everything the same. We are HOME!!!! Please continue as Manda wishes to pray for all CB families and friends!!! God Bless! Jacki

P.S. Jaden, Manda sends hugs and kisses. Hi, Jess. You are always in our thoughts and prayers!!!!
PSS: This is a special add on for Misty. I'm sooooo very sorry and embarrassed. How could I forget you??! And all that you have done for Manda. I LOVE you, and i'm sorry. We miss you, Misty, and thank you for everything. Please forgive me for not mentioning your name.

SUNDAY, AUGUST 03, 2008
Hi All!
It's me, Amanda. i'm feeling much better today, and i'm a bit bored right now, so my mom and dad suggested i update. there's not much really to tell medical-wise. I'll just tell you what i did last night.

Last night i was a bit bored also, so my family decided we would do some fireworks. My dad got all these fireworks for the 4th of July back in June, and i was in for the 4th, so we have a ton of fireworks to blow off. We only did the ones i wanted to last night, but i saved some more for tonight with Pippi. Yes, Pippi's here!!! She's staying until i fall asleep. There's not much else that's going on. i think i've watched all of the Disney shows that were on today and more. OK, well, i'm going to think of what I can do for boredomness...lol.

"The whole of life is but a moment of time. It is our duty, therefore, to use it, not misuse it." --Plutarch
Have a B+ day!
Amanda :-) B+ :-)

TUESDAY, AUGUST 05, 2008
HI All!
I didn't get a chance to update yesterday because i was off my TPNs for two days, and i was down all day (until 10:00PM. that's when i started perking up.) So, everything went good with Pippi (Bethany). i think so, at least! She looked kind of different without her scrubs on. Maybe next time i'll ask her to wear my Tinkerbell ones for me (just kidding!) One of my lumens had a nice clot in it last night. we weren't getting any blood back, and it's just hard pushing in. So my mom wasn't going to let me go another night without my TPNs, so she switched to another lumen. So far, everything's steady. i'm not sure if my mom got a blood return yet, but i'm hoping she did.

I'm still VERY nauseous today. There're these two medicines for my nausea that make me sleep like a rock and sometimes make me loopy. So i only try to use them for emergencies. like this morning, i think i was about to throw up...thank goodness i didn't, though. I'm running a low-grade fever. it's running from 99.3-

99.6°. I'm trying to think positive because tomorrow night is [the] "American Idol" [concert at the Times Union Center]!!!!!   I'm excited. probably not as much as Carolyn, but i'm excited for her! I don't think there's anything else going on in the medical world.

My [grandmother] Minnie is here today, and she rented three movies for me to watch because i'm saving ALL my spoons [energy] for tomorrow night so i can scream![11] She rented College Road Trip, Nims Island and She's the Man (a favorite!).   I'll probably watch one or two later.

I wanted to mention Carrie's video that she made.   Carrie, yesterday i was kinda sleeping and dozing off when my mom came in and asked me to watch your video. I watched it, and it is AMAZING!!!!!!!   Your video is sooo beautiful, and Thank You for including me in it. I'll try to stop by your site later.
Please continue to pray for all my CB buddies, especially Penelope, who is in the hospital, and Erik is in as well.

"Whatever the mind of a man can conceive and believe, it can achieve."   --Napoleon Hill
Have a B+ Day!
Amanda :-) B+

THURSDAY, AUGUST 07, 2008
Hi All!

---

[11]Amanda would ration her strength and energy as if she only had a certain number of spoons to use every day. Once they were gone, she had to begin using the next day's spoons in order to keep up but would then have to work harder to make up the difference.

I'm soooo sorry i didn't update yesterday. i was saving all of my spoons for the concert (American Idol). You guys have no idea how much fun i had last night and how i felt "normal" for those four hours. And i can't wait to tell you all the big surprise (i'm talking BIG!)

Medical news first as always. I'm a little low on spoons today because i used all of them last night, but i just woke up, and i'm feeling pretty good (yes, i slept in until 1:00PM). Two of my lines have blood clots in them, so Tony's coming in a little while to TPA them. Not much else medical-wise! Now i can tell you all about my brilliant night out!

So, yesterday i dressed up (well it was for me), i had on my favorite skirt and top, and, thanks to Christine, my cousin, i had some flip-flops to wear. We left (my mom, Carolyn, Pippi my nurse, Kim, Phil, Brittany, and Brianna) around 5:30 (the concert was at 7:00). We had to have special parking because of my wheelchair, and this guy escorted us to our seats, which were NOT our seats! We originally were going to sit with Kim and Phil, Brittany, and Brianna up in these seats which were near the stage but not up so close we could touch them, but this nice guy put us in front row seats!!!!! I thought he was joking when he said, "those are your seats," but he wasn't! I was up sooo close, i could hear them breathe!

Anyways, i'm not going to get into all the details, but the concert was GREAT. i needed my pain button a lot more than usual, but i got through it GREAT, and i screamed as loud as i could through the whole thing. During the middle of the show, my mom told me, "don't use up all of your film because we're going to meet them all backstage after the show!!!!!!" I thought she was kidding at first, but then she told me again, and i was, like, so confused and excited. It was just a special feeling you get when you're so excited!

My favorite performance was "Apologize" by my American Idol David Archuleta. David Cook did a GREAT job, and he even recorded our cheering because he's doing a documentary on all his shows. So, i'm getting to the good part now. After the show, another guy escorted us to a special room where they were all going to meet after the show (there was no one else there yet except me, Carolyn, Pippi, and my mom). Carolyn and I were taking loads of pictures when one of them came out. we were asking for autographs immediately! When my mom told me not to look, i new David A. was coming out! We had pictures taken together, and he signed my poster and shirt. He's so much funnier in person, though. he's still shy like he was on the show, but he's sooo much funnier.

Then David C. came flying in on a skateboard, and Carolyn was, like, going nuts because she's obsessed with him. She was going up to all of them like they were her family or something. Syesha was resting her vocal cords, so she wrote on her hand to talk to me. I have all of their autographs except for Jason, Chickezie, and Brooke. When people started coming in, we left because we already had our time and stuff. I can't even explain how happy i was last night and excited. I don't think i'll ever be as excited again or have that special smile i put on last night. it was like i made another wish again, and it came true. I'm putting a lot of pictures up, and, Rina, i was thinking of you the whole night, and i promise i will send you lots of pictures. I'll print extras and send them to you.

I want to thank a couple of people for making this possible for me: My Aunt Pat and the "American Idol" tour for making this happen, and Pippi, Kim, Phil, Brittany, and Brianna for going.
Kim, Phil, Brittany, and Brianna: Thank you for my Jonas Brother shirt (i'm going to wear it tonight!).
If i forgot anyone, i'm sooo sorry!
Please continue to pray for all my CB friends.

"Yesterday is but a dream,
And tomorrow is only a vision.
But today well lived makes
Every yesterday a dream of happiness
And every tomorrow a vision of hope.
Look well, therefore, to this day."
                  --Sir William Oser

Have a B+ Day!
Amanda :-) B+

SATURDAY, AUGUST 09, 2008 10:01 AM,

Hi all. It's Jacki. What a night. To see Manda and Carolyn Rose smile. It's like time stopped and I was trying to take it ALL in!!!! What a BLESSING to have that night! Now to medical things, as Manda tries to get over. Last night, we found out Manda's bone marrow is involved. Manda's H's are dropping, which happens, but usually they can do a blood transfusion. Not this time. Manda's red blood count is 1.2 [Normal red blood cell count for children is 4.6 to 4.8 million cells per microliter (million/µL)]. Extremely low, so they can not transfuse her. This leaves Manda open to EVERYTHING!!!! She has nothing to fight infection. Dr. Adams is speaking with hematology to see if we can use a drug called Procrit to help raise her H's. Can't promise anything also because of her liver. So we will see.

Now to the GOOD news. Manda was on such a high after the ["American Idol"] concert. It was the most WONDERFUL thing to see. (Thanks, Tammy, for the phone call to say how happy and great Manda looked. That meant sooo much.) Every moment means something!! Manda has been in good spirits and sitting up watching movies with Minnie and making a present for her dad's birthday this Wed. Today, though, she's weak, tired, sleepy, and nauseous. It's the weekend and off TPN's and lipids. With her H's being so low, it is going to be a tough weekend. (At least with a transfusion, it helped make her more comfy.)

That's it for now. Please, as Manda wishes, continue to pray for ALL CB friends and families!! Thanks to Bethany also, for all your help, love, and support!! And to All the AMC nurses who check in with Manda's CB page. She misses you all and LOVES to hear from you!!! God Bless. Jacki

P.S. How could Manda forget her SPECIAL time with her twin cousins last night?! Thanks Val and Tom. Kisses to Sophie and Natalie: xxx ooo. It was a wonderful visit.

Amanda Perrotta

At this point in Amanda's journey through Mitochondrial Disease, she began to experience a profound understanding of her time here with us on earth. While she always maintained an attitude of hope for her eventual recovery, she knew that her struggle was coming to an end. From the first, her strength dwindled, but by now, one by one, her organs began to shut down due to the systemic stresses induced by her condition. She developed terrible bedsores from lack of movement. Her bowels completely stopped moving and became increasingly more impacted, causing her constant pain. Her liver was diseased because of the high levels of proteins and lipids given to sustain her strength. This raised her ketone levels as she became less able to metabolize those proteins and lipids, resulting in more systemic damage to her organs and brain. She suffered a series of small, metabolic strokes that temporarily slurred her already-muted speech, and her lack of movement—walking and standing—caused her arms and legs to slowly atrophy and wither. Though her physical strength declined, her mental and spiritual strength remained strong, invigorating her will to pray continually for anyone suffering with Mito and for all of her friends on Caring Bridge.

Amanda was always thinking of others and was always more concerned for those whom she loved than for herself. She began to keep a hand-written journal about things dear to her. Because of her growing weakness in the last months of her life, she couldn't sit up and use the computer very often, if at all, so she began to write in a notebook, propped up with pillows or leaning against mom or dad.

Interspersed here and there among the CaringBridge computer journals that Amanda entered, in their proper places by date, are Amanda's journals from this notebook that she kept. Her words here are more private and introspective because she was writing things that would not be read publicly or online. She listed things she wanted to remember, recounted things she had yet to do, taught lessons of wisdom, and wrote letters of love and affection to all of the people close to her.

For instance, Mike Silvia, one of her friends from Wildwood School, had not spoken since he was a boy. He was withdrawn and silent. But after meeting Amanda, amazingly, he spoke. His life opened up to her and, through her outward nature and completely selfless guidance, began to open up to others as well. Amanda's journals do not reveal this friendship. She only mentions her "friend, Mike S," whom she was always happy to see and whom she missed terribly when she could not return to school.

Here, on August 9th, while her strength decreased and her medical problems increased almost exponentially, from her bed in Albany Medical Center Hospital, Amanda made her first hand-written journal entry. As always, her attitude and outlook are astounding. (Though her occasional grammar, spelling, and punctuation errors have been corrected, all of her thoughts remain as she wrote them, and clarification has been added only if required.)

> This journal belongs
> to Amanda Perrotta
> <u>Only read if necessary!</u>
>
> Please do not read if you weren't told to.

Lesson #1: "There's a reason for everything."
August 9th, 2008   16 years old

Today's a beautiful day! It's sunny out and perfect. I wish it was that beautiful in here. Right now, i'm kind of house bound. My H's are very low, and I can't have either a transfusion or a bone marrow transplant, so, for right now, I'm just sitting and waiting. I know God <u>chose</u> me to have this disease for a special reason, and I know I'll find out someday. I just wish I knew what it was so I could be more positive than I am right now. I'm very positive and try to be positive throughout this whole ordeal. i just wish no one had to be sick or die young. I've had more friends die than I think just about anyone.

I do know this, though: I am going to get through this, and, one day when I wake up, there's going to be a cure. OK, I could go on forever. Tonight, we're doing fireworks.

♥, Amanda B+

Lesson #2: "A Lesson Learned"

August 10th, 2008   16 years old

When things happen to you, just things that you never expect to happen to you, you usually ask, "why?" Ever since I was 10 and had seizures every day, I started to learn that even <u>bad</u> things happen for a reason to us who are <u>special</u>. That's why, last night, the last spark on one of the fireworks went right toward <u>my</u> oxygen tank. I immediately ~~tried~~ thought I was going to blow up and <u>die</u>. But I didn't. <u>God</u> was teaching <u>me</u> a lesson. He was telling me to not always trust that things will always go exactly as planned. That's one I didn't yet learn, and I know now. You know you're being taught a lesson when something bad happens, but you don't get hurt that bad. And that's one lesson I'll <u>never</u> forget.

♥, Amanda B+

MONDAY, AUGUST 11, 2008 10:01 AM,

Hi all. It's Jacki. Manda's worse day is always on a Monday. TPNs and lipids are withheld every Saturday and Sunday. By

Sunday afternoon, you can see the toll it takes on her body. She is doing OK, but she is very weak and tired. Tony (Manda's nurse) has been WONDERFUL!!! Manda's G-J tube came out Saturday night. Tony was not on call and came out to help hold us over until she has surgery to replace it either today or tomorrow. Manda also had another blood clot. Tony was here until I think 1:00 or 1:30AM helping me. We can NEVER thank him enough. I also want to thank Rose for coming to cut Manda's hair. She looks BEAUTIFUL!! We are still awaiting news for the use of Procrit (for Manda's H's). Other than that, not much.

Can't wait for Manda to update soon. To all, thank you for all you do everyday. It is truly appreciated from Louis and me. We don't know how we would get through this with out you all!! One quick add on. Manda is very excited about her sister, Dahea, coming home August 21st. She misses her, as we do, very much!! Da, if you're reading this, mom and dad love you and had fun talking with you last night. To all AMC nurses, Manda sends hugs and misses you very much!! Will update soon. Please, as Manda wishes, continue to pray for all CB friends and families. ESP: Manda's Jaden and Jess, Gina, Erik, Kiley and Josh, Sharon and the boys, Melissa, Rina, Emily, Natalie, and all else. God Bless! Jacki.

Lesson #3: "Something you never want to ask yourself"
August 11th, 2008   16 years old

You know those times when you don't want to answer a question, but you have no choice? Well, this is one of those times. I know someone's going to read this some time later, either if I'm 100 or 30. I'm watching a show right now, and this man had to go on a

vent [ventilator]. My mom asked me if I would want to ever <u>live</u> on one of those. I answered, "I don't know." I'm only 16. But when you have a life-threatening disease, you have to think about that because you never know, so here's my answer.... If I was put on one, <u>please</u> let me be on one if they say I'll get <u>better</u>. If they say I won't get <u>any</u> better, let me have the pleasure of finally getting to meet <u>God</u>. I know it would be <u>very hard</u> for all of you, but I did my job here on earth, and it's time for me to leave.
Thank you!
♥, Amanda B+

Started on August 11th, 2008. 16 years. Circled ones are VP! Very important[12].
Times I always want to remember:

8/11
- 1. Getting Abby (always my #1!)
- 2. My MAW [Make-A-Wish] trip to Disney.
- 3. Letting Dahea into our home.
  4. When I was able to eat and walk.
- 5. The Meet and Greet with the '08 AI's [American Idols].
  6. Dancing
- 7. Every little moment I have with my family.
- 8. People calling me an "Inspiration".
  9. Training Abby
  10. Going to school @ Wildwood.
  11. My 16th birthday @ Sunnyview.

---

[12] In her journals, the numbers were circled. Here, they are marked with a bullet. Also, all of these entries were added onto the same page of her journal between the 11th and 12th of August.

- 12. <u>Daddy</u> doing my hair every night.
- 13. Meeting <u>Mike S.</u> and having <u>him</u> for a <u>Best</u> Friend.
  13.[13] My 13th birthday. I won $5.00 in the money machine.
  14. <u>Mommy</u> cooking <u>dinner</u> every night.
- 15. <u>Mommy's</u> homemade mac + cheese.
- 16. Abby sleeping with me <u>every night</u>.
  17. Going to the <u>Bakery</u> on my days off.

8/14
18. Daddy's ∧[43] Birthday
19. Doing puzzles with Minnie.
20. Teach Henry [their parrot] the word "We Rock".
21. Taking a trip out to The Lake.
22. Watching movies + TV with my mom.

Things I want to do in 2009!
1. Go on my 1st date with someone I like.
2. Receive my 1st kiss from a <u>boy</u>.
3. Convince Carolyn to try out for either American Idol or So You Think you Can Dance. (Didn't work)
4. Receive my Class ring.
5. Go to a <u>real</u> party.
6. Publish my book, "Abby: The Service Dog."
7. Write a sequel to "Abby: The Service Dog."
8. Apply for a <u>summer</u> job.
9. Not be in the hospital for <u>any</u> holidays.
10. Go back to Walt Disney World on a train.

✶More to come!

---

[13] In her journals, there were two 13's.

Amanda Perrotta

Things I Want to do in 2009!
11. Get my 1st <u>official</u> boyfriend.
12. Throw Dahea a surprise 18th birthday party.
13. Get to eat soft foods for 1 day.

8/14/08	14. Hope for a cure to come soon.
	15. Spend 1 whole day with Carolyn.
8/15/08	16. Get my hair braided again.
8/24/08	17. Go skiing.
8/25/08	18. Learn how to sky + snowboard.
8/25/08	29. Change someone's life.

TUESDAY, AUGUST 12, 2008

Hi all. It's Jacki. Manda did not have her tubes replaced today. She was too weak and not feeling well. We are shooting for tomorrow at noon. We will see!! Not much else going on, just hanging on to every moment and trying to enjoy some family time!! Each day is a Blessing!!

Manda was scared last night (about the way her body feels), so Louis and I talked to her, and she just wanted to sleep near me (We snuggled). Manda seems more alert today and in good spirits!! Minnie came and brought the quilt she made for Manda's benefit. It is soooo beautiful!! All of Manda's colors, bright and soothing!! Thanks mom!! Today brings rest for tomorrow, hopefully. Also, Manda is working on a card for her dad's birthday tomorrow. She is recording a message on it. He will LOVE it!! That's it for today. Will update soon, or Manda will when feeling a little stronger. Please, as Manda wishes, continue to pray for all CB friends and families!! We love them all!! A special Thank

You to Emily for her package of gifts. Manda totally enjoyed them!! Thanks, Emily. You are so very sweet. God Bless!! Jacki.

Lesson #4: "The little things are the big things"   16 yrs.
August 12th, 2008

When I choose a topic every day, I try to write what I want to teach people in life. The #1 thing I really want to teach people is that the smallest things in life are the biggest things. I learned this lesson the hard way. I went to Carolyn's basketball games from being little to big in just <u>one</u> year. Last year, I really didn't care about Carolyn's basketball games. This year is totally different. I want to go to every single one I can get to. And now that I know that I can't get to every single one, it hurts because I know that I missed my chance last year and the year before.

So, that is my lesson for today. Even if you don't like going somewhere or doing something, do it because you never know if that little thing becomes big.

♥, Amanda B+

P.S. Sorry for the messy handwriting.

THURSDAY, AUGUST 14, 2008 o

Hi all. It's Jacki. Manda had her tubes replaced yesterday. She did great!! As always, after she is fine, as the day progresses, she is weak (like a high at first, then she crashes). She came home and made dad a cake and was so talkative. Manda's grandparents came down to visit, and she was happy that they tried her cake (carrot cake). What a baker. Just like her father, not me!!

Manda has been in a lot of pain the past couple of days (from the liver), so they had to raise her basal [pain medication] rate three times so far since we have been home. Yesterday didn't help with the tubes, but that is not where the pain is either. Today, Dr. Adams' office called with Manda's blood results. Not great, as usual, but now Manda is Neutropenic!! [Neutrophils, the most common of the white blood cells, serve as the primary defense against infection.] Her white blood count is so very low, nothing to fight with. Red blood count the same, so it is affecting her breathing. Her spirits are WONDERFUL!! as always. I know she is scared because she talks about it more and with Louis and me.

Not much else going on. Just trying to live LIFE every day. Thank you all for all you do. Love to all AMC nurses and staff!! (Dr. Hopkins, you, too). Please, as Manda wishes, continue to pray for all CB friends and families. Esp: Manda's Jaden, and Jess, who is back in (we love you guys). God Bless, Jacki.

P.S. To the Christine from Pinewoods, you did have Manda when she was two. Thanks for stopping by her site. Keep in touch!

Lesson #5: "The world would be a better place"   16 yrs.
August 13th, 2008

Today, I had to go to VIR to have my [feeding] tubes replaced. When I was waiting to go into the VIR recovery room, this young lady saw an older woman who was in a wheelchair and was on oxygen. So that young woman just watched that older woman try to get to where she had to go. So, that young woman didn't even bother to go help the other woman. It was <u>horrible</u> to watch! Finally, another woman who was there with her <u>very</u> sick son went over and brought the woman to where she had to go. So, the lesson for today is, even if you are occupied to the fullest, <u>always</u> be willing to help out a person in need. Because you <u>never</u> know if <u>you</u> yourself will be in that same position. I know I <u>never</u> thought that <u>I</u> would be in <u>this</u> position. Oh, Happy Birthday, Daddy. I ♥ you!

♥, Amanda B+

Lesson #6: "You can't keep everything in"   16 years
August 14th, 2008

I came up with this topic last minute. As you're reading this, know that I just learned this lesson today. Lately, I've been scared of what's going on with my body. And I've been keeping all of those scared feelings bottled up. So, today I decided to let everything run out of me. I went back to BK [a web site forum called Brave Kids] and just let everything go. And I feel so much better. I usually never talk much about my feelings with my mom or dad, but, lately, have been going to them and telling them how I feel about everything. And I feel so much better thanks to them and BK. I know now where to go. So, the lesson in that is: <u>never</u> hold your feelings back. It will make you feel so much better.

♥, Amanda B+

FRIDAY, AUGUST 15, 2008
Hi All!

My mom begged me to do my update today, and, since i'm feeling better, might as well update while i'm feeling good! OK, medical news first as always! So, my red blood cell count and everything else is the same (which is better than it getting lower). the only thing that got a bit lower was my H's. But hopefully we will see some changes with that soon because today we started Procrit, but Tony said that it won't show probably until next week. I'm really hoping that this will help my H's. My tubes are doing GREAT! And from now on, i'm always going to have a stat lock on it...lol [which keeps the feeding line stable to reduce clots and the risk of inflammation]. My PICC lines are doing well (thank goodness!). That's pretty much all the medical news.

This weekend, i'm really hoping to get out and go to PetSmart to get Abby some bones and do an ID Tag for my grandparents' dog, Sparky. I really wanted to go to the movies before the Sisterhood of the Traveling Pants II got out of the theaters. But I don't think that will happen anytime soon, so i guess i'll have to wait a couple months until it comes out on DVD. Camp Rock is coming out on DVD August 19th, so maybe i can get my dad to pick it up for me? My goal this weekend is to get to everyone's CB pages and see what's going on with all of you.

I want to thank you all for your prayers and signing my guest book. i really love reading it when i can't update.
Please continue to pray for all of my CB friends, and I need a special prayer for my friend, Rachel, who is going through a bump in the road. And for my Jaden, who is in the hospital.

"Times change, and we change with them"   --Latin Proverb
Have a B+ day!
Amanda :-) B+

Lesson #7: "You'll never be OK with your illness."
August 15th, 2008   16 years

I'm doing this topic today because it's how I've been feeling lately. I know that <u>any</u> child or adult will <u>never</u> be OK with their illness. I've had Mito for three years now, and I'm mad sometimes that I have it. I just recently found out why kids and adults that have done <u>nothing</u> <u>bad</u> in their lives have a life-threatening illness. I'm pretty sure that <u>God</u> picked us because we're the <u>special</u> ones who are going to <u>change</u> the world with our <u>positive</u> attitudes and how we approach things. We're the ones who, one day, will have to <u>confront</u> the <u>Lord</u>, and the Lord will clap and say, "<u>Thank You</u> for <u>changing</u> the world and making a difference in people." We're the <u>lucky</u> ones.

♥, Amanda B+

SATURDAY, AUGUST 16, 2008
Hi All!
Not much medical news today, but I figured I would update today because i have no TPN's until Monday night! So, it's going to be a rough weekend! Anyways, I really think the Procrit is helping!!!! I had a lot of muscle pain yesterday, so i'm really hoping that's a good thing! I think that's all the medical news..lol. WOW this is a short entry..lol.

So, I was going to go to PetSmart this weekend, but I think i'll go there another time because i'm going out to the town beach later on. that's where my fundraiser will be. I wanted to make sure you all knew that my fundraiser link is in the little box on top of the page. The tickets for the BBQ dinner are going fast, so if you're going to get a BBQ dinner, please call the phone number that's given on my fundraiser page.

Hmmm, not much else to say, i guess. Okay, well, i'm still hoping to get to everyone's page this weekend, but, if i don't, i'll definitely get to everyone's pages Tuesday. this weekend is going to be tough, so i would probably say Tuesday.

Please continue to pray for all my CB friends, and Thank you for praying for my friend, Rachel. she's doing better. please continue to pray for her.

"The Cure to Mito is living Life" --Amanda Perrotta
Have a B+ day!
Amanda :-) B+

PS: I left out a very special prayer for my buddy, Jaden (so, sorry Jaden!) He's in the hospital right now and wants to get to Disney very badly. please pray that he gets out of there soon and gets to go to Disney! Love ya, Jaden and Jess!

Lesson #8: "It's OK to be scared"
August 17th, 2008   16 yrs.

I thought long and hard about this subject. I wasn't sure whether this would be a good subject to teach because i'm still learning about this one. I've been scared ever since my disease started progressing. During this whole process, I made sure I was brave, and I made sure I didn't cry. i know I could cry, but chose not to until one day during spring, I broke down. I couldn't stop crying. that's when I learned that it's OK to cry. I know every kid or adult who has an illness wants to be Superman, but, if you try to be Superman, you'll eventually break down. So. please don't try to be brave because it will catch up to you sooner or later. That's my lesson for today.

♥, Amanda B+

MONDAY, AUGUST 18, 2008

Hi all. It's Jacki. We all know the weekends are very trying for Manda, so I am doing a quick update. Let me fist say (I know I am her Mother), Manda is the strongest young girl I have ever met!! She NEVER complains no matter what. Manda finds the good in every outcome. How many of us can say that? We complain about the little stuff on a daily basis. If there is one thing our family has learned, it is that NOTHING else matters in life than being together with the ones you love!! Treasure every day! For that we thank our Amanda!

Now for medical news. Manda is weak as expected. She has another blood clot. The nurse (Valerie) is coming out today to TPA it. Also, we started the Procrit IVs. They will be given on M, W, F hopefully. They will hold the H's and not let them drop any further. Thanks to all for everything you do. Thanks also to AMC nurses (Maude and Peggy) for your call the other night. Please, as Manda wishes, continue to pray for all CB friends and families!! God Bless. Jacki

Lesson #9: "A talk you never want to have"
August 18th, 2008   16 yrs.

So, this morning, I had a very scary dream that I <u>don't</u> want to have <u>again</u>! When I told my mom, she started a conversation you never want to have! She asked me: if the doctors told her that there was nothing more they could do, would I want to know? To tell the truth, I would want to know. There would be so much more I would like to experience. I would probably like to tell people how much they mean to me. And how much their prayers mean . I think people would choose what they want to do, and the parents should have nothing to do with their choice about that topic. OK, onto maybe good news?! So, lately my pee has been very light, so that might mean that my liver is getting better!

♥, Amanda B+

TUESDAY, AUGUST 19, 2008

Hi all. It's Jacki. I can't wait until Amanda finds the strength to write again. I love reading her entries!! Manda had a VERY rough day and night. Val could not get the clot to break up, so we are short a lumen. This throws Manda's schedule off A LOT!! I can't keep everything running like we want to, which does not help how she feels. Through it all, she is quiet but never gets discouraged. She goes with the flow! For now, we are just waiting for Manda's nurse, Tony, to get rid of the clot. If not, a trip to VIR to unclot it hopefully, and pray the PICC does not have to be removed and changed!! Manda will update soon. I can't WAIT!!

Please, as Manda wishes, continue to pray for all CB friends and families!! Esp: Her Jaden, she loves you! And a SPECIAL prayer for Natalie. Melody we are keeping you and your family always in our thoughts and prayers. To Melissa, thank you for our talk last night. Don't know what we do without ya!! Love ya. God Bless. Jacki.

WEDNESDAY, AUGUST 20, 2008
Hi Everyone!
It's Amanda, back in action! I was going to do my CB yesterday, but I ended up not feeling so well. Medical stuff first, as you all know. This afternoon, Kim and Val (nurses) are coming to try to get my clot out one more time. if they don't get it out, we're going to end up back in VIR and probably stay a day or two. And we all don't want that, especially since i have so much to do at home! I can't remember if there's anything else. if there isn't, that's pretty much a miracle!...lol.

I've been meaning to tell all of you who have an illness about one of my favorite sites called BraveKids. It has a child/teen forum, and it also has an adult one. I've been going there for three years now, and that forum is just GREAT! I've met soooo many friends through that. I just wanted to tell you all, in case anyone wants to meet other people who maybe have the same disease or illness as you. If you ever start an account on there, look me up. i'm "Dreaming101," and i'll make sure I hook you up with all of my friends and friends who have the same illness as you. It's totally child/teen/adult safe, and every forum has Moderators who make sure you're not saying anything bad etc. Here's the link: http://www.bravekids.org.. they also have a number of camps on the site that are very cool!

OK, so i think i'm going to head out. Please continue to pray for all of my CB buddies especially Jaden.

And my friend, Miss Natalie, who will be having surgery done in September.

"One way to get the most out of life is to look upon it as an adventure"   --William Feather
Everyone have a B+ day!
Amanda :-) B+ F.R.O.G. [Forever rely on God]

Lesson #10. "God is the one who will always answer"
August 20th, 2008   16 yrs.

I never really noticed that God either answers you 'yes,' or 'no.' Just recently, I discovered that God always answers—He either helps you out or goes down another road. Either way, he always puts you on that road you're supposed to be on.   He will <u>never</u> put you on a road that has too many or less obstacles that you can't handle. Even though sometimes you think, "I can't believe this is happening," or "why me?" just remember that God only puts you on a path that you yourself can handle.   Remember that, one day, <u>you</u> will find out why God put you on the path that you had. That was the lesson for today.
♥, Amanda B+

THURSDAY, AUGUST 21, 2008
Hi All!
So, you may be wondering right now, "why isn't Amanda in VIR?!" Well, that's because they had an emergency with a little boy who only has one line, and i have three, so they had to get him in there fast. They told my mom tomorrow for sure, unless they

have another Emergency person. Nothing medical-wise is really going on. I took my Procrit again on Monday. i forgot to tell you that, and i took it again last night. I get it three times a week—Mon., Wed., and Fri.! That's it for medical stuff!

OK, so I have a HUGE apology to give to someone. Emilie, i'm soooo sorry. everyday i've been meaning to mention your name, and then something comes up. but that shouldn't make a difference. Thank you for my box of goodies and all the cards you send me. they're greatly appreciated, and i LOVE getting mail from you. you always come up with the cutest cards!
Jenn Stacey-Thank you for my coupons. I actually ordered my Build-a-Bear a couple days ago (the day i got your coupons!...lol).
If i forgot anyone, please tell me because i'll feel terrible!

Nothing much is going on today. oh wait!!! Dahea (sister) is coming home!!!!!! i've missed her a lot, and i can't wait until i see her (which is not going to be in the hospital!). I'll tell you a quick joke inside our family. Every time Dahea leaves or comes back from Korea, I'm always in the hospital!!! So, Dahea and Carolyn always joke about me being in the hospital. But this is my first time NOT being in the hospital when she comes home, so I'm overly excited! Pippi (nurse) is coming over at 4:00PM to just keep an eye on me so i don't get into trouble! LOL

Please continue to pray for all my CB friends, especially Jaden, who is still a little tired, and my Miss Natalie, who will be having surgery in September.

"Happy are those who dream dreams and are ready to pay the price to make them come true"   --Leon J. Suenes
Have a B+ day!

Amanda Perrotta

Amanda :-) B+ F.R.O.G

Lesson #11: "Why I started this journal"
August 21st, 2008   16 yrs.

I started this journal because eventually I want to turn it into a book. I might not be able to in <u>my</u> lifetime, but i'm hoping when someone eventually comes across this journal, they would want to help me <u>teach</u> all the <u>lessons</u> that I'm teaching, help me to get them all out into the world. I really <u>want</u> to <u>help</u> teach everyone how they should live their lives. I would live to teach someone how to live their lives without <u>fear, regrets,</u> and without wishing that God had not put you on the wrong road. I want people to <u>change</u> the world into a much better place, where <u>everyone</u> <u>lives</u> like there's <u>no</u> <u>tomorrow</u>.
♥, Amanda B+

FRIDAY, AUGUST 22, 2008 1
Hi All!
OK, so as you all know, i probably only have two more days of updating until Tuesday. I'll try as hard as i can to update Saturday, but forget Sunday or Monday because i don't have TPN's this weekend.

So, Tony came out this morning to see if he could unclot the blood clot one more time. I prayed about 50 times when i woke up that the clot would vanish! And guess what?! Tony got a GREAT blood return back, and it started working again. that's a miracle itself. see what prayers can do! I also have some more good news! Tony got my levels back for red blood, bellyrubbon (?sp) [bilirubin, a breakdown product of normal blood function, can be measured to indicate abnormal hemoglobin/O_2 metabolism or liver dysfunction], and etc. the Procrit is now starting to work! about three of my levels came up tremendously! We're still waiting on my liver counts and some other things, but i'm hoping maybe they will get better. So i think that's all the medical news!

Dahea came home last night! I was sooo excited to see her! She looked great, and, as always, came home in a cute, fancy outfit. She brought the whole family home a present. She bought me a Rosary bracelet with real pearls and diamonds, and got it blessed. I was soo in shock because i never expect for her to bring home a present for me, but she always does! Thanks, Da, for my rosary bead bracelet.

Pippi (nurse) came to stay with me last night while mom and dad picked up Dahea and went out to eat. I FINALLY got to watch Step Up 2. it wasn't as good as the first one, but it wasn't boring either. Next movie up is College Road Trip! Thank you, Pippi, for staying with me.

Please continue to pray for my CB friends, especially Jaden, who is still feeling a little yucky, and his mom, Jess.
And for Miss Natalie, who is scheduled for surgery in Sept.
Aunt Kim-I did get the picture of Liam and Belle. i didn't get to reply to your email because i accidentally deleted it. I try to reply back to as many emails as i can during the day. I'll probably get back to you on Tuesday. is that OK?
Happy Birthday to you, Happy Birthday to you, Happy Birthday, dear Alicia, Happy Birthday to you!!

"God always answers. Even if things don't turn out the way you thought they would, he still answered."   --Amanda Perrotta
Have a B+ day!
Amanda :-) B+ F.R.O.G

Lesson #12: "There's good in every person"
August 22nd, 2008   16 yrs.

I didn't have any trouble picking this topic today! This lesson I learned about a year ago. I was sometimes a mean person a couple years ago, but that was only because of my disease. After I got over the anger stage, I realized that there is good in every person! You sometimes can't see it right away, but there is! I try to find the good in everyone now. Sometimes you have to look deep into their souls, but eventually you will find it. Sometimes when you can't find it, they might be sick with their own illness, and might even be going through their anger stage. So remember—everyone has their own reason.
♥, Amanda B+

Lesson #13: "You're the same as any other person...you just have some setbacks"
August 23rd, 2008   16 yrs.

Since I was 11 and had seizures, I never thought I could be a normal kid again. I was wrong! I started dance again, and, even though I went to a Special Education school, I started to play basketball and every other sport again! When I found out that I

had Mitochondrial Disease, I still played all the sports until I could no longer walk. I thought, since I can no longer walk, I couldn't play one sport. It took me six months to start taking steps again, and, even though I can't walk far distances, I play basketball still. I don't run or anything, but, with a lot of confidence, I just run in my chair. So, the lesson for today is: even though you have an illness, you're still a normal human. You just have some setbacks.
♥, Amanda B+

SUNDAY, AUGUST 24, 2008

Hi all. It's Jacki. It's the weekend, and Manda is weak, and her color has not been great. This is what happens, though. We are reconsidering stopping the TPN's and lipids at this point (on the weekends) because there has not been a significant change in her numbers with her liver enzymes. Why put her body through this if it is not going to help? Our goal is to keep Manda comfortable. We are going to do one more blood test, and, if no change, just keep her on seven days a week like before!! We did stop the L-Carnitine [for the rapid absorption of fats into the mitochondria] last week, too. We spoke with the doctors, and they agreed. Manda is under palliative care at home now [meaning that her care is now simply to relieve her pain and keep her comfortable].

Manda is asking a LOT more questions about her illness and telling us how her body feels. This is a very rough, sensitive, and emotional road to go on with her, but we are doing our very best as a family together!! Manda's spirits are so extremely inspirational to all of us. There's no time for any other thoughts!! This weekend brings time together making memories and cherishing each day!! Thanks to all for all you do, and for all your thoughts and prayers!! Please, as Manda wishes, continue to pray for all CB friends and families. We love you all. God Bless. Jacki.

"My dad is Superman"
August 24th, 2008   16 yrs.

This weekend and next week, I am starting my own <u>family</u> journal.

My dad would do anything for Carolyn, Dahea, and me. I wasn't as close to my dad, but that quickly changed when our family found out that I have Mitochondrial Disease. Ever since then, we're as close as we can be! My dad is an inspiration to all dads. If I needed something in the middle of the night, I know my dad would go and get whatever it was. If there was an award for "Best dad," my dad would take home all the medals. To <u>people</u>, he is a man, but <u>to me</u>, he is my <u>dad</u>! The special part is that he could be <u>Superman!</u>
♥, Amanda

MONDAY, AUGUST 25, 2008
Hi all. It's Jacki. Manda is still sleeping. That is what she needs now—as much rest as possible. I kid with her all the time. She will tell me she is not sleepy or tired in one breath and, in the next, say, "Mommy, just let me sleep for a little bit." Her sisters have been having fun with her (doing her and Abby's nails, puzzles, etc.) The 3-D puzzle is finally finished, and we have pictures, but Manda will have to put them up. Dahea stayed up

until two AM to finish, and Manda woke up with it next to her. Thanks, Dabe, mom loves ya.

Carolyn went shopping and brought back the Jonas Brothers CD for Manda, so that's all we have been listening to!! Thanks, 'C.' Love ya more than life for that one!! So, as you all can see, we are making loads of memories and making the best out of EVERY day and are truly grateful for them, and all of you on this journey!! Manda is quiet again but still has that fight, thank God!! Thanks to all for all you do. We love you!!

Please, as Manda wishes, continue to pray for all CB friends and families! Hi, Jess, and Mr. Jaden. We miss you two and love ya LOTS!! God Bless. Jacki.
P.S. A special Thank You to Aunt Kim for helping with Manda's bracelets. She LOVED them!!

"Carolyn"
August 25th, 2008   16 Yrs.

Today, I guess I'm going to tell you all about my biggest sister, Carolyn. I sometimes think an Angel sent her down to help support me through everything! Carolyn's the type of sister who would go overboard for me. She has helped me so much through this. She's very quiet and shy and a great friend to be around. I wish I could help as many people as Carolyn helped. i know some day I'll get to see her children help other kids like her mom did. I trust Carolyn with my whole heart. I love you, Carolyn! I love you to heaven and back. And I thank you for being one of my inspirations!

Amanda Perrotta

♥, Amanda B+

TUESDAY, AUGUST 26, 2008,
Hi All!
I thought i would change my background and my color since it's not really warm anymore, so i think i have to put up the autumn background (i know. :-( ). Hmm, medical-wise, everything is pretty much status quo. I have a couple of new things i want to share with you. My family, Drs., and etc. are waiting for my liver panels to come back. If they come back the same, then i get to go back on TPN's/lipids 24/7. If there is a tiny chance it will get better, then i'll just continue to have TPN's five times a week.

Today my parents are going out to the Town Beach where my fundraiser is going to be. I can't go because they want it to be a surprise for me, but i do get to hang out with the coolest people on earth....Brittany and Brianna! I'm very excited! I also made cinnamon mini muffins for the meeting. they're low sugar, low fat, and low carbs, and there's only like 70 calories for, i think, three. I never expected my muffins to be soooo tiny! You could probably have 100 of them and you would still have the exact calories in you...lol.

Nothing else is really going on. I'm saving all my spoons for this weekend. This weekend i'm going out to Utica to visit my Uncle, Aunt, and cousins! I really wanted to make them something here and bring it to them, but i'm sure they will keep me busy even if i'm just sitting! We could bring Abby, but i've been thinking about it, and i think I should leave her here. i don't need any drama while i'm trying to enjoy my cousins, Uncle, and Aunt.

Please continue to pray for all of my CaringBridge friends, especially Jaden, that he stays healthy so he can go to Florida! And for my Miss Natalie and for everyone else that needs prayers right now.

"You must be the change you wish to see in the world"
                                        --Mahatma Gandhi
Have a B+ Day!
Amanda :-) B+   F.R.O.G

"Dahea is a blessing to our family"
August 26th, 2008   16 yrs.

I knew I was going to write about Dahea next because she has been a blessing to our family. When Dahea first came, I thought she didn't like me. I was pretty much wrong, as usual. Soon enough, she started to talk to and play pranks on me. After that moment, she quickly became my second sister. Dahea has done so much for me. She has helped me through the good and bad. Even though she gets into trouble once in a while, or gets on my nerves, she is, and always will be, my sister. I hope that she knows how much she means to me. I know she has always been closer to Carolyn than to me, but I hope to change that one day. Thank you, Dahea, for being a perfect sister! I ♥ U!
♥, Amanda B+

WEDNESDAY, AUGUST 27, 2008

Amanda Perrotta

Hi All!
OK, before i get to the fun stories, let's see what's going on medical-wise. The Drs., mom, dad, and I agreed that they're keeping me on TPN's every day and every week! There are some bad things that come with that, and then there are some good things as well. Let's get the bad over first. If i'm on TPN's every night, that means my liver won't get any better. it will probably just get worse, but i'm prepared for that. The good thing is, if i'm on TPN's every night, i'll have much more energy to do stuff i want to do. And i won't have to feel icky on Sundays and Mondays!!!!

This morning, while Tony was here, i tried to take a nap, but, when i woke up, i felt extremely nauseous!!! Let's just say, about two minutes later, i was retching (nothing came up because there's nothing in my stomach), but i just retched for about five minutes, and then i felt fine. The reason I retched was because my tubes were all twisted!!! How silly of me! I don't think there's anything else going on medical-wise. Yessss!

I had a fun night last night. Brittany and Brianna came over while everyone else went to the fundraiser meeting. We made a blanket, which is soooooo warm! That's all i need for the winter! After it was finished, i was thinking maybe, for some of my Christmas gifts, i'll make those for some people. ?? I'm still thinking on it. Right now, i'm actually working on my friend, Rina's, Christmas gift and her birthday present. I might send them at the same time. maybe not though?

Tonight, i don't think we have anything planned. Just saving all my energy for Utica.

Please continue to pray for all my CB friends, especially Jaden, Natalie, and one of my friends on BraveKids whose name is Niki.
"Never say more then is necessary"   --Richard Brinsley Sheridan
Have a B+ Day!
Amanda :-) B+ F.R.O.G

"Super mom"
August 27th, 2008   16 yrs.
I always save my mom for last because she and my dad have been through a lot with me, and, through every obstacle, they (especially mom) have always believed in me. My mom was and is the type of mom who always makes positive of something, even if that something is bad. I think that's where I get my positive attitude and thinking. My mom never left me anywhere alone, even if I asked her. She knew more about me than I did when I was little. When I got sick, she always told me that everything will be OK and to still reach for my dreams. She told me that, even if I am sick, I can still have a bright future. Thank You mom for believing in me every step of the way! I LOVE YOU (more than life)!
♥, Amanda B+

THURSDAY, AUGUST 28, 2008
Hi All!
This might be the last time i update until either Sunday or Monday, but i'll definitely try to update tomorrow before i leave to go to Utica.

OK, so, some of my blood work came back today. My liver is status quo. red and white blood cell count is a bit lower than last week, but i'm hoping by taking the Procrit tomorrow it will get a little higher!   I was really sleepy this morning (mom says it's probably from my red and white blood cell count being low), but i'm fine now. I slept until about 12:00PM, so, if i get some extra sleep tonight, i'm sure i'll be rearing to go tomorrow with my little cousins. Everything else medical-wise is the same.

I'm still debating whether i should bring Abby to Utica with me. My aunty, uncle, and cousins just got a puppy a few months back, and i'm just not so sure.

I really wish i could make a blanket for each of my CB friends, but it's so hard to ship it.   but no worries, i'm still making small Christmas presents that i can send through mail.

Michele and Diane stopped by my house a little while ago, and we just talked for a bit. Michele is looking into getting a Tattoo guy to come in and do my tattoo!   I already know what i want. The whole family is getting one. So i'm very excited about that! OK, well, better get going. Please continue to pray for all my CB friends, especially Jaden, Carrie, Niki, and Miss Natalie.

"A road twice traveled is never as long"   --Rosalie Graham
Have a B+ weekend!
Amanda :-) B+ F.R.O.G

"My best friend Abby"
August 28th, 2008   16 yrs.
So, I forgot to mention my best friend in my family.   Two summers ago, I was looking for any terrier pups. When I found

Abby's owner in the paper, I knew I was going to have a Cairn Terrier. Once we got to the owner's house, I saw Abby, and she was the one! Ever since then, Abby and I have grown up together. I only have one best friend who is a guy, and now I have a girl best friend (except she's K). Abby has always been there for me through the good and the bad. Abby's not only my baby or best friend, she is now also my Service Dog. I love Abby to death. And if something ever happens to me, I want her owner to be Carolyn or Dahea.
♥, Amanda B+

FRIDAY, AUGUST 29, 2008
Hi All!
This is going to be a VERY quick update as i am getting ready to leave for Utica to see my aunt, uncle, and cousins! Everything medically is pretty stable right now. I've been having some little problems with my sugar lately, but i finally got the hang of that. Tony (nurse) came today to draw some more blood, change my dressing for my PICC, and etc.. Today is my last day of taking Procrit until Monday. OK, well, that's it medical-wise. i'll try to update either Monday or Tuesday.
Please continue to pray for all my CB buddies over the weekend, especially Jaden, Natalie, and Carrie!

"Where there is an open mind, there will always be an open frontier"   --Charles Kettering
Have a B+ weekend!!!
Amanda :-) B+ F.R.O.G

"How you know you have a true friend"
Dedicated to: Mike Silvia, my best friend! I love you, Mike, and always will.

August 29th, 2008   16 yrs.

Ever since I was little, I've had loads of friends. When you're only 10, you really don't know what a true friend is. Once I got my disease, people and friends walked in and out of my life. The year I started Wildwood, in 2002, I thought no one would want to be my friend. After a couple of years in Wildwood, and after I found out I had Mito, I finally realized what a true friend is. He/She is that kind of person who doesn't care what you look like or if you're different than other kids. And a true friend will always be by your side even if you have a life-threatening illness. So, before you start hanging our with a new friend, ask yourself, Would he/she stick with me through thick and thin?" That's my lesson for today!

♥, Amanda B+

SATURDAY, AUGUST 30, 2008

Hi all. It's Jacki. We made it!!! Ye-Ha. We are out at my brother's home in Utica. We left last night and arrived safely. Manda slept all the way. She did well but was extremely nauseous and in some pain. She made it, though. Manda is sleeping now and very tired. Spirits are great. She was so happy to see her cousins!! This is still going to be a tough weekend because they don't start TPN's and the lipid's seven days a week until next weekend. (Waiting for the appointment from Medicaid.) As always, it comes down to insurance, which is sooooo wrong, but life. I wonder what would happen if it was their child waiting?

Other than that, not much. Making lots of memories and trying to relax and enjoy family time between IV's. Pippi, Misty, Pegster, Ashley, Maude, Allie, Kathy, Elma: Manda misses you all soooo much. Not enough to come back to her room [at Albany Medical Center], though. Love to all!! Please, as Manda wishes, continue to pray for all CB friends and families!! God Bless! Jacki.
P.S. Pipi, Manda is looking for a visit. :}

"What family truly means"
August 30th, 2008   16 yrs.
I'm writing about this subject today because we're going to my uncle's, aunt's and cousin's house. I've seen some families that don't care about each other, abuse their kids, and etc. I'm lucky because I have a family that care [for] and love me. My mom always told Carolyn and me that we're rich with health, family, and friends. And even now, I still believe that. i may not have the health part, but I still know what family means. I may not have the picture perfect family, but at least I know that they are taking this emotional ride with me. If my family decided not to go on this ride, then they're not <u>really</u> my family. So always remember that, if your family truly loves you, they will be by your side every step of the way!
♥, Amanda B+

"You believe and then you see."
August 30th, 2008   16 yrs.
It took me a while to come up with this subject. When you were a little girl or boy, your mom always told you that either your fish or a family member went to Heaven. Then, your mom or dad tells you what Heaven is. I've believed there is and was a Heaven

my whole life. Lately, I've been questioning what Heaven looks like or if there even is one. I decided that I'm going to choose that Believing is not seeing. Even though I still wonder what Heaven looks like, I don't think you have to see to believe. God wrote in the Bible that we will each have our very own mansion. I believe that because I know God would never lie. My mom told me since I was little that I won't be sick when I earn my wings. So, the lesson for today is, "Believing is not seeing."

♥, Amanda B+

SUNDAY, AUGUST 31, 2008

Hi All!

It's Amanda, typing from Utica. I'm sorry I haven't checked-in yet. i've been busy playing with little cousins under the age of 8, so i'm sure everyone can sort of relate to that. My family and I were supposed to leave today but decided to stay an extra day. If i'm going on vacation, and i have to pack three loads of medical stuff, then it better be long...lol.

Medical-wise things are pretty stable. I just got another blood clot this morning in one of my lines, so i'm guessing tomorrow we're going to have to TPA it. Pretty much that's it!

I'm enjoying playing with my cousins every night and spending time with my uncle and aunt. Last night, we played the Wii and air hockey. It wipes me out, but it's too fun not to play! Thank you Aunt Kim, Uncle Bilbo, and cousins for letting me stay, and a special Thank You to Liam, for letting me sleep in your room.

I'm still checking in on everyone every chance i get. I might not sign your guest book, but believe me, i'm still looking after you all and saying prayers for all of you every night.

Please continue to pray for all my CB friends, especially Natalie, Jaden, and Carrie, and a special prayer for everyone in the path of the Hurricane, New Orleans, etc.

Everyone have a B+ day!

Amanda :-) B+ F.R.O.G

Lesson #7: "We never know how much time we have left"[14]

August 31st   16 yrs.

It took me a while before I came up with the subject. When people, kids, babies, etc. figure out that they have an illness or disease, we don't think it's anything. But the truth is that every living person has a time bomb inside them. But, with people who have a disease or illness, that time bomb ticks a lot more. i know myself that i won't be able to make it to my 21st birthday. My mom always told me, "if you have done your job on earth, then you will get your wings." It's hard knowing that I'm not going to live as long as my sister or even anybody else. So, the lesson for today is, even though you may not have a lot of time left, just keep living life!

♥, Amanda B+

MONDAY, SEPTEMBER 01, 2008

Hi all, it's Jacki. We made it home safe. Manda is very tired but truly enjoyed being out of the house and spending time with her cousins and Aunt Kim and Uncle Bilbo. Thank you guys for

---

[14] Amanda began her lessons again from #7.

making special time and memories with Manda and the rest of the gang!! We had such a relaxing time just hanging out, and taking naps for Louis. :-) Manda did well, then made the most of all her energy and would nap to rebuild!! We also loved little Ricky. He is the cutest puppy!!

Now for medical news. Manda has another clot, so I left Tony a message, and her sugar has been running high, making her body not feel that well. We will have to see about that. Other than that, it's the same pain/nausea, but she is a true FIGHTER!! Sleeping right now. Hopefully, Manda will update tomorrow. If not, I will. Please, as Manda wishes, continue to pray for all CB friends and families!! Also a special Thank You to Aunt Mimi for having a jewelry party with the proceeds going to Amanda's Journey. Thanks, Amy!! God Bless, Jacki.

Lesson #8: "Hope for the future."
September 1st, 2008   16 yrs.
I was scared I was running out of ideas and thoughts. So the MDA [Muscular Dystrophy Association] Telethon is on today, and i just heard the man say "hopefully in ten years, there will be a cure for every form of MD." What he said made me think, 'I wonder if there will be a cure for Mito in ten years'" I know researchers and doctors come up with 50 different meds every year. Hopefully, if I'm alive in ten years, I'll be one of those millions who will be cured. i wonder what it would feel like to play a sport again, have a <u>real</u> meal, and have to be hooked up to <u>nothing</u>! I don't think I would know what to do with myself! I'm so used to every conversation being medical. I just can't imagine

being so-called, "<u>normal</u>."   So, the lesson is, always look for the brighter future!
♥, Amanda B+

TUESDAY, SEPTEMBER 02, 2008
Hi All!
I feel like i'm playing yo-yo with my mom and the updates..lol. I'm home safely from Utica as most of you know. I decided my mom should update yesterday because i was tired from the ride home and playing with my cousins and a puppy!

Medical news first as always!   This morning, when I woke up i had that feeling you get before you throw up. needless to say, i did throw up (four times!). The first time i threw up, blood was coming out.   we all thought it was coming from my stomach. After about five minutes, we realized my nose was bleeding!   I had three nosebleeds today, but nothing was as BAD as the 1st one. it took about 40 minutes to get it under control. My mom called Tony (my nurse) first, and he said the bloody nose was probably caused by dry air, so we know what's going on with that. My mom called Cheryl, and she said the same thing about the bloody nose. she told my mom the vomiting might be from either a bug going around, an infection, the list goes on!   Cheryl told my mom, if i keep vomiting, then we'll have to go in to either the ER or they might just take me up to a room.

My line is still clotted, but we still have the other two working (knocking on wood!), so, we're grateful for that!   I think that's pretty much all the medical news. So, as you can see, i had an entertaining morning!

Amanda Perrotta

I'm planning on taking the rest of the day doing nothing! OK, so, as i'm typing this, my nose is bleeding, so i'm going to make it short for today!

Please continue to pray for all my CB buddies, especially Jaden, Natalie, and Carie.
Have a B+ day!
Amanda :-) B+ F.R.O.G

Lesson #9: "You have to have humor!"
September 2nd, 2008   16 yrs.
I came up with this topic pretty easily. When you have an illness that brings you into the hospital a lot, you usually start to get very depressed. Well, I try not to get depressed by joking around with medical humor. Every time I go into the hospital, I try to come up with different things to make me, nurses, and other people laugh. My humor varies from squirting saline to silly string. Why I do this is so that I can learn how to live the fullest, even if it's in a place I don't want to be. Another thing I want to teach people is to try to have humor in everything you do. Sometimes, things happen to you, and when those things happen, you don't want to become depressed. So try to make some humor about it!
♥, Amanda B+

WEDNESDAY, SEPTEMBER 03, 2008
Hi all. It's Jacki. Manda is sleeping right now. She had a very rough night. We are waiting to see if she has a line infection, and her platelet count is a little low (nose bleeds) [Platelets are blood cells that naturally form into clots to stop bleeding]. Not a great

amount, but, with Mito, everything is affected. I am waiting for a call from Cheryl to see what we want to do. Manda also has blood clots in one lumen, and the other one is hard flushing. Tony is coming in a while, and, between me, Cheryl, Dr. Adams, and Tony, we will know how to help Manda. Her spirits are still fighting and willing, and so are we as a family!! Manda or I will update soon. Please, as Manda wishes, continue to pray for all CB friends and families!! Jaden, Manda misses you and sends hugs!! God Bless!! Jacki.

P.S. Please say a special prayer for all Mito families, that God gives them the will and peace in making medical decisions every day. No parent or family should have to do this!! May God be with you all.

Lesson #10: "When one door closes, another one opens."
September 3rd, 2008   16 yrs.
It took me a <u>very</u> long time to come up with this subject. A friend that I know chose to earn his wings a bit too early. Or should I say, his mom decided that. I know it's not his time to leave yet. He would have had so many doors close on him, but he would also have many doors open for him. I want to fight this disease right to where I say, "I can't do this anymore!" I'm not planning on doing that any time soon, either. I dislike people who think they can't beat their disease or any illness. I personally think that's a sin. No matter how hard you want to quit, don't because God might have so many lessons he has to teach you before you die. So, the lesson for today is: never give up no matter how hard it gets"
♥, Amanda B+

Lesson #11" "You need a companion."
September 4th, 2008   16 yrs.

I'm doing this subject today to honor my best friend, Abby!
When I finally realized that my disease is life-threatening, I came
around and decided that I needed someone to share this with.
From the first day that I got here until now, she's always been
there for me. I lean on here for a lot of support, and she doesn't
run away like a person would, and she can't tell my secrets, so
that's why she's my best friend. I personally think everyone with
an illness should have a loyal friend who won't turn his or her
back on you. You could talk to them about anything, and they
won't say a peep about what you said, and they will go on the
adventure with you. That's someone everybody needs.

♥, Amanda B+

FRIDAY, SEPTEMBER 05, 2008

Hi all. Just a very quick update. Manda is not doing well at all
today. She had a very rough night and day today!! She is running
a fever and retching terribly. Tony drew labs today to see if she is
septic [has a blood infection], and we're just waiting on results.
Please pray for comfort and rest for our Manda; she is fighting this
battle with EVERYTHING she has in her!! I will let you all
know when we have some news. Please, as Manda wishes,
continue to pray for all CB friends and families! Esp: Jaden, who is
back in AMC and also fighting with all he's got!! We love ya, Jess
and Jaden, and our prayers and thoughts are ALWAYS with you
both!! Thanks to all. God Bless, Jacki, and, for Amanda, B+ and
F.R.O.G.!!

SATURDAY, SEPTEMBER 06, 2008,
Hi all. It's Jacki. Well, medical first. Cheryl just called and said, so far so good with the [blood] cultures; nothing is growing as of yet. We have three more days to wait, but it is looking good for NO infection!! Manda, on the other hand, is still retching and running a fever. We think it is more that her stool is backing up again, and for that there is nothing we can do. Dr. Adams did increase her pain meds (Dilaudid) and some of the other meds for nausea, and her Ativan from twice to four times a day.

Manda is also having a little more trouble breathing, so she sleeps sitting half way up, and we added the O_2 to her bipap when she sleeps. Manda is extremely weak and very tired and quiet. She just lays there, but every once in a while you see her BEAUTIFUL smile!! That's enough to get anyone through a day and the long nights!! Hoping and praying for comfort and rest for her. This is also going to be Manda's first weekend back on TPN'S and lipids yee-ha!! There is no need to stop them any longer on the weekends because it really did not help her liver enzymes go down. Why put her through it? We are doing EVERYTHING in our power to keep her comfy!! Well, enough of that. Can't wait for Manda to be strong enough to update!! Please, as Manda wishes, continue to pray for all CB friends and families, esp: Manda's Jaden and mom, Jess. God Bless. Jacki.
And for Amanda, B+ and F.R.O.G

P.S. A special thanks to Manda's nurse, Tony, who is more like family. I don't know what we would do with out him!! Also, Pipi, Manda loves you and can't wait to see you soon!!

Amanda Perrotta

MONDAY, SEPTEMBER 08, 2008

Hi all. Not much to report. Things are still the same here, the retching and fever with the bloody noses. Manda is exhausted. She is retching almost every two to three hours. We are trying EVERYTHING to keep her comfy, which is hard with the retching.[15] Her pain is well controlled, though, thank God!! Tony is coming today (on his day off), so we will see what he suggests. Nothing more at this time. Will update soon. Please continue to pray for all CB friends and families, esp: Manda's Jaden and mom, Jess, and all others in need!! Thank you all for all you do!! Please remember to check out Manda's link on the welcoming page if you have not done that yet. Her movies are BEAUTIFUL!! She worked hard on them. Thank you. God Bless. Jacki

Lesson #12: "You're going to win the fight"

September 8th, 2008   16 yrs.

I've been wanting to write about this subject for a while now, but I've been very sick. When you find out you have an illness, you immediately think you're going to be fine. In reality, though, you have to <u>fight</u> until you're too tired. With my disease, I have to fight every second for what I want or need to do. Some friends I've made over the years fight harder than I'll ever do. When you can't fight anymore and earn your angel wings, you still won the fight! The way I think of it is, if you fought the hardest that you could, and you earned your wings, you still won. God just wanted you to arrive a bit earlier than expected because you're special. So, never worry that you didn't win because you fought the good fight!

♥, Amanda B+

---

[15] At this point, Amanda began to throw up blood.

TUESDAY, SEPTEMBER 09, 2008
Hey Everyone!

It's Carolyn (Amanda's sister). My mom asked me to give a quick update since she is busy, and Amanda is too weak right now to update herself. Just wanted to let you all know that Amanda is pretty much the same. Very weak and sleepy, and continues to retch every couple of hours, which is very tough to watch. She continues to keep her head up, though, and faces every new challenge with a positive attitude. I'm so happy to have her as my sister. :o)

Tonight is the last meeting before Amanda's benefit, which will be held September 13th, this Saturday, at North Greenbush Town Beach (Snyder's Lake) from 12-7:30. It's going to be tons of fun, and I can't wait to see everyone! Thanks to everyone, especially the committee who put this together and gave up a lot of their own time to plan everything. We couldn't have done it without you guys. Thanks so much!

Please, as Amanda wishes.... Continue to pray for her Jaden, who is going through a lot right now, and for Jess (his mom) as well. Jaden...Manda loves you and misses you. Stay strong, little guy!

OK, well thanks everyone for all of your prayers and support. It truly means a lot to all of us. God Bless!
B+ and F.R.O.G
~Carolyn~

Amanda Perrotta

Lesson #13: "My inspiration"
September 10th, 2008   16 yrs.

I've been wanting to write about my inspiration: my friend Malisa. Malisa has Mito as well, just not the same form. She is the person who helped me get through the angry stage. I think God put her on this earth to help me and all other teens/adults with Mito. Malisa has hooked me up with so many new friends who sometimes are the same age/gender or even have the same form of Mito as I do! Malisa thinks I'm amazing and inspirational, but the truth is that she is the one who made a huge impact on me and will always be my inspirational amazing, life-changing hero. And for that, I applaud her. I hope some day I can be as amazing as she is.

Dedicated to Malisa.

♥, Amanda B+

THURSDAY, SEPTEMBER 11, 2008

Hi all. It's Jacki. Manda is still the same—fever and retching. Today, Dr. Adams is starting Manda back on Flagil, an antibiotic, but we have to stop the Procrit (for her H's). Dr. Adams upped Manda's Ativan from two to six times a day. Manda just lays here and sleeps most of the time. We have to get her doing more deep breaths if she can because she is now coughing up mucus, or trying to. Manda's O_2 has to be sent from her Bi-pap now, too, due to her low Oxygen stats and weakness in muscles. We are praying that we can even get her to her benefit this weekend!! Other than this, Manda is still maintaining a B+ attitude.

We are trying acupuncture tonight for the nausea, anything to help. Manda's pain is well controlled, though. They keep having

458

to go up on the Dilaudid, but we do whatever it takes to make her comfortable!! Thanks to all for EVERYTHING you do and for thoughts and prayers!! Will update soon. Please, as Manda wishes, continue to pray for all CB friends and families!!

For Manda, B+ and F.R.O.G. God Bless. Jacki.

FRIDAY, SEPTEMBER 12, 2008

Hi all. It's Jacki. Manda is still the same, but fever is higher. The fever and retching have been going on two weeks now. We know why. Manda's stool is backing up again. Manda does not have bowel movements at all. Her last BM was in April of this year. The stool just sits there (which means she is prone to infection). When Manda was in the hospital, Dr. Qualia went in to try to remove most of it, twice, but not with too much luck. There is nothing we can do about this except try to keep Manda comfortable and try Flagil (antibiotic) again prevent infection. Flagil will be running three times per day, seven days on, three weeks off, then seven days on from now on. Manda is lucky, though, because she has never had a line infection yet, and we have tried to keep her away from antibiotics when we can to reserve for later use, if you know what I mean. That would be the last thing to do for Manda, so we are very lucky there so far.

Manda is sleeping now and I think trying to save energy for tomorrow. We are still hoping to get her there [to the fundraiser], with the help from Pipi, her AMC nurse, and Tony, her VNA [Visiting Nurses Association] nurse. We want so badly for Manda to be able to share this memory with us!! We are truly grateful for all the support and love from our community and family and friends. Much love and thanks. Words can NEVER describe to any of you!! Also, a Thank You to Cheryl and Dr. Adams for your phone calls and love and support. We could not get through this without you all (Kate, you too!). So, enough for now.

Please know that Louis and I can never express the feelings we have for all who have been on Manda's Journey with our family. We love you all and keep you in our hearts forever!! Please, as Manda wishes, continue to pray for all CB friends and families. Jaden and Jess, Manda sends hugs and loves you!!
For Amanda. B+ and F.R.O.G. May God Bless you all!! Jacki.

SUNDAY, SEPTEMBER 14, 2008
Hi all. It's me Jacki. Well, Amanda made it to her benefit yesterday!! Even though she stayed inside the RV all day, her nurses got Manda out right at the end in time for Louis and me to thank everyone. The day was soooo beautiful!! Louis and I can NEVER even come close to thanking enough the Amanda's Journey committee and all the volunteers that came out to help. It was overwhelming to us as a family!! Thank you to Pippi and Tony, Manda's nurses, that made it even possible to have Manda there!! We love you both very much!! Also, to our families and friends. Thank you for being there for us. A special thanks to Karen and Kim, the heads of the committee, for going constantly to make this a special and memorable day for all of us!!

Now to Medical news, which I hate doing. Manda is still the same —fever, retching, bloody noses, and not really with it too much. Extremely sleepy, but pain is being controlled very well. Tony is continually upping Manda's Dilaudid and Ativan dosage. Manda is also getting Ativan now every three to four hours. Not much else to report, still the same here, just getting weaker and weaker.

Thanks to all for all thoughts and prayers, and your support. Please, as Manda wishes, continue to pray for all CB friends and families!! And, for Manda, B+ and F.R.O.G. God Bless. Jacki.

P.S. Thank you to Pastor Jim for all your love and support!! Louis and I want to say a special Thank You to all the AMC nurses that came yesterday. We love you all!! And to Erica, from Dr. Adams' office, thanks Erika and family!! And I did not want to forget Rich Becker and his family. Thanks Rich, and thanks for the coverage about National Mito week!!

Lesson #14: "Use and abuse it while you can"
September 15th, 2008   16 yrs.
I have been thinking about this subject for a while. When people get sick, whether it's a cough, sore throat, or disease, their first reaction is to lay down and hope that they'll feel better. The truth is, for kids/adults who have a life-threatening disease, well we don't just lay down all day and wish we weren't sick. As soon as we feel an inch better, we all get up on the horse again! When you just lay there in your bed, you're not going to get better just like that. You have to live to the fullest, even if you can't move. There are so many ways you can enjoy and live life to the fullest when you're sick. Always remember this, "If you feel better for even one second, use it and abuse it while you can."
♥, Amanda B+ F.R.O.G.

TUESDAY, SEPTEMBER 16, 2008
Hey Everyone!
It's Carolyn! (Amanda's sister for the people who do not know me.) Just giving a quick update because my mom is busy doing

461

stuff. This past weekend was amazing! My family and I had such a great time, and we are so thankful and truly happy for every single person who took part in it and gave up their time to come out and join us. :)

Amanda is pretty much the same. She's been sleeping a lot, and I guess now the TPN's (her nutrition) that keep her alive are not working with her body. That's why they think she is retching all the time. So, right now, the doctors are trying to figure it all out and to find a solution to the problem. So, please pray that everything there will work out. As many of you know, Amanda was interviewed last week with Benita Zahn. That will be showing this Thursday night at 5pm on channel 13. Nothing else is really going on. But, as Amanda wishes, please continue to pray for all of her CB friends as well as Tony, her nurse, who just had surgery. Hope you feel better, Tony! You're awesome! :-)

I thank everyone for being there, and checking in on Manda. She loves to hear from all of you! Hope everyone has an enjoyable week! :-) B+ and F.R.O.G.
~Carolyn~

WEDNESDAY, SEPTEMBER 17, 2008
Hi all. It's Jacki. Manda is not doing well as you all know. For over two weeks now, Manda sleeps all the time. She has been running a fever and retching. She is lucid and nods with her eyes closed most of the day and night. At this point, Manda's body is having a hard time with her only nutrient, the TPN's. There is nothing they can do about it. If we decided to stop, we all know

what that means! We, as a family, are NOT giving up!!! If our Manda can do this, then it would be a sin to give up on our child!!

Louis and I have always tried teaching the girls that Life is not always fair. Life may not always go where we want it to take us. There is a GREATER PLAN!! You do not have to like it, but we have to find some way to live with it and know that, out of something bad or hard, ALWAYS comes something good!! There is a reason for everything!! We might just not know what it is, but have faith!! This is something our Manda has taught us, especially Louis and me. Don't ever give up!! Fight till the end!!

Manda is a true fighter!! She left AMC in mid Aug. at the weight of almost 122.   As of today, she is almost 111. She is weak but still has the fight!! Please, as Manda wishes, continue to pray for all CB friends and families!! Also, a reminder: the week of Sept. 21-27 is National Mito week!!   Please know that Manda can't get to friends' sites too much any more, but don't think for one moment you are not all in our hearts!! For Manda, B+ and F.R.O.G!! God Bless. Jacki.

Lesson #15: "You can either write or talk about it"
September 17t, 2008   16 yrs.
When you have an illness or if you just have an issue, you should always either talk or write about it. That's one of the reasons I started this journal, this reason and a couple of others. I don't like talking to people much, so i feel like writing in this journal is like talking to a person. When I write about my feelings in here, I don't get as mad, sad, or frustrated as much. This is a very short lesson. But it needed to be told.
♥, Amanda B+ F.R.O.G.

Amanda Perrotta

THURSDAY, SEPTEMBER 18, 2008
Hi All! I just wanted to leave a short message while i'm feeling a tiny bit better. My mom is going to tell you all that's going on medical-wise, but i just wanted to thank you all for your prayers and for coming to my fundraiser. OK, well i don't have as much energy as i usually do, so everyone have a B+ day!! And know that i'm praying for all of you and i love you guys!
-Amanda :-) B+ F.R .O.G

~~~~~

Hi all. It's Jacki. I am not gonna add too much. It's Manda's day to update!! Medically, still the same. Let's just all enjoy Manda updating today. It's a good day when she has some energy to do!! I will leave it at that. Thanks, Peggy, for the beautiful flower arrangement. You are too sweet!! God Bless all!! Jacki.

Lesson #16:"An apple a day keeps the Dr. away"
September 19th, 2008   16 yrs.
These days, wherever you go, there are a lot of people who are obese and can't walk. To me, i think that's a sin, but to other people, well, they think it's completely normal. I don't know why they would want to become unhealthy and have to worry about medical problems like walking or breathing. Today, in this decade, there are <u>so</u> many diet options as well. Some people tend to feel bad for them, but I don't because God didn't give me a choice to <u>not</u> be able to walk sometimes or have respiratory

464

problems, but He let those people choose to have that lifestyle. I applaud those who are trying to live a healthier lifestyle!
♥, Amanda B+ F.R.O.G.

SATURDAY, SEPTEMBER 20, 2008

Hi all. It's Jacki. Did you not LOVE that update from Manda the other day? Yee-Ha for Manda!! I miss that sooo much! So, let's get medical out of the way. Manda is still the same, retching, fever, and more blood clots!! I just got off the phone with Dr. Adams. Manda's PICC line has to go. We are going to see what we have to do next, but she has to have something in order to get ALL her meds and nutrients. He is calling VIR to see if they can find access to a vein. We had no luck before but NEVER give up!! Now, Manda also is running very high potassium levels because nothing is being absorbed or metabolized in her system anymore. Dr. Adams said this is what is causing her chest pain and even more intense back pain. They are running another potassium level today. We had to stop all maintenance and TPN's. We will see what happens.

It is getting so much more involved taking care of Manda's needs at home to keep her comfortable, but we wouldn't have it any other way. Just to have her here is a true BLESSING! I do know that how Louis and I perceive "quality" has changed! Manda is holding on every day but struggles. For all of you that saw her on TV, that was taped three weeks ago. The day after, Manda started with all this and has continued!! She is so weak!! She sleeps all day, and then is aware but with eyes closed but still responds to our asking if she is awake. I don't know what's going to happen at this point. I just know that it is getting hard to see her this way!! We are going to try to take Manda to the ocean to stay at my aunt and uncle's house. We want her to see the ocean and remember the times we had as a family. Good times, and peaceful ones. We think this is important to her and to us as a family!! Let's just pray we can get her there!

Hey, on a much more lighter note, Manda wants to be Dorothy for Halloween, with Toto of course!! Her costume is amazing, the red shoes and all!! She wants to go trick-or-treating, but we will see!! We all know, if Manda has a goal, she does her best to achieve it!! That's it for now. Will update soon!! Thanks for all you do. As Manda wishes, please continue to pray for all CB families and friends!!

For Manda, B+ and F.R.O.G. God Bless. Jacki.

SUNDAY, SEPTEMBER 21, 2008
Hi All!
I wanted to type a quick message because i feel like i've abandoned you all. :-(I think about you all everyday, and i continue to pray for you all. It's been a bit tough lately getting on the computer because i've been so tired and nauseous, but, when i have even a second, i try to get on. Thank you everyone who is honoring my wishes and praying for all my CB and BK friends. I love you all and miss checking in on each of you. OK, well, i'm going to get going. Have a B+ night!
Amanda :-) B+ F.R.O.G.

~~~~~

Hi all. It's Jacki. I have a quick update. Not much better than yesterday. Manda's body is not metabolizing her TPNs anymore.

We had to stop for now. We are hoping they can come up with something, but they don't promise. Tony called this morning to check on Manda. Thanks Tony!! I don't think you really had a week off!! (sorry). There are a lot of other things going on too, but I am choosing to talk about them at another point. One step at a time. That's all we as a family can do. We are still holding on to Halloween and getting Manda to Maine!! A day in Manda's life is sleep, wake up around 4 or 5 PM, other than for meds during the night or day!! Manda is still fighting like us all, but it's getting soooo hard!!

On this note, I will leave you with one thought, for our Manda! "Yesterday is History. Tomorrow is a Mystery. TODAY IS A GIFT!" Thanks to all for love and support. It means MORE than you all will ever know!! This is the HARDEST thing we as a family have to endure!! But we will make it with the Grace of God, and for everything there is a reason!! Please, as Manda wishes, continue to pray for all CB friends and families. And for our Mare!! B+ and F.RO.G. For Manda the meaning of frog is: FOREVER RELY ON GOD!! May God Bless!! Jacki.

TUESDAY, SEPTEMBER 23, 2008 10:49 AM
Hi everyone!! This is Amanda's Aunt Kim here. I just talked to Jacki, and she will not have a chance, so she wanted me to update for her. As I am typing, the family is heading to the VIR because Manda's PICC line has to be pulled. Please, please pray that they are able to access her, since she has not had any TPN's since Friday and is now running a fever of 101. If Jacki cannot update later on this afternoon, I will do it for her...I know how much everyone cares about our Manda.

Amanda Perrotta

As Manda wishes, please pray for all of her friends!
Aunt Kim
B+ & FROG

TUESDAY, SEPTEMBER 23, 2008 03:40 PM,
Hello again everyone, it's Aunt Kim. I just wanted to let you all know the good news...that they were able to give Manda a new PICC line! They will be starting the TPN's back up tomorrow. So, as soon as she builds her strength, she will be updating personally!! :-) I know how you all love her updates!!
As many of you know, Manda is much wiser than her 16 years, and this world is a better place because of her!! I am very proud to be her aunt. Please continue your prayers for Manda and the whole family!!! Thank you.
Aunt Kim
B+ & FROG

WEDNESDAY, SEPTEMBER 24, 2008 10:27 AM,
Hi all. It's Jacki. Thanks, Aunt Kim, for the updating!! So, where do I start? First, thank God for access to a placement for a PICC. Manda now has EXTREMELY elevated ketones [a liver byproduct of fat/lipid breakdown. Excess ketones can cause coma and eventual death]—over 160 in urine!! [Normal is 0-160 mg/dl] Don't know at this point what we are doing, waiting to hear from Dr. Adams and Cheryl. Manda is still running a fever between 100.9 and 101. Has been off TPN's and lipids since Friday!!! Just hydration [water] at this point. Also elevated potassium levels [which can lead to improper water balance in the tissues and muscle spasms]. We have to wait and see!! She is now at 109 pounds and trying to keep her O2 levels up is getting

harder. Manda's heart rate is between 110 and 150 (at rest) [normal is 60 to 80 beats per minute at rest for women] for the past week!! We are going to see if they can up the bi-pap levels more. We also have O2 running with the Bi-pap now at all times!!

Right now, Manda is running the race for her LIFE!! What a fighter!! She told the doctor (during the procedure) yesterday to come out and check with us to see if we agreed where the PICC line was going! It was so funny. Of course we said yes to using the only vein [she has left], but Manda stood her ground!! She is so SASSY and STRONG!! Don't know what else to say, just PRAY!! Please!! Thanks to all for your on-going support. You will never know how it gets us ALL through the day to read Manda's page. It reminds us all that we are not alone in this, Amanda's Journey!! On a positive note, we got access to a new line yesterday!! YE-HAAAAAAA!! God Bless all. Jacki. And for MANDA, PLEASE CONTINUE TO PRAY FOR All CB FRIENDS AND FAMILIES!! AND REMEMBER TO always B + and F.R.O.G.

Lesson 17: "There's love and support everywhere"
September 24th, 2008   16 yrs.
I haven't written in a long time because I'm still retching and etc. When you become ill, you instantly try to find other people who are going through the same thing. Let me tell you from experience that finding adults/kids that have the same thing (illness) helps, but you also have to realize that you have family and friends that want to be there for you also. If you don't let your friends, family, or even your boyfriend in on what you're going through, they will just walk out. I bet you will find love and support everywhere you go if you let people in on your illness.
♥, Amanda B+ F.R.O.G.

THURSDAY, SEPTEMBER 25, 2008
Hi. Just a quick update. Manda is still the same: very high ketones in urine and having hard time keeping O2 levels up, especially when sleeping!! Heart rate is at 120's or higher while sleeping. Please, as Manda wishes, continue to pray for all CB friends and families!! Especially for Peggy and Lou, our thoughts are with you and Stephanie tomorrow night. Wish I could be there!! And for our Manda, B+ and F.R.O.G

"Minnie and Poppy"
September 25th, 2008   16 yrs.
I've notice that i have written a special page for most of my family members except my two sets of grandparents. So I thought I would start with Minnie and Poppy. Minnie and Poppy have always been there for me when I was or wasn't sick. I know it must be very hard for them to deal with all that's going on, but they never backed down and are always there for me. So, for that, I applaud them. I have no words to explain how thankful I am to have them as my grandparents. So, Thank You Minnie and Poppy for teaching me new things, for helping me grow, and for being the best grandparents ever! I LOVE YOU!
♥, Amanda B+ F.R.O.G.

SATURDAY, SEPTEMBER 27, 2008
Hey Everyone. It's Carolyn this morning because my mom is busy doing stuff for Manda.

She just wanted me to let everyone know that everything is still the same. Retching, fever of 101 or higher, and very high ketones. Dr. Adams started Amanda on TPN's separate from lipids. So far not going very well, but still holding out hope. Just asking for lots of prayers for her as well as my family. As Manda wishes, please continue to pray for all CB friends and families and for our Manda. B+ and F.R.O.G :) Thanks!

P.S. This is the last day for MITO awareness week. May God bless all and families!!
Love,
Carolyn

SUNDAY, SEPTEMBER 28, 2008
Hi all. It's Jacki. Things still the same mostly. Manda still running fever 100.5 to 101.8, retching, very tachy [tachycardia: irregular, fast heartbeat], sleeping rate of 130's and higher, and ketones still very high. Manda is still fighting. She sleeps until late afternoon or early evening and then wakes for a while!! Having a hard time keeping eyes open when awake!! She does respond to questions though. We did start the TPN's and lipids again, still retching. More so with the TPN's.

I spoke with Cheryl yesterday. We have a little room to play with the protein, but not much! We are trying everything. At this point, Manda's body is starving itself. Manda is quiet but still will let you know what she wants!! Especially lottery tickets. She LOVES to do scratch offs. How funny is that? A little gambler!! Still hoping for Manda to be comfortable!! Her pain is under control, just not the retching and levels!!

Please, as Manda wishes, continue to pray for all CB friends and families, especially Jaden, who leaves tomorrow for his Make-A-Wish trip. Enjoy, and have the time of your life guys!! Also for our Manda, B+ and F.R.O.G. God Bless!!! Jacki.

P.S. Manda has another blood clot in her PICC and arm. Please pray!! We got her out for a ride later in the day today. All she has wanted to do is pick apples!!! This is a family tradition. (We only picked two.) She did it !! Retching, fever, heart rate over 140 and O2's in the 80's [95-100% is normal while awake or any levels over 87% while sleeping]. She did it!! See? We can do whatever we put are minds to!! Just wanted to leave a happy note!!

MONDAY, SEPTEMBER 29, 2008

Hi all. A quick update that is not good. Manda has blood clots in both lumens. The VNA [Visiting Nurses Association] nurse was here last night and could only get one clot out. Not working great, though. The other lumen is still clotted. Also, Manda is very tachy, with heart rates in the 130's resting and sleeping, and her O2 levels we are trying to keep above 90's but having trouble. (That's with bi-pap and O2 on.) Please pray that her PICC doesn't have to go. It has not even been in a week!! Manda is taking very small amounts of TPN's and lipids, but something is better than none!! See, you have to HOPE!! Manda is FIGHTING for everything, and we will not give up until she says she is too tired!!

Still planning for Maine, a week from this Thursday. Manda wants to see the ocean!! And she will!! Thanks to all for everything you do.

Please, as Manda wishes, continue to pray for all CB friends and families, especially Melody and Natalie, who just had brain surgery. We love you both and are thinking of you. And Jaden, on his MAW [Make-A-Wish] trip. Keep him safe and healthy to enjoy it!! And for our Manda. B+ and F.R.O.G. God Bless. Jacki

P.S. Thank you, Cheryl, for all you do, and Dr. Adams, to keep our Manda comfortable and your phone calls Cheryl to check in!! A special Thank You to Misty for checking in on your girl and us!! Love you and miss you too!! See you soon!

"Nana and Poppy"
September 30th, 2008   16 yrs.
Since I told you about my other grandparents, I thought I would tell you about my other set of grandparents. Nana and Poppy have the most loving hearts. They may not show it sometimes, but, whenever I want to learn how to make or bake something, they're always there. Nana and Poppy have become close to me since I go my disease I think. I know Nana a Poppy would do anything for me if I needed it. And that's why I love them and am proud to be their granddaughter. Thank you, Nana and Poppy, for giving me the privilege of me being your granddaughter! I love you both!
♥, Amanda B+

WEDNESDAY, OCTOBER 01, 2008
Hi all. It's me, Jacki. I thought I would give a quick update. Things are still the same here with Manda. I wish there was more we could do. It is so hard to see her go through this. Tony is

coming back today!! Yahoooo!! We missed him. We are still planning our trip to the ocean!! Some good family time and a change of view for Manda. She can lay on the couch and look at the ocean. That would make anyone feel a little better. Please, as Manda wishes, continue to pray for all CB friends and families!! And for our Manda B+ and F.R.O.G. God Bless. Jacki

P.S. Thanks, Michele for the card and her scratch offs. She loved them. She even chuckled a little . :-)

~~~~~

Hi All! It's me, Amanda! I have a little bit of an energy spirit [spurt] in me right now, so i thought i would stop by and remind you all i'm still here, just not feeling as well. Thank you for all the prayers and support. The Drs. are hoping to get those TPN's back in order. I'm really looking forward to stopping by all of your sites and see how you're doing when i feel 100% better! You're all in my thoughts and prayers everyday! I Love you all! Please continue to pray for all my CB friends, especially Jaden, who is on his Make-A-Wish trip, praying he's having the best time he deserves!
Have a B+ Day!
Amanda :-) B+ F.R.O.G

PS: I have a couple people i need to thank. Emilie -Thank you for my cards and the package you sent about a month ago, I love all the crafts! Aunt Dawny-Thank you for my "Got Spoons" shirt, I'm waiting for a special occasion when i get out to wear it. If i forgot anyone please tell me. Natalie-there's a special package coming your way, so watch out!

THURSDAY, OCTOBER 02, 2008

Hi all. Was it not WONDERFUL to have Manda sign yesterday!! And she will again soon!! Thanks to all for your well wishes and you love and support. The Perrotta family will NEVER be able to tell you in words what it means to us. Please know we hold each thought and prayer close in our hearts!! Things are still the same. Manda is still not accepting the TPN's or lipids, but we still have a little room to play with. Let's just all pray and NEVER give up HOPE!! Manda does better on just normal saline to hydrate her but no nourishment. We know what that means without saying.

Manda woke up this morning with slurred speech, but she was up so much retching, let's hope it's just that and not another stroke. Her last metabolic stroke was the end of August. She is still fighting and is such an example to how we all should live!! (Sorry. I know she is my daughter, but how PROUD and HONORED and BLESSED to be the mother of this SPECIAL girl!!) I truly appreciated each moment with her and will NEVER forget anything she has taught our family!!) Well, enough for now. Let's just pray the Drs. can try to help Manda accept her nourishment. Please, as Manda wishes, continue to pray for all CB friends and families!! And for Our Manda. B+ and F.R.O.G. God Bless. Jacki.

P.S. Thanks, Aunt Val and Uncle Tom, and Natalie and Sophie (cousins) for the beautiful Dorothy and Toto doll!! Manda loved it!! Also, Gracie and family for the scratch offs!! Stewie and Kathy, she won $10 on yours. Thank you all!!

Amanda Perrotta

FRIDAY, OCTOBER 03, 2008
Hi all! This is Pippi! Just hanging out with Manda and decided to update for her. She is doing all right, talkative and her normal self. Slept until almost 4 PM, I think. She's been awake since I got here. That's all that matters! Still trying to figure out her TPN and lipids concoction, but the fluids are helping her hang in there. I can't believe how strong and upbeat she is! I love her, and she is a huge inspiration!
As always, a shout out to all her CB friends, especially Jaden on his Make-A-Wish trip! B+ and F.R.O.G.
Pippi

SUNDAY, OCTOBER 05, 2008
Hi all. It's me, Jacki. Manda's still the same. Thanks, Pippi, for updating for us Friday night. Manda still having trouble with metabolizing her TPN's and lipids. Still is only accepting her normal saline fluids. Not great!! Manda is sleeping more and more, but, when she is awake, she is still so positive!! Manda had more blood clots over the weekend and some metabolic strokes, but, through it all, she is still hanging on and making plans!! I know I have said it before, but Manda's spirit is so much stronger than this disease!! Thank God!! Amanda has to struggle every day to be here. We are still planning to leave for Maine on Thursday, God willing!! Please, as Manda wishes, continue to pray for all CB friends and families!! And for our Manda. B+ F.R.O.G. God Bless. Jacki.

TUESDAY, OCTOBER 07, 2008

Hi all. It's Jacki. Where do I start? Manda is not well at all now. She is hanging on. There is no reason she should be here with the nutrients she has been receiving the past month. It's hardly anything. Spoke with the Dr. Adams and Cheryl yesterday. Cheryl said she [Amanda] is waiting for something!! The TPN's and lipids she is not metabolizing at all!! Today is our last chance. Dr. Adams is lowering it for the last time. I am scared but have faith it will be what is supposed to be. On top of all this, Manda is having a LOT of neurological symptoms, eyes twitching and not dilating, slurred speech, double vision, and a hard time just seeing. Still running fever, retching, blisters on her toe. For the most part, Manda's pain is under control, it's just the nausea. Dr. Adams is starting a new med on top of the others for the nausea. Let's pray it works!! That's it for now. Please just keep Manda and all of family in your prayers at this time, that's all I ask. Thank you all for everything you do. Please, as Manda wishes, continue to pray for all CB friends and families. And for our Manda, B+ and F.R.O.G. God Bless. Jacki.

P.S. God willing, we are still planning for Maine on Thurs.

"How do you keep yourself occupied?"
October 7th, 2008
People always ask me, "How do you not get depressed when you're just laying around on the couch all day?!" Well, here's the answer...you have to keep yourself occupied 24/7. When I first started not going to school and staying home all day, I became very depressed. When I finally found out that I didn't want to feel that way anymore, I started taking up hobbies like doing a lot of crafts and scrap booking. So, please, if you start feeling that way, start some hobbies. And always remember to be positive!

Amanda Perrotta

♥, Amanda B+ F.R.O.G.

THURSDAY, OCTOBER 09, 2008

Hi all. It's Jacki. Just wanted to do a quick update before we leave for Maine. Yes, we are going!! Without saying much, we all know Manda is just holding on! Things are still the same. Manda's eyes now cross, and she is finding it very hard to see. She was still trying to get up and walk, but we have to hold her down. She will not give in and goes in her wheel chair to the bathroom!! She is fighting with EVERYTHING she has!!

Manda's new TPN's were delivered late last night. We don't know the outcome of them because she will start them tomorrow. Still just on IV fluids as of today. Will start lipids tonight when we are in Maine. Everyone pray that her body accepts her nourishment. Please, this is her last chance!! I am trying to be very positive yet realistic at the same time. My way is still hope! It is out of our hands! Only God knows. He has a plan of his own. I think this is the hardest thing Louis and I will EVER have to do!! Louis is not doing well with any of this. I think it's because daddies are suppose to able to fix everything. This can not be fixed, so keep him close in pray, please.

Everything is still the same, but we are taking our Manda to the ocean!! Ye-Haaaaaa!! To leave you all with something positive, it will be what it is meant to be, and, after reading Amanda's journals, she is at peace with everything! She has a page written for everyone.

Please, as Manda wishes, continue to pray for all CB friends and families!! And for our Manda, B+ and F.R.O.G God Bless. Jacki.

SATURDAY, OCTOBER 11, 2008 o
Hi all. It's me, Jacki. We made it!!! Manda slept the whole way here. We made a bed in the back of the van for her and hooked up her IV fluids. Well, for what you have probably been waiting to hear about, whether or not TPN's are being metabolized.... We ran them yesterday and could only get just a ¼ of them in her before she got sick. So that's not great, but it's something. We will take whatever we can get. Things are still the same otherwise: having a hard time seeing, her eyes crossed, cannot hold herself up, but wouldn't you think that would stop her. NO, not Manda!! We took her out on the beach yesterday and took some great family pictures. Abby LOVED the beach and the birds!! She was sooooo funny; we all laughed so hard! We bring the ocean water inside for Manda to put her feet in!! Is that not GREAT!! So she got to touch the water!!

Manda's will and fight are so touching to us as parents and family to see!! She is laying here right now on the couch looking out at the ocean. We are loving our time together and making pictures to keep in our heads and hearts forever!! What a gift to be given! Well, have to go. Will update later, but first, please, as Manda wishes, continue to pray for all CB friends and families. And, for our Manda, B+ and F.R.O.G. God Bless. Jacki.

SUNDAY, OCTOBER 12, 2008
Hi all. As you can see, this is an early update. Let's start with the good first. Manda took a little more TPN yesterday than the day

before!! Yipeeeeee. She fought it but held out as long as she could!! Now for the other. She no longer can bear weight on her legs or trunk, so we prop her up with pillows!! She is having a harder time hearing. We have to raise our voice, and even with that she is confused!! She is still having a hard time seeing, too, and her motor skills are off. Still very nauseous and feverish.

Now let's focus on the positive. I like that better. Manda's cognitive state might be altered at times, but she comes in and out. She is working on projects with Minnie, and she wants to go get Rina a birthday present!! Just when you start to feel like, "oh my God, how are we going to do this?" Manda says something funny and leaves you with no time for the "What are we gonna do?" Thank God. We go between the laughing and tears, but we don't let her see those!! I am so grateful for this time as a family, I can't even put it in words. I am sitting here watching the sunrise, and how beautiful and blessed I feel today!!

Well, just wanted to give an update. Will probably not update till we get home tomorrow. Thanks to all for your constant love and support. Thanks to Sheridan for the picture on your CB site for Manda. I loved it!! Please, as Manda wishes, continue to pray for all CB friends and families!! And for our Manda, B+ and F.R.O.G. God Bless. Jacki.

MONDAY, OCTOBER 13, 2008
Hi all. It's me, Jacki. Well we are leaving today. This has been an EXTREMELY emotional trip!! Very hard! Manda has regressed so rapidly over the weekend cognitively, she can hardly hear or see. She is extremely weak, can no longer do anything for herself!!

Manda's sisters are having a very hard time watching this, so keep them close in prayer, please!! All of us if you may!! I guess all that matters is, once again, Manda met her goal!! Maybe not the way she planned, but we got here!!

At this point, it is getting hard to update because we are always busy, so try to be positive. We will continue to update because that is what Amanda would want. I may not, but probably Aunt Kim. Praying for safe trip home. I wish we could stay forever. All good things come to an end!! Memories live on, though!! We have plenty of them!! I will leave you with that!! I know I said I would update when we got home, but I think I just wanted one more time to update here while i was looking at the ocean! How blessed today. Another day with our Manda!! Thank you all, and, as Manda wishes, please continue to pray for all CB friends and families. For our Manda, B+ and F.R.O.G. God Bless. Jacki.

P.S. Please say an extra prayer for Braden and his mom and dad and family as he has surgery tomorrow!! A special Thank You to my aunt and uncle for letting us stay here at their house!! We wouldn't have been able to come otherwise!! Thanks, Art and Cha!!

TUESDAY, OCTOBER 14, 2008
Hello everyone! It's Manda's Aunt Kim here. I just spoke with Jacki, and she wanted me to give everyone an update. Yesterday, they came home from their wonderful trip to Maine. Manda was able to sleep on the way home. Now, as Manda would do, here is the medical. Last night, Manda's heart rate was over 210 [beats per minute], and her O2 levels were between 40-50. She was taken by ambulance to Albany Med. They believe she was dehydrated and

is now resting comfortably. Jacki says that Manda is confused and having a very hard time seeing and hearing...but she is in NO pain! Thank God for that! They are planning on being released tomorrow.

I also wanted to tell everyone that, even if Jacki does not update (and I will probably be doing it), she still reads the messages left in the guest book. So, please keep them coming; they are inspirational and supportive and mean so much. Please continue to keep Manda and the family in your prayers.

Lastly, I wanted to say that Jacki & Louis truly are the most wonderful, caring parents you could ever know. I only hope that Bill (Uncle Bilbo) and my children are half as wonderful.
Aunt Kim
B+ & FROG
P.S. As Manda wishes, please continue to pray for her CB buddies.

WEDNESDAY, OCTOBER 15, 2008
Good Morning everyone! It's Aunt Kim. Just talked with Jacki for our morning update. They are getting ready to leave the hospital and will head home...just waiting for the ambulance. Manda's nurses will be there waiting for her, as she will be having a couple more machines to use: a heart monitor and a machine for suctioning [her tubes]. She has been sleeping a lot, but, as I said before, she is not in pain. Jacki wanted me to put it in a certain way...I'm trying to think of how, but I can't. Manda is a very, very sick girl. We are ALL thankful for every minute of every day that she is here. I will leave it at that.

Please keep her and the family in your prayers...pass on her site to everyone you know...let's see how many hits we can get to her site and if we can set a record number of messages. Jacki is still checking them and passes them onto Manda when she can. I think it will really boost their spirits!!

Also, Manda wanted me to tell everyone that, even if she can't get to your websites...you are always in her prayers.
If I need to update again, I will. Thank you all for everything you do. I wanted to leave you all with this beautiful saying: "Life is not measured by the number of breaths we take but by the moments that take our breath away."
Love,
Aunt Kim
B+ & F.R.O.G

Amanda Perrotta

Halloween was coming, so, even though Amanda knew that her ability to physically write a message was nearing an end, she made the effort to note what she enjoyed—dressing up. She could no longer type on the laptop computer, but she mustered the energy to make one of the last of her personal, hand-written journals. Though her characters tumble down the page in ragged lines, and her thinking is jumbled and somewhat repetitive, her spirit is alive and vibrant, thinking only of others and fun things to do. Here is her reconstructed entry for October 15th.

"Push the Fun"
10/15/08
Amanda
Happy early Halloween everyone.   Wondering why this girl is writing...well, I am finally home.

THURSDAY, OCTOBER 16, 2008
Good morning everyone!   It's me, Aunt Kim.   I just talked with Jacki to get 'our' morning update.   They arrived home safely yesterday afternoon, and Manda was able to get back to resting comfortably.   Now for the medical.   There are still problems with her increased heart rate while O2 levels dropping, so the alarms go off, but Manda is not even feeling this. As Jacki puts it, Manda is 'pleasantly confused.' Sometimes she thinks she is in other places or talking to someone. But, like we keep saying, she is in NO pain. So we are all grateful for that!

I want to thank everyone for filling the guest book yesterday! Manda's site had over 1,000 hits (but only less than 100 guest book entries).   I want to encourage everyone to still write. Jacki told me today that she loves reading them and that it really keeps her going. Also, this is hard to say...but, at the end of Manda's Journey, the family will be having a book put together from CaringBridge containing all the messages, so please, please keep them coming. I am sure they will be very comforting.

Now, as Manda wishes, please continue to pray for all her CB friends and family. Remember to B+ and F.R.O.G. God Bless!
Love,
Aunt Kim

P.S. I found this prayer the other day, and I thought it was beautiful.

<u>An Irish Prayer</u>
May God give you...
For every storm, a rainbow
For every tear, a smile
For every care, a promise
And a blessing in each trial.
For every problem life sends
A faithful friend to share
For every sigh, a sweet song
And an answer for each prayer.

FRIDAY, OCTOBER 17, 2008
Hello AFF (Amanda's Faithful Followers)! This is Aunt Kim. I just spoke with Jacki, so I wanted to do a little update. Everything is the same with Amanda right now...same heart rate issues and O2 levels dropping. She was awake more yesterday, and always manages a smile. She is such a strong girl through all of this!! The

amount of messages yesterday really had the family so excited. Jacki was so happy to tell Manda about them all and was surprised at those from other countries. Carolyn told me she had goose bumps reading them all. So, THANK YOU from the bottom of my heart for all of your notes and prayers, and please continue to do so!

Jacki would like me to say 'Thank You' to all of Manda's nurses and doctors at AMC for being so wonderful for Manda's last visit. You guys have become like family. Also, to Fr. Rodino, Thank you so much for your visit and blessing.

Now as Manda wishes, please pray for all her special friends on CB and their families. God Bless you all!!
Love,
Aunt Kim
B+ & FROG

P.S. I wanted to leave you again with a wonderful Irish saying:

Always remember to forget
The things that made you sad.
But never forget to remember
The things that made you glad.
Always remember to forget
The friends that proved untrue.
But never forget to remember
Those that have stuck by you.
Always remember to forget
The troubles that passed away.

But never forget to remember
The blessings that come each day.

October 17, 2008
Being handicapped has its day.

SATURDAY, OCTOBER 18, 2008 09:52 AM,
Good Morning AFF!! It's Aunt Kim. I was a little confused this morning and thought CB was shut down till Jacki called with our morning update. Thanks, Jacki, for keeping me in line!! I need it. Now, as Amanda would do, here are the medical issues. Her heart rate is still going up and O2 going down. She can hardly see or hear, but is still trying to color or read books!! Is she not amazing? She is in no pain lying down, but as soon as anyone moves her, she is in extreme pain. And she has to be moved every ½ hour. What happens is that, if you touch her, her muscles reflex and go tight, so it now takes more than one person to move her.

But, as Jacki says, Manda's almost gone back in time. She doesn't remember the situation she is in...she is in a happy place....does not get upset or angry. I believe that is something to be thankful for. We need to look at it in that way.

Also, please check out Manda's videos under the links section. She made them herself. Jacki recommends the 1st and 3rd ones. Once again, they are amazing...like our Manda!! I've been adding new pictures here and there. I hope you're enjoying them, even if they are embarrassing to the girls!! Sorry, Manda & Carolyn, but you were so darn cute!!! :-).

Amanda Perrotta

Thank you all for checking on and leaving Manda and the family messages. They cannot wait to get on the computer and see what everyone is saying. I thought a nice thing might be to tell them how Manda has affected your life...if you know her personally or just from the computer. That would be nice for their book.

Jacki says, "Thank you" to Pippi for her visit last night, and she hopes you found your costume for Halloween! Uncle Bill, the kids and I will be visiting the family tomorrow, so I will try to update from there! Maybe get some more 'adorable' pics!! :-)

Now, as Manda wishes...please continue to pray for all her CB friends and family. Thank you ALL for everything you are doing, it means so much to our family!
Love,
Aunt Kim
B+ & FROG

P.S.: Another little Irish prayer:

May God Grant you always a sunbeam to warm you, a moonbeam to charm you, a sheltering angel so nothing can harm you, laughter to cheer you, faithful friends near you, and, whenever you pray, heaven to hear you.

Here are Amanda's last three journals. They were not dated.

"Sorry I haven't written since I was too [sick"].
I'm sorry I haven't journaled. I'm actually not walking right now, but I know I'll get it back just like[before].

~~~~~

"Mad and scared"
Will only [be] a few more days until Halloween!! You may ask why I'm scared on Halloween? I'm mostly scared on Halloween of the costumes. They're usually always scary.

~~~~~

Pippi's favorite colors: pink, green, purple. Favorite character: Ariel.[16]

MONDAY, OCTOBER 20, 2008
Good Morning AFF!! It's Aunt Kim. Sorry for the lack of an update yesterday, but my husband (Uncle Bill) and our kids (Liam & Belle) were visiting with Amanda and the family. We had a wonderful family day together. Amanda stayed up the entire time...she doesn't want to miss out on a thing. :-) They even brought her a cookie sheet, and she made cookies with Carolyn and Belle...and they were yummy! I know Jacki has said it before, but when you witness it, it's so amazing. Manda's spirit is way,

---

[16]Amanda was thinking about making Christmas presents for everyone and trying to keep track of everyone's favorite things.

way stronger than this awful disease!   I don't think I've ever met anyone who would not give up, and who would keep fighting, no matter what.   But, of course Manda's busy day and not taking a rest hit her last night, after we left.   Her heart rate continues to rise and drop, and her O2 levels drop as well.   Sometimes she needs to be reminded to just take a breath.   She was resting comfortably when I talked to Jacki this morning, and she said Manda did good through the night.   So, that is a blessing!   Jacki told me that Manda doesn't like people to see her sick, so she was very strong for us...what a sweet girl!!   But, I always knew that.   :-)

The family is still so amazed at the outpouring of messages and visits to Manda's site.   She told me that she didn't mind my writing her updates either, so I take this very seriously.   :-)   I want to make her proud, so, please, please keep them coming.   And as I said before, if you have any special memories of Amanda or something funny she did, please tell us!   We all like a smile.   And continue to keep the family in your prayers.

As Amanda wishes, please continue to pray for all her CB friends and family. God Bless!
Love,
Aunt Kim
B+ & FROG

TUESDAY, OCTOBER 21, 2008
Good Afternoon AFF!   It's Aunt Kim. Sorry for the late update. (I had an appt.) I spoke with Jacki, and they had a very rough night last night. Amanda's heart rate was way up, and O2's way down. The alarms were going off all night. Now, her bladder is

shutting down as well. Her nurses are probably arriving as I type to see what is happening with her. She is having a lot of memory problems as well. Jacki and I were trying to find a positive thing to say...as we don't like dwelling on the bad. So, how's this...Amanda is still a typical teenager...she is still sassy to Jacki and is mad at her. Typically, it's not a good thing to be sassy to your mom (please note that, all you kids out there), but in this case, Jacki doesn't mind. :-)

Jacki also wanted me to remind everyone that she still reads Manda the messages and that, even though Manda can't get to everyone else's guest book, she still thinks about them and prays for them.

Manda wanted to say "Happy Birthday" to Jaden again. As always, please keep Manda and the family in your prayers as well as all her CB friends and their families. God Bless! And 'Thank You' all for everything.
Love,
Aunt Kim
B+ & FROG

P.S.: Ask and it will be given to you; seek and you will find; knock and the door will be opened to you. For everyone who asks receives, he who seeks finds; and to him who knocks, the door will be opened.

--Jesus, Matthew 7:7-8

WEDNESDAY, OCTOBER 22, 2008
Good Morning AFF!! It's Aunt Kim. I just spoke with Jacki and got our morning update. After speaking with the doctor, they

have determined that Amanda's bladder has shut down. Jacki now has to push on Manda's belly, which is why she gets mad at her. She slept all day yesterday except for about an hour. The heart rate and O2 levels are still an issue, and the alarms are going off more times during the day. Manda is not in pain when she is sitting still, but she needs to be moved every ½ hour, and that causes her a lot of pain. But, as Jacki and I talked about, even though Manda is very sick, she always, always finds something to smile about. They are taking one day at a time and enjoying every minute of every day together. Jacki says that when Amanda gives her a smile, she can't help but smile, too...her smile has always been contagious!! :-) Please continue to keep her and the family in your prayers, and don't be afraid to leave a message...they are still checking.

Thank you to Pippi for coming by yesterday. And Kim, TT, Mark and Pastor Jim and Karen, for your visits as well. Jacki said it was nice seeing you all!! Now, as Manda would say, please continue to pray for all her CB friends and family. God Bless!
Love,
Aunt Kim
B+ & FROG

P.S. Jacki told me she liked this prayer, so it's my choice for today:

Full Original Serenity Prayer:
God, give us grace to accept with serenity
the things that cannot be changed,
Courage to change the things
which should be changed,

and the Wisdom to distinguish
the one from the other.
Living one day at a time,
Enjoying one moment at a time,
Accepting hardship as a pathway to peace,
Taking, as Jesus did,
This sinful world as it is,
Not as I would have it,
Trusting that You will make all things right,
If I surrender to Your will,
So that I may be reasonably happy in this life
And supremely happy with You forever in the next.
Amen.[17]

THURSDAY, OCTOBER 23, 2008
Good Morning AFF!!! It's Aunt Kim. I just spoke with Jacki and had our morning update. Last night was a tough night for Amanda with the bladder issues. Jacki is going to speak with the doctor's office today (actually they might have been calling when we were getting off the phone) to see what they suggest she do. Manda was awake for a few hours yesterday, and the alarms for her heart rate and O2 didn't go off as much...that's a good thing!

Manda now writes on a wipe-off board since it's so hard for her take a breath to speak. Last night, she wrote that she wanted a party...an ice cream party!! So, that's what they did. Pop D. came over, and they had ice cream. Jacki said it was a 'little messy,' with ice cream all over the place! and Manda had to have a bath after! That must have been some party, guys!!   :-)

---

[17]Reinhold Neibuhr never copyrighted this prayer.

Special Thank You to Amanda Larkin and her mom for stopping by on Sunday with their gifts. Jacki says she is so sorry she forgot to mention you the other day. Also, Thank You to Aunt Dorothy and family for their support and gift for Amanda. Please keep Manda and family in your prayers, as well as all her CB friends and families. Thank you all for everything. God Bless!!
Love,
Aunt Kim
B+ & FROG

An Olde Irish Wish
May the raindrops fall lightly on your brow
May the soft winds freshen your spirit
May the sunshine brighten your heart
May the burdens of the day rest lightly upon you
And may God enfold you in the mantle of His love.

FRIDAY, OCTOBER 24, 2008
Good Morning AFF!! It's Aunt Kim. As with every morning, I spoke with Jacki so that I could update everyone. I am going to do the medical, which right now is not very good. Jacki said that last night was a "very, very bad night." Amanda's heart rate went up and O2 levels went down for at least 15 minutes before they could get them to regulate. Amanda is severely anemic right now, so much so that they are unable to take blood for testing. She cannot be exposed to any disease, as she has no way to fight it off. Jacki is now pushing on Manda's belly every 45 minutes. They have increased the pain meds, so she was comfortable yesterday.

Now, lets think of something positive. Last night, for the second night in a row, Manda had Poppy D. over for an ice cream social. Thank you Pop for coming and for the scratch offs, too!!! :-) Minnie is helping make Christmas presents for Manda's cousins...under Manda's direction of course! :-) Thank you, Minnie! Manda is also looking forward to her visit Sunday with cousins Woody and Sarah. They are going to model their Halloween costumes...the cuties!!

Jacki would like to say Thank You to Billy Ceresia for his gift to Amanda's Journey. I also needed to say that, if anyone wishes to visit the family, please call ahead as Amanda cannot be exposed to any sickness and is very weak. Jacki says, please, please don't be offended if they say it's not a good time. They so appreciate everyone's support, but sometimes the family just needs...family time. So, please just call ahead, and, if it's not possible to visit, keep praying...and leaving them messages right here in CB. They read the messages all the time. Jacki reads them to Manda...and Carolyn and Dahea check them, too! Jacki says it really helps them a lot to read the supportive messages.

I have been keeping track and noticed over 900 hits yesterday but only a little over 30 messages...please, please, don't be afraid to leave a message; even if it's just to say, 'hi,' it means so much. :-) Thank you all!!
As Amanda wishes, please pray for all her CB friends and families!
Love,
Aunt Kim
B+ & FROG

Amanda Perrotta

"The best and most beautiful things in this world cannot be seen or even heard, but must be felt with the heart."   --Helen Keller

SATURDAY, OCTOBER 25, 2008 10:56 AM,
Good Saturday Morning AFF!! It's Aunt Kim. I talked with Jacki and have a short update, mostly because not much has changed. Manda had an OK night, but her muscles are getting weaker and tighter, which causes a lot of pain. They have had to increase her pains meds once again, but if that is what's needed to keep her comfortable, they will do it. Jacki is also having to do a lot of suction, but she says she is getting better at it...no more almost sucking out Manda's teeth...yes, Jacki..that is a good thing!   :-) You are an awesome mom, Jacki!!!   I could write an entry on everything you've done for your daughter, but I think I'd run out of room. :-) So, I guess I'd better leave it at that (We love you)! \

Now, let's think about something positive. Although Manda slept a lot yesterday, she worked on the computer with Minnie. She also had a little ice cream with Pippi (thanks for the visit) and is looking forward to her cousins' visit tomorrow, and their Halloween costumes.

Please continue to keep Manda and the family in your prayers. They loved reading all the messages yesterday. Isn't it something how just writing that you are thinking about someone, or just saying, 'Hi,' makes their day a little better? It truly does with Manda and our family. So, I thank you all!! Also, if you haven't checked out all the videos under the 'links' icon, please do. Amanda has created three of the videos, and the last link was a story a local news station did on her for Mito Awareness Week.

As Manda wishes, please continue to pray for all her CB friends and families. God Bless everyone!!
Love,
Aunt Kim
B+ & FROG

"So much has been given to me, I have not time to ponder over that which has been denied."   --Helen Keller

SUNDAY, OCTOBER 26, 2008
Good afternoon AFF!! It's Aunt Kim. I hope everyone is having a great weekend. I just talked with Jacki...this is going to be short as there really isn't much change going on. Manda slept most of the day yesterday, although she did wake up for a little ice cream. :-) I told her she sounded like a pregnant woman, what with her ice cream cravings! Jacki said she smiled, so I asked if she wanted some pickles, too. She made a 'yuck' face. So it's just ice cream for Manda. :-) Lately, her heart rate has been dropping as well as going up. It went down as low as 33 and up to 245.[18] Her O2 levels are dropping a lot more during the day, too.

Today, Amanda is getting some visitors. As I was talking with Jacki, I heard, "Trick or Treat," from cousins Woody and Sarah...or I mean Ariel and Superman. :-) She will also be seeing her twin cousins Natalie and Sophie. So, the family will be enjoying some time together today.

Thank you for continuing to keep Manda and the family in your prayers. And please remember all her CB friends and families.

_____

Amanda Perrotta

God Bless everyone!!
Love,
Aunt Kim
B+ & FROG

"You think the only people who are people, are the people who look and think like you. But if you walk the footsteps of a stranger, you'll learn things you never knew you never knew."

--Pocahontas[19]

MONDAY, OCTOBER 27, 2008
Good Morning AFF!! It's Aunt Kim. I hope everyone had a great weekend. As always, I spoke with Jacki, so I can update everyone. Not much has changed. They have increased the pain meds but have the capability of raising it a few times more if needed, so they are confident Manda will be comfortable. Her heart rate is staying at an elevated level, and she is a little more confused; sometimes she forgets she can't eat regular food. But...Jacki says like clockwork at night, Manda will wake right up for her ice cream!! :-) Everyone has asked, so this is what she has: 1½ cups of sugar free vanilla, chocolate, or strawberry...and sometimes a tad of chocolate/peanut butter on top!! Yummy!

The family would like to thank everyone who has been calling ahead about visiting with Amanda. Please continue to do so, as Manda cannot be exposed to anything, and she tires so easy. As I said before..please, please do not be offended if someone tells you it's not a good time to visit. It's just always safer to call ahead.

---

[19] From the song "Colors of the Wind," © 1995, Disney records. Words and lyrics by Alan Menken and Stephen Schwartz.

And continue to keep Manda and the family in your prayers. Thank you all!!

Please continue to pray for Amanda's CB friends and family and she wishes. God Bless everyone!
Love,
Aunt Kim
B+ & FROG

"Life has to be lived. That's all there is to it."

--Eleanor Roosevelt.

TUESDAY, OCTOBER 28, 2008
Good Morning AFF!! It's Aunt Kim.
Well, I just spoke with Jacki. Things are pretty much the same. The heart rate and O2 levels are still going up and down; the alarms are going off all the time. Manda slept most of the day yesterday, except for about an hour and a half where she worked with Minnie on the computer and making Christmas presents for her cousins. Isn't she so special...making sure she takes care of her cousins? She also woke up around 8 for you know what!! Yeah, ice cream!! Poppy D. came too late for it, but he did bring her these googly eyes that make Halloween noises and hung them up on Manda's IV pole. Jacki says Manda just kept staring at them. :-) Thanks Pop! Manda is having some problems with her skin breaking down. The nurse, Marianne, is going to check it out today and come up with a plan.

Jacki had a cute story. She says that when Marianne was doing suction on Manda's mouth, she told her to just pretend she was at the dentist, and she opened up! :-) Oh, and Manda...the gambler...won again on the scratch offs...$38!!   I think I'm going to have her scratch off some for me!!!   :-)

Thank you everyone that has called ahead about stopping for a visit and respecting the privacy of the family. They are enjoying ever day and every minute together. Jacki and I were talking about how amazing it is that, in her 16 years, Amanda has affected so many people's lives. How many of us can say we've done the same? She truly was sent here for a purpose. I am so proud to be her aunt!!!

Please continue to keep Manda and the family in your prayers. Don't forget to leave a message. The family is always checking them. And keep in your prayers all her CB friends and families. God Bless everyone!
Love,
Aunt Kim
B+ & FROG

"All our dreams can come true, if we have the courage to pursue them."   --Walt Disney

WEDNESDAY, OCTOBER 29, 2008
Good Morning AFF. It's Aunt Kim. I spoke with Jacki already, so, I thought I would give you the update now. Manda's pain has increased, which then causes her heart rate to go way up. Tony will be coming today to increase the pain meds. They really want to get this pain under control, and, as I said before, they will have the ability to keep raising it. Jacki says they are looking at getting a special hospital bed for Manda's comfort. It will make it easier

to position her to maker her comfortable, especially because they now need to move her onto her left side and push her belly just to get some [urine] output. Otherwise she will be in pain because her belly gets distended. She has a couple sores, which happens when you do not move a lot, and Marianne is getting some cream to help with that.

OK, now lets talk about some positive things. Of course, Manda woke up last night for her ice cream. I believe on her own she is raising stock prices for ice cream!! :-) Maybe we should all go and invest in some! Ha-Ha. Her dad (Lou) brought her home the new Tinkerbell movie, so they hope to watch that today. We all know how she loves 'Tink'!

That brings me to a request...please, please pray that Amanda is able to enjoy Halloween. She has her 'Dorothy' costume and has been looking forward to putting it on. But, with the pain issues, it's making it hard to move. So, lets pray that it's under control, so she can enjoy this day! Thank you.

As Manda would say, please continue to pray for all her CB friends and families. I have a family and little boy I would like to mention today. My son, Liam, Manda's cousin, has a classmate who was diagnosed with a brain tumor. He is only 7 years old. We all know how much the messages left by everyone mean. Thank you again for all your support. Please continue to pray for Manda and the family. :-) God Bless!!
Love,
Aunt Kim
B+ & FROG

P.S. I think I left this one before...but, I like it so much:

Amanda Perrotta

<u>An Olde Irish Wish</u>
May the raindrops fall lightly on your brow
May the soft winds freshen your spirit
May the sunshine brighten your heart
May the burdens of the day rest lightly upon you
And may God enfold you in the mantle of His love.

THURSDAY, OCTOBER 30, 2008
Good Morning AFF! It's Aunt Kim. I just spoke with Jacki, so I'll give you the morning update. It was a rough night last night, and things are not going to well already today. Manda's heart rate is extremely high at rest, and she is very, very confused. The nurse found a few more sores, so they are getting a hospital bed today. That should help out a lot. Manda is also needing a lot of suction. To let you understand this, in case you don't know, the muscles in her mouth are very weak, so she cannot swallow. This is why she needs the suction.

I know it is hard to read these things. And let me tell you...as someone who knows and loves Manda...it's just as hard to write them. Jacki and I try to find a positive thing to say about every day. As a family, they try to focus on the little things and goodness in the day. Even if it's just Amanda giving them a smile. The truth that things are very bad is so hard to understand as adults, and for the kids it's even harder. Jacki wanted me to explain that Manda has a lot of young cousins, so we try not to dwell on or go into a lot of details of the bad things. I am sure you all understand.

Yes, Manda is working on crafts with Minnie, although she dozes on and off during this. Poppy D. came over for a little ice cream last night...sugar free of course!   :-)

Jacki wanted me to thank you all for all your messages to Manda and the family. Please continue to do so, and pass it on to as many people as you can. This is so good for the girls (Manda's sisters). It is the first thing the girls check when they come home from school, and sometimes they even check from school. We cannot wait to get the number of visits to hit 100,000!! Now, that would give Manda a huge smile!!   :-)   Thank you all for everything!!!

Please, as Manda wishes, continue to pray for all her CB friends and family. God Bless!!
Love,
Aunt Kim
B+ & FROG

P.S. This is a little saying I have in my house, and Jacki told me she really liked it, so I thought it was appropriate with my entry today: "Look for small miracles, and you'll find they're everywhere."

FRIDAY, OCTOBER 31, 2008
Happy Halloween!!!
Good Morning AFF! It's Aunt Kim...like you all don't know that by now! :-) I have your morning update. Amanda's new bed came yesterday!!! Jacki said it's awesome. It even helps move her...now that's some bed! Her pain is under control, so she is now comfy in that new bed. Jacki has to do a lot more suctioning lately. And, yesterday, Manda had a hard time breathing. She is very, very confused, but everyone just goes along with what she is

saying, and that satisfies her. Her heart rate and O2 levels are still an issue day and night. Jacki told me that Manda's dog, Abby, would not sleep all night because of the new bed. She sat and was guarding over Manda, and now, this morning, she's sleeping because Jacki is on guard. :-) Isn't that cute?

Jacki says tonight they will lay Manda's costume over her and take some pictures. It's just too difficult to get her into the costume. From her new bed, she will be able to see the kids in costumes from the window or even the front door. So, neighbors can stop by at the door. Pippi will be coming tonight, as 'Pippi Longstocking' of course. Manda is looking forward to that.

Thank you everyone for respecting the family's privacy and calling ahead. This is a very emotional time, and sometimes it takes everything they can do to just get through the day. Family privacy means everything sometimes. Jacki says, again, please don't take offense to being told that it's not a good time because they have a lot medically going on at any time of the day.

Please check out the new link we added. It's the very last one, and is a video showing the Family Fun Day that was celebrated in August. The video was done by Manda's Uncle Ed. He did a great job!! Thank you, Ed.

Thank you again for all your messages. Remember, if you can't visit in person, a message is the next best thing. They check them a lot during day and read them at night. They will be making all the messages into a book, so please keep them coming, and let's try to get that 100,000 visits!

Please continue to keep Manda and the family in your prayers as well as all her CB friends and families. Thank you all for everything!! God Bless! Have a wonderful Halloween!!
Love,
Aunt Kim
B+ & FROG

"God doesn't give us what we can handle; God helps us handle what we are given."

SATURDAY, NOVEMBER 01, 2008
Good Afternoon AFF. I hope everyone had a wonderful Halloween! I spoke with Jacki, and she said the family really enjoyed Halloween together last night. I will be posting some pictures as soon as I get them. I know everyone is looking forward to seeing them. :-) Jacki said they were able to cut Manda's costume so that they could just slip it on the front of her. If there is a will, there is a way, right? I guess you can see where Manda gets her determination. :-)
The overnight was rough. The machines for heart rate and O2 were going off all night. Manda is now in a lot of pain again, so they will have to increase the pain meds again today. Manda is very, very confused right now. She still is eating her ice cream, and it has to be fed to her, but she is still enjoying having it!

Jacki wants to thank everyone for the scratch offs...from what I hear, Manda is set for a while. :-) Also, thank you, to all the family, friends and neighbors who peeked in on Amanda and waved from the door.

Amanda Perrotta

Please continue to pray for Manda and the family. We are so excited about the number of visits!! We are almost at 100,000!! I know Manda will have a big smile when she hears that!! Please continue to pray for all her CB friends and families. God Bless!!
Love,
Aunt Kim
B+ & FROG

"To love means loving the unlovable. To forgive means pardoning the unpardonable. Faith means believing the unbelievable. Hope means hoping when everything seems hopeless."
                                                    --G. K. Chesterton

SUNDAY, NOVEMBER 02, 2008
Good Morning AFF!! This will be a very short entry, as Jacki and the family had some sad news this morning. Amanda's MITO buddy, Jaden, passed at 5:15 AM. Amanda's whole family has you, Jessica, Jaden, and your family in our thoughts and prayers. We are so sorry what this terrible disease is doing, especially to the children. Please know that the Perrotta family is taking today to think of Jaden and enjoy the family time that they have together.

As for Manda...she slept most of the day yesterday, and her pain is mostly under control. Same issues with the heart rate and O_2 levels going up and down.

Please continue to keep Manda and the family in your prayers. We are almost at 100,000 [visitor] hits. I'm hoping to get there today. It would give them something to smile about on such a sad day. God Bless everyone!

Love,
Aunt Kim
B+ & FROG

"Be content with what you have, for God has said, 'Never will I leave you; never will I forsake you.' So say with confidence, 'The Lord is my helper; I will not be afraid.'"

--Hebrews 13:5,6

TUESDAY, NOVEMBER 04, 2008

Good Morning AFF!! I say this is going to be a short entry, but then when I'm done, it's usually a little longer than I expected. I just spoke with Jacki. It was a very tough, emotional night, last night. Manda's breathing is very shallow now. They will be increasing the pain meds once again today.

Yesterday, she assisted Minnie (please read between the lines), with making cousin Sarah's Christmas present. Her dad, Lou, brought her home a singing/dancing Frosty the Snowman that is sitting in front of her, and she loves looking at now.

Thank you Fr. Rodino for visiting and talking with the family, and Pastor Jim. Both of your insight is so helpful when making decisions that parents should never have to make. Thank you to Amanda's cousin, Michael, for his beautiful poem, too. Also, thank you for respecting the family and their decision to no longer accept visitors.

Please continue to leave messages. Jacki told me that she reads them to Manda. It makes it easier knowing that Amanda has made a difference in people's lives. It's what gets them through the day when they read how she has touched someone's life. Please keep Manda and all her extended families, the Perrottas and Dedricks, in your prayers.

As Manda wishes, please continue to pray for all her CB friends and families. Everyone will see you tonight, Pippi!! :-)
Love,
Aunt Kim
B+ & FROG

"The steadfast love of the Lord never ceases, his mercies never come to an end; they are new every morning."
                                                    --Lamentations 3:22-23

TUESDAY, NOVEMBER 04, 2008
Good afternoon everyone. Jacki called me a little while ago and wanted me to do an update. Things are not to good with Amanda right now. There are two nurses at the house...Pippi and Maryanne. They are pulling the lipids that are given to Manda and limiting her fluids because of lack of output. Her respiration now is very, very low. They have been on the phone with Cheryl and Dr. Adams and making plans regarding whether or not they need to go to the hospital.

All we can ask right now is that everyone please, please pray! We need to focus everything on Amanda and the family. Thank you!! God Bless!
Love,
Aunt Kim
B+ & FROG

WEDNESDAY, NOVEMBER 05, 2008
Good Morning AFF!!! I see you have all been signing the guest book already this morning, so I thought I had better get my update out to you. Jacki said that everything is pretty much the same with Manda. Amanda is still holding on..what a fighter this girl is!! I've never seen anyone go through what she is and still be so strong. She is amazing!! Jacki says they are trying to stay home as long as possible, but when the time comes, provisions have been made for a direct admission to AMC. When Manda's respiration drops to a certain level and her output drops to a certain level, then they will head to the hospital.

Thank you cousin Woody for reading to Manda, and cousin Sarah for visiting. Please remember: only family will be able to visit Manda. But that doesn't mean to stop sending messages. Everyone in the family is still reading them...they mean so much. Thank You!! God Bless!!! I will update again if need be.
Love,
Aunt Kim
B+ & FROG

"The value of life lies not in the length of days, but in the use we make of them."

--Michel de Montaigne

Journey's End

THURSDAY, NOVEMBER 06, 2008 09:08 AM,

Amanda Perrotta

Good Morning AFF!!! Well, this is going to be a hard entry. I wish I never had to type this. Amanda has a high temperature, increased heart rate and blood pressure, a decrease in output, and very delayed responses. She slept almost all day yesterday. They had to increase her pain meds two times yesterday as well.

So, the plan is to try to hold out till tomorrow and then take her to Albany Medical Center where she will complete the end of her journey. It is so very devastating that it has come to this. At the hospital, they will only give her fluids and make her comfortable and pain free, and Jacki will have a chance to just be Manda's mom and not caregiver...which is how it should be. Jacki...I know I told you today, you are such a great mom. I don't know if I could ever do what you have done for your daughter. You are truly amazing.

Please know that there will be no visitors at the hospital at this time. But, please, please keep praying and keep leaving messages. Remember, everything will be made into a book for the family to read for years to come. I am sure it will be a source of comfort.

Jacki wanted me to thank everyone for their love and support over the years...and for being part of Amanda's Journey. Your thoughts and prayers are what will get our family through this. Please keep all of Manda's CB friends and family in your prayers as well. Especially Jessica and Angel, Jaden's family. You are in our thoughts today, Jessica. God Bless everyone!
Love,
Aunt Kim
B+ & FROG

"God says, 'Do not fear, for I am with you;
do not be dismayed, for I am your God.
I will strengthen you and help you;
I will uphold you with my righteous right hand.'"
                    --Isaiah 41:10 (New International Version)

FRIDAY, NOVEMBER 07, 2008
Good Morning AFF!!!   Once again, an entry that is not easy to
write But I will start out with the medical this morning. They
have now pulled Manda's fluids. She is resting comfortably and
has not woken up. They are just waiting to hear from the doctor
as to when to leave for the hospital. They have to make sure the
room is ready.

Thank you, Tony, for staying the night and for all the wonderful
care you've given to Manda. Also, to Marianne for coming today
on your day off and for the compassion you have given to Manda.

Thank you everyone for the beautiful messages and please keep
them coming. We all love reading them. Please continue to keep
Manda and the whole family in your prayers. God Bless!
Love,
Aunt Kim
B+ & FROG

We are not human beings on a spiritual journey. We are spiritual
beings on a human journey.

FRIDAY, NOVEMBER 07, 2008

Amanda Perrotta

Good evening AFF!! I am at AMC as I type, visiting Manda and the family. So, Jacki thought I should give a little update. They arrived to the hospital safely. The nurses had the room decorated, signs hanging up and even things that Amanda had made from her previous trips to the hospital. Thank you so much to all the nurses, you are so very special!!! Dr. Porter was in today, and everyone is hoping for a peaceful, restful night. Pippi is still here, and Aunt Mimi is staying with Jacki and Manda tonight...a little girls' night together. :)

Thank you all for your notes, we all appreciate them. Please keep them coming, and continue to pray for Manda and all the Dedricks and Perrottas.
Love,
Aunt Kim
B+ & FROG

SATURDAY, NOVEMBER 08, 2008
Good Morning AFF!! We had a wonderful visit yesterday with Amanda and family. She was awake for us and even gave her Uncle Bill a smile...something I know we will always treasure. She even asked for a 'Shirley Temple' drink last night...but never drank it. I talked with Jacki this morning and, unfortunately, they had a rough night. Manda has a high temperature and a very high heart rate. They have been up since 3AM.

Thank you all for your wonderful, supportive messages. Please keep them coming. Jacki has their computer at the hospital and was reading some messages last night. Please keep Manda and all the families in your prayers, too. God Bless!!!

Love,
Aunt Kim
B+ & FROG

"I will cause you to walk in the straight way. I will open to you the gates of righteousness, for whoever finds Me, finds life."
                              --Psalm 118:19; Proverbs. 8: 35-36

SUNDAY, NOVEMBER 09, 2008 o
Good Afternoon AFF!! I'm here at AMC, and thought I would do the update from here. OK here we go...Manda is getting closer to becoming an angel in heaven. We all know she is already one on earth. Yesterday, was a very emotional day. Manda's heart rate monitors went off for about a minute, and she came back. The family is trying to hold onto every minute together we all have with her. She is comfortable yet unresponsive. She is going through the natural stages to prepare for her eternal life.

Minnie and Pop are staying at home with the girls, and dad, Lou, is staying with Jacki at the hospital. Jacki says thank you to everyone for their love and support, especially Pippi, the nurses, doctors and staff at AMC for their unselfishness...for coming in on their days off. It means so much to the family. Please keep praying for a peaceful and painless transition. God Bless!!! Please continue to pray for all of Manda's CB friends and families.
Love,
Aunt Kim
B+ & FROG

MONDAY, NOVEMBER 10, 2008

Amanda Perrotta

Good Morning AFF!! This will be a very short entry. There has been no change with Manda. She is still holding on with everything she has. What a strong girl she is! They turned off her monitors, and her heart rate and O2 are so very low. She needs to have a lot of deep suctioning now. I hope God is prepared for our Angel Amanda...she's one tough cookie!

Thank you everyone again for your thoughts, messages, and prayers. Please continue to do so as the family will soon need them more than ever. And remember, all the messages will be made into a book.[20]
God Bless everyone...especially Manda!!
Love,
Aunt Kim
B+ & FROG

"It is love that makes the impossible possible."   --Indian Proverb

TUESDAY, NOVEMBER 11, 2008
Good Morning AFF!! Well, I have another short update. "Amanda the Amazing" is still fighting! She has a fever but is on a cooling mattress. Her lungs aren't opening up as much, so she is having a hard time breathing and is requiring a lot of deep suctioning. But she is very comfortable and in no pain!
Thank you all for your continued prayers and messages. Please keep them coming. And please remember all of Amanda's CB friends and family.

---

[20]Because there were over 200 pages of them, they have been trimmed to include only a sampling of the personal notes and poems, and any letters of special note.

Love,
Aunt Kim
B+ & FROG

"The strongest among the weak is the one who doesn't forget his weaknesses."   --Danish Proverb

WEDNESDAY, NOVEMBER 12, 2008
Good Morning AFF!! I just talked with Jacki, and I'm having a difficult time thinking about what to write, so please bear with me. Amanda's status is much worse this morning. The family is now spending this time praying and thinking about their wonderful memories with Manda. She has fought one heck of a fight and will be such a bright angel in heaven.

I know I've asked before, but Jacki and I were talking. If anyone has a special memory of Amanda that they would like to send, please do so. The guest book entries will be made into a book. The family will really appreciate reading how their Amanda has made such an impact on peoples lives. I thought I would give a little memory of my own since I've been writing this CB page for her. I've grown to appreciate all of you and your messages. I owe a story to all of you.

When all the family came out to visit my husband (Uncle Bill) and me in Utica, we had everyone over for dinner...Minnie, Pop, Jacki, Louis, Carolyn, Amanda, Amy, Ed and baby Woody. We knew we were expecting a baby, but Bill was finding it hard to say it. Leave it up to Manda...she just spits out, out of the blue, "Well, when are you going to have a baby?"

"How about next April?" Bill finally says. Everyone was in shock...but Amanda was quite proud of herself! God, I love her!
Love,
Aunt Kim
B+ & FROG

You gain strength, courage, and confidence by every experience in which you really stop to look fear in the face. You must do the thing which you think you cannot do.

--Eleanor Roosevelt

WEDNESDAY, NOVEMBER 12, 2008
Good Afternoon AFF! Jacki just called me and wanted me to update everyone....the doctors have come in and said that Amanda does not have much time left with us. It will be anytime now as she is having a very, very hard time. They agree that she is in no pain, and we are all thankful for that.

Please pray for our Angel Amanda...that she knows how much she is loved and will be missed. And for her entire family, that we will all be able to go on, because that is what she would want us to do. God Bless!!!
Love,
Aunt Kim

WEDNESDAY, NOVEMBER 12, 2008
6:42 PM

Good evening, "Amanda's Faithful Followers," AFF's. I am so very sorry that I have to type this...but Amanda, our Angel here on earth...earned her purple wings at 5:25 p.m. tonight.

The family would like to thank the nurses and doctors at AMC for all their support and kindness, over the years and especially over the last few days. Also, thank you to Fr. Rodino for your visit today.

Please keep Amanda's family in your prayers, as it's so hard to grasp life without her right now. We will get through this though as a family, because that is what Manda would want.

Love,

Aunt Kim

B+ & FROG

"Remembered Joy"

Don't grieve for me, for now I'm free!
I follow the plan God laid for me.
I saw His face, I heard His call,
I took His hand and left it all...
I could not stay another day,
To love, to laugh, to work or play;
Tasks left undone must stay that way.
And if my parting has left a void,
Then fill it with remembered joy.
A friendship shared, a laugh, a kiss...
Ah yes, these things I, too, shall miss.
My life's been full, I've savored much:
Good times, good friends, a loved-one's touch.
Perhaps my time seemed all too brief—
Don't shorten yours with undue grief.

Amanda Perrotta

Be not burdened with tears of sorrow,
Enjoy the sunshine of the morrow.

--An Irish Blessing

Very early in the morning, still the middle of the night after Amanda died, her father, Lou, sat in the quiet of their kitchen and let his heart and soul finally rest after his long yet loving journey with Amanda. These are his words as he remembered some of the distinctive points of Amanda's life.

~~~~~

My family and I were given the most devastating news in November of 2005. At first, we looked at each other and said, "What exactly is Mitochondrial Disease?" My wife searched quickly to find out more about his disease. This was just simply something we had never heard of, nor anyone else we knew. Quickly my wife responded with what seemed like an endless search. Finally we received the facts of this retched disease. Again, we looked at each other and stared into each other's eyes and said, "Just remember the reason why we always loved each other from the age of 16. We are both nurturers of children, and still are, and we will get through this, no matter how difficult it is."

We then sat our parents down around Thanksgiving and told them the news. At first they didn't understand what we were telling them because, for the past 14 years, we had doctors telling us that Amanda was only mildly autistic with complicated digestive problems that could be modified with proper early interventions.

We then enrolled Amanda in a Helping Hands program that seemed to help her in a small way. As she became a little older, we decided to transfer her into Pinewoods School for special needs children where my wife, Jackie, had previously worked for many years.

Amanda did well at Pinewoods Center until she had a bad seizure at the age of two. It was then recommended to us that we see a neurologist right away who then put her on anti-seizure drugs to try to control them. At that time, she had some good days and again some bad days. She also continued to have stomach and digestive problems. Again, my wife and I talked and decided to see a pediatric neurologist. The neurologist, Dr. Rieback, took very good care of Amanda in finding the right combination of anti-seizure drugs for quite awhile until she reached puberty.

At this time, she started having more frequent seizures that were a little more intense. We called Dr. Rieback to schedule an appointment to find out that he could no longer see any patients. After ten years, our doctor, whom we felt comfortable with, who gave us such comfort in helping Amanda, was sentenced to prison for life. We were devastated at a crucial time when we needed him the most.

At that time, Amanda was getting worse with seizures. We went to see Dr. Kelly Matone at Albany Medical Center, who was able to give us care under the circumstances. Amanda seemed to do okay again for a while and attended Oakwood Christian School with her sister, Carolyn. They both attended Oakwood for the first year in 2001 and really adapted quite well.

At the beginning of school in September 2002, Amanda returned home from a trip to South Carolina. That evening, she was playing outside and dropped right in front of the other children. We dialed 911. She had a very bad seizure that put her in the hospital for two weeks. Her seizures were getting worse. The doctors ran all kinds of tests, especially EEGs [electroencephalographs to monitor. Amanda's brain waves] After relentless testing, they couldn't give us any reason for Amanda's condition other than having a bad seizure disorder.

We then talked and decided just to treat the seizures as they occurred. Unfortunately, they were uncontrollable, to the point that she couldn't walk, talk, or even sit up. Her brain had seizures so much that she regressed to her toddler years, including crawling and wetting her pants—at age 11.

At this time, we decided to continue to still hope and pray that we would find the right combination of drugs to reduce Amanda's seizures. It finally worked, and Amanda was feeling better after a whole year of having constant, partial complex seizure activity.

She was then enrolled in Wildwood School, where she met many friends and staff whom she immediately took a liking to. She seemed to be doing quite well there until she began to have muscle cramping and weakness in her legs. She continued to go to school with AFO's [Ankle-Foot Orthoses] helping to support her legs as she walked. This was the time when we decided to seek more answers.

Our doctor, Anthony Malone, recommended to us a pediatric genetic specialist down in New York at Columbia-Presbyterian Hospital who could test for metabolic and mitochondrial disorders. Amanda had her muscle biopsy in August 2005. In November, we knew for sure that she had a terminal disease.

We just never believed that this most wretched disease was something that could cause us to watch this beautiful, young, inspiring little lady go from dancing intensely on stage with her sister to suffering from the shutting down of the muscles of her esophagus, to the point of not being able to swallow, and eventually shutting down her stomach such that she could never eat again. This disease then continued to shut down her bowels, intestines, and kidneys, and eventually her lungs and heart.

Through all of this, she always kept a smile and never complained. She was placed here with all of us that have been touched by her life. She was my daughter, friend, companion, and most of all, my little clown. I loved her so much, and that is why I felt the need to tell her story the way my wife and I witnessed it.

I am going to end on one last statement, and that is: God has a plan for each of us. Some have it harder than others, and some don't. But just remember Amanda's Journey at your times of need, and listen closely to your hearts. God is in everyone's heart. I believe that Amanda reached into hers and found God. She then realized that He was in control and gave her the courage, strength, and beautiful smile that followed her through her journey, right up to her last breath with her loving, supportive family by her side.

Even though it is hard as it is, it is the way it is.

Amanda and I love you all for all of your support and gratitude on this special day of her life.

Thank you.

Amanda's mother and father together, and her sisters, Carolyn and Dahea all wrote letters as well, calling her by her pet name, Mary. These were written after the new year, some time after Amanda died, to place some distance in their hearts from the events leading up to her death. Their love and admiration for her are evident through their words.

~~~~~

Dear Mary,

Before I came to America, I always wished to have a younger sister because I was the youngest. Now that you are my younger sister, Mary, I thank God every day for sending me such a special sister like you. Lots of people don't really understand how close you, Carolyn, and I are because we have only known each other for two years.

And sometimes I can't even explain how close we are when we have known each other only two years, though I think, sometimes, we can't explain everything. It's the love that is bonding the three of us so closely, and it's almost impossible for me to explain how strong our love for each other is.

You will always be my sister, FOREVER, and I miss you so much even though I know you are always with me.

I love you so much, MARY!! XXOO

Love, Dahea

Amanda Perrotta

Dear Mary,

In your journal entry about me, you talked about how you sometimes thought I was an angel sent down to help support you through everything. I think the real angel and blessing was you. Having you in my life for those short 16 years changed my whole perspective on how to live. Even though you were younger than me, you would often act a lot older than I. Your insight on life made me want to be just like you. And I intend to live the rest of my life being positive and forever relying on God. Not one day will go by where I won't think about you. I have way too many memories and pictures that are in my heart for a lifetime. I miss you more than anything, but I know you're with me, and sometimes I can even feel you holding my hand. I want you to know that you were not only my little sister, but also the biggest part of my life. Everything we did, whether getting in trouble or telling secrets, even our sleepovers at the hospital, were some of the best times. Thank you, Mary, for being not only my sister, but the best person you could with everything you went through. You will be in my heart always and forever. I love you to the moon and back.

Love,

Chunky Monkey (Sissy)

+ Abby (Service dog)

To our Manda, (Mare, Sweets),

Where do Daddy and I start. This letter is going in your book you wrote. Our reason for writing this is to let everyone know how proud we are to have been blessed and chosen to be your parents.

Mare, in your short time here on earth, sixteen years, you left and continue to leave your mark in people's lives every day.

Daddy and I hope, when people read your book, they see your light shine through. Your whole life's positive outlook was and will continue to be for all of us an amazing gift that God gave you. I only hope that you know how much of an impact you made on us and many other's lives.

There was so much more daddy and I wanted to say to you. We knew you were leaving us, and we didn't want to scare you. I know now that you also knew and were doing the same—protecting daddy and me. In the end, though, words don't and didn't matter; we all knew how much we were and are loved.

You were an angel on earth given to us for only sixteen years. It seems as though not enough time to have had you. We know now that God needed you more in heaven. Thank you, Manda and God, for the best sixteen years of our lives. We miss you but know you are always close in our hearts!

Mommy and daddy love you more than life and to the moon and back. Sleep with the angels, baby girl, and remember that we will all be together again; heaven has no time.

Mare, we will, I promise, as you taught us all, to B+ and F.R.O.G.

With all our love,
Mommy and Daddy XXOO

Amanda Perrotta

THURSDAY, NOVEMBER 13, 2008

Good Afternoon AFF!! I hope everyone has enjoyed the new photo of Amanda. It was from my wedding in 1999, and I always thought she looked like a little angel in it, so it made it most appropriate now to post it. I am also sorry that I didn't write more last night, I had planned to say a few more things, but couldn't seem to get my fingers to type it.

I just spoke with Jacki about the update, so here it is. The family is doing all right. They all miss Manda like crazy, of course. We also understand that now she is free, but that doesn't make the pain any easier.

The arrangements have been made for Monday, November 17th. The wake will be from 8:30 a.m. till 1:00 p.m. followed by the funeral Mass at 1:00 p.m. This will all take place at St. Jude The Apostle Church, 43 Brookside Ave., Wynantskill, NY. The family is asking for no flowers please, but donations in Amanda's name to UMDF, Make-A-Wish, or CaringBridge would be so appreciated. All three causes were so close to Amanda's heart. There will be an obituary in the Albany Times Union and in the Troy Record.

Thank you to all of our family, friends and the wonderful people at AMC for their help, prayers and kind words. There were so many people that have been so very kind and compassionate, that there are too many to list right now. Please know that our whole family thanks you and loves you.

Now I have a saying that Jacki would like me to write. It is a saying that she bought to hang up in their family room, and seems so fitting right now.

Our Family is a circle of love and strength.. With every birth and every union the circle grows. Every joy shared adds more love. Every crisis faced together makes the circle stronger.

Jacki & Louis...you have showed us all how strong and wonderful you two are as parents. I know I speak for everyone when I thank you for sharing Amanda with us. We love you guys and will always love Amanda.

Love,
Aunt Kim
B+ & FROG

The Celtic Cross

Grieve not nor speak of me with tears,
but laugh and speak of me as though I were beside you.
I love you so.
It was heaven here with you.

TUESDAY, NOVEMBER 18, 2008
Good Morning AFF!! I know it's been a few days, so Jacki and I thought we would give you all a little update. Yesterday was Amanda's Celebration of Life...and of course it was beautiful. Yes, there were tears, but a lot of smiles, too! There were pictures of Amanda everywhere, so how could you not smile? I even found

myself laughing when I would think about something Amanda did. She IS an amazing girl!

Thank you to everyone who showed your support yesterday...whether in prayer from miles away...or if you came in person. We as a family, appreciated every one of you. If you were there, you know of the large number of people who came...what a testament to the most wonderful 16-year old we know. Thank you to all the nurses from AMC, Dr. Adams and Cheryl, and especially Fr. Rodino, for the beautiful mass.

Please keep signing the guestbook. Jacki says they need to hear from everyone now more than ever. I am looking into having all the journal entries and guest book entries into a book, so if you really want to say something...please do it. :-) Don't be afraid. Thank you and God Bless!!!

Love,

Aunt Kim

B+ & FROG

WEDNESDAY, NOVEMBER 19, 2008

Good afternoon AFF!!! Well, please keep leaving messages or leave one if you have never done so before because, as I've said, we will be making all the entries into a book. Jacki is really looking forward to working on the book next week and so am I. We want it to be beautiful, just like Amanda.

Jacki wanted me to wish everyone "Happy Holidays" this year. And please continue to pray for all of Amanda's CB friends and families. God Bless!!

Love,

Jacki, Louis, Carolyn Rose, Dahea, Abby, The Dedricks, and the Perrottas

B+ & FROG

P.S. I wanted to say Thank You to everyone for your wonderful words about my keeping the CB site for Amanda. Everything I've said and done has been out of pure love for my niece. I hope I've done her proud...I'll love you forever, Manda! I received a card (thank you, Chrissy) that had a beautiful poem on it, and I want to share it with you.

Don't think of her as gone away—her journey's just begun.
Life holds so many facets—this earth is only one.
Just think of her as resting from the sorrows and the tears
In a place of warmth and comfort where there are no days and years.
Think how she must be wishing that we could know today
How nothing but our sadness can really pass away.
And think of her as living in the hearts of those she touched,
For nothing loved is ever lost—and she was loved so much.

FRIDAY, NOVEMBER 21, 2008
Good Morning everyone! I have a quick update for you since I just talked with Jacki. She said that they are having a very hard

time and miss Manda sooo much, but they are trying to stay positive, just like she did. She will get them through, and we are all sure that she is busy doing something good in heaven. We were just saying that she is probably doing some crafts and walking some dogs. :-)

We would like to ask that you please say some extra prayers for Manda's Mito friend Erik, mom Tammy, and family. And to Jess, you are in our thoughts and prayers, too!

Thank you all for your continued love and support. Please don't forget to leave a final message as this site will be closed next week. But Amanda's Journey site will remain open. The site will be used to help other Mito families in need. We want to continue Manda's good work. God Bless!
Love,
Aunt Kim
B+ & FROG

MONDAY, NOVEMBER 24, 2008
Good Morning AFF!! Jacki and I thought we would do an update today. The family is doing OK. Jacki has been working on getting the house in order, keeping Amanda's things the same. There are, of course, bad days, and then there are good ones. Everyone misses Manda terribly, and with the holidays approaching, it's even harder. But they are trying to stay positive because that is what Manda would want.

The Amanda's Journey website will be left open and offers the ability to send emails if you need to. This site will contain information on any upcoming events. Jacki is planning on having a Mito/Remembrance walk next fall. Also, a book of Amanda's journal entries is in the works. All proceeds will go to help Mito families.

Thank you everyone for you love and support, especially all the doctors and nurses. Thanks, Pippi, for helping decorate Amanda's pine blanket and for coming to dinner. :-) God Bless!!
Love,
Aunt Kim
B+ & FROG

P.S. Jacki wanted me to give this wonderful poem that was on a gift from Aunt Mimi when Manda was at Sunnyview for rehab a year ago this month. Thanks Aunt Mimi!

An Angel's Touch To Inspire

A feather fell to earth today and made my heart rejoice.
Its words of inspiration came to lift me with its voice.
You have the will to reach your goals, to be your very best,
To walk life's path with head held high, to pass each trying test.
Have faith that you are not alone. He keeps you in his sight,
Inspiring you along the way, to reach life's greatest height.[21]

WEDNESDAY, NOVEMBER 26, 2008
Good Morning AFF!!

---

[21]Copyright unknown but the poem can be traced to the Encore company.

Amanda Perrotta

This will be my final journal entry on CaringBridge. I want to thank everyone who has responded so wonderfully to my entries. I appreciated every comment you made. I know everyone, including me, would rather have it that Manda updated, but I hope I made her proud. Tomorrow, Jacki, Louis, and the girls will be doing an entry, and then we will close out the account. We want to make sure everyone understands that www.amandasjourney.org will be left open. Please feel free to send emails to this site. It might take some time, but this site will contain information on upcoming events that will help benefit other Mito families. We know this is something Amanda would be so proud of.

Please continue to pray for all of Amanda's CB friends and families. Have a wonderful Thanksgiving, enjoying your families, and don't forget to be thankful for all of our blessings.

Oh, and don't forget to watch the Thanksgiving Day Parade..it was Amanda's favorite thing to do on Thanksgiving...watch it...and remember her! I am sure she will be watching it tomorrow, and she could never have better seats!! God Bless!
Love,
Aunt Kim
Remember to always B+ and FROG

We will love you forever and ever, Amanda!!!

THURSDAY, NOVEMBER 27, 2008
Hi all. It's Jacki. It has been a while for me, so bear with me as this is so very hard to do and so final! First, Thank You, Aunt

Kim, for all of your dedication to Manda's CB site. For the beautiful way you word everything as only you could do. I love you for that. What a talent you have. So where do I even begin to start Amanda's Journey's last entry? I can only write from my heart, so here it goes. I have only wanted two things in my whole LIFE: To marry my husband, Louis, and be a mother!!! I was BLESSED with both!! I am very simple, yet very happy. I don't ask for much, just time together with my family. Now my (our) life has changed, and I am (we are) left to go on. How does someone do this? One day, one breath, one minute at a time for as long as you need. There is no wrong or right way. It's not like losing a child comes with a book of how you are supposed to handle it. I miss my Manda more than Life!! I know she's with me and us because I can feel her. We made Manda a promise at the end. We promised her to B+ and F.R.O.G. I/we are trying to honor this, even though it kills us sometimes. You have a bad moment, then you pick yourself up and go on, like Manda would want. Louis and I are asking EVERYONE to do the same when they get sad. Please remember: if Manda could do it, being sooo very sick and having to get through it, we have NO excuse!! It's OK to be sad or angry, or even cry, but, in the end, B+.

Now enough, as Manda would say. Louis and I, Carolyn Rose, and Dahea can never thank you all enough for all that you have given to Manda and our family!! Each one of you is so special in your own way and in what you have brought to us all!!

We will be updating www.amandasjourney.org and having some events to benefit Mitochondrial Disease. I will leave you all with this: we love you and keep you all close in our hearts always. And REMEMBER, as Manda wishes, ALWAYS B+ and F.R.O.G.

We Love you, Manda, Mare, Sweets. Sleep with the Angels, baby girl!! May God bless you all. Thank you, Manda, for being you!! With Love ,thankfulness, and gratitude to you all.
Louis, Jacki, Carolyn Rose, and Dahea. XOXOXOXO

SATURDAY, NOVEMBER 29, 2008
Hi all. I know we were going to close Manda's site Friday, but Erik Liddell, one of Manda's friends, went to be with her last night. He earned his wings, too!! How Mito affected our lives. Jaden Angel: November 2nd, 2008. Our Amanda Mary Francis: November 12th. Erik Liddell: November 28th. We loved them ALL!! Please continue to pray for us and for ALL the children with Mito!! May God bless them and their families!! God Bless. Jacki.

P.S. I felt the need to add this! We are all in this together!! Remember, for Manda B+ and F.R.O.G.

SUNDAY, NOVEMBER 30, 2008

Hi all. It's Jacki. We as a family have left the site open for a couple more days due to Erik Liddell's passing from Mito. We are in the final stages now of closing down the site, but it's going to take a couple days to copy all of this for the book. I don't know how many days the site will be open. At this point, I can't promise that if you leave a message it will be copied into the book, but our family and I would still appreciate a message from any of you.

Just a quick note to let you all know how we are doing. We miss Manda more than life.... Nights and mornings are the hardest. We go to sleep thinking about her and wake up thinking about her, but we know we have to keep that B+ attitude and F.R.O.G., for we made a promise to her. Thank you again for all your love and support. It means a lot. As Manda wishes, please continue to pray for all CB friends and especially the Mott/Lidell family. And the Weekes. May God Bless you All! Jacki.

Amanda Perrotta

Amanda's obituary for the Troy Record

Amanda Perrotta

On November 12, 2008, at Albany Medical Center Hospital, Amanda Mary Francis Perrotta, precious daughter of Edmund Louis Perrotta and Jacquelin Dedrick Perrotta, left with the angels for her home in heaven.

Amanda attended Wildwood School and enjoyed her school days surrounded by dedicated staff of caring teachers and therapists. When it was no longer possible for Amanda to physically attend school, she embarked on a mission to educate others about Mitochondrial Depletion Syndrome, the disease robbing her of the energy needed to sustain life.

Through her CaringBridge Web site, Amanda brought together others with chronic and life threatening illnesses to encourage them to live life to the fullest, and always with a smile.

Amanda is also survived by her beloved sisters, Carolyn Rose Perrotta and Dahea Lee; her grandparents Louis and Rosemary Perrotta and William L. and Carol Dedrick; her Godparents, Dawn MacGuinness and William M. Dedrick. She is the great granddaughter of Rose Cronin of Troy and the late Edmund Cronin, the late Ambrose and Julia Perrotta, William and Florence Dedrick and Edward and Polly Martin of Troy, as well as many loving aunts, uncles and cousins. Amanda was predeceased by her baby cousin angel, Emma Hamilton. Amanda will also be missed by her beloved service dog, Abby, who was trained by Amanda.

Amanda's entire family is so very grateful to all her doctors and the nurses of C-7 and D-7 at Albany Medical as well as Amanda's home health team nurses who attended with care and love to Amanda.

The funeral service for Amanda will be held Monday afternoon at 1 p.m. at St. Jude the Apostle Church, Brookside Avenue, Wynantskill, where a Mass of Christian Burial will be celebrated by Rev. Salvatore Rodino, pastor.

Relatives and friends are invited to attend and may call at the church Monday from 8:30 a.m. to 1 p.m. Interment St. Mary's Cemetery, Troy.

In lieu of flowers, donations in Amanda's Memory made to the United Mitochondrial Disease Foundation, 8085 Saltsburg Road, Suite 201, Pittsburgh, PA 15239, or made online to Make-a-Wish foundation would be appreciated.

Arrangements by the Bocketti Funeral Home, 336 Third St. Troy, NY.

Amanda Perrotta

When news spread that Amanda had earned her wings, tributes and condolences began to pour into her CaringBridge guestbook, literally from all over the world. Her faithful readers and fans responded with enthusiasm. The site was nearly overrun with postings. From a couple of days before Amanda died to nearly a month after, the letters, words of love, and rememberances streamed in unabated, representing 48 different states and over 15 countries. Here is a representative sampling of the wonder and inspiration that Amazing Amanda brought to everyone.

Tributes and Rememberances

WEDNESDAY, NOVEMBER 12, 2008
Perrotta family,

Amanda touched so many lives, and we are so grateful to have known of her for the time that we had. Baruch Dayan Emet..

Tamar Godel

WEDNESDAY, NOVEMBER 12, 2008
My sympathy to Amanda's family during this difficult time. I have been following Amanda's CB site for a short time. However, I have learned so much from this beautiful young lady. She is truly an inspiration to many people. She showed me how to persevere even in rough times. May God bring you peace and comfort.

Kathy Ghahkenshah
Amman Jordan

WEDNESDAY, NOVEMBER 12, 2008
My heart hurts with you. I don't even know the words to say right now. I know that Manda is dancing with Jesus, though! Every angel in heaven is celebrating her sweet spirit and her passion for life! Her life was a beautiful one and will remain so always! She is dear to our hearts! We are praying for ALL OF YOU! I can't even imagine the feelings you must have. Hugs to you all!

Mindy Pfohl

WEDNESDAY, NOVEMBER 12, 2008
Oh Manda...I am so sad, but so relieved you are spreading your B+ news to a crowd of angels who are already practicing it!! Well, my friend, you FROG-ed to the end, and now you are experiencing everlasting life in a healed body. I will be praying for your family. I wish I lived closer so I could be there to celebrate your life, but you will see me here in Texas celebrating for you, I promise. Now I am going to bed. Goodnight, my angel friend. Godspeed....

Zack Tavlin
The Woodlands, TX

WEDNESDAY, NOVEMBER 12, 2008
Dear Perrotta family,

Tonight at our Bible Study, my daughter, Katie, asked everyone to pray for Amanda and you. We have been going to the Caring-

Bridge site many times daily to check on Manda and see how all of you are doing. We are sad to hear that she has passed but know that she is with our Lord in heaven, where there is no sadness, no crying, no illness. We pray for those close to her who are grieving, that the joy of Manda's life would bring comfort, and we Praise God for the beauty, strength, and happiness she brought to so many. In the short time we were able to know her through this site, we were truly touched, and each of us has been changed by the strength she showed through her journey. May we all be as strong. Many thanks to Aunt Kim, who has been so faithful in keeping us updated. May God's peace be with you all.

Chantelle, Hannah, and Katie Macune
Corpus Christi, TX

WEDNESDAY, NOVEMBER 12, 2008
To my sweet and precious Amanda,

Fly away sweet girl. Fly away.
Sweet Perrotta Family, my heart breaks for you as I write this message with tears pouring down my face. My heart aches to know of the void that will forever be in my life. I pray that God will bless you with the strength to get through the many days ahead. I pray that you are comforted somewhat by knowing that Jaden was waiting at heaven's gates to welcome your precious angel. May you be wrapped tightly in God's loving arms.

Carrie Maniscalco
Jackson, MS

WEDNESDAY, NOVEMBER 12, 2008
To the Perrotta and Dedrick families,

My sympathy goes out to you all. You have all endured so much over the years and have had strength like no family I have ever met. I never saw any of you sad despite what life had handed you. Amanda and that famous smile shined everywhere she was and in every picture. The love shines through the sadness and suffering and proves that God made sure Amanda was an angel on earth and will now be a bright angel in heaven above. We love you all and our prayers are with you during this time.

Donna, Mary Rose, and Thomas Clark
Wynantskill, NY

WEDNESDAY, NOVEMBER 12, 2008
Dear Perrottas,

Words are of small comfort and little can ease the pain of loss. Please know that all, many who only knew her through these pages, will forever remember your daughter. She was, indeed, an angel on earth and is now an angel who will forever be a light to all, inspiring us to savor and appreciate life's moments. You are a remarkable family, and I want to thank you for sharing your daughter with us. She is now whole, holy, and free of pain. Her light will shine forever.

My thoughts and prayers are with you.

Linda Fisher

WEDNESDAY, NOVEMBER 12, 2008

I had another memory tonight about Sean Robert and Amanda. Remember when we came to visit you guys in AMC on C7 and Amanda had that balloon? She gave it to Sean Robert. I remember thinking, "Oh, no now I am going to have to take it home and listen to that song in the balloon over and over." Sean Robert LOVED it and would play it over and over, and I let him. Every time he smiled and laughed over that silly balloon, I too smiled. I am so sad that Amanda is not here! I want to say (as I am sure many of us do) that Amanda is "in a better place." I know she is where she belongs, and I believe that, but where we think a "better place" is isi n the arms of her family. How hard it is to believe and understand even though it has been happening before our eyes for weeks.

You all (and I mean everyone reading this and everyone in Manda's life) will be in my prayers! Remember how much I love you and thank you for teaching me so much and opening your heart to me the very first time we met!

God Bless you all!

Shannon Whelan
Slingerlands, NY

WEDNESDAY, NOVEMBER 12, 2008
Sweet Angel Amanda,

I hope you are at peace in Heaven with your Mito friend Jaden. Alexis will be joining you someday, and I know you will be there to welcome her. My thoughts are with you and your amazing family.

Love always,

Steph & Alexis Roung
St. George, ON Canada

WEDNESDAY, NOVEMBER 12, 2008
Sending heartfelt prayers and hugs as you all begin this new journey together. I have tried to imagine this point with Josiah and I can't, so I can't imagine what emotions you must have right now. I stand with you in the 'I hate Mito Club.' She fought a good fight, and she has finished the race, and Jesus stands and says, "Well done, my good and faithful servant, come in and rest." Rest well, sweet Amanda, rest well.

Jen Kovacevic
Lakeland, FL

WEDNESDAY, NOVEMBER 12, 2008
Dear Miss Amazing's Family,

I often think of the song, "My Wish" when I think of Amanda, and I think of all that that song represents....
"My wish for you is that this life becomes all that you want it to,
Your dreams stay big, your worries stay small.

Amanda Perrotta

You never need to carry more than you can hold. And while you're out there getting where you're getting to,
I hope you know somebody loves you and wants the same things, too,
Yeah, this, is my wish."

Even though Amanda's life was shorter than most, she lived each day with the most positive attitude, and she was LOVED by so many. She was amazing that way. I promise I will do my best to continue to carry her positive attitude in my heart and "live" my dreams to the best of my ability in her honor. This baby we are bringing into the world in six short months has Amanda's determined spirit already, and I know Amanda is a part of him or her already.

Thank you for allowing Amanda to be a part of my life and the lives of so many others. She will always be Amazing Amanda. Now she will just be "Angel Amazing Amanda," and she will always be my inspiration.

Hugs,

Malisa M

WEDNESDAY, NOVEMBER 12, 2008
"When it is all over, you will not regret having suffered; rather you will regret having suffered so little and suffered that little so badly."—Blessed Sebastian Valfre

I can just say congratulations to Amanda as she has received her wings today. Something all of us strive for. She did it with such strength. Thank you, Aunt Kim, for thinking of us, people you have never met, and keeping us updated. We are indebted to all of your amazing family.

God's peace to you F.R.O.G

Lee and Lori True
Parker, CO

WEDNESDAY, NOVEMBER 12, 2008
I did not know Amanda but have been monitoring her site reading her story all throughout the evening. I found it through a link from a friend. I have been praying all day for your precious girl. I know he has a better plan for her, and that doesn't help right now, but take comfort knowing she is no longer in pain. There are no words that can help ease the pain you are experiencing, but know in your hearts that she is loved by so many and that millions of prayers have been sent her way. We will continue to pray and send warm wishes to you and your family. May God bless you and keep you,

The Jennings: Sam, Sandy, Michael, Jonathan and CJ
Cashiers, NC

WEDNESDAY, NOVEMBER 12, 2008
I am grieving for your whole families now as I couldn't imagine what it must be like to lose such an amazing lady in your life. I knew when I opened your page today that she had moved on be-

cause of the background change. She was so full of life and happiness with everything she did and went through, it was an honor and a pleasure to get to follow you all on this adventure of Amanda's life.

Lisa Simmons
Davie, FL

WEDNESDAY, NOVEMBER 12, 2008
Our thoughts and prayers are with you all.
We will miss Amanda so much but will never forget her positive outlook, her smile, her Caring, and her spirit. Amanda gave us so many special moments and memories. She also taught us many life lessons—many that I will strive to teach my own children, my students, and anyone else I can get to listen!
We love you Amanda!

Chris Stanley and Family

WEDNESDAY, NOVEMBER 12, 2008
Dear Perrottas,

I know you are hurting. I hope you can find some comfort in knowing that Amanda is no longer suffering.

I will continue to pray for the Lord to comfort you at this time.

I feel so lucky to have known Amanda even though it was only in passing in the halls of Wildwood. She was always sweet and friendly.

Thank you for sharing such a wonderful girl with us.
Love,

Kia Cheek

WEDNESDAY, NOVEMBER 12, 2008
I'm sure I'm the poorer for not having known Amanda and her
wonderful family. Stacy and Ari wrote about how amazing
Amanda was with Rina. She clearly had a gift and has passed it on
to others. May you be strengthened by her love and the love of
those around you.

A friend of the Goldbergs,
Muriel Horowitz

WEDNESDAY, NOVEMBER 12, 2008
Dear Perrotta Family,

I'm a mom and grandma in Utah who's been following Amanda's
story for some time. I am so sorry for your loss. Your beautiful
Amanda was a unique and amazing spirit who had such maturity
and wisdom for one so young. I ran across her CB page about
Christmas time last year. I remember she was in a rehab center
and had been there or in the hospital for quite some time. I was
initially surprised that she seemed to take things so lightly, but as I
got to 'know' her, I came to realize that her attitude was
deliberately chosen—she chose to 'be positive,' no matter what
her day presented. I have prayed for her constantly since that time

Amanda Perrotta

and have read her every entry, and never once has she failed to find something positive to share. I loved her 'LOLs' in every entry, her ability to laugh at herself and her circumstances rather than crying and complaining.

My family has some history with depression, and I have not been spared completely, although, for the most part, I'm fine. But a few weeks ago a series of events put me in a tough place, and I was really struggling. This was about the time that Jacki was doing most of the updating. But one day, Amanda managed to update for herself, as sick as she was. I couldn't believe it! She was STILL positive! No complaining. Just looking for the good, asking for prayers for others. For the first time in my life, I thought maybe my 'depression' was controllable from within, so I decided to try to B+. It took me exactly 2 days to regain my usual positive outlook instead of the few weeks it might have taken for the low spot to pass on its own. Wow! Thank you, Amanda! I might never have realized the power of the human spirit without your wonderful example.

I will continue to pray for all the family. You must be wonderful parents to have raised such amazing children. Best wishes always.

Shelley Chaves
UT

WEDNESDAY, NOVEMBER 12, 2008
Dear Jacki, Lou, Carolyn and family,

Right now, I don't really have words of my own, so I will borrow this passage from someone whose name I don't know but whose words seem to fit when I think of Amanda and your loving family. Please know that I care very deeply for your family and hope that I can be a source of comfort in the coming days, weeks, and difficult months ahead. Amanda was one of those special people who come along once in a lifetime. She was loved by me and by so many. I am so very, very sorry for your loss.

'I'll lend you for a little while,
a child of mine,' God said,
'for you to love the while she lives,
and mourn for when she's dead.

It may be two or three short years,
or twenty-two or three,
but will you, till I call her back,
take care of her for me?

She'll bring her charms to gladden you,
and, should her stay be brief,
you'll have her lovely memories
as solace for your grief.

I cannot promise she will stay,
since all from earth return,
but there are lessons taught down there
I want this child to learn.

I've looked the wide world over
in my search for teacher's true,
and from the throngs that crowd life's lanes,
I have selected you.

Amanda Perrotta

Now will you give her all your love?
Nor think the labor vain?
Nor hate me when I come to call,
to take her back again?'

God fancied he heard the parent's say,
'Dear Lord, thy will be done.
For all the joy the child shall bring,
the risk of grief I'll run.

I'll shelter her with tenderness,
I'll love her while I may,
and for the happiness I've known
forever grateful I'll stay.

But should the angels call for her,
much sooner than I planned,
I'll brave the bitter grief that comes,
and try to understand.'[22]

Denise LaBier

WEDNESDAY, NOVEMBER 12, 2008
Amanda,

The smile in your picture will not be forgotten. Although we
have never met you have touched my heart with your courage. I

---

[22] Poem by Edgar A. Guest

am so happy you are now pain free, but my heart aches for your family. You will all be in our prayers.
With Love,

April and Wayne Bryant and Family
Hayden Lake, ID

WEDNESDAY, NOVEMBER 12, 2008
Amanda's family,

I have never met any of you and you do not know me. I have been following Amanda for the past couple of months. She has proved to be a 'Brave Little Soul.' She has helped people around the world and across the US to learn about Mito. May she be at peace with no pain or suffering. Your family will be in my thoughts and prayers.

Kristie Grote
Maryland Heights, MO

WEDNESDAY, NOVEMBER 12, 2008
Although I only met her once, Amanda touched my heart, and she moved me. I am so sorry for your loss.

God bless you Perrotta family,

Mary Rose Clark
Wynantskill, NY

Amanda Perrotta

WEDNESDAY, NOVEMBER 12, 2008

2 Timothy 4:6-8:

"...and the time has come for my departure. I have fought the good fight, I have finished the race, I have kept the faith. Now, there is in store for me the crown of righteousness, which the Lord, the righteous Judge, will award to me on that day."

Dear Perrottas,

Words cannot express how deeply sorry I am for this tremendous loss. I pray that you find moments of peace and are comforted by the many memories you have as a wonderfully close family. Should there be anything that I could do to help you during this difficult time, please don't hesitate to let me know. I love you guys.

Love,

Diane Kunz F.R.O.G.

WEDNESDAY, NOVEMBER 12, 2008

Amanda,

You were a huge inspiration in my life, and you were my family. I know deep down you are no longer in pain and at peace, but the tears still roll down as I think of you. The thought of no longer hearing your voice and sassiness or seeing your beautiful smile.... These thoughts and memories will last forever in my heart and mind. I love you very much!!

Jacki, Lou and girls, we love you guys and will be there for you every step of the way. Remember, you are family to us, and we will do everything we can for you. Love you lots and lots!!

Love and peace always,
Neice and Keith Boniface

WEDNESDAY, NOVEMBER 12, 2008
Amanda is victorious.

Praise God for her.

We'll see her again someday.

Fly free, special little lady, fly free.

Monika Y
Clifton Park, NY

WEDNESDAY, NOVEMBER 12, 2008
Our deepest sympathy is with you during this difficult time. Your family will continue to be in our prayers. We are better for having known Amanda through this site these past weeks. She clearly was an angel on earth and now is an angel watching over all. Praying God's peace and comfort for all of you.

The eternal God is your refuge, and his everlasting arms are under you. --Deuteronomy 33:27

Love, The South Family
FL

Amanda Perrotta

WEDNESDAY, NOVEMBER 12, 2008
To you all, my heart aches for you. There are no words that I can
offer to you and this time other than to say you are in our
thoughts and prayers and Amanda was such an inspiration to my
boys, especially Jake, who is 15. He looked up to her and enjoyed
reading her journal entries and thanked her immensely for the
spoon theory article she led him too.

Hugs,
Sharon Goldin and the boys
Lorton, VA

WEDNESDAY, NOVEMBER 12, 2008
To the whole Family,

I wish there were something we could say or do, but I know
nothing will fill that gap right now, so please know we love you.
We will be lighting a candle in honor of Amanda tonight. Erik
sends his love to you all! Please let us know when services will be
held as we would like to pay our respects and give you a hug.
LOVE AND HUGS

The whole Mott/Liddell family
Tammy Mott
East Branch, NY

WEDNESDAY, NOVEMBER 12, 2008

As we sit together with tears overflowing, we want to share with you the tribute we wrote to Amanda on Rina's CB site journal entry this evening. It speaks for itself.

Hi all. Things here with Rina remain the same in terms of her virus and fatigue. That being said, while we use this site to keep you all updated on how she is doing, today we chose to dedicate this space to a remarkable young woman: Amanda Perrotta. Amanda lost her battle with Mito and passed away. The CB community has become a unique family to us with a bond like no other.

Our dear friend, Malissa, connected Amanda and Rina just about a year ago because she knew what they could do for each other. Instantly, a unique friendship and sisterly bond formed as they shared their daily stories with each other of, as they called it, "boring medical stuff" and the "fun stuff." Amanda became a big sister to Rina. She taught her how to live each moment with light and laughter even at the most challenging times. Rina and Amanda shared the same perspective on life on how to continue living each day to its fullest while dealing with the complexities of being a young tween living with Mito. Together they came up with fun names for their medical equipment, and made play lists of songs that carried special meaning and positive messages. How they laughed thinking about their doctors and nurses singing those songs while in procedures. Amanda taught Rina B+. It was Rina's choice to have a huge sign made with B+ on the door of her room, and we will forever think of sweet Amanda when in the room. There are not enough words to express the impact Amanda had on Rina or how our circle of CB friends will miss her. Our hearts are heavy with overwhelming sadness of such an incredible life taken at such a young age and the gaping hole it leaves. But we know that "Amazing Amanda" would want Rina and all of her CB buddies to continue living each day with hope and promise and a smile on their faces. Amanda's spirit will forever live on in our home and hearts. Please pray for her family, and let them feel the love around the world envelop them at this time.

Stacy, Ari and Rina
Cheltenham, PA

WEDNESDAY, NOVEMBER 12, 2008
Dear Amanda & family,

I talked to your Aunt Kim this morning as she dropped off Isabella for preschool (I am her teacher and was also Liam's), and she told me an update on you, and I've been striving to think of words ever since to let you know that I'm thinking about all of you and praying for you. Faith enables you to make it through absolutely anything, so keep your trust in God that He shall guide you through this chapter of your life here on Earth, and, with your arrival into Heaven, He'll continue to help you as you embark on your brand new journey of eternal life, forever with Him in the peace and joy of Heaven. God bless you all!

Amy Boulrice
Stittville, NY

WEDNESDAY, NOVEMBER 12, 2008
Oh, my sweet SuperManda,

I am crying my eyes out at the thought of losing you, at the fact that I will never hear your sweet voice again, but I know that the Lord Jesus has you in His arms as we speak and is getting ready to call you home. You have blessed me and all who know me so much, and you will NEVER be forgotten! Have fun up there, and be free as a bird without Mito! I LOVE YOU MY SUPERMAN —DA AND I ALWAYS WILL!

Rachel J
NY

WEDNESDAY, NOVEMBER 12, 2008
Jacki and family,

I am sitting here and crying to myself. Amanda was so wonderful and inspirational, and for being only 16. Wow. I know she will be a beautiful angel with so much grace as down here with us. I also know all her suffering will end, but I will miss her and reading her daily journal entries. She not only showed so many what the importance of life is, but how to make the best day out of that day. Some would say she could make the sweetest lemonade out of lemons. I feel Amanda is a major loss not only to your family, but to all the lives she touched. This is why my heart is breaking the same as yours. While I am sharing tears with you now, know if I could put my arms around you to comfort you I would. My heart is breaking for the heartache you and your whole family is feeling. I am praying as she flies off that Gods surrounds you with peace and strength. If you ever need to talk feel free to call. Just e-mail and I will call you. Love in Christ and through Amanda,

Amanda Perrotta

Dainta Deardorff
South Bend, IN

WEDNESDAY, NOVEMBER 12, 2008 03:21 PM, CST
Stopping by to tell Amanda good-bye. May the angels carry her
high to her God that will be waiting to meet her. Then she will
forever be free, healthy, and a wonderful 16-year old that can
walk, talk, sing, and dance. I am so proud of you, Amanda! You
gave so many others hope to go on when they was down. You
will forever be in my heart. Hugs to you my friend.

Drema Pearson

WEDNESDAY, NOVEMBER 12, 2008
Sweet, sweet girl, may the angels watch over you now and keep
you safe in your eternal sleep. Thank you for being such a presence
in our lives. You have left angel prints on our hearts.
Jacki, Lou, Carolyn, and Dahea, may God's love and warm em-
brace surround you now. God bless you.
With much love and prayers,

Marie, Bill and Sarah Barhold

THURSDAY, NOVEMBER 13, 2008
Jackie and Lou,

My husband, Josh, and I had the joy and privilege of meeting
Amanda at PetSmart in 2006. I started training Emmet with the

hope of having an obedient dog. Little did I know that I would leave that class with a good dog (usually), good friends, and life lessons from a special girl. I loved Amanda from the day I met her. She had an even stronger will than her stubborn little Abby! We had so much fun in class together, and even on her tough days--she was there. Never, in all the time I spent with Amanda, did I hear her complain.

Emmet always wiggled his tale so hard when he saw her, his whole body would shake. And Amanda always had a loving hug for him, even when he wasn't following directions in class. Josh, Emmet, and I had so much fun at the graduation picnic. Amanda's pictures with Emmet, Abby, and Maggie are forever a part of our photo albums and our cherished memories.

When I think of Amanda, I remember who she was to me: she was the embodiment of love, of joy, of determination. She shined with the Light of our Lord. So often I wanted to call, to visit, to share in her light. I let life get in the way, I worried that I might call on a bad day, I was afraid I might make her sick. So many excuses, and none of them right. Please know that I thought of all of you so often, prayed for you all, and spoke of your wonderful family.

I look forward to the day that I get to see her again. To hug her and tell her how much she meant to me, how she changed my heart. In honor of Amanda, I will work each day to look past the minor burdens of this world and let God's light shine through me the way she did EVERY DAY.

I'm sure you are so proud of your daughter, but I still feel the need to tell you how amazing she was. While some of that was just who she was, much of it came from the both of you and the love you gave to her. God bless your family during this time of parting. May you find peace in knowing she's gone to Heaven, where you'll see her again.

With all our love and prayers,

Josh & Heather Carpenter, and the pups Emmet & O'Malley
Kinderhook, NY

THURSDAY, NOVEMBER 13, 2008
Hi Amanda's Family,

I don't know you and you don't know me. In fact the only way I got to your CB site is because I was bored at work (I am a NICU nurse in Indiana) and was looking through CB history for some of our kids here and found your site listed on someone else's. I am so sorry to hear the loss of your darling daughter, sister, cousin, angel on Earth. I have been reading Amanda's site for hours now and just felt compelled to leave a note of sympathy for the family and of joy for Amanda. I know she is now awake, happy and healthy and playing with all her friends in heaven. You are an amazing family with amazing strength and I hope God is now putting your minds at ease. Please know you will now be in my prayers and i will check back on occasion to see how you all are doing. Take care of yourselves and of each other, Amanda will be watching.

Love,

Stephanie Murray
Fishers, IN

SATURDAY, NOVEMBER 15, 2008

This is a paper I wrote in my English comp class a few months ago about Amanda. The assignment was to write about someone who helped you in a time of need. I was always too shy to share it with people, but I figured it was selfish not to at this time. I am sure as many of you who read this blog like I do, Amanda changed your life for the better. I know that I am better for being able to share a portion of this life with Amanda and her family. So with nothing but love and complete admiration I want to say thank you to Amanda. I miss you, but I will also never forget you.

Mark Rosa

Two roads diverged in a yellow wood. This is a fitting way to begin the story. Standing at a crossroads in my life, I faced a choice much like the choice in the famous Robert Frost poem. Whether I understood the choices at the time is irrelevant. In the mirror stood a twenty one year old man confused and convincing himself that he was alone in the world with his problems.

I was never a bad student but had recently become burned out with school much like a candle lit at both ends. I traveled to college with the false belief that vast amounts of money ensured happiness. I soon realized that I had made a mistake in going to college to find a way to make money. Since I did not enjoy what I was doing, I eventually dropped out of school.

Unsure of what direction my life was going in I decided to move home. Like a tree with many branches, school was not my only problem. Legal and personal troubles I was going through at the same time began to put more and more pressure on other branches in my life and I feared that like school they would begin to break.

My life as I knew it was beginning to unwrap at the seams. Feeling failure breathing down my neck like a sharp cold rush of air, I began to make poor life decisions. Drugs and depression began to eat away my physical and mental health. I was spending more time destroying my life than embracing it. Confused, scared, and alone I stood in the darkness. Without knowing it, I was sent an angel to help light my way back to the path.

This is not your typical help in a time of need story. It differs in the fact that the person who changed my life does not know, and probably never will, the extent in which they affected it. Her name is Amanda.

I began working at a summer extension program at a school for children with disabilities following my first year of college. With a title of teacher assistant, I was entrusted with the responsibility of teaching the children. What I would come to realize is that, over time, "teacher" became student and the student became teacher. In the process, Amanda taught me more about life than any book or professor could ever dream.

When I met Amanda, she was a happy teenage girl who, even with her health and developmental problems, always had a smile on her face and a smart witted comment for you. No matter what the weather or what was going on in your day-to-day life, Amanda brought a simple happiness to everyone around her. I quickly found myself enjoying going to work every day for the opportunity to work with someone with such a positive outlook on life. Little did I know that this outlook would be tested.

A few months after moving home from college, I began working in Amanda's classroom full time. She looked like any other "normal" teenager would. A girl of average height and weight, Amanda truly enjoyed coming to school every day to be with her teachers and classmates. As months went by, Amanda began missing more and more school days to visit doctors. One day we were told that we had a meeting after school. Knowing how schools worked this was nothing new. After making sure the children had all gone home on their individual buses, I returned to the classroom to find the desks moved into a giant circle. There were more people in this meeting than usual, and Amanda's parents were there along with the school's nurses and some administrators. I instantly knew this was not going to be good.

We sat down and the meeting started. They told us they had some bad news. The air in the room was heavy. Amanda's mother said, "Amanda has been diagnosed with Mito." I was shocked. I admit that at the time I did not know what it meant, but knew it could not be good. The meeting went on. Amanda's parents and the nurses did their best to explain what the disease is.

After the nurses and Amanda's parents had finished explaining the disease there was silence. Then the question came. Is she going to die? The answer was yes, that in the end this disease would cause her death. I was speechless. It was like being stuck in a painting. Nobody was moving or speaking, everyone trying their best to absorb the information. Finally, the meeting was over and I walked to my car. The thoughts bounced around in my head like a tennis ball at Wimbledon. How do you tell a child that they are going to die?

Over the next few months, Amanda still came to school. We were told to talk to her about her disease but not to let he know it is life threatening. That did not last long. Amanda was too smart to be kept from the truth. She embraced this obstacle. She learned all she could about the disease and reached out to people like her. She created her own personal website, which allowed her to vent her feelings and emotions along with keep people up to date with her life since she was becoming less and less mobile.

Over the next year, Amanda came to school less frequently. She soon spent more time in and out of hospitals than at school. Her body began to change over the months as well. Eating and swallowing foods became very difficult. Eventually her stomach would not work properly, causing her to lose weight. The girl now standing in front of me was less than 100 pounds. Wanting to remain as "normal" as she could she would walk herself to exhaustion. Then finally she accepted the fact that her body would not allow her and she would need help. She was told she would have to use a wheel chair when she did come to school to conserve her energy.

Instead of allowing the teachers to address the class and tell them about the changes that they noticed in Amanda, Amanda chose to tell the class herself. It was a true example of her strength and courage to see her stand up in front of a classroom and explain to her friends, classmates, and even some teachers that even though there were some changes going on with her body, she was still the same Amanda.

I will never forget the wheelchair she brought in. It reminded me of the wheelchairs you see at hospitals. It must have reminded Amanda of that too, or maybe she just wanted to make it her own, because she asked us if she could paint the wheelchair. That afternoon a few teachers and I stayed after work to paint the wheelchair. That ugly black wheelchair transformed into a vibrant purple extension of Amanda with one simple can of spray paint. Even though Amanda's body was becoming weaker, her spirit and will only got stronger. She never let you feel sorry for her or complained once. Even with scars on her body from surgeries and needing tubes to feed her body, she would care more about asking you about your life, talking about TV shows or Harry Potter books. The simple things in her life that everyday people take for granted became a daily struggle.

Seeing a person facing a life of unfair struggles and limitations made me realize that I had no reason to feel sorry for myself. I began to understand that no money, fame, or personal success would automatically ensure happiness, but rather family, friends, and quality of living. I was privileged to see how a beautiful strong young girl could handle all these lives obstacles like waves crashing down repeatedly, and never let them take her under. It is life and how you choose to live it that will make you happy. You cannot afford to dwell on the bad times because you will end up missing all the beauty out there in the world. Every moment given to us is special and should be embraced.

With the help of a special friend unknowingly guiding me out of my personal darkness, I began to change my life. I am a better person for having the opportunity to share this life with Amanda. I will forever be thankful that our paths crossed. Two roads diverged in a yellow wood, and I, I took the one less traveled by, And that has made all the difference.

Mark Rosa

SATURDAY, NOVEMBER 15, 2008
I just came across Amanda's CB site and I'm so sorry for your loss. She is beautiful!!! Our prayers are with you all. God bless. Thank you so much for sharing her story. She was a strong and very brave little girl!

Donette Warren
Andover, MN

Amanda Perrotta

FRIDAY, NOVEMBER 14, 2008
To Amanda's family:

I am a relative of Tom and Valerie (first cousin of Val) Perrotta. I did not know Amanda, but from all I have heard and read, what a privilege to have been a part of her life. So sorry for the sadness in your hearts, but so glad that Amanda had the opportunity to influence so many. What a sweet and gentle soul. Amanda's spirit will live on.
God bless your family.

Liane Corbett-Densmore
Averill Park, NY

FRIDAY, NOVEMBER 14, 2008
Rina wanted us to buy her a Tink and friends figurine set to keep in her room, Tink being Amanda, of course, and the other three being Rina, Malisa and Natalie so they can continue to be together. You all remain close in our hearts and thoughts. When Rina told her doctor about Amanda, the doctor shared the following with Rina: many people pass thru your life. Some just pass thru, some stay with you forever and always be with you no matter. So many of our friends have shared how Amanda touched their lives thru Rina's CB. Thinking of you this weekend.

Stacy, Ari, and Rina B+
Cheltenham, PA

MONDAY, NOVEMBER 17, 2008
Dear Perrottas,

I have said it before but Amanda has really helped me put things into perspective. I have a much easier time playing with the hand I have been dealt...and with grace as Amanda has.

Once I heard about her CB site I immediately became one of the "AFF"!

Thinking of you and praying for you.

Love,
Kia Cheek

MONDAY, NOVEMBER 17, 2008

Hello family. I am so glad I got to see you all today. I'm sorry I couldn't stay for the service, I know my limits, and my loss is still fresh. But I couldn't let the day go by and not stop By. Jackie, continue to keep your head up, I know at times it seems like the pain will never end, but I know what you feel. If you ever need to talk you know that I am here. Jaden and Amanda have taught so many people so much, but if one person could take anything from this, I would want them to take the love that our children had for us and others. I love you guys, and you will always be a part of my heart.

Jessica Weekes, Proud mom of Jaden, and Proud friend of Ms. Amanda
Schenectady, NY

Amanda Perrotta

About the Amanda's Journey Foundation

The Perrotta family started the Amanda's Journey Foundation to raise awareness and understanding of Mitochondrial Disease. To this day, many who are eventually faced with the diagnosis of with Mito tell of doctor after doctor passing off the symptoms as psychological, or merely futile attempts to gain sympathy. Often the signs of Mito are so hard to distinguish from normal fatigue, or the progress of the disease so slow, that blame is actually passed to the parents or other loved ones as though they are forcing a misdiagnosis.

Research and increased awareness of Mito are important steps at reducing the number of these misdiagnoses and bringing the cure for this disease within the reach of the 1 person every hour who faces this tragic news. Though there are many forms of Mitochondrial Disease, some of them more chronic and long-term than Amanda's invasive form with depletion, further work is necessary to develop advanced treatments and solid research-based cures for Mito so that families remain healthy and, more importantly, whole.

Please consider supporting the Amanda's Journey Foundation generously. You can visit the associated website at **www.amandasjourney.org** for information about benefit walks and events, or you can search "amandasjourney" on Facebook for more pictures, including ones that did not make the final edit of this book. As of late 2009, Amanda had more than 250 Facebook friends worldwide.

As Amanda said, "The cure for Mito is living life." Together, we must find a way to keep a life worth living within the reach of those with Mito.